oF 8

OXFORD STUDIES IN ANCIENT PHILOSOPHY

OXFORD STUDIES IN ANCIENT PHILOSOPHY

EDITOR: BRAD INWOOD

VOLUME XXXV

WINTER 2008

OXFORD
UNIVERSITY PRESS

OXFORD
UNIVERSITY PRESS

Great Clarendon Street, Oxford OX2 6DP

Oxford University Press is a department of the University of Oxford.
It furthers the University's objective of excellence in research, scholarship,
and education by publishing worldwide in

Oxford New York

Auckland Cape Town Dar es Salaam Hong Kong Karachi
Kuala Lumpur Madrid Melbourne Mexico City Nairobi
New Delhi Shanghai Taipei Toronto

With offices in

Argentina Austria Brazil Chile Czech Republic France Greece
Guatemala Hungary Italy Japan Poland Portugal Singapore
South Korea Switzerland Thailand Turkey Ukraine Vietnam

Oxford is a registered trade mark of Oxford University Press
in the UK and in certain other countries

Published in the United States
by Oxford University Press Inc., New York

British Library Cataloguing in Publication Data

Data available

Library of Congress Cataloging in Publication Data

Oxford studies in ancient philosophy.—
Vol. xxxv (2008).—Oxford: Clarendon Press;
New York: Oxford University Press, 1983–
v.; 22 cm. Annual.
1. Philosophy, Ancient—Periodicals.
B1.O9   180.'5—dc.19   84–645022
AACR 2   MARC-S

Typeset by John Waś, Oxford
Printed on acid-free paper by
the MPG Books Group in the UK

ISBN 978–0–19–955779–0
ISBN 978–0–19–955780–6 (Pbk.)

ADVISORY BOARD

Contributions and books for review should be sent to the Editor, Professor Brad Inwood, Department of Classics, University of Toronto, 125 Queen's Park, Toronto M5S 2C7, Canada (e-mail brad.inwood@utoronto.ca).

Contributors are asked to observe the 'Notes for Contributors to Oxford Studies in Ancient Philosophy', printed at the end of this volume.

Up-to-date contact details, the latest version of Notes to Contributors, and publication schedules can be checked on the *Oxford Studies in Ancient Philosophy* website:

www.oup.co.uk/philosophy/series/osap

EDITORIAL

This volume of *Oxford Studies in Ancient Philosophy* marks a transition to new editorship. It is a distinct honour, though an intimidating one, to succeed David Sedley in this capacity. Under his leadership (from 1999 to 2008) the series has added a second volume per year and carried on the traditions of high quality and innovative philosophical scholarship established by its founding editor, Julia Annas, and her successor, Christopher Taylor. My aim will be to continue those traditions, to encourage the publication of challenging new work across the full range of ancient Graeco-Roman philosophy, and to maintain the high standing and distinctive character which the series has established under its first three editors.

I want to thank David Sedley, not only for his support and encouragement over decades of friendship, but also for his generous assistance in the process of editorial transition. Roughly half of the material in this volume is the outcome of his editorial labours, not my own. The articles in Volume XXXV range in time from Hesiod to Plotinus and cover themes in ethics, physics, metaphysics, and logic broadly construed. There is a pleasing but unintended balance in the philosophers and periods covered. I hope that there will be something for everyone to enjoy, to learn from, and to disagree with. I want to close by expressing my gratitude to John Waś for his exceptional helpfulness and continued excellence in the processes of copy-editing and production and to the departments of Classics and Philosophy at the University of Toronto for their practical assistance.

CONTENTS

HESIOD, PRODICUS, AND THE SOCRATICS ON WORK AND PLEASURE

DAVID WOLFSDORF

1. Socrates and Hesiod's *Works and Days* 287–319

SINCE poetry, especially the epic poetry of Homer and Hesiod, was central to Greek culture in the late archaic and classical periods, those individuals engaged in the formation and early development of philosophy, in many ways a reaction and alternative to conventional culture and forms of expression, inevitably engaged with their illustrious predecessors. Plato's criticism of poetry in the *Republic* is the most obvious example. But in general, philosophers' engagements range from criticism of the poets as established authorities to employment of them, in various ways, as constructive models or as corroborators of their ideas. In all cases, interpretation of the poetry itself was required, and this too ranged from the conventional to the idiosyncratic. The aim of this paper is to shed light on the ways that one passage in Hesiod's *Works and Days* particularly served Prodicus and in turn the Socratics in the formulation of their ethical thought.

The encomium on work in Hesiod's *Works and Days* 287–319 was much discussed in Socratic circles. Socrates himself seems to have been one important impetus to this discussion. Evidence comes from Xenophon's response to accusations made against Socrates:

his accuser said that he selected from the most renowned poets the most base verses and used them as evidence in teaching his associates to be malefactors and tyrants. For example, Hesiod's line 'No work is a disgrace,

© David Wolfsdorf 2008
I am grateful to Grace Ledbetter, Thomas Blackson, David Sansone, and an anonymous referee for their comments on earlier drafts. Thanks also to David Sedley for a range of helpful philological, philosophical, and expository suggestions.

but idleness is a disgrace'.[1] His accuser said that Socrates explained this line as an injunction by the poet to refrain from no dishonest or disgraceful work, but to do even these for gain. Now when Socrates agreed that it is a benefit and a good to a person to be a worker, harmful and bad to be an idler, and that work is in fact a good, while idleness is bad, by 'working' and 'being a worker' he meant doing something good, and it was those who gamble or do anything else that is wicked and harmful that he called idle. On these assumptions, it would be correct to say: 'No work is a disgrace, but idleness is a disgrace.'[2]

In this case, the accuser claims that Socrates misappropriated lines of poetry to authorize his own corrupt ethical views. In defence, Xenophon claims that Socrates drew on the poets for salutary wisdom. Contrast Xenophon's account with Libanius', which attributes to Socrates the use of Hesiod's line in a *reductio* of the poet:

And in his cross-examinations Socrates pursues the following sort of method . . . [He] asks his interlocutor whether Hesiod is wise, and the latter, under the influence of common opinion, is compelled to agree. 'But doesn't Hesiod praise all work and claim that no work is a disgrace?' When Socrates poses this second question, one cannot deny it. 'So a burglar or tomb-robber has a wise man, Hesiod, as his witness that he does no wrong.' . . . But no one hurries off from this conversation bent on sordid profit; exactly the opposite happens. For since the poet has been proved wrong . . . they know that one should not engage in every sort of work without exception. (*Decl.* 1. 86)

Libanius has Socrates use Hesiod's line critically, not only to undermine the poet's authority, but also to affirm his own ethical principle.

Again, Plato deploys Hesiod's line in *Charmides* in his own provocative and ironic manner. Critias, future leader of the Thirty Tyrants, has submitted τὸ τὰ ἑαυτοῦ πράττειν as a definition of sound-mindedness. The phrase literally means 'doing one's own things'; but it is more naturally taken as idiomatic for 'minding one's own business' and so as an antonym of meddlesomeness (πολυπραγμοσύνη). As such, in late fifth-century Athens τὸ τὰ ἑαυτοῦ πράττειν is a catchphrase for anti-democratic sentiment: withdrawal

---

[1] The line ἔργον δ' οὐδὲν ὄνειδος occurs at *WD* 311. The natural reading is to take οὐδέν as modifying ὄνειδος, viz.: work is no disgrace. But Socrates takes οὐδέν as modifying ἔργον, viz.: no work is a disgrace.

[2] *Mem.* 1. 2. 56–7. Cf. Eust. *In Il.* 1. 382. 28; *In Od.* 2. 143. 4.

and quietism follow disenchantment with Athenian politics.[3] In response to Critias' definition Socrates initially takes the phrase in its literal sense and presents an argument to show that making things for others may also be sound-minded. Then, in defence of his definition, Critias insists on distinguishing doing (πράττειν), working (ἐργάζεσθαι), and making (ποιεῖν):

'Tell me,' [Socrates] said, 'do you not call making and doing the same thing?' 'Not at all,' [Critias] replied, 'nor working and making either. I learnt this from Hesiod, who says that no work [ἔργον] is a disgrace. Now, do you suppose that if he had given the names of working and doing to such things as you were mentioning just now, there would have been no reproach in shoemaking, selling salt fish, or owning a brothel? . . . For it is things honourably and usefully made that he called works [ἔργα]. (*Chrm.* 163 A–C)

Critias defends his definition of sound-mindedness by arguing, on the alleged authority of Hesiod, that ἔργον means something well done and beneficial. In this respect Critias' use of Hesiod is akin to Xenophon's in his defence of Socrates. But Critias' use has an ideological edge, for Critias explicitly distinguishes occupations of the lower, predominantly democratic, class from good work.[4] In short, Critias cites Hesiod approvingly, but gives a distorted interpretation of ἔργον. In turn, Plato's use of Hesiod's line is ironic precisely because a future tyrant employs it in the expression of an anti-democratic sentiment, just as Socrates' accuser alleged that Socrates himself misused the line to promote malfeasance and tyranny.

2. Some Prodicean distinctions in Plato

In his response to Critias in *Charmides*, Socrates refers to Prodicus:

'Critias,' I said, 'you had hardly begun when I grasped the significance of your speech: you call one's proper things and one's own things good things and the making of good things you call doings. Indeed, I have heard Prodicus make countless distinctions among words.' (163 D)

Socrates' point may simply be that Critias' attempt to distinguish making, doing, and working is akin to Prodicus' well-known prac-

---

[3] See L. B. Carter, *The Quiet Athenian* (Oxford, 1982).

[4] Socrates then interprets Critias' definition, to Critias' satisfaction, as doing good things.

tice of making semantic distinctions. On the other hand, it is likely that the texts in view of which Prodicus made his semantic distinctions were canonical works of the poetic tradition, including Hesiod's *Works and Days*. Generally speaking, this is consistent with the ὀρθοέπεια we know other sophists, such as Protagoras, practised.[5] Thus, possibly, the distinction that Critias in *Charmides* introduces echoes one that Prodicus himself made in discussing the Hesiod passage.

In Plato's *Protagoras* Protagoras criticizes and Socrates attempts to defend the consistency of Simonides' Scopas ode. Protagoras claims that Simonides contradicts himself by criticizing Pittacus' maxim that it is hard to be (ἔμμεναι) good, while elsewhere in the ode claiming that it is hard to be (γενέσθαι) good (339 A–D). Socrates defends Simonides by arguing that the verbs ἔμμεναι and γενέσθαι mean 'be' and 'become' respectively. Accordingly, Simonides is arguing that it is difficult to become good, but, having once achieved goodness, it is not difficult to remain in that condition. In support of his defence, Socrates calls on Prodicus and cites Hesiod, *WD* 289–92:

> Now, as our friend Prodicus says, Protagoras, being and becoming are not the same thing. And if [so], then Simonides does not contradict himself. Perhaps Prodicus and many others might say with Hesiod that to become good is hard, for the gods have placed sweat before excellence. But when one reaches the summit, then it is easy, although it was hard. And when Prodicus heard this he gave me his approval. (340 C–D)

In line 292 of *Works and Days* Hesiod uses the poetic verb πέλει in speaking of the ease of possessing goodness, and the regular participle ἐοῦσα in speaking of the difficulty of the attempt to possess goodness: ῥηιδίη δὴ ἔπειτα πέλει, χαλεπή περ ἐοῦσα. Possibly the historical Prodicus used Hesiod's line to distinguish words for being and becoming.[6]

Again, in Plato's *Protagoras*, immediately before the discussion of Simonides' ode, Prodicus and other members of the audience at Callias' house deliver speeches to encourage Socrates and Protagoras to resume their suspended discussion regarding the partition

---

[5] See D. Fehling, 'Protagoras und die ὀρθοέπεια', in C. J. Classen (ed.), *Sophistik* (Darmstadt, 1976), 341–7; C. J. Classen, 'The Study of Language amongst Socrates' Contemporaries', ibid. 215–47 (Classen treats Prodicus at 230–8).

[6] If so, I would assume that Prodicus argued that πέλει here means 'become'. In that case, Prodicus' assent to Socrates in *Protagoras* would be dramatically ironic.

of goodness.[7] Within his speech, Prodicus distinguishes ἡδονή and εὐφροσύνη, the latter of which I translate as 'appreciation':

we in the audience would be extremely appreciative [εὐφραίνεσθαι], not pleased [ἡδοίμεσθα]—for being appreciative [εὐφραίνεσθαι] is a condition of learning something and partaking of understanding [φρονήσεως] with the intellect [διανοίᾳ] itself, whereas being pleased [ἥδεσθαι] is a condition of one eating something or experiencing some other pleasure [ἡδύ] with the body [σώματι] itself. (*Prot.* 337 C 1–4)

Prodicus' statement indicates an explanation for his distinction. The use of the word φρόνησις suggests that the basis for Prodicus' distinction is etymological. In fact, we have a report from Galen in support of the view that at least some of Prodicus' semantic distinctions had this kind of etymological basis.[8] In *Protagoras* Prodicus' distinction between pleasure terms is not connected to Hesiod's *Works and Days*. However, as we shall see, there is reason to believe that Prodicus' interest in Hesiod's encomium on work might have encouraged these distinctions as well.

3. Prodicus on the distinction between pleasure terms

In *Topics* Aristotle suggests a criticism of an interlocutor who mistakenly treats co-referring expressions as though one could be predicated of the other:

In addition, look and see if he has stated a thing to be an accident of itself, taking it to be different because it has a different name, as Prodicus used to divide pleasures into joy [χαράν], delight [τέρψιν], and good cheer [εὐφροσύνην]; for all these are names for the same thing, pleasure. And if anyone says that joy [τὸ χαίρειν] is an accident of good cheer [τὸ εὐφραίνεσθαι], he would be declaring it to be an accident of itself. (112ᵇ21–6)

Aristotle thus confirms Prodicus' interest in semantic distinctions between pleasure terms. On the other hand, Aristotle's description does not agree with Plato's treatment. We also have a testimony regarding Prodicus' distinction of pleasure terms from Alexander's comments on Aristotle's passage:

---

[7] Here and throughout I translate ἀρετή as 'goodness'. This is rather anaemic, but very convenient given the wide range of senses which this word bore from the time of Hesiod to the 4th cent.

[8] *Nat. fac.* 2. 9.

For ἡδονή and χαρά and εὐφροσύνη and τέρψις are the same thing with respect to their underlying nature and significance. But Prodicus tried to distinguish particular significances for each of these words, just as the Stoics did; for they say that χαρά is rational elation, whereas ἡδονή is irrational elation, and that τέρψις is ἡδονή through the ears, while εὐφροσύνη is ἡδονή through discourse. (*In Top.* 2. 96 Wallies)

But Alexander's report can be explained away. While Alexander states that Prodicus distinguished various pleasure terms, the distinctions he proceeds to clarify are Stoic, not Prodicean.

This leaves the discrepancy between Plato and Aristotle. Prodicus surely distinguished pleasure terms, but Plato probably adapted Prodicus' distinctions for his own purposes.[9] In general, we should be wary of attributing to Prodicus the exact distinctions Plato associates with him. In fact, this is consistent with our conclusion regarding the distinction between πέλει and ἐοῦσα. Plato makes Socrates speak of a distinction not between these words, but between ἔμμεναι and γενέσθαι. Finally, it is also possible that Prodicus distinguished ἔργον from other senses of 'work', but not necessarily as Critias does.

4. Prodicus' *Choice of Heracles* and Hesiod's *Works and Days*

Although our evidence that Prodicus drew distinctions between words for work and being and becoming on the basis of Hesiod's *Works and Days* is indirect, to say the least, and although we have as yet seen no evidence that Prodicus drew distinctions between words for pleasure on the basis of Hesiod's *Works and Days*, we have good evidence that Hesiod's poem, in particular lines 287–319, influenced Prodicus. The central idea of Prodicus' *Choice of Heracles*, in which the hero must decide between the paths of good-

---

[9] Note that Plato reuses the distinction he attributes to Prodicus in *Protagoras*. In *Timaeus* Timaeus discusses the experience of harmonious and inharmonious sounds: 'so they produce a single experience, a mixture of high and low. Hence the pleasure [ἡδονήν] they bring to the ignorant [ἄφροσιν] and the appreciation [εὐφροσύνην] they provide—by their expression of divine harmony in mortal movement—to those of understanding [ἔμφροσιν]' (*Tim.* 80 B 4–8). Note here again that the use of εὐφροσύνη, in contrast to ἡδονή, is related to the word φρόνησις. Consider also the *Timaeus* passage in relation to Socrates' etymology of εὐφροσύνη in the *Cratylus*: 'εὐφροσύνη needs no explanation, for it is clear to everyone that since it is conveyance [φέρεσθαι] of the soul in concord with the world, its name derives from εὐφεροσύνη' (*Crat.* 419 D 4–9).

ness and badness, is an allegorical adaptation of the metaphor of the two paths in *WD* 287–92:

> It is easy to get hold of badness in abundance. The road to it is smooth, and it dwells close by. But between us and goodness the immortal gods have placed the sweat of our brows. Long and steep is the path that leads to it, and it is rough at first. But when one reaches the summit, then it is easy, although it was hard.[10]

These lines occur in the context of Hesiod's exhortation to Perses to cease his idleness and injustice and to devote himself to honest toil. But while justice plays an important role in Hesiod's exhortation, M. L. West, among others, correctly emphasizes that goodness and badness in this particular passage refer less to morality than to prosperity, poverty, and social class. In particular, the fruits of toil are not virtue itself, but an ample store of grain and produce.[11]

Prodicus' allegorization of Hesiod's metaphor of the two paths accords with the ethical-political concerns of his age as well as serving his professional interests. Prodicus' *Choice of Heracles* was an epideictic work, composed above all for the sons of wealthy citizens and their guardians in an effort to win students for his more costly lecture course.[12] Prodicus casts Heracles' choice between good and bad as between civic virtue and somatic pleasure.[13] The

---

[10] Compare David Sansone: 'It would appear (a) that this Hesiodic passage provided the text on which Prodicus based his sermon (so W. Nestle, "Die Horen des Prodikos", *Hermes* 71 (1936) 151–70 at 164–5; E. Dupréel, *Les Sophistes. Protagoras, Gorgias, Prodicus, Hippias*, Neuchâtel, 1948, 121) and (b) that the historical Socrates was influenced by both the Hesiodic text and the use to which Prodicus put it' ('Heracles at the Y', *Journal of Hellenic Studies*, 124 (2004), 125–42 at n. 48). For a more general discussion of the two-paths theme in Greek literature, see J. Alpers, *Hercules in bivio* (diss. Göttingen, 1912); M. C. Waites, 'Some Features of the Allegorical Debate in Greek Literature', *Harvard Studies in Classical Philology*, 23 (1912), 1–46 at 12–19; G. K. Galinsky, *The Herakles Theme* (Oxford, 1972), 101–3, 162. Sansone cites a number of additional references at nn. 1–2. For a critique of Sansone's thesis that Xenophon presents Prodicus' *Choice of Heracles* more or less verbatim, see V. Gray, 'The Linguistic Philosophies of Prodicus in Xenophon's "Choice of Heracles"?', *Classical Quarterly*, NS 56 (2006), 426–35.

[11] 'κακότης and ἀρετή are not "vice" and "virtue" but inferior and superior standing in society, determined principally by material prosperity' (*Hesiod: Works and Days*, ed. M. L. West (Oxford, 1978), 229).

[12] Compare the comment of Aristippus to Antisthenes, on the latter's *Heracles*, in *Socr. ep.* 9. 4: 'I will send you large white lupins so that you will have something to eat after you have produced your *Heracles* for the youths.' (The Socratic epistles are assembled and translated in *The Cynic Epistles*, ed. A. Malherbe (Missoula, Mont., 1977).)

[13] I use the phrase 'somatic pleasure' here and below to refer, above all, to pleasures of eating, drinking, and sex.

path of badness is replete with, so to speak, lower sensual pleasures, while the fruits of civic virtue above all include social recognition:

> The young enjoy the praises of their elders. The old are glad to be honoured by the young. They recall their past deeds with pleasure, and they take pleasure in doing their present deeds well. . . . Because of me [Virtue] they are dear to the gods, loved by their friends, and honoured by their native land. And when their appointed end comes, they lie not forgotten and dishonoured, but flourish in memory and song for all time.[14]

Prodicus' casting of badness as endorsing somatic pleasure and goodness as endorsing pleasure in social recognition, a kind of cognitive pleasure, would have provided him with a good opportunity to reflect upon semantic distinctions between pleasure terms, even if he did not in fact apply them. Indeed, in Xenophon's recounting of Prodicus' *Choice of Heracles* all four of the pleasure terms Aristotle attributes to Prodicus occur, but not consistently with the meanings Aristotle attributes to them.[15]

5. Prodicus, Hesiod, and Xenophon

Prodicus' allegorization, in terms of the values of somatic pleasure and civic virtue, of Hesiod's two paths in turn influenced the Socratics' considerations of Hesiod's encomium on work. Most explicitly, in *Memorabilia* 2. 1 Xenophon makes Socrates cite *WD* 287–92 to Aristippus in an effort to exhort Aristippus to cease his self-indulgent lifestyle and to devote himself to goodness (2. 1. 20). Xenophon is explicit that Hesiod's lines have the same meaning as Prodicus' *Choice of Heracles*, which he makes Socrates subsequently paraphrase at length: 'the wise Prodicus expresses himself in the same way concerning goodness' (2. 1. 21).

The somatic pleasure of the path of badness in Prodicus' *Choice*

---

[14] *Mem.* 2. 1. 33. Goodness also includes some material comforts, peaceful sleep, and the pleasures of simple meals. But the emphasis is on what might be called social pleasures of recognition.

[15] Badness says that Heracles will taste all pleasures (τερπνῶν) and will delight (τερφθείης) in sounds and sights (2. 1. 23, 24). Badness speaks of enjoying (εὐφρανθείης) sex, then later criticizes the hard-won pleasures (εὐφροσύνας) that Goodness recommends (2. 1. 24, 29). Finally, Goodness uses the verb cognate with χαρά to refer to the pleasures that the young enjoy (χαίρουσιν) in receiving praise from their elders (2. 1. 33).

of Heracles and retrospectively in Hesiod's *Works and Days* well suits the identity of Socrates' interlocutor Aristippus, whose hedonistic development of Socratic ethics troubled most Socratics. On the other hand, Xenophon's reading of Hesiod under the influence of Prodicus' allegorical adaptation of Hesiod is objectionable. Consider again lines 291–2:

[The long and steep path to excellence is] rough at first [τὸ πρῶτον]. But when one reaches the summit, then it is easy, although it was hard.

The significance of these lines seems to be twofold. First, unless idleness led to more suffering than a life of labour *per se*, exhortation to toil with no reward would be absurd. Yet Hesiod does not view life in the Iron Age as necessarily devoid of pleasure. Honest toil does yield enjoyable rewards. This point is confirmed by the second reason why lines 291–2 are significant: if the achievement of goodness did not relieve difficulty and suffering, the unacceptable conclusion would follow that the life of the gods in particular would be distressing. But in the poem Hesiod is explicit that the life of the gods, as of mortals in the Golden Age, is free from toil and replete with enjoyment:

First, the immortal gods who dwell in Olympian chambers made a golden race of mortal men . . . And these men lived just like the gods [ὥστε θεοί] without sorrow in their hearts, remote and free from toils [πόνων] and grief. Miserable old age did not oppress them, but, their limbs ever strong, they always took pleasure in feasts, beyond the reach of all badness. (109–15)[16]

In short, Hesiod's lines are consistent with a form of hedonism that Xenophon rejects. Hesiod endorses a rationally tempered pursuit of somatic pleasure. Moreover, given Prodicus' distinction between pleasure terms, it is doubtful that Prodicus himself would have viewed the contrast between the paths of badness and goodness simply as one of self-indulgence and self-sacrifice. Thus, despite the fact that the somatic pleasure-seeker is the butt of Xenophon's appropriation of Prodicus' adaptation of Hesiod's lines, Aristippus had grounds for debate.

---

[16] Compare the following statement attributed to Aristippus: 'If it were base to live luxuriously, it would not occur among the festivals of the gods' (D.L. 2. 68).

6. Aristippus and Hesiod

There is direct evidence that Aristippus himself was drawn into the discussion around Hesiod's encomium on work and that his conception of these verses was informed by Prodicus' allegorization. In his commentary on Hesiod's *Works and Days* Plutarch refers to Aristippus in the context of his own comments on lines 293–7. Hesiod's lines, which immediately follow the description of the paths of good and bad, run:

That man is altogether best who considers all things himself and marks what will be better afterwards and at the end. And he, again, is good who heeds a good adviser; but whoever neither thinks for himself nor keeps in mind what another tells him, he is an unprofitable man.

Hesiod thus ranks three characters from best to worst: the self-sufficient wise person, the person who follows the good counsel of another, and the person who does neither. Plutarch comments:

Zeno the Stoic changed the lines around and said: 'That man is altogether the best who heeds a good adviser; and that man is also good who considers all things himself.' [In saying this,] he gave the first prize to heeding well and the second prize to wisdom. In contrast, Aristippus the Socratic said that it is worse to seek an adviser than to beg. (Plut. fr. 42 = *Schol. vet. in Op.* 293–7)

Further, though less direct, evidence of Aristippus' engagement with Hesiod's encomium on work comes from Diogenes Laertius. Diogenes reports that Aristippus identified pleasure with smooth motion (λεία κίνησις, 2. 85).[17] This report is credible because, given the Socratics' interest in definitions, it is reasonable to suppose that Aristippus would have been inclined or compelled to offer a definition of goodness as he viewed it.

Diogenes also reports that the Cyrenaics identify pain as rough motion (τραχεία κίνησις, 2. 86). If Aristippus identified pleasure as smooth motion, it is likely that the Cyrenaic view of pain also derives from him. Now, among surviving Greek fragments and literature to the end of the fifth century, the only instance of the use of the adjective λεῖος contrasted with τραχύς in an ethical context is

[17] Cf. Cic. *Fin.* 2. 18; Clem. *Strom.* 2. 20. 106. 3; S.E. *PH* 1. 215. More precisely, Diogenes, Cicero, and Clement report that pleasure is smooth motion that is perceived or sensed.

Hesiod's *WD* 287–92.[18] Moreover, as we have seen, Hesiod's lines are consistent with a kind of hedonism: pleasure is toil's reward. Finally, Hesiod, like Aristippus, values somatic pleasure. In short, by identifying pleasure with smooth motion, Aristippus is treating Hesiod's smooth path—itself a metaphor, and one that Prodicus subsequently allegorized as a life of self-indulgence—as a metaphor for the nature of pleasure itself.

These results encourage consideration of the meaning of Aristippus' comment on *WD* 293–7 and Aristippus' attitude towards Hesiod's encomium generally.[19] To begin, Diogenes Laertius attributes to Aristippus an apophthegm similar to the comment on *WD* 293–7: 'It is better, [Aristippus] said, to be a beggar than to be uneducated; the one needs money, the other needs humanity' (D.L. 2. 70). In other words, wisdom or education is more valuable than money. Accordingly, Aristippus' comment on Hesiod would mean that one who needs an adviser and thus lacks wisdom is worse off than one who needs money.[20]

While this much is clear, it is unclear why Aristippus would comment on Hesiod's lines in this way. First, it is unclear why Aristippus mentions begging. Immediately following the lines in question, Hesiod's poem continues:

But always remember my charge, high-born Perses: work, so that Hunger may hate you . . . Both gods and men are angry with him who lives idly, for in nature he is like the stingless drones who waste the labour of the bees, eating without working . . . Through work men grow rich in flocks and substance, and working they are much better loved by the immortals. Work is no disgrace, but idleness is. (*WD* 298–311)

In the context of Hesiod's injunction to Perses to work and desist from idleness, the contrast between heeding a counsellor's advice and begging now appears as the distinction between accepting Hesiod's injunction to work and rejecting it at the risk of destitution. Still, Aristippus' comment remains puzzling; it appears to suggest that Perses would be better off as a beggar than heeding his counsellor Hesiod's advice.

Here it is helpful to consider two points regarding Aristippus'

---

[18] This result was derived from a TLG search.
[19] Here, of course, conclusions must be more speculative.
[20] Cf. Plato, *Ap.* 30 B.

hedonism and lifestyle. The first relates to Aristippus' view of the role of fortune in human life:

[Aristippus] revelled in the pleasure of the present. He did not toil in seeking the enjoyment of what was not present. (D.L. 2. 66)

Aristippus appeared to speak with great force when he exhorted people not to belabour the past in retrospect or the future in anticipation, for this [not belabouring] is the sign of a contented soul and a demonstration of a cheerful mind. He enjoined people to focus their thought on the day at hand and more precisely on that part of the day when they are acting or deliberating. For he used to say that the present alone is ours; neither is what has passed, nor what lies ahead. For the one has perished; and in the case of the other, it is unclear whether it will be. (Ael. *VH* 14. 6)[21]

Further evidence for Aristippus' view of the obscurity of the future, specifically in conjunction with the problem of fortune, derives from some of the titles of his writings listed in Diogenes Laertius, in particular *On Fortune*, but also *The Shipwrecked*, *The Exiles*, and *To a Beggar*.[22] In short, Aristippus would have rejected Hesiod's injunction to toil now in order to secure pleasure in the future.

Second, Aristippus dismissed his civic ties and thus a conventional means of making a living. In Xenophon's *Memorabilia* Socrates begins his exhortation to Aristippus by insisting that the education of a political leader requires self-restraint and abstinence. Socrates falsely assumes that Aristippus aspires to political success. Instead, Aristippus condemns the burdens of political participation as ruler or subject and advocates freedom from political obligations altogether:

I believe there is a path between both ruling and servitude, and it is the path that I try to walk. It runs through neither, but through freedom, which above all leads to well-being . . . I do not confine myself to a political constitution; I am a foreigner everywhere. (Xen. *Mem.* 2. 1. 11–13)[23]

Aristippus evidently believed that a pleasant life with a certain

[21] Cf. Athen. 12, 544 A–B.

[22] Perhaps the quotation in Plutarch came from *To a Beggar*.

[23] Cf. Plut. *An virt.* 439 E; and consider the comments of Giannantoni on Aristippus' *The Exiles* (*Socratis et Socraticorum reliquiae* (4 vols.; Naples, 1990), iv. 160–1). Compare also *Socr. ep.* 8, where Antisthenes begins his criticism of Aristippus with these words: 'It is not right for a philosopher to associate with tyrants and to devote himself to Sicilian tables. Rather, he should live in his own country and strive for self-sufficiency.'

kind of independence was possible without civic ties and without the literal or figurative cultivation of one's patrimonial land or homeland.[24] In forgoing such conventional securities, Aristippus, like other itinerant sophists, must have had an outstanding capacity to deal with a variety of people and circumstances. In his *Life of Aristippus* Diogenes seems to capture this capacity:

[Aristippus] was capable of adapting himself to place, time, and person and of playing his part appropriately under whatever circumstances. Hence he found more favor with Dionysius than with anybody else because he could always turn the situation to good account. He derived pleasure from what was present. (2. 66)[25]

Aristippus' comment on Hesiod's *Works and Days* 293 ff. and his attitude to Hesiod's encomium generally may now be explained as follows. The counsellor in *Works and Days*, Hesiod himself, enjoins toil for long-term gain. Aristippus rejects this counsel and conventional, burdensome means of making a living. While Hesiod or Xenophon might admit that toil for long-term gain itself is not free from some risk, they would emphasize that the alternative is certain destitution and beggary. But Aristippus maintains that there is an alternative to the conventional life, an alternative in which one can enjoy the present. The capacity to live such a life, namely wisdom, is more valuable than wealth. In short, both Aristippus and Hesiod endorse somatic pleasure, tempered by rationality. But whereas Hesiod conservatively emphasizes traditional labour to secure pleasure in the future, Aristippus emphasizes unconventional means of enjoying the present.[26]

[24] For references to Aristippus' itinerant intellectualism and Dionysius' patronage of him, see testimonia IV A 1–14 in Giannantoni, *Socratis et Socraticorum reliquiae*, ii. 3–8.

[25] C. J. Classen refers to Aristippus' 'Kosmopolitanismus' ('Aristippos', *Hermes*, 86 (1958), 182–92 at 188). Compare O. Gigon's discussion of the distinction between Aristippus' and his contemporaries' cosmopolitanism (*Kommentar zum zweiten Buch von Xenophons Memorabilien* (Basel, 1956), 35–6).

[26] In the light of this, we can also see why Aristippus would have appropriated Hesiod's adjectives λεῖος and τραχύς to identify pleasure and pain respectively, even though Hesiod himself condemns the smooth path. Note, however, that it remains obscure precisely how Aristippus understood the smoothness of pleasure and the roughness of pain.

7. Prodicus and Phaedo

Phaedo is another Socratic who seems to have engaged with Prodicus' *Choice of Heracles* and perhaps Hesiod's *Works and Days* under
the influence of Prodicus' allegorical adaptation of it. In *Socratic
Epistles* 12 and 13 Simon and Aristippus exchange letters. In *Epistle*
12, Simon to Aristippus, Simon rebukes Aristippus for ridiculing
him by making fun of his life as a shoemaker:

> I hear that you ridicule our wisdom in the presence of Dionysius. I admit
> that I am a shoemaker and that I do work of that nature, and in like
> manner I would, if it were necessary, cut straps once more for the purpose
> of admonishing foolish men who think that they are living according to
> the teaching of Socrates, when they are living in great luxury. Antisthenes
> will be the chastiser of your foolish jests. For you are writing him letters
> which make fun of our way of life.

In *Epistle* 13 Aristippus begins his reply to Simon:

> I am not the one who is making fun of you; it was Phaedo. He said that you
> were better and wiser than Prodicus of Ceos, when you refuted him with
> regard to Prodicus' encomium on Heracles.

Neither of these letters is authentic. None the less, the contents of
the epistles are most likely based on the works of historical figures
and traditions that developed from them.[27] In particular, we know
that Phaedo composed a dialogue called *Simon*.[28] Thus, given Aristippus' comment, it seems likely that in Phaedo's dialogue *Simon*,
Simon *qua* handicraftsman was criticized and that the criticism
concerned the value of Simon's work.

Phaedo's criticism of Simon might have occurred in the context
of consideration of the role of work in the good life. As we have
seen, in Prodicus' *Choice of Heracles* good work is associated with
civic virtue. Of course, the Socratics debated the identity of civic

---

[27] Since the excavation of Simon's shop near the agora, the historicity of Simon
the shoemaker has been corroborated (D. B. Thompson, 'The House of Simon the
Shoemaker', *Archaeology*, 13 (1960), 234–40). Whether Simon composed Socratic
dialogues remains controversial (John Sellars, 'Simon the Shoemaker and the Problem of Socrates', *Classical Philology*, 98 (2003), 207–16; R. S. Brumbaugh, 'Simon
and Socrates', *Ancient Philosophy*, 11 (1991), 151–2; R. F. Hock, 'Simon the Shoemaker as an Ideal Cynic', *Greek, Roman and Byzantine Studies*, 17 (1976), 41–53).

[28] D.L. 2. 105. Diogenes also mentions a work called *Cobblers' Talks*, which 'some
also attribute to Aeschines' (ibid.).

virtue as well as the relation between civic virtue and well-being (εὐδαιμονία). Prodicus' *Choice of Heracles* and Hesiod's encomium on work thus provided the Socratics with an opportunity to reflect on the question of good work. Consider the question of Simon's occupation in relation to Critias' question in Plato's *Charmides*:

'Now do you suppose that if he [Hesiod at *WD* 311] had given the names of working and doing to such works as you were mentioning just now, he would have said there was no reproach in *shoemaking*, salt-fish selling, or running a brothel?' (*Chrm.* 163 B, emphasis added)[29]

In *Choice of Heracles* Prodicus advocates the cultivation of civic virtue to attain social recognition. I assume that in Phaedo's *Simon* Phaedo, Prodicus, Socrates, or some other interlocutor emphasized the same point. However, as Aristippus suggests in the epistle, Simon manages to achieve this end through a different kind of work; thus, he refutes Prodicus:

No, I do admire and praise you since, although you are but a shoemaker, you are filled with wisdom and you have long persuaded Socrates and the most handsome youths to sit with you, youths such as Alcibiades son of Cleinias, Phaedrus the Myrrhinean, and Euthydemus son of Glaucon, and of the men of public affairs, Epicrates, Sacesphorus,[30] Euryptolemus, and others. I also think Pericles son of Xanthippus was with you when he did not have to carry out the duties of a general or when there was not a war ensuing. (*Ep.* 13. 1)

I do not, on the basis of this, infer that Phaedo's point in *Simon* was that social recognition is a valuable object of desire; nor do I infer that Phaedo advocated a life of menial labour. Both positions are un-Socratic. I am merely noting that in *Simon* Phaedo made use of Prodicus' *Choice of Heracles* in the context of examining the relation between labour and success. This idea, of course, is central to Hesiod's *Works and Days*, and it is one of Prodicus' principal debts to Hesiod.

---

[29] On Phaedo's *Simon* compare U. von Wilamowitz-Moellendorff, 'Phaidon von Elis', *Hermes*, 14 (1897) 187–93, 476–7 (repr. in *Kleine Schriften*, iii. *Griechische Prosa*, ed. F. Zucker (Berlin, 1969), 41–8); L. Rossetti, *Aspetti della letteratura socratica antica* (Chieti, 1977), 146–53; and Giannantoni, *Socratis et Socraticorum reliquiae*, vol. iv, nota 11, esp. 119–25.

[30] This name is not found elsewhere, which suggests that the manuscripts are corrupt.

David Wolfsdorf

8. Conclusion

The preceding discussion has suggested that Hesiod's *Works and Days* 287–319 provided Prodicus and, under the influence of Prodicus' allegorical adaptation in *Choice of Heracles*, the Socratics with a framework for ethical reflection. Hesiod's encomium gave rise to the following question: To what type of work should one devote oneself? In answering this question himself, Hesiod assumes the value of material goods and derivatively social status. His concern is how these goods are best achieved and maintained. Hesiod's answer conforms with the values of an aristocratic community whose social stratification is tied to an agricultural economy. Hesiod recommends assiduous farm labour as a means of securing prosperity. The rewards of toil are pleasures, indeed, bodily pleasures.

Prodicus in *Choice of Heracles* adapts Hesiod's metaphor of the two paths into an allegory of Heracles' ethical dilemma. Prodicus endorses Hesiod's encomium on work, but emphasizes that the work in question involves the cultivation of civic virtue rather than the relatively private practice of farming one's land. As such, Prodicus casts Hesiod's metaphor in relatively moralistic terms. I say 'relatively moralistic' because conventional conceptions of civic virtue in the classical period remained far more ethnocentric than more modern and abstract appeals to rationality, autonomy, and agency. Furthermore, Prodicus degrades self-indulgence by associating it with the path of badness. The reward of the cultivation of civic virtue, above all, is social recognition, a kind of cognitive pleasure. Indeed, Prodicus seems to have distinguished various terms, including pleasure terms, specifically through his examination of Hesiod's encomium on work.

Xenophon reads Hesiod's encomium under the influence of Prodicus' *Choice of Heracles* and thus casts Aristippus as a notorious somatic pleasure-seeker inclined to pursue the path of badness. But Aristippus himself rejects a Prodicean interpretation of Hesiod's encomium, in two respects. First, Aristippus abandons political ties and thus dismisses the pursuit of civic virtue. Second, like Hesiod, and unlike Prodicus or Xenophon, Aristippus values somatic pleasure. On the other hand, with his concern over the obscurity of the future and the role of fortune, Aristippus rejects Hesiod's particular form of rationality, present work for future pleasure. Instead, he endorses the unconventional cultivation of pleasures of the present. This Aristippus recasts as Hesiod's smooth path, and so identifies pleasure itself, metaphorically, with smooth motion.

Finally, Phaedo in *Simon* adverts to Prodicus' allegorization of Hesiod in the context of examining the value of work. Possibly, Phaedo criticizes Prodicus on the grounds that Simon achieved the goal of civic virtue, social recognition, even though he laboured as a lowly shoemaker. In this context it is worth noting—although we have not discussed the subject in this paper—how central consideration of craft-labour is for Plato, as he himself attempts to conceptualize the nature of civic virtue as a kind of knowledge in his early dialogues. Plato, like Critias in *Charmides*, might have a disparaging attitude towards craftsmen such as shoemakers, but the grounds of his anti-democratic, aristocratic sentiment differ from those of Critias. The particular difficulty for Socratics such as Plato, but also, for instance, Antisthenes, is how to make sense of good work if one rejects conventional conceptions of excellence as civic virtue as well as ethical hedonism in both its somatic and cognitive forms. In other words, at this point these heirs of Socrates must transcend their Hesiodic and Prodicean inheritance and forge a new conception of ethical value.

Temple University

BIBLIOGRAPHY

Alpers, J., *Hercules in bivio* (diss. Göttingen, 1912).

Brumbaugh, R. S., 'Simon and Socrates', *Ancient Philosophy*, 11 (1991), 151–2.

Carter, L. B., *The Quiet Athenian* (Oxford, 1982).

Classen, C. J., 'Aristippos', *Hermes*, 86 (1958), 182–92.

—— 'The Study of Language amongst Socrates' Contemporaries', in C. J. Classen (ed.), *Sophistik* (Darmstadt, 1976), 215–47.

Dupréel, E., *Les Sophistes: Protagoras, Gorgias, Prodicus, Hippias* (Neuchâtel, 1948).

Fehling, D., 'Protagoras und die ὀρθοέπεια', in C. J. Classen (ed.), *Sophistik* (Darmstadt, 1976), 341–7.

Galinsky, G. K., *The Herakles Theme* (Oxford, 1972).

Giannantoni, G., *Socratis et Socraticorum reliquiae* (4 vols.; Naples, 1990).

Gigon, O., *Kommentar zum zweiten Buch von Xenophons Memorabilien* (Basel, 1956).

Gray, V., 'The Linguistic Philosophies of Prodicus in Xenophon's "Choice of Heracles"?', *Classical Quarterly*, NS 56 (2006), 426–35.

Hock, R. F., 'Simon the Shoemaker as an Ideal Cynic', *Greek, Roman and Byzantine Studies*, 17 (1976), 41–53.

Malherbe, A. (ed.), *The Cynic Epistles* (Missoula, Mont., 1977).

Nestle, W., 'Die Horen des Prodikos', *Hermes*, 71 (1936), 151–70.

Rossetti, L., *Aspetti della letteratura socratica antica* (Chieti, 1977).

Sansone, D., 'Heracles at the Y', *Journal of Hellenic Studies*, 124 (2004), 125–42.

Sellars, J., 'Simon the Shoemaker and the Problem of Socrates', *Classical Philology*, 98 (2003), 207–16.

Thompson, D. B., 'The House of Simon the Shoemaker', *Archaeology*, 13 (1960), 234–40.

Waites, M. C., 'Some Features of the Allegorical Debate in Greek Literature', *Harvard Studies in Classical Philology*, 23 (1912), 1–46.

West, M. L. (ed.), *Hesiod:* Works and Days (Oxford, 1978).

Wilamowitz-Moellendorff, U. von, 'Phaidon von Elis', *Hermes*, 14 (1897), 187–93, 476–7; repr. in *Kleine Schriften*, iii. *Griechische Prosa*, ed. F. Zucker (Berlin, 1969), 41–8.

HERACLITUS' CRITIQUE
OF PYTHAGORAS' ENQUIRY
IN FRAGMENT 129

CARL A. HUFFMAN

1. Introduction

HERACLITUS is famous for his harsh critiques of predecessors and contemporaries. Homer (frs. 56 and 42), Hesiod (frs. 57 and 40), Archilochus (fr. 42), Hecataeus (fr. 40), and Xenophanes (fr. 40) are all objects of his scorn. It was above all Pythagoras, however, whom Heraclitus singled out for abuse (frs. 40, 81, and 129). In this paper I shall argue that two standard assumptions about his attack on Pythagoras in fragment 129 are mistaken and have led to a false interpretation of the nature of Pythagoras' philosophy. These assumptions have to do with the meaning of two words, ἱστορίη and συγγραφή. Most of my paper will be taken up with a detailed study of the usage of these two words, particularly in Herodotus, who provides the best parallel for Heraclitean usage. My analysis of fragment 129 also has more general implications for what was meant by 'enquiry' (ἱστορίη), a central term in most scholarly accounts of the intellectual history of sixth- and fifth-century Greece, and hence for why Heraclitus was critical of Pythagoras' practice of enquiry. I shall also have a new suggestion to make concerning the identity of the writings, συγγραφαί, which Heraclitus says that Pythagoras selected in order to make his own wisdom.

© Carl A. Huffman 2008

An earlier version of this paper was given in June 2006 at a conference on Heraclitus in Mexico City organized by Enrique Hülsz, whom I would like to thank for his kind hospitality.

2. The standard interpretation of ἱστορίη in fragment 129

Fragment 129 is preserved in Diogenes Laertius (8. 6) and runs as follows:

Πυθαγόρης Μνησάρχου ἱστορίην ἤσκησεν ἀνθρώπων μάλιστα πάντων καὶ ἐκλεξάμενος ταύτας τὰς συγγραφὰς ἐποιήσατο ἑαυτοῦ σοφίην, πολυμαθίην, κακοτεχνίην.

Pythagoras, the son of Mnesarchus, engaged in enquiry most of all men and, by selecting these things which have been written up, made a wisdom of his own,[1] a bunch of things learnt from others, an evil conspiracy.[2]

The passage is included among the doubtful fragments in Diels and Kranz because of problems raised by Diels and some other early scholars. Kranz himself argues, in a note, that the fragment is, in fact, authentic,[3] and it is universally accepted as authentic by more recent scholars (e.g. Guthrie, Robinson, Mansfeld, Marcovich, Kahn, KRS, and Barnes).[4] If we accept the current consensus that the fragment is authentic, however, several thorny problems

---

[1] J. Burnet, *Early Greek Philosophy* [*Early*] (New York, 1930), 134, and then H. Cherniss, review of H. Diels, *Die Fragmente der Vorsokratiker*, in *American Journal of Philology*, 60 (1939), 248–57 at 250, citing Hdt. 1. 129. 2, argue that ἐποιήσατο must be translated 'claimed as his own'. There is no reason, however, to assume that ἑαυτοῦ must be taken closely with ἐποιήσατο, as these scholars appear to do, rather than as simply modifying σοφίην. Powell's lexicon lists some 25 uses of ποιέω in which the middle appears to be used in the same way as the active (B 2), and that may be the case here, so that the translation is simply 'he made a wisdom of his own'. In Burnet's translation, moreover, the passage is a much less forceful critique of Pythagoras, since it says that he 'claimed for his own wisdom what was but a knowledge of many things and an imposture', which makes the polymathy and malpractice things for which Pythagoras was not responsible but which he rather borrowed from others.

[2] My translations of πολυμαθίην and κακοτεχνίην are justified at the end of the paper.

[3] DK i. 181.

[4] Diels had two main reasons for doubt (DK i. 181). First, he had understood Diogenes to be quoting the fragment as evidence that Pythagoras had written treatises. Since modern scholarship had shown that all treatises ascribed to Pythagoras are likely to be later forgeries, Diels assumed that fragment 129 had also been forged in order to authenticate the forgeries. Fragment 129, however, does not, in fact, assert that Pythagoras wrote anything, but at most that he enquired into and selected some writings of others: Burnet, *Early*, 134 n. 2; W. Burkert, *Lore and Science in Ancient Pythagoreanism* [*Lore*], trans. E. Minar (Cambridge, Mass., 1972), 131; J. Mansfeld, 'Fiddling the Books (Heraclitus B 129)' ['Fiddling'], in K. J. Boudouris (ed.), *Ionian Philosophy* (Athens, 1989), 229–34 at 230 (repr. in J. Mansfeld, *Studies in the Historiography of Greek Philosophy* (Assen, 1990), 443–8). Malcolm Schofield, in an unpublished paper ('Pythagoras the Plagiarist'), has moreover suggested persuasively that Diogenes was not in fact quoting Heraclitus as evidence that Pythagoras left writings. Diels's second reason for doubting the fragment has to do with what

of interpretation still present themselves concerning the terminology that it employs; two of these problems will be the focus of this paper. I shall begin with what is meant by 'enquiry', ἱστορίη, when Heraclitus says that Pythagoras 'engaged in enquiry most of all men'. The standard answer to this question can be seen in the two most important recent books on Pythagoras, those by Kahn and Riedweg. Kahn identifies ἱστορίη as 'a standard designation for Milesian science', and he goes on to list 'geometry, astronomy, geography and history' as examples of this science.[5] Kahn here translates ἱστορίη as 'enquiry' rather than 'science', although in a more recent article he translates it as 'scientific enquiry', as did Burnet and Marcovich.[6] Kahn's thesis that ἱστορίη does refer to Milesian science is a crucial premiss in his argument that fragment 129 provides reliable early evidence that Pythagoras participated in the tradition of Presocratic natural science and that, if he had written a book, it would have been 'intermediate between that of Anaximander and that of Philolaus'.[7] Riedweg similarly argues that ἱστορίη is not just any sort of enquiry but the enquiry 'characteristic of the earliest Ionian thinkers'.[8] Since Heraclitus 'unambiguously attributed'[9] ἱστορίη to Pythagoras in fragment 129, Kahn concludes that Pythagoras belonged to 'the intellectual world created by the new Milesian cosmology' and Riedweg that he had a 'natural philosophy of his own'.[10]

he perceived as an awkwardness in having the phrase 'these writings' refer back to 'enquiry'. Many scholars have followed K. Reinhardt, *Parmenides und die Geschichte der griechischen Philosophie* [*Parmenides*] (Bonn, 1916), 235 n. 1, in regarding the awkwardness as simply a characteristic of archaic Greek style, and it is hard to see why it should be taken as a sign of forgery. I shall argue below, moreover, that there is no particular awkwardness in the phrase when it is understood properly. Mansfeld ('Fiddling', 232) argues that fragment 129 is a parody of the standard beginning of books in the 6th and 5th cents. and that this is a good reason for regarding the fragment as authentic.

[5] C. Kahn, *Pythagoras and the Pythagoreans* [*Pythagoras*] (Indianapolis, 2001), 17.

[6] C. Kahn, 'Writing Philosophy: Prose and Poetry from Thales to Plato' ['Prose'], in H. Yunis (ed.), *Written Texts and the Rise of Literate Culture in Ancient Greece* (Cambridge, 2003), 139–61 at 140; Burnet, *Early*, 134; M. Marcovich, *Heraclitus: Greek Text with a Short Commentary* [*Heraclitus*] (Merida, 1967), 68.

[7] Kahn, *Pythagoras*, 17.

[8] C. Riedweg, *Pythagoras: His Life, Teaching and Influence* [*Pythagoras*] (Ithaca, NY, 2005), 78.   [9] Ibid.

[10] Kahn, *Pythagoras*, 17; Riedweg, *Pythagoras*, 78. Kahn and Riedweg are hardly alone in adopting this understanding of the word ἱστορίη. As already noted, Burnet and Marcovich explicitly translate it as 'scientific enquiry', and in G. S. Kirk, J. E. Raven, and M. Schofield, *The Presocratic Philosophers* [KRS] (Cambridge, 1983),

Kahn and Riedweg make two main assumptions about ἱστορίη:
(1) it implies a certain subject-matter, i.e. the natural world in
general and cosmology in particular; and (2) it implies a certain
methodology, that of the new Ionian science, which takes a rational
and critical view of traditional Greek mythological accounts of the
world. Another fragment of Heraclitus causes some difficulty for
this attempt to associate Pythagoras with Ionian rationalism. In
fragment 40 Heraclitus says:

πολυμαθίη νόον ἔχειν οὐ διδάσκει· Ἡσίοδον γὰρ ἂν ἐδίδαξε καὶ Πυθαγόρην αὖτίς
τε Ξενοφάνεά τε καὶ Ἑκαταῖον.

Much learning from others does not teach one to have insight. For it would
have taught Hesiod and Pythagoras and again Xenophanes and Hecataeus.

As Burkert has emphasized, the structure of Heraclitus' sentence
clearly associates Pythagoras and Hesiod as one pair and Xenophanes and Hecataeus as another.[11] Hesiod and Pythagoras are first
joined by a simple καί and then Heraclitus clearly marks the fact that
he is adding another distinct pair both by introducing them with
αὖτίς τε, 'and again', and also by joining Xenophanes and Hecataeus
with τε καί, which suggests that attention is being drawn to them
as a pair rather than simply joining them (LSJ s.v. II). Heraclitus
cannot be joining Pythagoras to Hesiod on grounds of chronology,
since Hesiod flourished 150 years before Pythagoras, while Xenophanes and Pythagoras are almost exact contemporaries. Thus, the
pairing with Hesiod suggests that Heraclitus saw some similarity in
outlook or approach between Pythagoras and Hesiod; Pythagoras
belongs not to the new world of Ionian rationalism represented by
Xenophanes and Hecataeus but rather to the mythological view of
the world found in Hesiod. Here the importance of the interpretation of ἱστορίη in fragment 129 emerges again, because Kahn uses
his interpretation of it as Milesian science to override the pairing
of Pythagoras and Hesiod in fragment 40, concluding that 'there is
no reason to suppose that the great learning ascribed to Pythagoras
is limited to theological genealogy in the style of Hesiod'.[12]

My first point is that ἱστορίη understood as the standard designation for Ionian science is an invention of modern scholarship. I
am not calling into question the existence of Ionian rationalism,

218, it is glossed as 'the voracious and critical practice of enquiry characteristic of
Ionian intellectuals'.

[11] Burkert, *Lore*, 210.   [12] Kahn, *Pythagoras*, 17.

but rather the contention that the Greek word ἱστορίη picks out this new mode of thought. In Herodotus, who provides the best parallel for Heraclitean usage, ἱστορίη is a general word for enquiry that does imply an active curiosity and desire to know things but is not limited to a specific subject-matter or to a rational outlook on the world. It can just as easily refer to enquiry into various versions of a myth or into religious practices as into natural phenomena, and need not imply any interest in rationalizing those myths or religious practices. Nor is ἱστορίη usually based on eyewitness reports, as has sometimes been suggested. The uses found in Herodotus suggest that it in fact emphasizes enquiry into hearsay evidence, into what people say or have written. Let us look at the evidence.

3. The meaning of ἱστορίη in fifth- and fourth-century Greek

ἱστορίη (ἱστορία in Attic), the cognate verb ἱστορέω, and the cognate agent noun ἵστωρ are relatively uncommon words in Greek epistemological vocabulary. Most surprising of all, if ἱστορίη was indeed the standard word for Ionian natural science, the verb never appears in the fragments of the Presocratics, and the two nouns appear only once each. ἱστορίη itself appears only here in fragment 129 of Heraclitus.[13] This might not seem too surprising, since almost nothing of the earliest Ionian texts by Anaximander and Anaximenes has survived. It is puzzling, however, that the word that is regarded as central to the Ionian rationalism on which the Presocratic tradition is based does not appear anywhere later in that tradition except in Heraclitus' critique of Pythagoras in fragment 129. Nor is the word particularly common outside Presocratic texts. It appears four times in Hippocratic treatises that are likely to be early, three times in Plato, and twice in Isocrates. Interestingly, it is never used by Thucydides. It is more common in Aristotle, appearing between thirty and forty times, depending on which treatises of Aristotle are regarded as authentic.[14]

What, then, has given rise to the common idea that ἱστορίη is

---

[13] ἵστωρ appears only in fragment 35 of Heraclitus. ἱστορέω appears only in fragment 299 of Democritus, which is usually regarded as spurious.

[14] I shall concentrate on uses of ἱστορίη itself, noting the evidence for ἵστωρ and ἱστορέω only where relevant. These other two words are just as rare or even rarer, however. Neither of them appears in Thucydides. ἱστορέω is never used by Plato, and ἵστωρ appears just twice.

the standard word for Ionian natural science? The answer lies in a
passage from Plato's *Phaedo*. At 96 A Socrates reports that in his
youth he desired 'this wisdom which they call enquiry concerning
nature' (περὶ φύσεως ἱστορίαν). The sorts of issues considered by
those engaged in this 'enquiry concerning nature' are clearly the
things considered in typical Presocratic cosmological texts, i.e. the
phenomena of heaven and earth in general (96 C τὰ περὶ τὸν οὐρανὸν
καὶ τὴν γῆν πάθη) and in particular such questions as whether we
think with blood or air or fire. What is it legitimate to conclude
about the use of ἱστορία from this passage? First, some people at
the beginning of the fourth century, when Socrates is supposed to
have said these words, called Presocratic natural science περὶ φύσεως
ἱστορίαν, 'enquiry concerning nature'. There is no indication that
Plato intends us to understand this as the term used by the first
Presocratics in the sixth century. The expression 'they call' is vague
regarding a subject and is most naturally taken as indicating either
the common usage of the time when Socrates is speaking or the
usage of experts in the field at that time. It is even more crucial
to note that there is not the slightest indication that the bare term
ἱστορία, which is what is found in Heraclitus fragment 129, could be
used to refer to Presocratic natural science. It is not 'enquiry' that
is the technical term for Ionian science in the *Phaedo* but 'enquiry
concerning nature'.

The relatively rich Aristotelian evidence for the usage of ἱστορία
clearly suggests that the qualifying phrase 'concerning nature' is
indeed crucial to pick out Ionian science. Aristotle once only, in *De
caelo* (298^{b}2), uses Plato's expression περὶ φύσεως ἱστορία in order
to refer to natural science as what deals with elements such as earth
and fire but also the heaven and its parts, as well as plants and
animals, i.e. the general subjects dealt with in Presocratic cosmology. This, however, is just one sort of enquiry, one sort of ἱστορία.
In the biological treatises Aristotle frequently (e.g. *GA* 716^{b}31)
gives cross-references to what he has said ἐν ταῖς ἱστορίαις ταῖς περὶ
τῶν ζῴων, 'in the enquiries concerning animals'.[15] In a couple of
places in the biological treatises he refers just to what he has said
in 'the enquiries', where the context makes it clear that this is simply a shorter way of referring to 'the enquiries concerning animals'
(e.g. *GA* 719^{a}10). Yet another type of enquiry is specified in the

---

[15] These are references to the treatise whose title is often incorrectly translated
as *The History of Animals*.

De anima, where Aristotle once refers to 'the enquiry concerning soul' (402ᵃ4). All the uses so far have been applied to natural science. In the *Rhetoric*, however, Aristotle moves on to talk about 'the enquiries of those writing about human actions' (1360ᵃ37), which is a reference to what we would call history, to the writings of Herodotus and Thucydides. In the *Poetics* Aristotle uses the bare word ἱστορία several times as a shorthand to refer to this sort of enquiry (1451ᵇ2, 1451ᵇ11). There are two passages in Aristotle where ἱστορία is used without any indication of subject-matter, expressed or implied by the context (*Pr. An.* 46ᵃ22; *HA* 491ᵃ2). In both cases the word clearly has the general meaning 'enquiry (of whatever sort)' and does not pick out Ionian science or any other particular type of enquiry. Aristotle's usage thus shows that ἱστορία is, in itself, a general term meaning 'enquiry', which can be applied to a wide range of subject-matters by adding a qualifying phrase. There is no evidence whatsoever that the bare term ἱστορία would have normally conveyed a reference to Ionian science.

In LSJ three senses of ἱστορία are listed. The first is the use we have been examining, 'enquiry', and the last is the relatively rare use, at least in the early texts, meaning 'written account of one's enquiries'. In the second use, the other common one, ἱστορία refers to the knowledge obtained by the enquiry and thus is often translated 'information' or 'learning'. In this usage as well the bare term refers to learning in general and does not pick out a specific type of learning.[16] In the *Panathenaicus* (*c.*339 BC) Isocrates puts into the mouth of one of his students a critique of his speech on Athens and Sparta as being 'difficult and hard to understand, bursting with much learning and philosophy' (πολλῆς μὲν ἱστορίας γέμοντα καὶ φιλοσοφίας, 246. 6). There is not room to unpack all the nuances in the language here, but it is clear that, given the subject of the speech, ἱστορία must be either history in the modern sense, i.e. learning about events of the past, or more likely learning in a general sense that would include observations on a wide variety of topics, such as the constitutions of Athens and Sparta. What is

---

[16] The second of Plato's three uses of ἱστορία belongs to this class. In the *Phaedrus*, in a passage discussing prophecy, Socrates explains the name given to divination by use of birds and other signs, *oionoistic*, as resulting from the fact that 'it uses reasoning to bring intelligence [νοῦν] and learning [ἱστορίαν] into human thought [οἰήσει]' (244 C–D; trans. Woodruff and Nehamas). Plato's third use (*Crat.* 437 B) does not shed much light on the issues discussed in this paper. A fanciful etymology is given for the word as 'it stops the flow' (ἵστησι τὸν ῥοῦν).

again extremely unlikely is that ἱστορία is a reference to Presocratic science.[17]

Before turning back to the earliest uses of ἱστορίη, those in Herodotus, two further passages need to be examined, one from the late fifth century and one considerably later again. First, fragment 910 Nauck[2] of Euripides is often cited, along with the passage from the *Phaedo* discussed above, as evidence that ἱστορία means Ionian science, since the fragment describes one who has gained understanding of ἱστορία as 'beholding the ageless order of undying nature'. It is important to look at the whole fragment, however:

> ὄλβιος ὅστις τῆς ἱστορίας
> ἔσχε μάθησιν
> μήτε πολιτῶν ἐπὶ πημοσύνην
> μήτ' εἰς ἀδίκους πράξεις ὁρμῶν
> ἀλλ' ἀθανάτου καθορῶν φύσεως
> κόσμον ἀγήρων . . .

Happy is he who gains understanding of learning, not for the harm of the citizens nor for entering into unjust acts, but beholding the ageless order of undying nature . . .

The last phrase clearly does refer to the Presocratic cosmological tradition and shows that Ionian science is one sort of ἱστορία, one sort of learning. The fragment does not show, however, that the bare word ἱστορία indicates this sort of enquiry. Scholars jump quickly from the first two lines of the fragment, 'happy is he who gains understanding of learning', to the description of the happy man as 'beholding the ageless order of undying nature' in lines 5 and 6. In lines 3 and 4 we are told that the happy man does not gain learning 'for the harm of the citizens nor for entering into unjust acts'. It is possible that Euripides is envisaging someone as gaining learning about the cosmos in order to commit unjust acts or to harm the citizens, but it is surely more likely that he is thinking of learning

---

[17] The other use of ἱστορία in Isocrates picks out a specific field of learning. Isocrates' *Letter to the Rulers of Mytilene* begs the rulers to allow his grandson's music teacher, Agenor, to return from exile. Isocrates praises Agenor as the foremost man of the present day 'in the learning that belongs to this branch of education' (4: περὶ τὴν ἱστορίαν τῆς παιδείας ταύτης). We can thus add *mousikē* to the disciplines that can be picked out by ἱστορία, if the proper qualifying phrase is added. Three of the four uses of ἱστορίη in early Hippocratic treatises also bear the general meaning 'learning' (*Art* 1. 2; *Precepts* 13. 9; 13. 12), although in a fourth case the learning is specified as knowledge of 'what man is and through what causes he arises' (*On Ancient Medicine* 20).

of a different sort, learning such as the sophists retailed, the skill in
oratorical tricks and eristic reasoning, which was commonly viewed
as leading to unjust behaviour. Thus fragment 910 says that it is not
the person who pursues learning in areas that lead to the harm of
fellow citizens who is happy but rather he who pursues the learning
that focuses on the order of nature. Study of the cosmos is a possible
type of enquiry or learning, but fragment 910 provides no evidence
that ἱστορία used by itself picked out this specific sort of enquiry.

The final passage is over a hundred years later in date but still
crucial for understanding the meaning of ἱστορία. As Burkert has
emphasized, Hermesianax of Colophon, a Greek poet of the early
third century BC, specifically connects Hesiod to ἱστορίη, describing him in fragment 7 (Athen. 13, 597 B) as 'the keeper [or master]
of all learning' (πάσης ἤρανον ἱστορίης).[18] Nothing in the context
suggests that Hermesianax sees Hesiod as engaging in Ionian natural science. By far the most likely interpretation of Hesiod's vast
'learning' is his familiarity with the mythological traditions about
the gods reflected in the *Theogony* and with wisdom literature such
as is presented in the *Works and Days*. The crucial point is that the
standard interpretation of fragment 129 has used the word ἱστορίη
as evidence that, despite Heraclitus' pairing of Pythagoras with
Hesiod in fragment 40, Pythagoras must be distinguished from
Hesiod and instead joined with practitioners of Ionian natural science such as Xenophanes. The passage from Hermesianax shows
that this is a problematic argument, since Hesiod too is described as
practising ἱστορίη, thus making it perfectly plausible that Heraclitus saw both Hesiod and Pythagoras as practising ἱστορίη, although
labelling Pythagoras as even outdoing Hesiod. The pairing with
Hesiod suggests, however, that Pythagoras' learning was not specifically Ionian science but rather the sort of learning we find in the
Theogony and *Works and Days*. It is puzzling that neither Kahn nor
Riedweg, nor anyone else advocating the standard view, has discussed this passage of Hermesianax. Perhaps they simply regard
the passage as too late to provide evidence for usage at the time of
Heraclitus; it is time to turn to that usage now, and it will emerge
that the Hermesianax passage is perfectly in accord with the early
usage as revealed in Herodotus.

Herodotus provides our best parallel for Heraclitus' usage for
several reasons. He did write before Plato or Aristotle, in the 420s

---

[18] Burkert, *Lore*, 210.

or earlier. Even more importantly, he wrote in the Ionic dialect used by Heraclitus. In addition, he clearly made use of earlier Ionian writers such as Hecataeus, so that his usage of ἱστορίη is the closest we are likely to get to what Heraclitus might have meant by the term. Indeed Kahn, in his now classic book on Heraclitus, argues that for 'the normal usage of . . . words in Ionic prose, their "ordinary" meaning for Heraclitus' original audience . . . our best guide will be the usage of Herodotus'.[19] Herodotean usage of ἱστορίη largely conforms to the later usage studied above; it refers to enquiry in general and does not refer to a specific subject-matter or methodology. Herodotean usage does suggest, however, some connotations as to the nature of the enquiry that are particularly relevant to Heraclitus' usage of the term in fragment 129.

The usage of ἱστορίη in Herodotus has received particular attention because of his status as the founder of the discipline we call history. Much attention has been paid to the etymology of the word. The standard view is that it is related to the root *wid-* meaning 'to see',[20] although a derivation has also been suggested from ἵζειν 'to seat', which would refer to the role of the official known as an ἵστωρ in convening people in order to hear evidence.[21] To some extent, however, the proposed etymologies, and in particular the dominant etymology from the root meaning 'to see', have led to misleading generalizations, such as the idea that ἱστορίη always involves eyewitness evidence,[22] which is contradicted by Herodotus' actual usage,

[19] C. H. Kahn, *The Art and Thought of Heraclitus* [*Art*] (Cambridge, 1979), 92.

[20] E. J. Bakker, 'The Making of History: Herodotus' *Historiês Apodexis*' ['Making'], in E. J. Bakker, I. J. F. De Jong, and H. Van Wees (eds.), *Brill's Companion to Herodotus* (Leiden, 2002), 3–32 at 13.

[21] E. D. Floyd, 'The Sources of Greek ἵστωρ "Judge, Witness"', *Glotta*, 68 (1990), 157–66. W. R. Connor, 'The Histor in History', in R. M. Rosen and J. S. Farrell (eds.), *Nomodeiktes: Greek Studies in Honor of Martin Ostwald* (Ann Arbor, 1993), 3–15, has drawn attention to the similarities between Herodotus' own behaviour as an enquirer, particularly in the earlier books of his history, and what we know of the functions of the ἵστωρ from authors such as Homer. Like the ἵστωρ, Herodotus sets himself up as an arbitrator, who adjudicates between rival views. One wonders, however, how far it is legitimate to push the parallel since the noun ἵστωρ is never used by Herodotus.

[22] H. Fränkel, 'Xenophanes' Empiricism and his Critique of Knowledge (B 34)', in A. P. D. Mourelatos (ed.), *The Pre-Socratics* (Princeton, 1993), 118–31 at 125, identifies the realm of *historiē* as what can be reliably investigated in contrast to legend and translates it 'direct acquaintance' (130). Although Herodotus clearly regards Croesus as a more reliable place to begin one's discussion of the cause of the war, there is no indication that he regards the various myths about figures such as Io and Europa told by the Persians, Greeks, and Phoenicians, with which he begins

in which he distinguishes what he has seen from what he has learnt by enquiry (2. 99. 1). The most recent studies conclude that in Herodotus ἱστορία is 'a means to gain information through hearing'.[23] 'The core of the concept is not so much seeing yourself as acquiring knowledge through the interrogation of others',[24] so that it is literally the collection of 'hearsay evidence'.[25]

What is the Herodotean evidence? Surprisingly, ἱστορίη appears only five times. The verb ἱστορέω is more common, being used seventeen times. I shall begin with the five uses of ἱστορίη. The most famous is in the first sentence of Herodotus' book, in which he announces that 'this is the setting forth of the enquiry [ἱστορίης ἀπόδεξις] of Herodotus of Halicarnassus'. The context is so general here that it is hard to draw conclusions, but two observations are important. First, there is a difference between the enquiry and the publication of the enquiry. The setting forth of his enquiries includes the organization of his material and conclusions drawn from it, but the ἱστορίη proper is the investigations he undertook.[26] Second, the use of ἱστορίη in the first sentence, as an introduction to the whole work, suggests that it here has a very broad sense, including all the enquiries Herodotus made: enquiries he made of other people, texts he consulted, and things he saw. It will then include topics that Herodotus shares with Presocratic cosmologists, such as the reasons why the Nile floods in the summer (2. 19–27),[27] but it will also include the myths about Io and Europa with which

his history, as separate from his enquiry. Surely it would be odd for Herodotus to state that he is presenting the results of his enquiries and then immediately go on to list legends which he did not consider part of his enquiries.

[23] Bakker, 'Making', 15.   [24] Ibid. 16.

[25] A. B. Lloyd, 'Egypt', in Bakker, De Jong, and Van Wees (eds.), *Brill's Companion to Herodotus*, 415–35 at 419. Bakker still stresses that the others whom you interrogate are presumed to have been eyewitnesses, although this is in tension with his statement that ἱστορία is a means of getting information about 'what is beyond perception, remote in space or time' ('Making', 16). He also stresses that the listening is 'critical listening' ('Making', 15). As I hope to show below, however, the evidence really suggests that ἱστορίη proper is simply making enquiries without any limitation to eyewitnesses, and that, while Herodotus makes critical judgements about his enquiries, ἱστορία proper focuses on the enquiries rather than the judgements.

[26] See also 7. 96, where Herodotus says that he will not report information gained by enquiry, i.e. the names of the leaders of the native contingents in the Persian army, because these names are not necessary 'for the account of his enquiry' (ἐς ἱστορίης λόγον).

[27] See D. W. Graham, 'Philosophy on the Nile: Herodotus and Ionian Research' ['Nile'], *Apeiron*, 36/4 (2003), 291–310.

Herodotus begins his book (1. 1–5), as well as his reports of the customs of various peoples and his accounts of strange animals.

More specific insight can be gained into the meaning of ἱστορίη from two passages in book 2, in which Herodotus describes not his own ἱστορίη but that of the Egyptian priests. Herodotus reports (2. 118) that he asked the Egyptian priests whether the Greek account of the events at Troy was true. The priests then gave an account of the events that they said they knew from Menelaus himself on the basis of enquiries (ἱστορίῃσι φάμενοι εἰδέναι παρ' αὐτοῦ Μενέλεω). The crucial point to note is the subject-matter of these enquiries. They are not enquiries about natural science but about traditional stories, i.e. myths, in this case the central myth in the Greek tradition, that of the Trojan war. Thus, for Herodotus the collection of different versions of myths is a perfectly legitimate activity for ἱστορίη.[28] An even clearer indication about the connotations of the word ἱστορίη comes at the end of the Egyptian priests' account of Helen and Menelaus (2. 119). Herodotus comments that the priests told him that they knew (ἐπίστασθαι) some of these things by enquiries (ἱστορίῃσι) but that other things they knew with certainty (ἀτρεκέως ἐπιστάμενοι), since they had occurred in their country (παρ' ἑωυτοῖσι γενόμενα). Here ἱστορίη is used of enquiries made about events that occurred outside Egypt and that are thus more remote and less reliably known than information that the priests were able to obtain from sources inside Egypt itself. Thus ἱστορίη has the connotation of enquiries that go beyond what is readily at hand and thus that require effort and probably travel but which are also less likely to yield certain knowledge.

A third passage from book 2 describes Herodotus' own enquiry rather than that of the priests and is crucial, in that it distinguishes ἱστορίη from other aspects of Herodotus' methodology. In the middle of book 2 (99) Herodotus says that what he has said up to this point in the book is the result of 'what I have seen, my judgement, and my enquiry' (ὄψις τε ἐμὴ καὶ γνώμη καὶ ἱστορίη). These would then seem to be the three main tools that Herodotus relies on in his account of Egypt: what he has seen himself, his judgements about what he has seen and heard, and what he has learnt from making enquiries of others. This passage shows that,

---

[28] The Egyptian priests' claim to have knowledge from Menelaus himself would have to be based on their confidence that they had uncovered an oral tradition or written document that ultimately went back to him.

properly speaking, ἱστορίη is not based on autopsy, nor is it constituted by Herodotus' judgements about what is reasonable; ἱστορίη
is instead constituted by what we see most in Herodotus, his reports of what various people say in response to his enquires, i.e.
hearsay evidence. In this passage of book 2 Herodotus goes on to
say that in the rest of this book he will tell the Egyptian accounts
(Αἰγυπτίους . . . λόγους) in accord with what he has heard (κατὰ τὰ
ἤκουον). What follows makes it clear that he is referring to what
he has heard from the Egyptian priests. At first sight it is hard to
understand what the distinction is between his enquiries up to this
point in book 2, i.e. what he has heard from people he asked, what
he learnt by ἱστορίη, and the information he presents in the rest
of the book as what he has heard from the Egyptian priests. The
crucial difference may well be that the material presented in the
second half of the book is material that Herodotus reports on the
basis of just one source, without making further enquiries. ἱστορίη
would thus seem to have the connotation of active collection of
what people say on a given topic rather than simply reporting one
source: that is, it is a 'survey' of opinions on the topic.[29]

It is important once again to note the wide range of topics covered
by the enquiries that constitute ἱστορίη for Herodotus. In the first
half of book 2, which Herodotus labels as the result of his ἱστορίη, he
does enquire about topics in natural science such as the behaviour of
the Nile (2. 19–27); he also enquires, however, into ritual practices,
such as the Thebans' custom of sacrificing goats but refusal even to
touch sheep (2. 42); and he enquires about the myths of Heracles
that justify this ritual practice, on the grounds that Heracles was
allowed to see Zeus but only when Zeus was wearing the head and
fleece of a ram. The ram is thus held sacred and not sacrificed. In
most cases, what Herodotus reports is the result of what people
tell him orally in response to questions, but it seems likely to me
that some of his enquiries were directed to written sources and that
some of 'what people say' was what they said in writing. Thus,
when Herodotus reports the three different Greek explanations of
the flooding of the Nile, he may well be relying on what he has read
in Greek authors such as Hecataeus and Anaxagoras.[30]

These are all five uses of ἱστορίη in Herodotus; they show that it is
the active collection of what people say on a given topic. It can deal
with natural phenomena, but topics such as myths and religious

---

[29] I owe the translation 'survey' to David Sedley.   [30] See Graham, 'Nile'.

practices are in fact more common. ἱστορίη is, moreover, not limited to rational explanations of natural phenomena or human behaviour. The Thebans' behaviour regarding sheep is not rationalized but rather explained in terms of a myth. The seventeen uses of the verb ἱστορέω amply confirm these results concerning ἱστορίη, although I shall not go through them in detail. The verb is used primarily of questioning a person or making enquiries of a number of people. Many of the uses have nothing to do with Herodotus' practice of ἱστορίη but refer to questions that one person asks another in the course of human life, e.g. a father enquiring of a son as to what his grandfather had said (3. 51). In some cases these enquiries require travel, but the emphasis is on what is discovered by asking people rather than on what is seen as part of the travel.[31]

What, finally, does Herodotean usage, and the usage of other fifth- and fourth-century authors, tell us about what Heraclitus is likely to mean by ἱστορίη in fragment 129?[32] First, there is absolutely no support for the idea that Pythagoras' practice of ἱστορίη refers specifically to Ionian science. This conclusion would be justified

[31] Powell lists seven uses in which a specific person or group of persons is questioned, often with an accompanying indirect question. In another nine cases the verb is used absolutely, without specifying any person that was asked. Croesus is portrayed as making enquiries (ἱστορέων) as to who were the most powerful of the Greeks (1. 56). The connection of ἱστορίη with hearing as opposed to autopsy appears again in Herodotus' report at 2. 29 that, regarding the sources of the Nile, his account was based on his own travel and sight (αὐτόπτης ἐλθών) as far as Elephantine, but beyond that point his account is based on 'enquiring by hearsay' (ἀκοῇ . . . ἱστορέων).

[32] In fragment 35 Heraclitus uses the noun ἵστωρ, which is the agent noun related to ἱστορέω and ἱστορία: χρὴ εὖ μάλα πολλῶν ἵστορας φιλοσόφους ἄνδρας εἶναι ('It is necessary that men who love wisdom have knowledge of a good many things'). I follow Kahn (Art, 105) in assigning all the wording to Heraclitus. Unfortunately, in this case we cannot appeal to Herodotus for insight, since he never uses the word. Most historians of ancient philosophy translate ἵστωρ as 'enquirer' (e.g. Kahn, Robinson, KRS), because of its etymological connection to ἱστορία, but I cannot find a parallel for such a translation. The closest is the usage as 'arbitrator' (Hom. Il. 23. 486; cf. 18. 501). Such an arbitrator would have to make enquiries but is still not equivalent to an enquirer tout court. The most common usage in both earlier and later Greek is as an adjective describing someone as 'skilled' in some area (for example, in the Homeric Hymn to Selene, line 2, the Muses are 'skilled in song') or as 'having knowledge' (for example, the chorus in Sophocles' play calls Electra wretched and Electra responds (850) that she 'knows this, knows this all to well'— τοῦδ᾽ ἵστωρ, ὑπερίστωρ; cf. Hes. Op. 792 and West ad loc.). This suggests that ἵστορας in fragment 35 of Heraclitus should be translated 'having knowledge', but it is hard to know whether Heraclitus is mocking the new term φιλόσοφος (H. Granger, 'Heraclitus' Quarrel with Polymathy and Historiê' ['Quarrel'], Transactions of the American Philological Association, 134 (2004), 235–61 at 250), which a questionable later tradition said Pythagoras coined, or adopting it himself.

only if Heraclitus had said that Pythagoras had practised ἱστορίη περὶ φύσεως more than most men. Both Herodotean usage and later practice suggest that the Greek reader of fragment 129 would have taken ἱστορίη as a quite general term meaning enquiry, which did not imply any specific subject-matter or methodology in dealing with the world.[33] Herodotean usage suggests that Heraclitus' audience would have understood him to be saying that Pythagoras was actively engaged in collecting what people say on a number of topics, in making enquiries, and that he created his wisdom out of this hearsay evidence. Granger has recently made a convincing argument that, if Heraclitus were familiar with an early version of the brief maxims on ritual and mythology known as the Pythagorean *akousmata* or *symbola*, he 'would have good reason . . . to think that Pythagoras borrows many of his ideas from others and is merely a compiler of opinions'.[34] Burkert in particular has shown that the *akousmata* are not radically new in content but draw on earlier ritual practices.[35] Indeed, two of our other early sources for Pythagoras stress precisely his vast learning of the opinions of others and his 'borrowing' of those opinions. Ion of Chios thus says that Pythagoras 'above all knew and mastered the opinions of men' (fr. 4. 3–4). Herodotus attributes the doctrine of metempsychosis to the Egyptians and reports that some Greeks have used it as something unique to themselves (2. 123). There is little doubt that Herodotus is here referring in part to the most famous exponent of metempsychosis in the Greek tradition, Pythagoras, and accusing him of the same thing as Heraclitus is, i.e. collecting the opinions of others, in this case of the Egyptians, and claiming them as his own. Heraclitus' use of ἱστορίη, far from connecting Pythagoras to the tradition of independent and rational thought which is characteristic of Ionian cosmological speculation, instead portrays him as the consummate enquirer into and collector of the opinions of others. Such opinions might include those of the Ionian natural philosophers, but the use of the word ἱστορίη is no indication that they did, and they are just as likely to have included the religious practices and myths that are reflected in the *akousmata*. This conclusion in turn leads us to the other central problem in the fragment. What are the συγγραφαί which Pythagoras selected from his enquiries in order to

---

[33] Modern scholars would be well advised either to use ἱστορίη περὶ φύσεως or to find a new expression to designate the Ionian practice of rational enquiry into nature.
[34] H. Granger, 'Quarrel', 247–8.   [35] Burkert, *Lore*, 177 ff.

construct his own wisdom, the wisdom that Heraclitus regards as at best a bunch of things learnt from others and at worst as an evil conspiracy (κακοτεχνίη)?[36]

4. The meaning of συγγραφή in fifth-century Greek

Before addressing the usage of συγγραφή in fragment 129, it is necessary to clarify some problems with the grammar of the sentence in which it occurs. When Heraclitus says that Pythagoras made a wisdom of his own 'by selecting these writings', a central problem of interpretation has been understanding the force of the demonstrative pronoun 'these'. It might be a reference to writings that Heraclitus had mentioned in a passage of his book shortly before fragment 129. The fragment seems otherwise self-contained, however, and it is hard to find parallels for such a reference from one fragment to another or to find any appropriate writings mentioned in the extant fragments, to which 'these' in fragment 129 could be referring. One solution to the awkwardness has been to emend the text and either to remove the whole phrase 'these writings' or to replace it with 'these things' and assume a reference to the end of the sentence (that is, these things are 'wisdom', 'polymathy', and 'evil conspiracy'), but neither of these solutions has won many followers.[37] Another approach has been to assume that 'these writings' are not some writings that Heraclitus has mentioned elsewhere but the writings that Pythagoras consulted in his enquiry. Some scholars have found it difficult to find the antecedent of 'these writings' in the simple word 'enquiry',[38] but others have taken it as an example of archaic style.[39] A more serious difficulty is that, if 'these writings' refer to those that Pythagoras consulted in his enquiry,

---

[36] For this translation of κακοτεχνίη see my argument later in the text.

[37] KRS, 217 n. 1; but this emendation may have appeared first in Zeller (Marcovich, *Heraclitus*, 67). The strongest argument against the emendation is that on the standard reading of Diogenes, as Mansfeld has pointed out ('Fiddling', 229), συγγραφάς must have been in the text used by Diogenes' source, since the fragment is quoted precisely to show that Pythagoras wrote. If ταῦτα rather than συγγραφάς was in the text, no one would have thought that the fragment provided evidence that Pythagoras wrote. The emendation is also awkward because, since ταῦτα still has to be the object of ἐκλεξάμενος, it portrays Pythagoras as finding these things, i.e. polymathy and evil conspiracy, in others and picking them out to be his own, whereas it is more plausible to suppose that Pythagoras creates the polymathy and evil conspiracy on the basis of what he borrows from others.

[38] e.g. Diels in DK i. 181.   [39] Reinhardt, *Parmenides*, 235.

then the participle 'selecting' (ἐκλεξάμενος) needs to be translated 'selecting from', since it would not make sense for Heraclitus to say that he *selected* all the writings that he consulted in his enquiry. If he used all the writings, he would not be making a selection. Herodotus, whose history provides the best parallel for Heraclitus' Ionic prose, does use ἐκλέγομαι seven times, but it never means 'to select from'; the object of the verb is always the things selected rather than the things selected from.[40] 'These writings', then, are writings that Pythagoras selected as a result of his enquiry, and it is still necessary to explain the force of 'these'. West suggested that 'these' was a contemptuous reference to certain texts.[41] This is the best solution to the problem, because it does not require us to look outside the fragment for the antecedent of 'these', and it allows ἐκλέγομαι to be used according to its normal sense. For his readers to understand the reference, however, 'these συγγραφαί' would have be well known and recognized from the mere use of the term συγγραφή. West implies that they were Orphic treatises. Kahn, however, has argued that συγγραφαί are technical handbooks or treatises 'of astronomical lore, physical speculation, and applied mathematics',[42] and Schofield is similarly attracted to the idea that συγγραφαί referred to systematic treatises in prose and would particularly connoted Ionian cosmologies such as those by Anaximander and Anaximenes but also the cosmogony of Pherecydes, which is sometimes identified as the first prose book.[43]

Underlying Kahn's, Schofield's, and many other interpretations of what 'these writings' might be is the assumption that 'συγγραφαί

---

[40] Marcovich (*Heraclitus*, 69) notes that 'ἐκλεξάμενος is well documented in Herodotus', but does not recognize that the difficulty is not that Heraclitus used the word but that he used it with the meaning 'to select from', which is not paralleled in Herodotus. Hussey as reported by Kahn (*Art*, 309 n. 79) noted the difficulty with supposing that ἐκλέγομαι could mean 'select from'. Kahn responds by appealing to Reinhardt's claim that this is a sign of archaic style. Reinhardt, however, used archaic style as an explanation of how ἱστορίην could serve as the antecedent for συγγραφάς and not as an explanation of how ἐκλέγομαι could mean 'select from'.

[41] As a parallel for this usage of οὗτος he cites Heraclitus' contemptuous reference to 'these statues' (τοῖς ἀγάλμασι . . . τουτέοισιν) to which mortals pray (fr. 5). Further support for this interpretation can be found in LSJ s.v. C I. 3, where they note that 'οὗτος is used emphat., generally in contempt while ἐκεῖνος denotes praise' and provide further parallels.

[42] Kahn, 'Prose', 152.

[43] 'Pythagoras the Plagiarist' (unpublished paper, delivered on Samos in July 2005).

are probably prose treatises'.[44] This assumption has again led to
the conclusion that Pythagoras was working in the tradition of Ionian natural science, since the only prose treatises that we know
of which Pythagoras could have consulted are the books of Pherecydes, Anaximander, and Anaximenes or technical treatises on architecture, such as the books by Theodorus and Rhoecus on the
Samian Heraion and Chersiphon and Metagenes on the temple of
Artemis at Ephesus (Vitruv. 7, praef. 12).[45] Pherecydes' book presented a cosmogony of a more mythical sort, but it is specifically
cosmogonical and in combination with the Ionian prose treatises
would suggest a special interest in cosmogony and cosmology on
Pythagoras' part. Since Heraclitus refers to more than one writing
that Pythagoras selected, then given the scarcity of prose treatises,
he cannot be referring to Pherecydes alone, and it is inevitable
that the Ionian cosmologists would have to be included, which in
turn would show that Pythagoras was indeed involved in the world
of Ionian natural science. The assumptions that the συγγραφαί to
which Heraclitus refers in fragment 129 are prose treatises and
that they must have been reasonably numerous for Heraclitus to
describe Pythagoras as making a selection of them lead Kahn to
the hypothesis that by the middle of the sixth century there was
'a fairly widespread use of written prose for largely practical purposes, including technical notes or memoranda . . . produced by
and designed for specialists in astronomy, geometry, architecture,
sculpture and music'. Kahn supposes that many prose writings of
the sixth century were lost and that the books of Pherecydes, Anaximander, and Anaximenes are 'the tip of the iceberg', and perhaps
'signal . . . the moment when technical material begins to be presented in the form of literary prose'.[46] Clearly, assumptions about
the meaning of συγγραφή are playing a very significant role in the
reconstruction of sixth-century thought.

My second major point in this paper is that συγγραφή has been
misinterpreted in important ways. Although by the end of the fifth
century it was typically used to refer to prose treatises, (1) it did
not, even then, mean 'prose treatise' but was a more general term
meaning 'composition', and (2) the earliest uses of the noun and
the related verb, which are found in Herodotus, show that it re-

---

[44] Marcovich, *Heraclitus*, 69; so also Kahn, *Art*, 113; 'Prose', 148.
[45] See R. Hahn, *Anaximander and the Architects* (Albany, NY, 2001).
[46] Kahn, 'Prose', 151, 152–3.

ferred to anything written down, including verse as well as prose.
Thus, the συγγραφαί which Pythagoras selected need not have been
Ionian prose treatises and could have included Orphic poems as
well as Homeric and Hesiodic poetry.[47] There is no reason to suppose that συγγραφαί is a technical term for Ionian cosmological
and technical treatises and hence that Pythagoras was primarily a
cosmologist. Herodotus' usage further suggests, moreover, (3) that
συγγραφαί were typically written records of very short texts such as
oracles. This usage provides the basis for a speculative suggestion
as to what 'these things which have been written up' might be in
a Pythagorean context. Before spelling out this suggestion, however, it is first necessary to examine the usage of συγγραφή in some
detail, in order to show that it supports my contentions about the
meaning of συγγραφή in fragment 129.

As is the case with ἱστορίη, fragment 129 of Heraclitus is the
earliest surviving Greek text to use the word συγγραφή. Herodotus
uses συγγραφή itself only once, but he uses the related verb συγγράφω
six times and the related noun form σύγγραμμα once, so we may
be able to gain important insight from him as to the meaning of
συγγραφή in fragment 129. In the later fifth century the agent noun
συγγραφεύς also appears. I shall start from texts of the later fifth and
early fourth centuries, where the evidence is more plentiful, in order
to give an idea of the range of meanings that developed for these
words, before returning to the earlier uses in Herodotus. LSJ give
as the first meaning 'a writing or noting down', but the majority
of examples of the word refer to the result of this writing, i.e. 'that
which is written'. Within the class of what is written, there are then
two basic types of writing to which συγγραφή can refer. First, that
which is written can be a 'book, esp. in prose, history, narrative'. It
is undoubtedly this comment in LSJ, that συγγραφή was especially
applied to prose works, that has led to the standard remark by
commentators on Heraclitus 129, that a συγγραφή was usually a
prose work.[48] Second, what is written can be much shorter texts

---

[47] M. L. West, *The Orphic Poems* [*Orphic*] (Oxford, 1983), 8. Mansfeld translates
ταύτας τὰς συγγραφάς as 'the literature involved' and appears to think that essentially
all of Greek literature available at the time is meant ('Fiddling', 229–31). I agree
that in itself συγγραφαί can have this breadth of reference, but it is not clear to me
that the demonstrative pronoun can be translated as 'involved' or how Mansfeld is
taking account of its limiting force.

[48] Kahn ('Prose', 148 n. 21) cites K. J. Dover, *The Evolution of Greek Prose Style*
[*Prose*] (Oxford, 1997), 183–4, as evidence for 'the restriction of *syngraphê* to works

which record agreements of some sort, such as decrees, contracts, bonds, regulations, or specifications. I shall return below to this important second type of writing.

The evidence does indeed show that, when referring to a book, a συγγραφή was usually a prose treatise, just as συγγράφω usually meant to compose in prose and a συγγραφεύς was usually a prose author. In fragment 6 the sophist Hippias says that he will make a speech by putting together things which were said 'some by Orpheus, some by Musaeus . . . some by Hesiod, some by Homer . . . and some by others of the poets [ποιητῶν] and some in compositions [ἐν συγγραφαῖς] by Greeks and foreigners'. Here the contrast between what was said by the poets and what was said in συγγραφαί clearly indicates that Hippias intended us to understand that these compositions were in prose. Plato makes exactly the same contrast using the verbs ποιεῖν and συγγράφειν when, in the *Lysis* (205 A), he has Hippothales deny that he has been making poems (ποιεῖν) and compositions (συγγράφειν) in honour of his beloved.[49]

The evidence thus shows that συγγραφή and the related verb were usually applied to prose treatises, often in explicit contrast to poetic works. None the less, it is important to note that the word is not likely to have literally meant 'prose composition'. This is clear for two reasons. First, on occasion both the verb συγγράφω and the noun σύγγραμμα could refer to a poetic composition. Thus, in the first sentence of the *Eudemian Ethics* Aristotle refers to something that Theognis composed (συνέγραψεν) for the propylaion of the temple of Leto on Delos, but goes on to say that he composed it in verse (ποιήσας) and quotes two lines of poetry. Similarly, in the *Laws* (858 D) Plato uses συγγράμματα to refer to compositions both with and without metre (ἄνευ μέτρων καὶ μετὰ μέτρων).[50] Second, the statement in the *Suda* (=DK 7 A 2) about Pherecydes that 'some report that he was the first to publish a composition in prose'

in prose'. Dover does observe that a composition in prose was usually denoted by συγγράφειν but also notes exceptions to this general pattern. More importantly, he stresses that this is 'usage of the fourth century and the late fifth; earlier terminology was different' (184). Dover does not himself go on to examine the earlier uses of συγγράφειν etc. in Herodotus as I do below. Kahn ('Prose', 148 n. 21) refers only to the lone use of συγγραφή in Herodotus and does not examine the uses of συγγράφειν and σύγγραμμα, for which see below.

[49] See also Plato, *Parm.* 128 A; Diog. Ap. fr. 4; D.L. I. 112. At Thuc. I. 97 συγγραφή is naturally translated 'history' (similarly D.H. *Thuc.* 5).

[50] See Dover, *Prose*, 184, for further examples.

(συγγραφὴν ἐξενεγκεῖν πεζῷ λόγῳ) makes no sense if συγγραφή simply means 'composition in prose'. There would be no need to add the words πεζῷ λόγῳ, which mean precisely 'in prose'.[51] The best way of describing the situation seems to be that, in the late fifth and fourth centuries, a συγγραφή is a composition; the normal implication is that it is in prose and this implication is sometimes made explicit by adding a phrase such as πεζῷ λόγῳ. συγγραφή is thus quite close to the English 'composition'. If I say that I am giving you my composition, you would normally expect it to be in prose, but the word 'composition' does not mean 'prose composition' and it is possible that my composition is in fact a poem.

There is a second major use of συγγραφή, with parallel uses in the verb and agent noun, according to which 'that which is written' is not a book or a treatise but something shorter, frequently a written version of what was often originally an agreement expressed orally. Here συγγραφαί are contracts, agreements, bonds, regulations, or specifications. In book 5 Thucydides reports that the Spartans proposed dates to the Athenians on which those states not agreeing to a treaty would become enemies of both Sparta and Athens, but he says that they proposed the dates ἄνευ συγγραφῆς, 'without having written them up', 'without a written agreement'. Lysias (30. 17) refers to carrying out sacrifices 'according to what has been written up' (κατὰ τὰς συγγραφάς), i.e. 'according to the written regulations'. There is only one use of συγγραφή in Aristotle, where it is a reference to 'contracts' (*Rhet.* 1335[b]7). In late fifth-century Athens there were boards of συγγραφεῖς ('commissioners') appointed to draw up συγγραφαί, which were memoranda serving a number of functions, such as defining the terms of treaties, stating rules regarding religious ritual, or giving building specifications.[52] In summary then, a συγγραφή refers to something written up, usually but not invariably in prose, which can either be (1) a long composition such as a history or a treatise such as that of Diogenes of Apollonia or (2) much briefer writings, which sometimes express agreements originally reached orally, such as the terms of a treaty or religious regulations. A natural English translation for these briefer writings is often 'documents'.[53]

---

[51] The first use of πεζός with regard to prose is found already in Plato (*Soph.* 237 A). See Dover, *Prose*, 185.

[52] See M. Munn, *The School of History* (Berkeley, 2000), 88 and 378 n. 63.

[53] I owe this suggestion to David Sedley.

With this background in mainly Athenian usage in the late fifth and early fourth centuries, it is now time to turn to the earliest evidence outside of Heraclitus, the history of Herodotus. In Herodotus too, a συγγραφή turns out to be something recorded in writing, but it is clear that the writing can be either in prose or in verse. Moreover, none of the examples refers to long writings such as books or treatises. All are recordings in relatively brief written texts of pieces of information or short utterances such as oracles. There is only one use of συγγραφή itself. At 1. 93 Herodotus reports that Lydia does not have many marvels ἐς συγγραφήν, 'for writing up', 'for recording', 'to document'. The verb συγγράφω is used with a similar meaning in its two uses in the active voice. In one passage Herodotus says that he is unable to record exactly (ἀτρεκέως συγγράψαι) who was brave and who was a coward in a given battle (6. 14); similarly, in book 3 he says that he will not record (οὐ συγγράφω) the appearance of the camel, since the Greeks are familiar with it already (103). In each of these three cases what is at issue is the recording of some quite limited item of information, such as the description of a camel or a list of those who distinguished themselves in a battle.

There are four further uses of the verb, all in the middle voice, and all used of recording or writing up an oracle that was delivered orally. At 1. 47–8 Herodotus tells the story of Croesus' famous test of the most prominent oracles. Croesus' envoys were to keep close track of time during their journey and then ask the oracle what Croesus was doing on a specific day and at a specific time. They were then to 'write down' (συγγραψαμένους) what the oracle said and bring it back to Croesus. Herodotus goes on to report the five-line oracular response given by the priestess at Delphi in hexameter verse and says that the Lydians, 'having written down' (συγγραψάμενοι) the oracle, returned to Sardis. After all his envoys return, Croesus opens each of the scrolls and surveys 'what was written down'. The word used here is not συγγραφή but rather the close synonym σύγγραμμα.[54]

Herodotus' use of συγγράφω of recording oracles has important implications. First, most oracles were given in verse, and Herodotus explicitly cites the verse text of the oracles in two cases (1. 47; 7. 141). Thus, in Herodotean usage, a σύγγραμμα and presumably a συγγραφή can just as easily be something written in verse as some-

---

[54] There are two further uses of συγγράφω of 'writing down' oracles: 7. 141 and 8. 135.

thing written in prose. Second, both in the case of the oracles and
in the other cases discussed above, a συγγραφή is not a book but
rather a short record of some sort. Finally, in the case of the oracles,
the soldiers who fought in the battle, and the wonders of Lydia, the
information was presumably originally provided orally and then
recorded in the συγγραφή. Herodotus' usage thus shows most similarity not to the later meaning of 'book' or 'treatise' but rather
to the writing up of oral agreements conveyed by the meanings
'regulations', 'contracts', and 'specifications'.

5. The meaning of συγγραφή in fragment 129

What then does this Herodotean usage suggest about the meaning of fragment 129 of Heraclitus? First, in referring to 'these
συγγραφαί' which Pythagoras selected, even if we suppose that he
means books, it is not at all clear that Heraclitus meant us to understand that these books were in prose rather than poetry. Since
Herodotus uses συγγράφω for writing in both prose and poetry,
Heraclitus could have used συγγραφαί to refer to anything written
up, whether in poetry or in prose. Second, Herodotean usage in fact
suggests that it is more likely that Heraclitus was referring to short
records of information of some sort than to book-length writings
or treatises. As argued above, the grammar of Heraclitus' sentence
is most reasonably read as saying that Pythagoras, after engaging in
enquiry most of all men, made his own wisdom by selecting 'these
συγγραφαί', where 'these' indicates that the συγγραφαί were notorious in some way and that Heraclitus was contemptuous of them.
Scholars have been frustrated by a lack of a clear context from which
to determine what these συγγραφαί are. There is, however, a clear
context provided by the fragment itself, which scholars have overlooked: the enquiry of Pythagoras. To what selection of notorious
short records of Pythagoras' enquiry might Heraclitus be referring?
Once it is recognized that συγγραφαί need not be treatises, an answer
leaps to mind. We have seen above that Heraclitus' description of
Pythagoras as practising enquiry most of all men makes sense in the
light of the content of the Pythagorean maxims known as *symbola*.
Why not suppose, then, that 'these writings' is a sarcastic reference
to those most famous brief texts in the Pythagorean tradition?
The *symbola* were used as passwords intelligible only to those

initiated into the Pythagorean way of life and were later seen as
in need of 'symbolic' interpretation.[55] They circulated orally, as
indicated by their other name, ἀκούσματα ('things heard'), but also
came to be written down in collections. Anaximander of Miletus
(the younger) wrote a book around 400 BC entitled *Explanation
of Pythagorean Symbola*,[56] which must have been based on some
written collection of the *symbola* either by Anaximander himself or
by someone else. It is possible, however, that already in the period
when Heraclitus was probably writing, 500–490, around the time
of Pythagoras' death, some of these brief maxims of Pythagoras
promulgating ritual taboos had been recorded in writing and were
circulating. Aristotle later collected a number of them in his works
on the Pythagoreans, and Iamblichus appears to rely on Aristotle
in a long passage on *akousmata* in *On the Pythagorean Life* (82–6).[57]
Some describe a mythical cosmology (e.g. 'What are the isles of
the blest? Sun and moon', 82), a great number focus on religious
ritual (e.g. 'do not sacrifice a white cock, for he is a suppliant and
sacred to the moon', 84), and others govern the smallest details
of life (e.g. 'one must put the right shoe on first', 83). Heraclitus
is suggesting, then, that Pythagoras derived the ritual taboos and
mythological interpretations of the world found in these oracular
sayings, which had been written up, 'these συγγραφαί', from his
extensive enquiries. Moreover, once it is seen that the συγγραφαί are
'what got written up', it becomes clear that Pythagoras need not
have practised his enquiry just by reading books and that he could
have spent as much or more time in oral questioning of a variety of
authorities, who were probably, given the content of the *symbola*,
mostly connected to religion.

   Is Heraclitus suggesting that Pythagoras himself wrote up a collection of these *symbola*? The fact that Heraclitus does not make
Pythagoras the subject of a verb like συγγράφω at least leaves open
the question of who did the writing, and rather implies that it was
someone else. Moreover, as was first noted by Mansfeld, fragment
129 of Heraclitus has the form of an incipit of an archaic book. It
starts with the name of the author and his patronymic (the *sphragis*),
then gives the subject-matter (Pythagoras' great enquiries), following which the archaic reader, schooled in Hesiod and Hecataeus,
would expect a claim to truth, whereas Heraclitus plays on those

   [55] Burkert, *Lore*, 176.
   [56] Ibid. 166.   [57] Ibid. 166 ff.

expectations to provide a stunning denunciation of Pythagoras instead. This incipit structure gains even more force if Pythagoras did not write a book, since, as Mansfeld notes, 'it is . . . a nice touch that someone who did not write is presented as a writer who failed'.[58]

In fragment 129, then, Heraclitus may be saying something like this to his reader: 'You know these things of Pythagoras that have been written up and are in circulation—he just selected them out of his extensive enquiries into the views of other people.' Heraclitus then condemns Pythagoras on three distinct grounds. These are expressed in the last words of fragment 129 by the qualifications added to three normally positive terms: wisdom (σοφίη), learning (μάθησις), and skill (τέχνη). First, wisdom. There are in fact two related problems with the wisdom that Pythagoras constructed, both connected to the reflexive pronoun ἑαυτοῦ 'his own', which modifies σοφίην: (1) what in reality came from others he made his own, i.e. he plagiarized, and (2) he constructed a wisdom that was 'his own' rather than recognizing the wisdom that is common and available for all to see, the wisdom that Heraclitus himself proclaims (see fr. 2: 'Although the *logos* is common, the many live as if they had a private understanding').[59] This 'privacy' of Pythagoras' teachings makes particular sense if Heraclitus is thinking of the *symbola* which were used as Pythagorean passwords.

Second, learning. The problem with Pythagoras' learning is that it does not lead to the unified understanding of the world which Heraclitus regards as crucial (fr. 50), and instead produces 'a bunch of things learnt from others', a *polymathia*. *Polymathia* is what you get from practising *historia*, from making enquiries of others rather than searching yourself as Heraclitus did (fr. 101); it is the product that you would expect from *historia*.[60] In fragment 40 Heraclitus famously joins Pythagoras to Hesiod, Xenophanes, and Hecataeus as someone whose *polymathia* did not produce real insight. Hesiod's enquiries into the myths concerning the origins of the gods, Hecataeus' similar enquiries into the mythological genealogies of

---

[58] Mansfeld, 'Fiddling', 232. The evidence from the rest of the ancient tradition makes it overwhelmingly likely that Pythagoras did not write any books (Burkert, *Lore*, 218–20). Riedweg (*Pythagoras*, 42–3, 53) has recently tried to argue that Pythagoras did write books, but for a response see my review forthcoming in *Ancient Philosophy*.

[59] See also Granger, 'Quarrel', 258 ff.

[60] Thus I am in agreement with Granger ('Quarrel') that Heraclitus would not have seen himself as practising ἱστορίη.

prominent Greek families, Xenophanes' and Hecataeus' wide tra-
vels that led to their broad ethnographical enquiries, all of these
similarly lead to *polymathia* rather than to a unified understanding of the world. Here in fragment 129, however, Heraclitus uses
the Pythagorean *symbola* (ταύτας τὰς συγγραφάς), with their striking heterogeneity, as evidence that Pythagoras' enquiry, and thus
presumably his *polymathia*, went beyond all others.[61]

Third, art or skill. Pythagoras' selections from others are not just
a base plagiarism, which fails to comprehend the unity of reality
that is accessible to all. Pythagoras uses this idiosyncratic hotch-
potch of the views of others as the foundation for trickery, for κακοτεχνίη. As Schofield suggests, the trickery involved may in part be
Pythagoras' plagiarism and his attempt to trick people into thinking that he is presenting something new.[62] It is important, however,
to look carefully at the word κακοτεχνίη. The usage in fragment 129
is again the earliest. In Plato (*Laws* 936 D 6) and the orators (Dem.
47. 1; 49. 56) the plural, κακοτεχνίαι, is a legal term, which refers
to a fraudulent conspiracy, especially one involving bribery of witnesses to perjure themselves. Herodotus does not use the noun, but
he uses the related verb κακοτεχνέω to describe Cleomenes as 'having conspired' to depose the Spartan king Demaratus (6. 74). This
conspiracy involved the bribery of the Pythia at Delphi (6. 66). It
is thus tempting to suppose that in fragment 129 the reference is
to the Pythagorean society as a conspiracy, which is based on false
testimony about the Pythagorean doctrine of the immortality and
transmigration of the soul. Herodotus' story of Zalmoxis, whom
the Greeks thought to be a slave of Pythagoras, shows the type
of trickery that might have been involved (4. 95). Zalmoxis pre-
tends to die, hides himself in an underground chamber, and later
'returns to life' in order to convince the Thracians of the immortality of the soul. The willingness of Greeks to associate Pythagoras
with Zalmoxis suggests that Heraclitus was not alone in regarding
Pythagoras as a charlatan. The later tradition tells a similar story
about Pythagoras himself.[63] Thus, for Heraclitus, Pythagoras per-

---

[61] Typical translations for *polymathia* in fragment 129 ('much learning' Kahn,
'learning of many things' KRS) fail to give it the negative connotation it clearly
has. My suggested translation 'a bunch of things learnt from others' tries to bring
out the sarcastic reference to the lack of unity in the learning by the use of 'bunch'
and at the same time to emphasize that the learning derives from others rather than
from one's own insight.

[62] 'Pythagoras the Plagiarist'.   [63] Burkert, *Lore*, 156.

verts art or skill (τέχνη) into trickery, which is manifested most fully
in the evil conspiracy (κακοτεχνίη), based on false testimony about
the next life, that is the Pythagorean society.

6. Conclusion

Thus, neither the use of ἱστορίη nor the use of συγγραφή in fragment
129 provides any evidence that Pythagoras was engaged in Ionian-
style cosmology. The two words instead create a picture of Pythagoras as basing his supposed wisdom on an extensive collection of the
opinions of others, which were written up in brief maxims that are
the foundation of the fraudulent Pythagorean life. Those maxims
show that Pythagoras primarily enquired into religious ritual and at
most promulgated a mythic cosmology. This picture of Pythagoras
is consistent both with fragment 40 of Heraclitus, where he is paired
with Hesiod, and with the other early testimony about Pythagoras
found in authors such as Ion and Herodotus. Herodotus agrees
with Heraclitus in emphasizing Pythagoras' extensive enquiry, in
so far as he calls him 'not the least of the wise among the Greeks',
but he also, like Heraclitus, situates this apparent praise in a context
that is at least implicitly critical of Pythagoras, i.e. Zalmoxis' trickery regarding the fate of the soul (4. 95). Ion of Chios is in close
agreement with Heraclitus in emphasizing Pythagoras' extensive
collection of the opinions of other men: 'beyond all [he] knew and
learnt the opinions of men'.[64] The context of Ion's comment, the
fortunes of Pherecydes in the next life, shows that these opinions focused not on cosmology but on the same topic to which Herodotus
(4. 95 and 2. 123) connected Pythagoras, the fate of the soul after
death. Ion differs from Heraclitus only in regarding Pythagoras'
polymathia as something positive.

Schofield argues that Heraclitus was so vitriolic about Pythagoras because he saw him as a close competitor and because there were
real similarities in their philosophies that some might suppose to be
due to plagiarism on Heraclitus' part.[65] The analysis of συγγραφαί
given above suggests another important area of similarity and com-
petition between the two. Just as Pythagoras may have been known
primarily through a collection of brief maxims that were in circu-

---

[64] Fr. 4. For the proper text see Burkert, *Lore*, 123 n. 13.
[65] 'Pythagoras the Plagiarist'.

46 *Carl A. Huffman*

lation, so Heraclitus was known for his brief oracular aphorisms. Perhaps Heraclitus chose the form of his philosophy partly under the influence of the collections of the Pythagorean *symbola* in circulation and thus felt it incumbent on himself to distinguish his philosophy sharply from that of Pythagoras, which was, in form at least, so similar to his own.

DePauw University

BIBLIOGRAPHY

Bakker, E. J., 'The Making of History: Herodotus' *Historiês Apodexis*' ['Making'], in E. J. Bakker, I. J. F. De Jong, and H. Van Wees (eds.), *Brill's Companion to Herodotus* (Leiden, 2002), 3–32.

Barnes, J., *The Presocratic Philosophers* (London, 1982).

Burkert, W., *Lore and Science in Ancient Pythagoreanism* [*Lore*], trans. E. Minar (Cambridge, Mass., 1972).

Burnet, J., *Early Greek Philosophy* [*Early*] (New York, 1930).

Cherniss, H., review of H. Diels, *Die Fragmente der Vorsokratiker*, in *American Journal of Philology*, 60 (1939), 248–57.

Connor, W. R., 'The Histor in History', in R. M. Rosen and J. S. Farrell (eds.), *Nomodeiktes: Greek Studies in Honor of Martin Ostwald* (Ann Arbor, 1993), 3–15.

Diels, H., and Kranz, W., *Die Fragmente der Vorsokratiker*, 6th edn. (3 vols.; Berlin, 1951).

Dover, K. J., *The Evolution of Greek Prose Style* [*Prose*] (Oxford, 1997).

Floyd, E. D., 'The Sources of Greek ἵστωρ "Judge, Witness"', *Glotta*, 68 (1990), 157–66.

Fränkel, H., 'Xenophanes' Empiricism and his Critique of Knowledge (B 34)', in A. P. D. Mourelatos (ed.), *The Pre-Socratics* (Princeton, 1993), 118–31.

Graham, D. W., 'Philosophy on the Nile: Herodotus and Ionian Research' ['Nile'], *Apeiron*, 36/4 (2003), 291–310.

Granger, H., 'Heraclitus' Quarrel with Polymathy and Historiê' ['Quarrel'], *Transactions of the American Philological Association*, 134 (2004), 235–61.

Guthrie, W. K. C., *A History of Greek Philosophy*, vol. i (Cambridge, 1962).

Hahn, R., *Anaximander and the Architects* (Albany, NY, 2001).

Huffman, C. A., review of Riedweg, *Pythagoras*, forthcoming in *Ancient Philosophy*.

Kahn, C. H., *The Art and Thought of Heraclitus* [*Art*] (Cambridge, 1979).

—— *Pythagoras and the Pythagoreans* [*Pythagoras*] (Indianapolis, 2001).

—— 'Writing Philosophy: Prose and Poetry from Thales to Plato' ['Prose'], in H. Yunis (ed.), *Written Texts and the Rise of Literate Culture in Ancient Greece* (Cambridge, 2003), 139–61.

Kirk, G. S., Raven, J. E., and Schofield, M., *The Presocratic Philosophers* [KRS] (Cambridge, 1983).

Lloyd, A. B., 'Egypt', in E. J. Bakker, I. J. F. De Jong, and H. Van Wees (eds.), *Brill's Companion to Herodotus* (Leiden, 2002), 415–35.

Mansfeld, J., 'Fiddling the Books (Heraclitus B 129)' ['Fiddling'], in K. J. Boudouris (ed.), *Ionian Philosophy* (Athens, 1989), 229–34; repr. in J. Mansfeld, *Studies in the Historiography of Greek Philosophy* (Assen, 1990), 443–8.

Marcovich, M., *Heraclitus: Greek Text with a Short Commentary* [*Heraclitus*] (Merida, 1967).

Munn, M., *The School of History* (Berkeley, 2000).

Powell, J. E., *A Lexicon to Herodotus* (Hildesheim, 1966).

Reinhardt, K., *Parmenides und die Geschichte der griechischen Philosophie* [*Parmenides*] (Bonn, 1916).

Riedweg, C., *Pythagoras: His Life, Teaching and Influence* [*Pythagoras*] (Ithaca, NY, 2005).

Robinson, T. M., *Heraclitus: Fragments. A Text and Translation with a Commentary* (Toronto, 1991).

West, M. L., *The Orphic Poems* [*Orphic*] (Oxford, 1983).

DOES SOCRATES CLAIM TO KNOW THAT HE KNOWS NOTHING?

1. Introduction

EVER since antiquity, some have found it tempting to suppose that Socrates claims to know that he knows nothing.[1] Here is a contem-

© Gail Fine 2008

Thanks to Lesley Brown, Terry Irwin, and audiences at Marquette University, Oxford University, and St Andrews University for helpful discussion; and to Christopher Taylor, Brad Inwood, Alex Long, Gary Matthews, and Hayden Pelliccia for helpful written comments.

[1] Or so we are told. I do not know when this claim was first attributed to Socrates. One early source often thought to do so is Cicero, *Acad* 1. 16: 'nihil se scire dicat nisi id ipsum'. Cf. 1. 44–5: 'itaque Arcesilas negabat esse quicquam quod sciri posset, ne illud quidem ipsum quod Socrates sibi reliquisset, ut nihil scire se sciret'. (Notice that the only cognitive terms Cicero uses are forms of *scire*.) Cf. 2. 74. For this reading of what Cicero says, see J. Annas, 'Plato the Skeptic', in P. Vander Waerdt (ed.), *The Socratic Movement* (Ithaca, NY, 1994), 309–40 at 310. For a recent challenge to this reading, see M. F. Burnyeat, 'Antipater and Self-Refutation', in B. Inwood and J. Mansfeld (eds.), *Assent and Argument* (Leiden, 1997), 277–310 at 290–300; see further n. 5 below.

At *Acad.* 1. 44–5 Cicero says that Arcesilaus attributed some version of the claim to Socrates; if Cicero is right, some version of the attribution goes back at least that far. (I say 'some version' because there is dispute about precisely what claim Cicero takes Arcesilaus to have attributed to Socrates. Unfortunately, it is not clear precisely what Arcesilaus' own formulation was.) A. A. Long, in 'Socrates in Hellenistic Philosophy', *Classical Quarterly*, NS 38 (1988), 150–71, repr. in id., *Stoic Studies* (Cambridge, 1996), 1–34 (latter pagination), argues that Arcesilaus is the 'effective creator of the totally sceptical Socrates' (12). However, it is not entirely clear how Long conceives of scepticism. He is certainly right to say that Aristotle says that Socrates disavows knowledge (*SE* 183ᵇ7–8: ὡμολόγει γὰρ οὐκ εἰδέναι). But it is one thing to disavow knowledge, and another to claim to know that one knows nothing: see n. 4, and the end of sect. 5 (on the knowledge account of assertion). My primary concern here is with the latter claim.

See also Lact. *De ira Dei* 1: 'ait se nihil sciri nisi unum, quod nihil sciret'. Like Cicero, the only cognitive terms Lactantius uses are forms of *scire*. However, Lactantius seems to go on to use *intellexit* to mean something different from what he seems to want to convey with forms of *scire*. He seems to go on to say that Socrates denies that there is such a thing as human wisdom; yet in (T4) (for which see below) Socrates claims to have human wisdom. Perhaps Lactantius thinks that Socrates'

porary example: I was recently on holiday in Capri; and, on one of my walks, I went to the Parco Filosofico. It was divided into such areas as Realismo and Idealismo, with suitable quotations decorating the paths. In the Realismo section, the following quotation was attributed to Socrates (though no specific reference was given): ἓν οἶδα, ὅτι οὐδὲν οἶδα—'I know one thing, that I know nothing'. Apparently T-shirts with this Greek 'quotation' are popular in Greece.

There are also more scholarly examples. For example, in their book *The Delphic Oracle*, Parke and Wormell say that Socrates thought he was wiser than others 'because whereas all men thought they knew something and did not, Socrates knew that he knew nothing'.[2] At least three articles in the recently published Blackwell *Companion to Socrates* also ascribe the claim to Socrates. Harold Tarrant, for example, says that '[t]he most famous claim of Socrates is that he knows that he knows nothing'.[3]

The claim that one knows that one knows nothing seems to be a contradiction. For if one *knows* that one knows nothing, one knows

human wisdom is not genuine wisdom: which agrees with my interpretation in sect. 7.

See also Jerome, *Ep.* 57. 12 (where, again, just forms of *scire* are used). The letter's primary concern is 'the best method of translating'. Jerome defends himself against the charge that he does not render word for word, saying that 'in translating from the Greek . . . I render sense for sense and not word for word', noting that Cicero did the same. He also says (quoting himself in another work) that 'each particular word conveys a meaning of its own, and possibly I have no equivalent by which to render it'. (He is not talking about his brief remark about Socrates, which is not at all his main concern in the letter.) I agree with the general point. But using the same Latin word for two different Greek words can obscure the sense of the latter; and, in the case to hand, there are different cognitive Latin words that Jerome (and Cicero and Lactantius) could have used. I return to this issue below.

[2] H. W. Parke and D. E. Wormell, *The Delphic Oracle* (2 vols.; Oxford, 1956), i. 402. Presumably by 'all men', they mean 'all humans other than Socrates'.

[3] 'Socratic Method and Socratic Truth', in S. Ahbel-Rappe and R. Kamtekar (eds.), *A Companion to Socrates* (Oxford, 2006), 254–72 at 263. He takes *Ap.* 22 E–23 B to make this claim. (T4) below is part of this passage; so we can evaluate Tarrant's interpretation of the passage when we turn to (T4). (So far as I can tell, it would not be plausible to say that in the part of the passage immediately preceding (T4), Socrates claims to know that he knows nothing; if Tarrant is right, it would be on the basis of (T4).) According to R. Janko, Socrates 'famously claimed that he knew nothing except that he knew that he knew nothing' ('Socrates the Freethinker', in Ahbel-Rappe and Kamtekar, 48–62 at 58; cf. 59, 60). Janko does not say what passage or passages he has in mind. And, as phrased, he seems to iterate levels of knowledge once too often for the point he wants to make. In 'Socrates in the Italian Renaissance' (Ahbel-Rappe and Kamtekar, 337–52), J. Hankins also seems to attribute the claim to Socrates or, at any rate, to think that Ficino does so, though the passage he cites from Ficino does not do so: see 349.

something: in which case it seems it is not true that one knows nothing. Conversely, if one knows nothing, it seems one could not know that fact. For if one knew it, one would know something, in seeming contradiction to the hypothesis that one knows nothing. Even if the claim can be interpreted so as to be consistent, it at least sounds paradoxical. It is therefore worthwhile to ask whether Socrates makes the claim and, if he does, how it is to be interpreted.

Of course, not everyone attributes the claim to Socrates. In his recent book *Socrates*, for example, Christopher Taylor says that doing so 'is a clear misreading of Plato'.[4] In what follows, I shall try to steer a middle course. I shall suggest that attributing the claim to Socrates does not involve a *clear* misreading of the text. None the less, on balance it is better not to attribute it to him— though explaining why this is so takes some work. In assessing the evidence, I shall focus on the *Apology*, which is the main place where Socrates has been thought to claim that he knows that he knows nothing.

2. Some preliminaries

The Greek 'quotation' that I saw in Capri—ἓν οἶδα, ὅτι οὐδὲν οἶδα— does not occur in the *Apology* or, indeed, anywhere else in Plato.[5]

---

[4] (Oxford, 1998), 42. The passage just quoted in the text continues as follows: 'Though Socrates frequently says that he does not know the answer to the particular question under discussion, he never says that he knows nothing.' I assume Taylor means that if Socrates never says that (*a*) he knows nothing, then he never says that (*b*) he knows that he knows nothing. But it is useful to distinguish (*a*) from (*b*). For Socrates could claim to know nothing without claiming to know that fact: or so it might seem. I consider this below, in discussing the knowledge account of assertion at the end of sect. 5. Burnyeat, 'Antipater and Self-Refutation', 290–1, and Annas, 'Plato the Skeptic', 310, also say that Socrates never claims to know that he knows nothing, though neither discusses the matter in detail, since their main concerns lie elsewhere. See also G. Vlastos, *Socrates, Ironist and Moral Philosopher* (Cambridge, 1991), 82–3 n. 4, retracting the view in his 'Socrates' Disavowal of Knowledge', *Philosophical Quarterly*, 35 (1985), 1–31, and reprinted in G. Fine (ed.), *Plato 1: Metaphysics and Epistemology* (Oxford, 1999), 64–92 at e.g. 91. See also M. Stokes, *Plato:* Apology (Warminster, 1997), 18–21.

[5] I do not know when the sentence first occurs in Greek, whether as something Socrates allegedly said or in some other context. A TLG search did not turn up any occurrences. Nor did it cite any occurrences of οἶδα ὅτι οὐδὲν οἶδα or of οἶδε ὅτι οὐδὲν οἶδε. According to D.L. 2. 32, Socrates said καὶ εἰδέναι μὲν μηδὲν πλὴν αὐτὸ τοῦτο [εἰδέναι], which is close. (I follow the OCT in bracketing εἰδέναι.) So far as I can tell, this is ambiguous as between (*a*) Socrates knows that, for all *p*, he does not know that *p*; and (*b*) there is a *p* such that Socrates knows that *p*: namely, for all *q*,

Gail Fine

But it does not follow that the English sentence 'I know one thing, that I know nothing'—or: 'I know that I know nothing'—does not correctly translate something Socrates says. After all, *eidenai* (εἰδέναι, the infinitive of which οἶδα acts as the first-person singular of the present tense) is just one of many Greek words that are generally translated as 'to know'.

But when is it appropriate to translate a given Greek word as 'knowledge'? There are, after all, disputes about what knowledge is, and so there are also disputes about when it is appropriate to say that someone has, or lacks, knowledge. This, in turn, has led to disputes about which words should be translated as 'knowledge'. Myles Burnyeat, for example, argues that *epistēmē*, which is often translated as 'knowledge', should instead be translated as 'understanding'. One of his reasons is that he thinks the conditions for having *epistēmē* are more demanding than the conditions for having knowledge. That is true as Burnyeat conceives of knowledge. But it is not true on every conception of knowledge.[6]

For the purposes of this paper, I shall assume that for some-

where *q* is not identical to *p*, Socrates does not know that *q*. (*a*) is a contradiction (if 'know' is used univocally), but (*b*) is not. Unfortunately, there is not enough context in Diogenes Laertius to allow us to know which way to understand the remark. For the distinction between (*a*) and (*b*), see Burnyeat, 'Antipater and Self-Refutation', 291. He argues that Varro ascribes (*b*) but not (*a*) to Socrates. Whether or not the claim that Diogenes ascribes to Socrates is self-contradictory, it does not occur in Plato.

See also Metrodorus 70 B 1 DK, for which Diels–Kranz cite both Cicero's Latin from *Acad.* 2. 73 and Eusebius' Greek from *PE.* 14. 19. 9 Mras. Unfortunately, it is not clear what the Greek original said (though whatever it said, the surviving formulations suggest it was very different from the claim to know that one knows nothing). DK records seven, not obviously equivalent, formulations (see DK 69 A 2, 70 A 23, 70 A 25, 70 B 1, and 72 A 1); they are discussed in detail by J. Brunschwig 'Le fragment DK 70B1 de Métrodore de Chio', in K. Algra, P. van der Horst, and D. Runia (eds.), *Polyhistor: Studies in the History and Historiography of Ancient Philosophy* (Leiden, 1996), 21–38. I owe the reference to Brunschwig to C. Brittain, *Cicero, On Academic Scepticism* (Indianapolis, 2006), 43 n. 103.

⁶ Burnyeat seems to conceive of knowledge as justified true belief, where justification does not imply truth and is not especially difficult to come by: see his 'Aristotle on Understanding Knowledge', in E. Berti (ed.), *Aristotle on Science* (Padua, 1981), 97–139 at e.g. 102 with 115. By contrast, in 'Socrates' Disavowal of Knowledge', 71 n. 25, Vlastos says that most people nowadays deny that knowledge is justified true belief.

Burnyeat's article focuses on Aristotle's use of *epistēmē* and *epistasthai* in the *Posterior Analytics*. But in sect. VI he discusses Plato's *Theaetetus*. He argues that at the beginning of the dialogue *epistēmē* 'must be translated as "knowledge"' since it 'has plenty to do with certainty and justification' (133), but that later on, it 'verges towards understanding' (134). He then suggests that Plato believes that you 'know

one to be talking about knowledge, they must be talking about a truth-entailing cognitive condition that is appropriately cognitively superior to mere true belief.[7] Let us say that this is the basic *concept*

a thing if and only if you have systematic and scientific understanding of it in terms of its first principles' (135).

In discussing Aristotle, Burnyeat eventually says that *epistēmē* is 'that type of knowledge which is secured by understanding', and that 'in the end it will not do too much damage to go back to the traditional rendering of *epistēmē* as "scientific knowledge". But only in the end. If we are not to be badly misled, we need first to think away a welter of assumptions about the aims of the theory of knowledge as a philosophical enterprise' (132). Hence Burnyeat's considered view seems to be that Aristotle uses *epistēmē* in the *Posterior Analytics* for a kind of knowledge, though not for knowledge as such, whereas he seems to think that Plato (in some places in the *Theaetetus*) identifies knowledge as such with understanding; Aristotle's insight is to see that not all knowledge requires understanding. I myself do not favour translating *epistēmē* as 'scientific knowledge' even in the end, since neither Plato nor Aristotle restricts the word to knowledge in the scientific realm, as 'science' is understood nowadays. But I have no objection to translating it as 'knowledge'—except in so far as one might wish to translate (e.g.) *eidenai* as 'to know', and one might well want to use different English words to translate different Greek words.

Though Burnyeat's considered view seems to be that for Aristotle in the *Posterior Analytics* *epistēmē* (or unqualified *epistēmē*) is a kind of knowledge, at places he seems to suggest that *epistēmē* (or unqualified *epistēmē*) is understanding rather than any kind of knowledge. See e.g. 100–3, where he says that knowledge involves justification, whereas understanding involves explanation, as though these are disjoint.

J. Lesher, 'Socrates' Disavowal of Knowledge', *Journal of the History of Philosophy*, 25 (1987), 275–88, suggests that, in at least one passage in the *Apology* (=my (T3)), *epistēmē* 'may not count strictly speaking as knowledge ("skilled", "artistic abilities" are equally legitimate options)' (281). G. S. Kirk, *Heraclitus: The Cosmic Fragments* (Cambridge, 1954), 155, notes that Herodotus (1. 22; 3. 139; 8. 25) does not always use *epistamai* veridically: in which case it does not amount to knowledge, as knowledge is generally conceived. Thanks to Alex Long for calling my attention to the Herodotus passages; and see now his 'Wisdom in Heraclitus', *Oxford Studies in Ancient Philosophy*, 33 (2007), 1–17 at 9. On this view, *epistēmē* is sometimes used for a lower-level cognitive condition than knowledge, whereas Burnyeat's suggestion, by contrast, is, in effect, that it is sometimes used for a more demanding cognitive condition than knowledge as such (as Burnyeat conceives it).

There is also some dispute about whether *eidenai* and its cognates are always used for knowledge. For example, in 'Aristotle's Theory of Definition', in E. Berti (ed.), *Aristotle on Science*, 359–84 at 366, J. L. Ackrill suggests that in the *Posterior Analytics* Aristotle may sometimes use *eidenai* for mere true belief. However, he does not press the point; and he more often suggests that Aristotle uses the word for a weak sort of knowledge. In *Socratic Wisdom* (New York, 2000), H. Benson suggests that some of Socrates' avowals of knowledge are 'unconsidered, careless, or vernacular expressions' (236). Some of the passages he thinks can be read in this way use *eidenai*; hence he thinks that Socrates does not always use *eidenai* to indicate genuine knowledge.

[7] There are two ways in which this view of knowledge is broader than the justified-true-belief account of knowledge. First, it does not say that knowledge is a species of, or even implies, true belief, though it leaves both possibilities open. Secondly, it does not require justification to be the factor that makes knowledge appropriately

of knowledge. It leaves room for dispute about the precise *criteria* for knowledge: about the precise way in which knowledge is cognitively superior to mere true belief.

If we think of knowledge in this way, then, when Plato, in *Meno* 97 A ff., asks what *epistēmē* is, and what it is to *eidenai* something, he is discussing knowledge. For he asks there what distinguishes true belief (*orthē doxa, alēthēs doxa*) from a truth-entailing cognitive condition that is more valuable than mere true belief. He calls this condition *epistēmē*; and, in 97 A ff., he speaks interchangeably of having *epistēmē* and of knowing (*eidenai*).[8] At least in the *Meno*, then, Plato uses forms of *epistasthai* and the cognate noun, as well as forms of *eidenai*, for knowledge, as I am conceiving of knowledge here.[9]

cognitively superior to mere true belief. On the other hand, the account of knowledge I assume here is not committed to the view that being in a truth-entailing cognitive condition and having just any old justification are sufficient for having knowledge. It leaves open the possibility that some true beliefs are justified to some extent, but not justified enough to constitute knowledge. It also leaves open the possibility that, of two people both of whom know, say, a mathematical theorem, one might know it better than the other does—by, for example, being able to relate it to a wider range of related propositions, or by being able to give a deeper and fuller explanation. I return to this issue later.

It would do for my purposes to say that knowledge is true belief plus something, where there is room for dispute about precisely what must be added to true belief so as to yield knowledge. I use the less familiar and somewhat more awkward phrasing in the text so as to sidestep questions about whether knowledge is a species of, or implies, true belief, since such questions lie apart from my concerns here. Despite the somewhat unfamiliar phrasing, the basic idea underlying the view of knowledge assumed here is widespread. But it is not uncontroversial. For example, in 'The Concept of Knowledge', in P. A. French, T. E. Uehling, Jr., and H. K. Wettstein (eds.), *Causation and Causal Theories* (Midwest Studies in Philosophy, 9; Minneapolis, 1984), 529–54, C. McGinn says that knowledge is a 'subrational achievement' that is 'more primitive than belief' and that requires 'less cognitive sophistication' (547). (I owe the reference to Benson, *Socratic Wisdom*, 192 n. 15.)

    [8] See my 'Knowledge and True Belief in the *Meno*', *Oxford Studies in Ancient Philosophy*, 27 (2004), 41–81.
    [9] Earlier in the dialogue, however, he sometimes seems to use forms of *eidenai* more broadly than for having *epistēmē*, as *epistēmē* is defined in 98 A; see e.g. 91 D 2. By contrast, *epistēmē* seems to be consistently used in conformity with the definition given in 98 A. (Forms of *epistasthai* and of the cognate noun are not used in the *Meno* until 85 D 1, though forms of *eidenai* are used frequently before then.) I ask about the *Apology* later. Of course, we might not want to use 'knowledge' ('to know') to translate both words; for we might want to use different English words to correspond to different Greek words (Jerome notwithstanding: see n. 1). Be that as it may, at *Meno* 97 A ff., when Plato uses forms of *epistasthai* and the cognate noun, and forms of *eidenai*, he is talking about knowledge, as knowledge is being conceived of here, however we in the end choose to translate these two words. Nor is it unique to Plato

It therefore seems *prima facie* reasonable to assume that when, in the *Apology*, Plato uses forms of *epistasthai* and the cognate noun, and forms of *eidenai*, he is talking about knowledge.[10] To be sure, even if he uses these words for knowledge in the *Apology*, it might assume different views about knowledge from those articulated in the *Meno*. But that is a different issue from whether it uses these words for knowledge, as knowledge is being conceived of here.

Although the use of forms of *epistasthai* and the cognate noun, and of forms of *eidenai*, is *prima facie* sufficient for Plato to be talking about knowledge, it may not be necessary: perhaps he also uses other cognitive words to indicate knowledge. That is an issue I address in due course. All I have said so far is that in order to decide whether he is talking about knowledge, we need to decide whether he is talking about a truth-entailing cognitive condition that is appropriately cognitively superior to mere true belief; and I have suggested that it is reasonable to think that he uses forms of *epistasthai* and the cognate noun, and forms of *eidenai*, in this way.

Let us now turn to the *Apology*, to see whether Socrates says anything that should be translated as 'I know one thing, that I know nothing' or as 'I know that I know nothing'. Even if he does not, he might say things that imply such a view. So let us ask about that too.

---

to use these words for knowledge—that is, for a truth-entailing cognitive condition that is appropriately cognitively superior to mere true belief. To take just one pre-Platonic example, Xenophanes says: 'No man [ἀνήρ] has ever seen, nor will anyone ever know [εἰδώς], the truth [σαφές] about the gods or about any of the things I speak of. For even if someone should in fact say what is really the case, still he would not know [οἶδε] it. But belief [δόκος] is allotted to all' (21 B 34 DK).

It is awkward that Plato does not use a noun cognate with *eidenai* (e.g. εἴδησις, for which see the opening lines of Aristotle's *De anima*) and that there is no verb cognate with *sophia/sophos*. Even when verbs are at issue, I shall sometimes speak of knowledge (rather than using e.g. 'to know' or 'knowing'); and I shall sometimes contrast e.g. *epistēmē* (a noun) with *eidenai* (a verb).

[10] One might argue that I am not justified in assuming this, on the ground that it is not until the *Meno* that he explicitly distinguishes knowledge from true belief; hence the distinction cannot be assumed earlier than that. See J. Beversluis, 'Socratic Definition', *American Philosophical Quarterly*, 11 (1974), 331–6; cf. his 'Does Socrates Commit the Socratic Fallacy?', *American Philosophical Quarterly*, 24 (1987), 211–33 at 217 ff. However, the distinction antedates Plato: see previous note. Moreover, one can observe distinctions one does not explicitly draw. Even if one should not assume in advance that forms of *eidenai* and *epistasthai* (*epistēmē*) indicate knowledge, as knowledge is being conceived of here, we shall see as we proceed that the assumption is reasonable in the end—which is not to say that forms of *eidenai* are never used colloquially: see n. 6.

3. Setting the scene

I shall consider five central passages in detail. I begin by setting them briefly in their context. Socrates explains that his friend Chaerephon went to the oracle at Delphi and asked whether anyone was wiser than Socrates; the oracle replied that no one was.[11] Socrates was perplexed by this reply. For, he says:

(T1) ἐγὼ γὰρ δὴ οὔτε μέγα οὔτε σμικρὸν σύνοιδα ἐμαυτῷ σοφὸς ὤν. (*Ap.* 21 B 4–5)

> I am aware [*sunoida emautōi*] of being wise [*sophos ōn*] in nothing, great or small.[12]

Though the oracle cannot lie (21 B 6–7), it can be difficult to interpret (21 B 3–4). Socrates therefore decided to try to find out what it meant, by cross-examining others with reputations for wisdom. After cross-examining an unnamed politician, he concluded:

(T2) πρὸς ἐμαυτὸν δ᾽ οὖν ἀπιὼν ἐλογιζόμην ὅτι τούτου μὲν τοῦ ἀνθρώπου ἐγὼ σοφώτερός εἰμι· κινδυνεύει μὲν γὰρ ἡμῶν οὐδέτερος οὐδὲν καλὸν κἀγαθὸν εἰδέναι, ἀλλ᾽ οὗτος μὲν οἴεταί τι εἰδέναι οὐκ εἰδώς, ἐγὼ δέ, ὥσπερ οὖν οὐκ οἶδα, οὐδὲ οἴομαι· ἔοικα γοῦν τούτου γε σμικρῷ τινι αὐτῷ τούτῳ σοφώτερος εἶναι, ὅτι ἃ μὴ οἶδα οὐδὲ οἴομαι εἰδέναι. (*Ap.* 21 D 2–8)

> [a] As I was going away from this man, I reasoned to myself that I am indeed wiser than he is. [b] It is probable [*kinduneuei*] that neither of us knows [*eidenai*] anything fine and good [*kalon kagathon*]; [c] but he thinks he knows something when he does not, whereas I, just as [*hōsper*] I do not know, neither do I think I know. [d] Indeed [*goun*], it seems that I am wiser than he to this small extent, that what I do not know, neither do I think I know.[13]

[11] There is dispute about the accuracy of the oracle story, in any of its versions; see M. Stokes, 'Socrates' Mission', in B. S. Gower and M. Stokes (eds.), *Socratic Questions* (London, 1992), 26–81; and his *Plato: Apology*, 115 ff. See also n. 61.

[12] The passage is sometimes translated in a more non-committal way: 'In no way, great or small, am I aware [*sunoida*] of being wise [*sophos*].' See e.g. Long, 'Socrates in Hellenistic Philosophy', 14; Stokes, *Plato: Apology*, 18; Burnyeat, 'Antipater and Self-Refutation', 290. The translation given in the text seems to me to be a more natural reading of the Greek (though Stokes, *Plato: Apology*, 18, cites Arist. *NE* 1172^{b}31–2 as a parallel for the non-committal reading). It also fits the context somewhat better: Socrates has just learnt that the oracle said that no one is wiser than he is; and he is expressing his surprise at that. His surprise seems more natural if he *sunoide* that he is not wise than if he does not *sunoide* that he is wise. Further, (T1) is parallel to (T3[a]) (discussed below), which is unambiguously positive.

[13] I have inserted '[a]', '[b]', '[c]', and '[d]', for ease of reference.

Socrates next cross-examined poets, then craftsmen. He went to the latter because, he explains:

(T3) ἐμαυτῷ γὰρ συνῄδη οὐδὲν ἐπισταμένῳ ὡς ἔπος εἰπεῖν, τούτους δέ γ᾽ ᾔδη ὅτι εὑρήσοιμι πολλὰ καὶ καλὰ ἐπισταμένους. καὶ τούτου μὲν οὐκ ἐψεύσθην, ἀλλ᾽ ἠπίσταντο ἃ ἐγὼ οὐκ ἠπιστάμην καί μου ταύτῃ σοφώτεροι ἦσαν. (*Ap.* 22 C 9–D 4)

[a] I am aware [*sunoida*] that I know [*epistamenōi*] practically [*hōs epos eipein*] nothing. [b] But I knew [*ēidē*] that I should find them [the craftsmen] knowing [*epistamenous*] many fine [*kala*] things; and in this I was not mistaken [*epseusthēn*], since they knew [*ēpistanto*] things that I did not know [*ouk ēpistamēn*], and in that respect they were wiser than me.[14]

As a result of his cross-examination of others, Socrates became widely disliked, as he explains in the following passage:

(T4) ἐκ ταυτησὶ δὴ τῆς ἐξετάσεως, ὦ ἄνδρες Ἀθηναῖοι, πολλαὶ μὲν ἀπέχθειαί μοι γεγόνασι καὶ οἷαι χαλεπώταται καὶ βαρύταται, ὥστε πολλὰς διαβολὰς ἀπ᾽ αὐτῶν γεγονέναι, ὄνομα δὲ τοῦτο λέγεσθαι, σοφὸς εἶναι· οἴονται γάρ

[14] Some further features of this passage, beyond those I discuss in the text below, deserve comment:

　1. In (T3[a]) Socrates claims positively to be aware of something: as he also does in (T1), on my translation of it. See n. 12.

　2. (T1) and (T3[a]) both use forms of *suneidenai*. But whereas (T1) uses *sophos*, (T3[a]) uses forms of *epistasthai*. This supports a suggestion I shall make later: that, in the *Apology*, both *sophos* (*sophia*) and forms of *epistasthai* and the cognate noun are used for a high-level sort of knowledge that is difficult to attain.

　3. The craftsmen are said to know *kala*, but they are not explicitly said to know *kala kagatha*. One might think the difference is significant, on the ground that if the craftsmen were said to know *kala kagatha*, that would conflict with Socrates' seeming claim in (T2) that neither he nor an unnamed politician knows anything *kalon kagathon*; nor, as becomes clear, does he think anyone else knows anything *kalon kagathon* (as that claim is meant here). However, as we shall see, in 20 B he says that equestrians, for example, know *kala kagatha* about horses, in that they know how to make horses achieve their proper *aretē*. So I do not think we can make anything of the fact that (T3) has *kala* rather than *kala kagatha*. But Socrates is none the less consistent, if (T2) tacitly restricts the scope of *kala kagatha* to human *aretē*. The craftsmen mentioned in (T3) know *kala kagatha* in their domains; but they do not know anything *kalon kagathon* in the moral sphere—at least, not in the way at issue in (T2).

　4. Socrates says he knows (*eidenai*) that the craftsmen know (*epistasthai*) their crafts; yet he denies that he knows (*epistasthai*) them. According to Burnyeat, '[t]he Platonist must rather deny (an argument at *Charmides* 171 AC does deny) that *A* can ever know that *B* knows that *p* unless he knows that *p* in the same sort of way as *B* does' ('Socrates and the Jury', *Aristotelian Society*, suppl. 54 (1980), 173–91 at 184–5). Here, however, Plato allows that *A* can know (*eidenai*) that *B* knows (*epistasthai*) that *p*, even if *A* does not know that *p* in the same sort of way as *B* does.

58 *Gail Fine*

μέ ἑκάστοτε οἱ παρόντες ταῦτα αὐτὸν εἶναι σοφὸν ἃ ἂν ἄλλον ἐξελέγξω. τὸ δὲ κινδυνεύει, ὦ ἄνδρες, τῷ ὄντι ὁ θεὸς σοφὸς εἶναι, καὶ ἐν τῷ χρησμῷ τούτῳ τοῦτο λέγειν, ὅτι ἡ ἀνθρωπίνη σοφία ὀλίγου τινὸς ἀξία ἐστὶν καὶ οὐδενός. καὶ φαίνεται τοῦτον λέγειν τὸν Σωκράτη, προσκεχρῆσθαι δὲ τῷ ἐμῷ ὀνόματι, ἐμὲ παράδειγμα ποιούμενος, ὥσπερ ἂν ⟨εἰ⟩ εἴποι ὅτι "Οὗτος ὑμῶν, ὦ ἄνθρωποι, σοφώτατός ἐστιν, ὅστις ὥσπερ Σωκράτης ἔγνωκεν ὅτι οὐδενὸς ἄξιός ἐστι τῇ ἀληθείᾳ πρὸς σοφίαν." (*Ap.* 22 E 7–23 B 4)

[*a*] As a result of this investigation, Athenians, I have acquired much unpopularity, of the most troublesome and unpleasant kind. The dislike has given rise to many slanders, and to my being described by this word, 'wise'. This is because, each time, the bystanders think that I am myself wise in subjects in which I refute someone else. [*b*] But what is probable, gentlemen, is that in fact the god is wise and that in that oracle he is saying this: that human wisdom is worth little or [*kai*] nothing. [*c*] And he seems to be speaking of Socrates here before you, and to use my name, taking me as an example, as if he were to say: 'This one among you, men, is wisest who, just like Socrates, has realized [*egnōken*] that in respect of wisdom he is, in truth, worth nothing [*oudenos axios*].'[15]

Socrates also explains why he acquired his reputation in the following passage:

(T5) ἐγὼ γάρ, ὦ ἄνδρες Ἀθηναῖοι, δι᾿ οὐδὲν ἀλλ᾿ ἢ διὰ σοφίαν τινὰ τοῦτο τὸ ὄνομα ἔσχηκα. ποίαν δὴ σοφίαν ταύτην; ἥπερ ἐστὶν ἴσως ἀνθρωπίνη σοφία· τῷ ὄντι γὰρ κινδυνεύω ταύτην εἶναι σοφός. οὗτοι δὲ τάχ᾿ ἄν, οὓς ἄρτι ἔλεγον, μείζω τινὰ ἢ κατ᾿ ἄνθρωπον σοφίαν σοφοὶ εἶεν, ἢ οὐκ ἔχω τί λέγω· οὐ γὰρ δὴ ἔγωγε αὐτὴν ἐπίσταμαι, ἀλλ᾿ ὅστις φησὶ ψεύδεταί τε καὶ ἐπὶ διαβολῇ τῇ ἐμῇ λέγει. (*Ap.* 20 D 6–E 3)

I have, Athenians, acquired this reputation [*onoma*] on account of nothing other than a sort of wisdom [*sophian tina*]. What kind of wisdom [*poian dē sophian*] is that? The one which is presumably [*isōs*] human wisdom [*anthrōpinē sophia*]. In fact, I probably [*kinduneuō*] am wise in that. But perhaps [*tach' an*] the others I mentioned just now are wise with a wisdom that is more than human, for otherwise I cannot explain it [*ouk echō ti legō*]. For certainly I do not know [*epistamai*] it, and whoever says I do is lying.

[15] In the text, I have inserted '[*a*]', '[*b*]', and '[*c*]' for ease of reference. There are various difficulties about the passage that need not detain us here. For discussion, see Stokes, *Plato*: Apology, note ad loc.

4. Socrates' pre-oracle belief: (T1)

Let us now ask how best to interpret these passages, beginning with (T1).

However we interpret (T1) in the end, it is not formally or explicitly contradictory: for it uses two different phrases, *sunoida emautōi* and *sophos ōn*. The passage would, however, be implicitly contradictory if these phrases were synonymous, or if being aware of something implied being wise with respect to it. This is how Richard Kraut understands the passage. He translates *sunoida* not as 'aware', but as 'know'; and he says that 'you cannot know that you are not wise even in a small way; for to know something is to have a small amount of wisdom'.[16] He concludes that (T1) involves a contradiction.[17]

However, having some knowledge would not normally be thought sufficient for having *sophia* or for being *sophos*. It would not normally be inferred from the fact that someone knows that today is Tuesday, that he has even a small amount of *sophia* or is at all *sophos*. As Burnyeat puts it, '*sophos* usually indicates an expertise or specialized knowledge that most people do not have'.[18] And this seems to me to be how Plato uses *sophos* in (T1). So, for example, he at least sometimes uses *sophia* interchangeably with *epistēmē*.[19] And, in the *Apology*, he consistently uses *epistēmē* for a

---

[16] *Socrates and the State* (Princeton, 1984), 272 n. 44.

[17] However, he softens the blow by adding that (T1) is just Socrates' pre-oracle belief, which, according to Kraut, Socrates abandons in favour of a consistent position once he understands what the oracle meant. See n. 51. In sect. 7 I ask whether Socrates abandons his pre-oracle belief.

[18] 'Antipater and Self-Refutation', 290. So also Stokes, *Plato: Apology*, 19; J. Lyons, *Structural Semantics: An Analysis of Part of the Vocabulary of Plato* (Oxford, 1963), 227–8.

[19] See esp. *Ap.* 19 C 6–7. Cf. *Theaet.* 145 D 11–E 7, where the identification is accepted in advance of knowing what *epistēmē* is. See Vlastos, 'Socrates' Disavowal of Knowledge', n. 4. Lyons notes that '*sophia* is frequently used convertibly with *epistēmē*, but only in contexts where *epistēmē* is graded "upwards"' (*Structural Semantics*, 228).

There are just eight occurrences of forms of *epistasthai* or the cognate noun in the *Apology*: 19 C 7, 20 A 8, B 4, 5, C 3, E 2, 22 D 1, 2. 19 C 7 is the only place where *epistēmē* is explicitly used interchangeably with *sophia*; but the other occurrences of forms of *epistēmē* seem to have the same force as in 19 C 7. *Sophia* (*sophos*) is used quite often in the *Apology*. It has been argued (by e.g. Vlastos, 'Socrates' Disavowal of Knowledge') that Socrates uses it in more than one sense; contrast Lyons, *Structural Semantics*, 227. Even if Vlastos were right (though I do not think he is), all I need for present purposes is that Plato sometimes uses it interchangeably with *epistēmē*,

high-level sort of knowledge that most people lack.[20] For example, at 20 B Socrates says that only equestrians have *epistēmē* of how to make horses fine and good (*kalon kagathon*)—that is, of how to make them acquire their proper virtue (*aretē*). This involves their having the relevant craft or skill (*technē*, 20 C 1): a specialized, systematic, synoptic grasp of a given domain.

Socrates goes on to speak of the *technē* and of *epistēmē* of how to make humans achieve their proper virtue (*aretē*), and of what being *kalon kagathon* consists in for them. But, he says, he does not know (*epistasthai*) such things (20 C 3). When Socrates says in (T1) that he *sunoide* that he is not *sophos*, he means that he *sunoide* that he lacks *sophia* so understood: he *sunoide* that there is no domain or area about which he has systematic, synoptic understanding.

Now, to be *sophos* in this sense is to have knowledge, at least of a sort. So in claiming, in (T1), that he is not at all *sophos*, Socrates is claiming to lack knowledge, at least of a sort.[21] But does he claim to *know* that he lacks (this sort of) knowledge? He would do so if to *suneidenai* something were to know it. And, according to Paul Woodruff, that is Plato's view.[22] His reason is that at *Phaedrus* 235 C 6–8 Socrates says: 'I know well [*eu oida*] that none of these ideas has come from me—I *sunoida* my own ignorance [*amathia*]'. Here, Woodruff suggests, '*sunoida* is at least as strongly epistemic as *oida* ("I know")'. Since to *eidenai* something is to know it, to *suneidenai* something is also to know it.[23]

---

where *epistēmē* is, as Lyons puts it, 'graded "upwards"'; and that it is reasonable to think he so uses it in (T1). I discuss *sophia* in more detail in sect. 7.

[20] Outside the *Apology* Plato does not always use forms of *epistasthai* and the cognate noun for a high-level cognitive achievement (though he often does so); see e.g. *Euthd.* 293 B–C. As noted in the introduction, here and elsewhere in this paper my remarks are largely confined to the *Apology*.

[21] I leave open for now the question of whether, in the *Apology*, Socrates takes *epistēmē* and *sophia* to be just an exalted kind of knowledge, or knowledge as such. If the latter is the case, he has demanding standards for knowledge such that someone who lacks *epistēmē* and *sophia* has, at best, true belief. If the former is the case, he takes *epistēmē* and *sophia* to be a kind of knowledge, but admits lower-level knowledge as well—i.e. knowledge that does not amount to *epistēmē* or *sophia*, as they are conceived of here, but that none the less crosses the threshold from mere true belief to knowledge. I ask later which of these two views Socrates seems to favour in the *Apology*.

[22] 'Plato's Early Theory of Knowledge', in S. Everson (ed.), *Epistemology* (Companions to Ancient Thought, 1; Cambridge, 1990), 60–84 at 62. For a different reason for taking *suneidenai* to be knowledge here, see Stokes, *Plato:* Apology, 18.

[23] 'Plato's Early Theory of Knowledge', 62 n. 3. The passage in the *Phaedrus*

Now *eidenai* does indeed often indicate knowledge. And if that is how it is being used here, then Woodruff's reading of the passage is right. For Socrates says that it is because he *sunoide* his own ignorance that he *eu oide* that none of the ideas he is discussing comes from him; the fact that he *sunoide* something grounds his knowing it well (*eu eidenai*). Hence, in this passage, *suneidenai* is at least as cognitively strong as *eidenai* is. So if *eu oida* is being used here for genuine knowledge, then in this passage to *suneidenai* something is to know it. However, later I shall suggest that Plato sometimes seems to use *eu oida* colloquially, or for something like confident belief for which one has reasonable grounds, though not grounds that are good enough for genuine knowledge. If that is how it is used here, then the passage is not evidence for the claim that Plato uses *suneidenai* for genuine knowledge, since the use of *eu oida* would not, in this case, indicate genuine knowledge here.

Even if the *Phaedrus* passage provides evidence for the claim that Plato sometimes uses forms of *suneidenai* for genuine knowledge, it does not follow that he so uses *suneidenai* in (T1). For he does not always use *suneidenai* in such a strongly epistemic way. Consider, for example, *Laws* 870 c 8–d 4:

many a murderer has been prompted by the cowardly fears of a guilty man. When a man is committing some crime, or has already committed it, he does not want anyone to *suneidenai* about it; and if he cannot eliminate a possible informer in any other way, he murders him. (Trans. T. Saunders, lightly revised)

reads: ὅτι μὲν οὖν παρά γε ἐμαυτοῦ οὐδὲν αὐτῶν ἐνενόηκα, εὖ οἶδα, συνειδὼς ἐμαυτῷ ἀμαθίαν. Woodruff and Nehamas translate as follows: 'I am well aware that none of these ideas can have come from me—I know my own ignorance.' Their translation may be found in J. Cooper (ed.), *Plato: Complete Works* (Indianapolis, 1997). In *Plato:* Phaedrus (Warminster, 1986), C. J. Rowe translates the passage in much the same way: 'I am well aware that none of them has its source in my own mind, because I know my own ignorance.' It is somewhat curious that they all use 'well aware' for *eu oida*, and 'know' for *sunoida*. The reverse seems preferable, as in my translation in the text, and as in R. Hackforth (trans. and comm.), *Phaedrus* (Cambridge, 1952). In the *Phaedrus* passage, as in (T1), Socrates uses two different cognitive terms: he *sunoide* his *amathia*. According to Lyons, *Structural Semantics*, '[t]he constant and closest relation to be registered in the analysis of the meaning of *sophos* (*sophia*) is its antonymy with *amathēs* (*amathia*). These terms are explicitly gradable, and perhaps graded, antonyms' (*Structural Semantics*, 227–8). So perhaps in this passage, when Socrates claims to *suneidenai* his *amathia*, he means that he *sunoide* that he is not *sophos*, where *sophia* is to be 'graded "upwards"' (Lyons, 228). On this reading, even if *suneidenai* is used for knowledge, the passage is neither explicitly nor implicitly contradictory.

The sort of person Plato has in mind does not just want no one to *know* that he is a criminal; he does not want anyone to be aware of the fact at all.[24]

Can we tell how *suneidenai* is being used in (T1)?[25] One might think that considerations of charity should lead us to suppose that it is used for less than knowledge in (T1). For otherwise, would not Socrates in effect be saying that he knows that he knows nothing? And would not that be a contradiction? It would be if, as Kraut believes, *suneidenai* were being used for knowing something *in the sense of being sophos with respect to it*. But it would not be if *suneidenai* were being used, as it easily can be, for knowing something in a lower-level way. For (or so one might think) one can quite consistently have low-level knowledge that one lacks high-level know-

[24] As against this interpretation, Tim Williamson writes (not in connection with Plato, but as a general philosophical point): 'A notorious criminal may try to eliminate all those who know that he killed the policeman, because they are potential witnesses against him in court. He will not bother to eliminate those who merely believe truly that he did it, because their confidence that he did it, however great, is no threat to him, given the rules of forensic evidence' (*Knowledge and its Limits* (Oxford, 2000), 87). That might be true if the rules of forensic evidence were always strictly and correctly followed; but, alas, they are not. Of course, a criminal might not be (too) worried about someone who had the mere true belief that he committed the crime, if the true belief is a mere lucky guess with no reasons to back it up at all. But he might be worried if the person with mere true belief has some good reasons to back it up, even if the reasons fall short of those needed for knowledge.

[25] Forms of *suneidenai* occur just three times in the *Apology*: in (T1), (T3), and 34 B 5. I discuss (T3) below. Its use in 34 B 5 is lower-level than *sophia* and *epistēmē*. For if Socrates lacks all *sophia* and *epistēmē*, he does not have *sophia* or *epistēmē* of the fact that Meletus is lying. If he does not, presumably others do not either. (It is true that he thinks the craftsmen are wise in their domains; so it is not that he thinks no one has any wisdom. But it seems plausible to suppose that if he lacks wisdom in the case at issue in 34 B 5, so too do others.) It is more difficult to say whether *suneidenai* is used in 34 B 5 for low-level knowledge or for awareness that falls short of knowledge. (To say that *suneidenai* is used in these two ways is not to say that the term is ambiguous or has different senses. Rather, it has a broader sense than 'to know'; but a given context might make it clear whether the sort of awareness at issue is tantamount to knowledge or falls short of it.)

One might think that if *suneidenai* is used for knowledge in the *Phaedrus* passage just explored, then, given the closeness of that passage to (T1), *suneidenai* is also used for knowledge in (T1). However, we must look at each passage in its overall context, to see what reading best fits that context. Perhaps the *Phaedrus* and *Apology* assume different epistemological views, in such a way that similar-sounding claims should in the end be interpreted differently. Both the middle books of the *Republic* and *Theaetetus* 184–6 deny that perception is knowledge; but there is less agreement here than meets the eye, because (or so I believe) perception is understood differently in the two contexts. Nor, I have suggested, is it entirely clear that *suneidenai* is used for knowledge in the *Phaedrus* passage.

ledge.[26] For example, I can have good grounds for my true belief that I lack mathematical expertise: grounds that are good enough to count as my knowing that I lack it. Perhaps I know that an expert mathematician must be able to do elementary sums correctly, and that I myself cannot do them, as my repeated mistakes make all too clear. I then have low-level knowledge that I lack mathematical expertise. Or again, I might know that I lack high-level knowledge of Russian: for I know that I have never learnt the language at all. But the knowledge I have of these facts is not itself a piece of *sophia*. It is not specialized expertise of a given domain; it does not involve a systematic, synoptic grasp of a field; it is too atomistic to count as wisdom, as wisdom is conceived of in the *Apology*.

And it seems to me that *if suneidenai* indicates knowledge in (T1), it is knowledge that falls short of having the *sophia* Socrates claims to lack; his grasp of the fact that he is not *sophos* is lower-level. He does not, in his view, have a deep and systematic enough grasp of a given domain to count as having *sophia* of the fact that he is not *sophos*. Grounds of charity also suggest this reading: for *suneidenai* can be used for less than having *sophia*; and if it is used for less than having *sophia* here, we avoid attributing a contradiction to

---

[26] Of course, one might hold epistemological views that preclude this possibility. It is sometimes thought that Plato holds such views in the *Charmides*. See also n. 14, point 4 above, though the issue there is somewhat different. Whether or not Plato holds such views in the *Charmides*, it is a different question whether he holds them in the *Apology*. My suggestion is that *if* one thinks that, in the relevant contexts, Plato uses *suneidenai*—and *gignōskein* in (T4)—for knowledge, then one should also think that he allows one to have low-level knowledge that one lacks high-level knowledge: that one can know (*suneidenai, gignōskein*) that one lacks *sophia* and *epistēmē*, without thereby having any *sophia* or *epistēmē*. If, however, Plato uses *suneidenai* and *gignōskein* in the relevant contexts for awareness that falls short of knowledge, then we do not know, from the *Apology*, whether he thinks one can have low-level knowledge that one lacks high-level knowledge. For in this case the issue is not broached.

Even if Plato does not broach that issue, he might none the less implicitly distinguish between lower and higher levels of knowledge, and claim to have low-level knowledge of something, even if not of his own cognitive condition. Later I shall suggest that he sometimes seems to use *eidenai* for low-level knowledge. (But, in the *Apology*, he never explicitly claims to *eidenai* that he lacks knowledge.) Since he does not explicitly say what it is to *eidenai* something in a way that falls short of having *sophia* or *epistēmē* of it, any attempt to spell out the differences is somewhat speculative. What matters for my purposes here is not that we be able to give a precise account of how Socrates implicitly distinguishes lower- from higher-level knowledge, but that we see that it is reasonable to attribute some such distinction to him, whether in connection with his description of his own cognitive situation (if we think *suneidenai* and *gignōskein* indicate low-level knowledge) or in connection with *eidenai*, when it is used in a way that falls short of having *sophia* or *epistēmē*, or both.

Socrates.[27] So even if Socrates claims to *know* that he is not *sophos*, we need not take him to be even implicitly contradictory; for even if he claims to know that he is not *sophos*, he does so in a way that falls short of being *sophos*.

But it is not clear that he claims to *know* that he is not *sophos*: his awareness that he is not *sophos* might fall short of knowing, in even a low-level way, that he is not *sophos*. This need not mean it is a lucky guess: not all true beliefs are mere lucky guesses. Some of them are backed by good reasons, even if these reasons are not good enough to constitute knowledge. In the geometry lesson in the *Meno*, for example, Meno's slave eventually comes up with the right answer; but Socrates denies that he knows the right answer (85 B–D). The slave has grounds for his true belief: he worked it out himself and followed a proof, of sorts, at least to some extent. But, in Plato's view, he has not done so in a way that gives him knowledge.[28]

---

[27] It is true that later, Socrates says that the fact that he *gignōskei* that he is not wise gives him human wisdom. But, as we shall see in sect. 7, that is not to say that he has genuine wisdom or is genuinely wise.

[28] I have now in effect distinguished different kinds, or levels, of mere true belief (lucky guesses vs. well-grounded true beliefs that fall short of knowledge), and of knowledge (low-level vs. high-level). The basic idea is certainly not foreign to Plato. For example, in the Divided Line at the end of *Republic* bk. 6 he describes two kinds of belief (*eikasia* and *pistis*) and two kinds of knowledge (*dianoia* and *noēsis*). (*Eikasia* and *pistis* are two kinds of belief as such, not two kinds of *true* belief; but some beliefs at each level are true.) Perhaps the slave at the end of the geometry lesson in the *Meno* has *pistis* about the particular geometrical question they have investigated (though not about morality). *Noēsis*, as conceived in the *Republic*, is certainly sufficient for the high-level knowledge (*sophia*, *epistēmē*) discussed in the *Apology*; but it does not seem to be necessary for all *sophia*. For the craftsmen (i.e. good, skilled craftsmen) are said to be *sophoi* in their domains; yet they are not at the highest level of the Divided Line. (But perhaps even in the *Apology* Plato thinks that something like *noēsis* is necessary for being *sophos* as such or as a person, as opposed to being *sophos* in a given domain. For the distinction between being *sophos* about a given domain such as geometry, and being *sophos* as such or as a person, see sect. 7.) I am not sure the Divided Line countenances the sort of lower-level knowledge the *Apology* seems to admit. (I discuss lower-level knowledge in the *Apology* further below.) For even *dianoia* goes beyond it; but, in the Divided Line, anything that falls short of *dianoia* is at best belief. But my intention is not to read the Divided Line into the *Apology*. The point is just that it shows that Plato sometimes countenances higher and lower levels of knowledge and of true belief; and that makes it reasonable to assume that the same is true in the *Apology*, even though there is no explicit theorizing about it, and even if the precise kinds, or levels, of belief and knowledge are not exactly the same.

The view that the *Apology* distinguishes higher and lower levels of knowledge is widespread, though there are different accounts of how one should characterize them. For one clear and succinct account which is close to my own, see Taylor, *Socrates*, 42–8. I discuss the Divided Line in 'Knowledge and Belief in *Republic*

I have suggested that in (T1) *suneidenai* is used either for awareness that falls short of knowledge or for low-level knowledge that falls short of having *sophia* or of making one *sophos*. I prefer the first reading; and later I shall suggest some reasons in its favour, though they are far from decisive. Be that as it may, for now let me just note a few points about each reading.

On my preferred reading, Socrates does not claim, in (T1), that he knows that he knows nothing. Rather, he claims to be aware, in a way that falls short of knowing, that he lacks high-level knowledge: he is aware that he is not at all wise. However, if, contrary to my preferred reading, *suneidenai* indicates low-level knowledge in (T1), then there is a sense in which he implies that he knows that he knows nothing. But the sense in which he does so does not involve a contradiction. Rather, he in this case implies that he has low-level knowledge that he lacks high-level knowledge.

It is important to distinguish the second of these two interpretations from another one with which it might easily be confused. In his justly famous article 'Socrates' Disavowal of Knowledge', Gregory Vlastos argues that Socrates uses 'know' in two different senses, what he calls certain and elenctic knowledge (Kc and Ke, respectively); and he argues that when (as he thinks) Socrates claims to know that he knows nothing, he is at any rate not contradicting himself, because he means that he has Ke that he lacks Kc, and this is not a contradiction.[29] This, however, misleadingly suggests that Socrates uses a *single* word in two different senses. In fact, however, he uses two *different* words, *suneidenai* and *sophia*, in two different senses. My suggestion is *not* that Socrates uses a single word in two different senses. Rather, he uses two different words non-synonymously. These are very different claims.[30]

V–VII', in Everson (ed.), *Epistemology*, 85–115, repr., with minor modifications, in *Plato on Knowledge and Forms*, 85–116.

[29] 'Socrates' Disavowal of Knowledge', 68 n. 13, 82–4, 91. In n. 4 Vlastos mentions several Greek cognitive words; he seems to think that they are all synonymous with one another, and that each of them is ambiguous as between Ke and Kc.

[30] Socrates uses two different words (*suneidenai, sophos*) non-synonymously on both of the interpretations I have suggested. For on neither of them does it follow from the fact that he *sunoide* that he is not *sophos*, that he is *sophos* about that lack.

As I noted above (n. 1), some of the Latin attributions also use forms of just one cognitive word, *scire*. So the problem is not new with English. Indeed, the terms in which the debate is now cast in English—asking whether Socrates knows that he knows nothing, using just a single English word, 'know'—may ultimately be due to Cicero's repeated use of forms of *scire* in this connection. Though I agree with

My criticism of Vlastos is quite different from one levelled by
Lesher. He objects to Vlastos that it would be 'thoroughly "un-
Socratic"' to distinguish two senses of 'know'; for doing so would
violate his alleged '"semantic monism": that whenever we employ
a word, there is a single quality designated by that term which, once
properly identified, can serve as a distinguishing mark for all the
things designated by that term'.[31] But whether Socrates endorses
semantic monism is irrelevant here. For, again, Socrates uses two
different, non-synonymous words, for two different cognitive conditions.[32]

5. Socrates cross-examines a politician: (T2)

In (T2[a]) Socrates certainly does not say that he knows that he
knows nothing. Nor does he say this in [b]. Rather, he says that *it
is probable* that neither he nor the person he cross-examined knows
anything *fine and good*.

One might argue that saying that it is *probable* that he does not
know anything fine and good falls short of saying that he does not
know anything fine and good: in which case, so far from disclaiming
all knowledge in [b], he would not even clearly be disclaiming *any*
knowledge.

But even if—as I believe (see n. 35)—'probable' is not used to
avoid a definite commitment, Socrates does not say in [b] that he
knows nothing. Rather, he would in this case be saying that he
knows nothing *fine and good*. Saying that he does not know anything

Jerome that we need not always translate word for word, using just one non-Greek
word—whether in Latin or English or in any other language—to render two different
and non-synonymous Greek words leads to confusion in the case at hand.

[31] Lesher, 'Socrates' Disavowal of Knowledge', 278.

[32] C. D. C. Reeve, *Socrates in the Apology* (Indianapolis, 1989), 58–62, agrees with
Lesher that Socrates is a semantic monist; this leads him to suggest that Socrates
distinguishes, not different senses of 'know', but different kinds of knowledge, where
'knowledge' has a single meaning. The second of my two interpretations—on which
suneidenai indicates low-level knowledge—in effect involves distinguishing kinds,
or degrees, of knowledge, one conveyed by *suneidenai* and the other by *sophia* and
epistēmē. But that interpretation is not motivated by Socrates' alleged semantic
monism. For, again, he uses different cognitive words for different levels, or degrees,
of knowledge (if, contrary to my view, *suneidenai* indicates knowledge here at all).
To be sure, I have suggested that *sophia* and *epistēmē* are used interchangeably. My
point is that to *suneidenai* something is not to be *sophos* with respect to it or to have
epistēmē of it.

fine and good falls short of saying that he does not know anything at all;[33] hence it falls short of saying that he knows that he knows nothing.

Actually, Socrates probably does not mean to disavow knowledge even of everything that is fine and good; he is speaking elliptically. For earlier, as we have seen, he used the phrase 'fine and good' in connection with equestrians, who enable horses to achieve their proper *aretē*; he went on to ask who has the corresponding skill about how to make humans achieve their proper virtue, saying he lacks it (20 c 1–4). 'Fine and good' in [*b*] probably refers just to what is fine and good in the human sphere, in connection with moral virtue. For presumably Socrates was not cross-examining the unnamed politician about how to make horses achieve their proper *aretē*, but about how to enable humans to do so. So I take (T2[*b*]) to be saying that neither he nor the unnamed politician has moral knowledge. Since that falls short of saying that he has no knowledge whatsoever, it falls short of saying that he knows that he knows nothing.

Socrates is sometimes thought to disclaim all knowledge in [*c*]. However, it seems better to take [*c*] to say that, though neither Socrates nor his interlocutor knows anything fine and good, his interlocutor takes himself to know something fine and good, whereas Socrates does not take himself to know anything fine and good: 'just as I do not know' is elliptical for not knowing anything fine and good which, in turn, refers, here, just to moral knowledge.[34] So

[33] At least, this is so unless he thinks one cannot know anything at all unless one knows something fine and good. So far as I can see, however, nothing he says in the *Apology* commits him to this view. One might argue that he is committed to it in the *Republic*, if his view there is that one cannot know anything unless one knows the form of the good (which is fine and good). However, even if, in the *Republic*, knowledge of the form of the good is needed for the best sort of knowledge, I do not think that, even there, it is required for knowledge as such. Be that as it may, we cannot assume that the *Apology* has the same view as the *Republic*.

[34] For the view that the passage disclaims knowledge only of what is fine and good, see Lesher, 'Socrates' Disavowal of Knowledge', 281; Stokes, *Plato:* Apology, 18 (though the translation he gives there differs from the one he gives on 49); T. Brickhouse and N. Smith, *Plato's Socrates* (Oxford, 1994), 33; and, by implication, Vlastos, *Socrates*, 237 n. 5. However, there is dispute about what is involved in disclaiming knowledge of what is *kalon kagathon*. In *Socrates*, 237–9, and in 'Socrates' Disavowal of Knowledge', 88–91, Vlastos implies that it involves disclaiming all moral knowledge, where, however, the knowledge at issue is just Kc. Lesher, by contrast, does not think Socrates is disclaiming all moral knowledge; neither does Kraut, *Socrates and the State*, 272. However, Lesher and Kraut suggest different exceptions. Brickhouse and Smith think Socrates is disclaiming more than moral

read, [c] follows on naturally from [b]. By contrast, if in [c] Socrates
were suddenly to claim that he knows (*eidenai*) nothing at all, the
logic of the passage would be quite odd.[35]

In [b], Socrates says that neither he nor the unnamed politician knows anything *kalon kagathon*. In [c], he says that just as
he does not know anything *kalon kagathon*, so he does not think
he does, whereas the unnamed politician falsely believes he knows
something *kalon kagathon*. In [d], Socrates explains how [b] and
[c] make him wiser than the unnamed politician: he is wiser than
the unnamed politician because, when he does not know something
(*kalon kagathon*), neither does he think he does; whereas this is
not true of the unnamed politician. Socrates is not claiming that
he knows nothing, let alone that he knows that he knows nothing. Rather, he means (i) that he does not know anything *kalon
kagathon*, and does not think he does; and (ii) that this makes him
wiser than the unnamed politician, since the latter falsely believes
that he knows something *kalon kagathon*. Socrates is wiser than
the unnamed politician in that he lacks a false belief the politician
has. Moreover, it is a particularly bad false belief to have, since, as
the *Meno* explains at length, it makes the one who has it lazy and
disinclined to enquire—which, however, one must do in order to
acquire the knowledge needed for virtue.

knowledge. For they think the craftsmen's wisdom is included within the scope of
what is fine and good, so that when Socrates claims to lack knowledge of what is
fine and good, he means to claim (among other things) that he lacks the knowledge
craftsmen have.

[35] In 'Socrates' Disavowal of Knowledge' Vlastos translates [c], not as I have
done, but as: 'But he, having no knowledge, thinks he knows something, while
I, having none, do not think I have any' (67 (=his (T8)). (He gives a different
translation in *Socrates*, 82.) It might seem that on this translation Socrates disavows
all knowledge (*eidenai*), which is how Vlastos interprets the passage in 'Disavowal'
(where, again, he thinks the knowledge disavowed is just all Kc). However, even on
Vlastos's translation, the passage can still be taken to say just that Socrates has no
knowledge of what is *kalon kagathon*. That is how Vlastos understands the passage
in *Socrates*: see previous note.

Gary Matthews has suggested to me that we should not supply 'fine and good' in
[c], on the ground that it would be odd if Socrates first said that it is 'probable' that
neither he nor his interlocutor knows anything fine and good, only to add, in the
very same sentence, that he himself does not know anything fine and good, omitting
the 'probable'. Matthews therefore takes [c] to make a more general claim. However,
it seems to me that if 'probable' expresses a qualification or hesitation, its omission
in [c] would be odd whether the passage is read as I read it or as Matthews reads
it. I therefore doubt that 'probable' indicates a qualification or hesitation; certainly
it does not always do so. If it does not do so here, its occurrence does not tell in
favour of Matthews's reading.

Though this seems to be all (T2[*d*]) means, Socrates may believe a stronger claim. For in *Ap.* 29 A 5–B 5 he says:

τὸ γάρ τοι θάνατον δεδιέναι, ὦ ἄνδρες, οὐδὲν ἄλλο ἐστὶν ἢ δοκεῖν σοφὸν εἶναι μὴ ὄντα· δοκεῖν γὰρ εἰδέναι ἐστὶν ἃ οὐκ οἶδεν. οἶδε μὲν γὰρ οὐδεὶς τὸν θάνατον οὐδ᾽ εἰ τυγχάνει τῷ ἀνθρώπῳ πάντων μέγιστον ὂν τῶν ἀγαθῶν, δεδίασι δ᾽ ὡς εὖ εἰδότες ὅτι μέγιστον τῶν κακῶν ἐστι. καίτοι πῶς οὐκ ἀμαθία ἐστὶν αὕτη ἡ ἐπονείδιστος, ἡ τοῦ οἴεσθαι εἰδέναι ἃ οὐκ οἶδεν; ἐγὼ δ᾽, ὦ ἄνδρες, τούτῳ καὶ ἐνταῦθα ἴσως διαφέρω τῶν πολλῶν ἀνθρώπων, καὶ εἰ δή τῳ σοφώτερός του φαίην εἶναι, τούτῳ ἄν, ὅτι οὐκ εἰδὼς ἱκανῶς περὶ τῶν ἐν Ἅιδου οὕτω καὶ οἴομαι οὐκ εἰδέναι.

For to fear death, gentlemen, is nothing else than to think one is wise when one is not; for it is to think one knows [*eidenai*] things one does not know. For about death, no one knows whether it is in fact the greatest of all goods for man; but they fear it as though they know well [*eu eidotes*] that it is the greatest of bad things. And yet, how can this fail to be the disgraceful ignorance of thinking one knows things one does not know? But I, gentlemen, on this point and in this respect, am presumably superior to most men, and indeed if I were to claim to be wiser than someone in some respect, it would be in this respect: that, not knowing sufficiently [*eidōs hikanos*] about the things in Hades, I also think I do not know this.

If this is a claim about something fine and good (in the moral sphere), then it is another example of Socrates' claiming that, when he does not know something fine and good (in the moral sphere), he does not think he does, whereas others falsely believe they know something fine and good (in the moral sphere).[36] If, however, the

---

[36] In (T2[*d*]) Socrates says that when he does not know something (*kalon kagathon*), neither does he think he does. In the passage just cited in the text, he says instead that when he does not know something, he thinks he does not know it. The latter remark presumably does not mean that he thinks he does not know e.g. quantum mechanics, under that description: for he has never even heard of quantum mechanics, and hence cannot have the *de dicto* thought that he does not know quantum mechanics. Perhaps he means that when he has carefully considered some subject-matter without achieving knowledge of it, he is aware that he has not achieved knowledge of it. The higher the level of knowledge, the more plausible this claim is. By contrast, if his claim is that when he does not know something, he does not think he does, that could mean that *either* he is aware of not knowing it *or* he has never even considered the relevant subject-matter and so *a fortiori* does not think he knows it, since he does not even have beliefs on the matter.

The claim that when one does not know something neither does one think one knows it might be taken to be equivalent (by contraposition) to the claim that when one thinks one knows something, one knows it. If Socrates is in this position, he is very well off, cognitively speaking, given that he says that when he does not know something neither does he think he does. For in general, as Socrates is at pains to point out, thinking one knows something is not sufficient for knowing it.

claim is not about something fine and good (in the moral sphere), then Socrates implies that he is wiser than others because, even outside the domain of what is fine and good (in the moral sphere), when he does not know something, he does not think he does, whereas others sometimes believe they know something when they do not. This does not imply that others do not know anything.[37] Nor does it imply that others are never correct in their claims about what they do and do not know. Rather, Socrates is always correct in making such claims (or is at least always correct in making them in important cases, where these extend outside the moral sphere to, for example, whether there is life after death, but perhaps not also to trivial empirical matters of fact), whereas others are not, since they make mistakes about the extent of their knowledge not only in the moral sphere but also in other important cases, such as whether there is life after death.

In (T2) Socrates says he does not *eidenai* some range of things. This contrasts with (T1), where he claims that he is not *sophos*. As we have seen, *sophia*, like *epistēmē* (as it is used in the *Apology*), indicates high-level knowledge. By contrast, in some passages in the *Apology eidenai* is used more broadly. For example, when Socrates says 'I know well (*eu oida*) that wherever I go, the young will listen to what I say' (37 D 6–7), he presumably does not mean that he has *sophia* of that fact: he does not have a deep, synoptic, explanatory grasp of a domain. Rather, he has good grounds for saying what he does, about this one fact. When he tells the jury to know well (*eu iste*) that what he says is true (28 A 4–8), he is not telling them to acquire specialized expertise of that fact. Rather, he wants them to grasp the reasons why what he says is true, where doing so does not give them *sophia* or *epistēmē*. When he tells the jury that they know (*iste*) Chaerephon (20 E 8, 21 A 3), he is not ascribing *sophia* or *epistēmē* to them. Rather, they know who he is just in the sense

---

[37] However, at 23 C 7 Socrates speaks of people who think they know (*eidenai*) something, but know (*eidenai*) little or nothing; and in 23 D 8–E I he speaks of people who claim to know (*eidenai*) something, but in fact know (*eidenai*) nothing. Yet, as we shall soon see, Socrates often takes various people to know (*eidenai*) something or other. There are various resolutions. The two most plausible seem to me to be that in 23 C–E he means either that the people at issue think they have high-level knowledge, are experts, when they are not, whereas the knowledge he ascribes to various people is lower-level than that; or that 'knowing nothing' in 23 is elliptical for knowing nothing about the topics under discussion, which is compatible with their knowing something in other areas. Cf. Stokes, *Plato: Apology*, note on 23 D 7–E I.

that they have met him, can generally identify him, are aware of some of his salient character traits, and so on.[38]

It would be reasonable to think that some of these passages use *eidenai* colloquially or loosely, rather than for genuine knowledge. At least, the question of who has or lacks knowledge or wisdom is not to the fore, as it is in our key passages. Nor would anything be lost if Socrates had said 'what I say is true' (omitting 'know well that'), or if he had said 'you're aware of who Chaerephon is'. (Forms of *eu eidenai* are also used at 30 c 6–8, 31 d 6–e 1, 33 b 6–8.)

However, it is also possible that *eidenai* is being used for genuine knowledge that, however, falls short of *epistēmē*. Whether or not it is so used in the passages just mentioned, I suggest in Section 6 that that is a plausible reading of its use in (T3); and I shall shortly suggest that it also a plausible reading of its use in 29 b 5–7 (cf. 28 b 8–9, 37 b).[39]

Even if *eidenai* is sometimes used colloquially, in (T2) it seems to be used for genuine knowledge. If so, we need to know whether Socrates is saying he does not know anything *kalon kagathon* in even a low-level way, or whether he is saying he does not know anything *kalon kagathon* in a high-level way. Though I think it is difficult

---

[38] Cf. 24 A 6–7, though σχεδόν may weaken the seeming claim to knowledge.

[39] Is it plausible to say that Socrates has low-level knowledge of e.g. Chaerephon or of some moral facts (for the latter claim, see 29 B, which I discuss briefly below), but is only aware that he is not *sophos* (which is my preferred reading of (T1))? Perhaps he thinks it is relatively easy to acquire low-level knowledge of a person, or of a few moral facts. For the former, for example, perhaps all one needs to do is to meet the person, interact with him a bit over time, and have a reasonable grasp of some of his salient traits. For low-level knowledge of a few moral facts, see the next note. But perhaps he thinks it is difficult to have even low-level knowledge that one is not at all *sophos*. (Above, I suggested that *if suneidenai* indicates knowledge in (T1), then we should say that it is low-level knowledge; and I explained how one might have low-level knowledge that one lacks high-level knowledge. But I did not commit myself to saying that Socrates means to use that in (T1); nor did I commit myself to saying that he thinks it is possible. Rather, I sketched the sort of view one should have *if* one thinks *suneidenai* in (T1) indicates knowledge, and one wants to interpret the passage in a way that avoids contradiction.) Certainly Socrates thinks many Athenians do not even have the true belief that they lack *sophia*, whereas he happily accords them knowledge (*eidenai*) of various things. Though he thinks he has the true belief that he is not *sophos*, perhaps he thinks his grasp of that fact is not deep and synoptic enough to constitute any sort of knowledge. But if one thinks it is implausible to suppose that Socrates knows Chaerephon but not that he is not *sophos*, the two best alternatives seem to me to say either that *eidenai* is used colloquially or loosely in the relevant contexts or that *suneidenai* and, as we shall see, *gignōskein* are used in the relevant passages for low-level knowledge. On none of the suggested readings does Socrates contradict himself either explicitly or implicitly, though the explanations differ, depending on our understanding of the cognitive words at issue.

to be sure about this, the second alternative seems better. For as we have seen, in 19 E–20 C Socrates was concerned with high-level knowledge, with whether anyone has a deep, synoptic, explanatory grasp of what is *kalon kagathon*, especially in the moral sphere. The present discussion follows on from that one; it is therefore reasonable to assume that the same kind, or level, of knowledge is at issue in both.

A further reason for taking *eidenai* to be high-level knowledge in (T2) is that at 29 B (cf. 28 B 8–9, 37 B) Socrates claims to know (*eidenai*) a moral truth. This would seem to be inconsistent with (T2), if the latter disavows all moral knowledge (*eidenai*) of even a low-level sort. But the two passages are consistent if, in (T2), Socrates disclaims only high-level moral knowledge and if, in 29 B (and in 29 B 8 and 37 B 8), he claims merely to have low-level moral knowledge.[40]

But even if, in (T2), Socrates denies having any knowledge at all, whether moral or non-moral, and whether high- or low-level, he does not say that he *knows* that he knows nothing. Rather, he says

---

[40] For this suggestion see, among others, Taylor, *Socrates*, 45. Why might Socrates think he has low-level knowledge of a moral truth, but lacks high-level moral knowledge? One reason might be that high-level knowledge is synoptic, and involves a grasp of basic moral principles and of answers to the relevant 'What is *F*?' questions. Perhaps at least in the *Apology*, Socrates thinks one can know a few moral truths without answering a relevant 'What is *F*?' question. Perhaps he thinks repeated use of the elenchus can confer low-level knowledge in such a case. This is not to say that he thinks high-level moral knowledge is won through other means than the elenchus. It is to say only that perhaps he thinks one can practise it enough to have low-level knowledge that falls short of high-level knowledge. Perhaps even further use of the elenchus would enable one to achieve high-level knowledge. Cf. *Meno* 85 C 9–D 1.

There are many explanations of how to square (T2) with the occasional avowals of moral knowledge (which are always made with forms of *eidenai*), including the view that Socrates is inconsistent. I shall not explore this matter here, since it lies apart from my central concern, which is whether Socrates ever claims to know that he knows nothing.

Even if Socrates uses forms of *eidenai* for both high- and low-level knowledge, that is no help to those who want to argue that, though Socrates claims to know that he knows nothing, he does not contradict himself. For he never claims to *eidenai* that he does not *eidenai* anything. More generally, he does not use forms of *eidenai* to describe the cognitive attitude he has to his cognitive condition. If he uses forms of *eidenai* in two ways, that might help us avoid contradiction between (T2) and the occasional avowals of moral knowledge; but that is a *different* possible contradiction from the one I am concerned with here. Interestingly, in the *Charmides* Socrates explores the notion of knowing (*eidenai*) what one does and does not know (*eidenai*). But he does not say, in either the *Charmides* or the *Apology*, that he or anyone else knows (*eidenai*) that they know (*eidenai*) nothing.

that when he does not know something (fine and good), neither does he think he does. I am inclined to think this supports my preferred interpretation of (T1), on which *suneidenai* indicates a sort of awareness that falls short of knowledge. For if Socrates took himself to *know* when he lacks knowledge, we might have expected him to say here that he knows that he does not know anything (fine and good). But he conspicuously does not say that.[41]

One might argue that even if he does not say this explicitly, he implies it. Here it is worth mentioning the knowledge account of assertion, according to which knowledge is the norm governing assertion.[42] If one accepts this view, one would not assert that *p* unless one took oneself to know that *p*.[43] If Socrates accepts the knowledge account of assertion, then, were he to assert that he

---

[41] So also Stokes, *Plato:* Apology, 18.

[42] Thanks to Nick Sturgeon for suggesting the relevance of the knowledge account of assertion in this context. For a defence of the knowledge account of assertion, see T. Williamson, 'Knowing and Asserting', *Philosophical Review*, 105 (1996), 489–523. For a recent criticism of the knowledge account of assertion, see J. Lackey, 'Norms of Assertion', *Nous*, 41 (2007), 594–626. She defends the Reasonable to Believe Norm of Assertion, according to which '[o]ne should assert that *p* only if (i) it is reasonable for one to believe that *p*, and (ii) if one asserted that *p*, one would assert that *p* at least in part because it is reasonable for one to believe that *p*' (608). This is closer to the view I think Socrates assumes than is the knowledge account of assertion.

[43] At least, one would not do so *ceteris paribus*. But even on the knowledge account of assertion there are circumstances in which it would be appropriate to assert that *p* even if one does not take oneself to know that *p*. If, for example, one thinks a train is about to run someone over, though one might not claim to know this (if, say, one has very high standards for knowledge), one might shout 'Move; otherwise the train will run you over'. Though knowledge remains the norm for assertion, something might require one to violate the norm. See Williamson, 'Knowing and Asserting', 508. So one might argue that Socrates accepts the knowledge account of assertion, but thinks he is required to violate the norm governing it, perhaps in an effort to get his interlocutors to focus on the more important things—the state of their souls—that he thinks they are all too inclined to ignore. In *The Midwife of Platonism: Text and Subtext in Plato's* Theaetetus (Oxford, 2004), 31 ff., David Sedley argues that in the *Theaetetus* Socrates does not make assertions when he takes himself to lack knowledge or wisdom; so Sedley in effect thinks Socrates accepts the knowledge account of assertion in the *Theaetetus*. Sedley is well aware that in the *Theatetus* Socrates makes many assertions; he argues that in these cases Socrates takes himself to have knowledge. Sedley says, however, that he doubts that any single interpretation of Socrates' disavowal of knowledge fits every dialogue (31); he does not say how he interprets the *Apology* on this point. For my own part, I doubt that Socrates ever accepts the knowledge account of assertion, though defending that view lies outside the scope of the present paper. However, I go on to give reasons for supposing that he does not accept it in the *Apology* or the *Gorgias*.

knows nothing, he would in effect be committed to the view that he knows that he knows nothing.

But Socrates does not accept the knowledge account of assertion. He often makes very strong claims, yet tells us up front that he lacks knowledge. Perhaps the most striking example of this is in the *Gorgias*, where he claims to have proved something with arguments of iron and adamant (508 E–509 A), yet proceeds to say that he lacks knowledge (509 A 4–6).[44] There is also an example in the *Apology*. At 29 A he says that no one, himself included, knows (*eidenai*) whether death is good or bad (for the person who dies). Yet later he says there is strong evidence (μέγα τεκμήριον, 40 C 2) that it is good, and that he has much hope (πολλὴ ἐλπίς, 40 C 5) that it is. So he is willing to assert something quite strongly, while at the same time claiming not to know it. Hence, even if, in (T2), he asserts that he knows nothing, he is not committed to the view that he knows that he knows nothing. We cannot add the knowledge account of assertion to the disavowal of knowledge so as to get an implicit contradiction or paradox.[45]

6. Socrates and the craftsmen: (T3)

Like the other passages we have explored so far, (T3[*a*]) does not involve an explicit contradiction either. For once again, different cognitive words are used: this time, forms of *suneidenai* and *epistasthai*. But once again, one might argue that to *suneidenai* something is to know it; and one might think that, in that case, (T3[*a*]) involves an implicit contradiction, given that to *epistasthai* something is to know it. There is, however, a by-now familiar reply to this by-now familiar argument: to *suneidenai* something might fall short of

---

[44] Cf. 506 A 3–4: 'I do not have knowledge [*eidenai*] any more than you have when I say what I say' (trans. Irwin, in his *Plato: Gorgias* (Oxford, 1979)). In 'Socrates' Disavowal of Knowledge' (83; see his (T30)) Vlastos translates the passage as follows: 'I do not assert what I assert as one who knows', which sounds like an explicit rejection of the knowledge account of assertion. The word Vlastos translates as 'I assert' is λέγω, which Irwin translates as 'I say'.

[45] One might argue that in *Gorg.* 509 A and *Ap.* 40 C he is disavowing only high-level knowledge but implying that he has low-level knowledge. Even if this argument were correct (though I do not think it is), Socrates would not be either explicitly contradictory (since he does not explicitly claim knowledge in either passage) or implicitly contradictory (since he would be implying only that he has low-level knowledge that he lacks high-level knowledge).

knowing it; but even if to *suneidenai* something is to know it, it can be knowing it in a way that falls short of having *epistēmē*. Either way, (T3[*a*]) is not even implicitly contradictory.

Another way to avoid contradiction would be to say that 'practically' (*hōs epos eipein*) introduces a qualification. For if Socrates merely claims to be aware of knowing *practically* nothing, that falls short of claiming to know nothing; and so it falls short of claiming to know that he knows nothing. Perhaps one of the few things he knows is that he knows a few things.[46] Indeed, one might think that inconsistency can be avoided *only* by pressing 'practically' into service. For in (T3[*b*]) Socrates says he knows (*eidenai*) that the craftsmen know (*epistasthai*) their crafts: in which case, he knows something.

However, in (T3[*a*]) Socrates claims not to *epistasthai* (practically) anything. In (T3[*b*]), by contrast, he claims to *eidenai* that the craftsmen know (*epistasthai*) their crafts. And, as we have seen, at least in the *Apology eidenai* has a broader scope than *epistasthai* does. Hence we need not take 'practically' to introduce a qualification. An alternative is that, in claiming to *eidenai* that the craftsmen know their crafts, he is not claiming to *epistasthai* that they do so; he knows that they do so only in a lower-level way.[47] This allows Socrates to say, in (T3[*a*]), that he does not *epistasthai* anything, without contradicting (T3[*b*]).

Let us assume that 'practically' does not introduce a qualification. We still need to know whether, in (T3[*a*]), Socrates claims merely to *be aware* (in a way that falls short of knowing) or to *know* that he does not *epistasthai* anything. As we have seen, *suneidenai* can be used both ways. If it is read the first way, Socrates does not claim to *know* that he does not *epistasthai* anything. But if it is read the second way, one might be tempted to say that he claims to know that he knows nothing. Once again, however, it would be

---

[46] For this suggestion, see Lesher, 'Socrates' Disavowal of Knowledge', 281; Stokes, *Plato: Apology*, 18.

[47] On this interpretation, *eidenai* is used more broadly in (T3[*b*]) than in (T2). This does not imply either that it is used in different senses or that the different ways it is used are the ones Vlastos favours. Nor need we be disturbed by the double use of *eidenai*: so long as we pay proper attention to the context, we can see how the word is being used.

Another possibility is that *eidenai* is being used loosely or colloquially, not for genuine knowledge. Though I am sympathetic to the view that *eidenai* is sometimes used loosely or colloquially, in the present passage the context seems too theoretically laden for that to be a reasonable option here.

misleading to describe his claim in that way, since doing so involves using just one cognitive term ('know') when the Greek has two (*suneidenai, epistasthai*). But if one none the less insists on ascribing that claim to him, one should at least add that there is no explicit contradiction, since the Greek uses different cognitive terms. Nor is there an implicit contradiction since, again, the knowledge he (on this reading) claims to have can easily be taken to fall short of the knowledge he disclaims: he might have low-level knowledge (*suneidenai*) that he does not *epistasthai* anything, where the latter involves having high-level knowledge.

Can we choose between these two readings? Here it is relevant to consider (T3[*b*]) more carefully. Socrates says he knows (*eidenai*) that the craftsmen know (*epistasthai*) their crafts. He then says (somewhat curiously, to my ear) that he was not mistaken in thinking this, and that the craftsmen know (*epistasthai*) things he does not know (*epistasthai*). One might think he takes himself to know (*eidenai*) not only that the craftsmen know (*epistasthai*) their crafts, but also that he himself does not. And if he claims to know (*eidenai*) that he does not *epistasthai* the crafts, one might think he likewise thinks he knows that he does not *epistasthai* anything at all. It would then be reasonable to think that, in (T3[*a*]), *suneidenai* is used for (low-level) knowledge.

This line of argument can be resisted. First, even if Socrates claims to know that he does not *epistasthai* what the craftsmen do, it does not follow that he would claim to know that he does not *epistasthai* anything at all. Perhaps it is easier to know that one does not *epistasthai* a given craft than it is to know that one does not *epistasthai* anything at all. Secondly, though Socrates explicitly claims to know (*eidenai*) that the craftsmen know (*epistasthai*) their crafts, he does not explicitly claim to know (*eidenai*) that he lacks their knowledge. To be sure, he claims to lack it. But he does not say that he *knows* (*eidenai*) that he lacks it: *eidenai* does not carry over to the ἀλλά clause. Perhaps he avoids saying that he knows (*eidenai*) that he does not know (*epistasthai*) what the craftsmen do, precisely because he does *not* take this to be something he *knows*. If that is right, then presumably *suneidenai*, in (T3[*a*]), is awareness that falls short of knowledge.

7. Socrates and wisdom: (T4) and (T5)

(T1) expresses Socrates' pre-oracle belief about his cognitive condition. (T2) and (T3) express his belief about his cognitive condition once he has heard the oracle, but is still trying to figure out what it means. (T4) and (T5) describe the belief he arrives at after deciding what the oracle meant. Let us now look at them.

In (T5) Socrates tells us he has human wisdom.[48] In (T4) he says that his human wisdom consists in his realization that in respect of wisdom, he is worthless.[49] One might think that these passages involve a contradiction. On the one hand, Socrates says that he has human wisdom, which might suggest that he takes himself to have some wisdom. On the other hand, he says that he is worthless in respect of wisdom, which might suggest that he takes himself to lack wisdom altogether.

One way to resolve this seeming inconsistency is to say that Socrates does not mean that he has no wisdom at all. Rather, he means that the wisdom he has is worth a lot less than the god's wisdom.[50]

---

[48] He says that he probably ($\kappa\iota\nu\delta\upsilon\nu\epsilon\acute{\upsilon}\omega$) has human wisdom. Once again, one might argue that he is distancing himself from the claim; once again, I doubt that he is doing so. I think Socrates' human wisdom consists *only* in his realization that he lacks wisdom, which, in turn, is closely related to the claim that, when he does not know something, neither does he think he does. Cf. T. Irwin, *Plato's Ethics* (Oxford, 1995), sect. 17; Benson, *Socratic Wisdom*, 170. In *Socrates in the* Apology, 34–6 and 53, Reeve argues that there must be more to human wisdom than this, since '[o]therwise it seems that anyone who recognized that he lacked such knowledge would possess human wisdom and be as wise as Socrates, even if his recognition was a result of general skepticism or below-normal intelligence' (35). I agree that to have human wisdom, one must realize the extent of one's lack of wisdom in an appropriately reflective way and for the right reasons (though, as I go on to say, this realization can, and in Socrates' case may well, fall short of any sort of knowledge). Merely having the true belief that one lacks wisdom is not sufficient for having human wisdom, if the belief is based on e.g. general skepticism about the possibility of knowledge or just on general modesty. However, Reeve thinks Socrates' human wisdom also includes low-level knowledge of various moral truths, whereas I do not think it includes this. Indeed, *Ap.* 29 A–C seems carefully to distinguish his having an instance of human wisdom (viz.: given that he does not know whether death is the greatest of all blessings for a human being, he thinks he does not know this) from his knowledge (*eidenai*) that it is bad and shameful to do wrong, to disobey one's superior be he man or god: the δέ at B 6 is very telling on this point.

[49] Strictly speaking, he says that the god says this; but he thinks that whatever the god says is true.

[50] The view that Socrates disclaims only divine wisdom has a long and distinguished pedigree. See, for example, the Anonymous Commentator on the *Theaete-*

One might object that if we say this, (T4) and (T5) would conflict with (T1). For as we have seen, in (T1) Socrates claims to lack
wisdom altogether. However, it would be unfair to call this a contradiction. After all, (T1) is Socrates' pre-oracle belief. (T4) and
(T5) express his settled post-oracle belief. Perhaps, after hearing
and coming to understand the oracle, he decided that he has some
wisdom after all.[51]

On an alternative I prefer, Socrates continues to believe that he
lacks all wisdom. For he says in (T4[b]), not that he is worth a lot
less than the god in respect of wisdom, but that he is worth *nothing*
in respect of wisdom. A natural explanation of this claim is that he
takes himself to have no wisdom at all.[52] This explanation receives

tus, who suggests, as one interpretation of *Theat.* 150 C, that 'if "having no wisdom"
is to be understood in an absolute sense, it will be that he [Socrates] is not wise in
the wisdom which he attributes to god, or the one which other people attribute to
the sophists' (54. 31–8). The translation is by D. Sedley, in 'The *Theaetetus*: Three
Interpretations', in C. Gill and M. M. McCabe, *Form and Argument in Late Plato*
(Oxford, 2000), 79–103 at 99 n. 44. For the text of, and commentary on, the Anonymous Commentary on the *Theaetetus*, see G. Bastianini and D. Sedley, in *Corpus
dei papiri filosofici greci e latini*, vol. iii (Florence, 1995), 227–562.

  See also the *Anonymous Prolegomena to the Philosophy of Plato*, ed. L. G. Westerink (Paris, 1990), 10. 60–5: 'When he says "I know nothing", he is comparing his
own knowledge with that of the gods, the latter being in a different class from the
former. Ours is mere knowledge, while god's is practically applied. And god's knowledge knows by simple attention, whereas we know through causes and premisses'.
The translation is again due to Sedley, op. cit. The author of the *Prolegomena* does
not say what passage(s) he has in mind.

  Vlastos thinks Socrates distinguishes two senses of 'wisdom', human and divine.
He takes human wisdom to be elenctic knowledge and divine wisdom to be certain
knowledge ('Socrates' Disavowal of Knowledge', 88–92); and he thinks Socrates
disavows the latter but not the former. Cf. *Socrates*, 238–9. Here it is worth noting
that, though Socrates uses the phrase 'human wisdom', he does not use the phrase
'divine wisdom'. He simply says that the god is wise. Perhaps this tells in favour of
the view that he is not distinguishing different senses of 'wisdom' or even different
kinds of wisdom. Cf. Lyons, *Structural Semantics*, 227.

  [51] So Kraut: 'Socrates is significantly modifying . . . [(T1)]. His initial reaction
to the oracle is that he has no reason whatsoever to be considered wise. But in [(T2,
4, and 5)] he concedes that he is wise after all—though in a small way' (*Socrates
and the State*, 271; cf. 272 n. 44). (Where I have inserted '(T2, 4, and 5)', Kraut
mentions just (T2), but the surrounding discussion suggests he thinks (T4) and
(T5) make the same point.)

  [52] In (T4[a]) Socrates says that human wisdom is worth *little or nothing*; in (T4[b])
he says that he is worth *nothing* in respect of wisdom. There are two differences between (T4[a]) and (T4[b]). First, (T4[b]) omits 'or [καί] little'. However, (T4[a])
might mean that human wisdom is worth little, even (καί) nothing, taking καί epex-
egetically. (Contrast J. Riddell, *The Apology of Plato* (1877; repr. New York, 1973),
note ad loc., who takes καί to be disjunctive.) So read, (T4[a]) does not mean to leave

support from the fact that in 38 C Socrates repeats that he is not wise. Rather than saying that he has a little wisdom, he reiterates his pre-oracle belief that he is not wise.[53]

But how can that be? Does he not say that he has human wisdom? Yes, but it is not genuine wisdom. He calls his human wisdom *tis sophia*, a kind of wisdom. '*tis F*' can mean 'a kind of *F*', that is, a species of *F*.[54] But it can also mean 'something like *F*, but not genuinely *F*'.[55] On this latter reading, *tis* and so, presumably, 'human' have a cancelling force: Socrates has something like wisdom; but he does not have the real thing. On this reading, he is not saying that he has genuine wisdom. On the contrary, he says that he has something like wisdom, but lacks the real thing. If this is what he means, he is not retracting his earlier claim that he entirely lacks

open the possibility that human wisdom is worth at least a little. Secondly, (T4[a]) says that human wisdom is worth little or (*alt.*: even) nothing, whereas (T4[b]) says that Socrates is worth nothing in respect of wisdom. As I go on to say in the text, (T4[b]) leaves open the possibility that human wisdom is worth something, even a great deal; it is just that it is worthless *as wisdom*. (T4[b]) expresses what Socrates wants to say more clearly than (T4[a]) does.

[53] Contrast Stokes, *Plato:* Apology, note ad loc. At *Ap.* 29 A 4–5 Socrates again at least implies that he does not take himself to be wise, though one might take him to mean just that he does not take himself to be wise with respect to the matter at hand. In 23 A (= T4[a]) he says that as a result of his investigations, many slanders about him arose—including the claim that he is wise. If he thinks it is slanderous to claim that he is wise, then he does not take himself to be wise. However, the rest of (T4[a]) might be taken to suggest that the claim is restricted to the areas where he has disproved others' claims to wisdom. (T4[b]–[c]), however, suggest a complete disavowal of wisdom.

[54] As it does in e.g. *Meno* 73 E 1, where Socrates distinguishes virtue as such from particular kinds of virtue; cf. 73 E 4–5.

[55] In the second case, τις functions as an *alienans* qualification. See Stokes, *Plato: Apology*, note on 20 D 7, though I am not sure whether he in the end endorses this reading. On the one hand, he says that if human wisdom does not imply knowledge, that 'would suit the second alternative [= *alienans*] better'. On the other hand, he also says that the *Apology* contains 'at least three different applications of the words "wise" and "wisdom", *sophos* and *sophia*. In just one of them [= Socrates' human wisdom] "wisdom" does not imply knowledge' (19). He goes on to say that in '23 A–B there are three different "wisdoms": god's wisdom, "ordinary human 'wisdom'"', and Socrates's human wisdom, which does not imply knowledge'. (On 124, note on 23 B 5–6, Stokes speaks of uses of 'wise', rather than of applications; he also here mentions senses of the term.) This might mean that, though Plato uses the word 'wisdom' here, he is not using it for a kind of wisdom. But it might instead mean that human wisdom is a kind of wisdom that does not imply knowledge.

For possible *alienans* uses of τις in Plato, see *Euthd.* 285 B 1; *Phaedo* 69 B 7; *Rep.* 583 B 5. The first of these references is due to M. F. Burnyeat, 'Enthymeme: Aristotle on the Rationality of Rhetoric', in A. Rorty (ed.), *Essays on Aristotle's Rhetoric* (Berkeley, 1996), 88–115 at n. 8. He also cites *Ap.* 20 D 7.

wisdom. Nor is he distinguishing different senses of 'wisdom' or different kinds of wisdom. Rather, he distinguishes wisdom from something that is like wisdom, but is not wisdom at all.

One advantage of this reading is that it allows us to solve the following puzzle: Socrates plainly thinks he is better off than others are, precisely because he has, but they lack, human wisdom. How, then, can human wisdom be worthless? The answer is that it is worthless *as wisdom*: because it is not wisdom. It does not follow that it is worthless, or even that it is worth just a little.[56] It may be worth a lot—as something other than wisdom. Fake fur is worthless if what you want is genuine fur. But a fake fur coat might still be quite expensive. And if one is opposed to killing animals to make fur coats, but likes the feel and warmth of fur, one would prefer a fake fur coat to the real thing.[57]

One might think that if human wisdom is not genuine wisdom, the oracle turns out to be wrong. For does it not say that Socrates is wise, where that means that he has genuine wisdom? In fact the oracle does not clearly say that Socrates is wise.[58] Chaerephon went to the oracle and asked if anyone was wiser than Socrates; the oracle said that no one was (21 A).[59] To say that no one is wiser than Socrates is not to say that he is wise. Just as one person can

---

[56] It is true that he says his human wisdom makes him wiser than others in just a small way (21 D 6); so one might argue that human wisdom is worth just a little. But even if his human wisdom makes him only a little wiser than others, it might be worth a great deal: it might be worth a lot to come a little closer to genuine wisdom. Whether his human wisdom is worth a lot or just a little, the point is that it is worth *nothing—as wisdom*. That allows it to be worth something (in either a large or a small way, as the case may be) as something other than wisdom that, however, brings him closer to wisdom.

[57] This might make it sound as though, by analogy, one should in some cases prefer non-genuine wisdom to genuine wisdom. And there is a way in which Socrates thinks this, though there is also a way in which he does not do so. In his view, one should prefer genuine wisdom about moral virtue over mere human wisdom about it. On the other hand, he says he is better off with his ignorance than he would be with the wisdom the craftsmen have (22 E 1–5). For though they have genuine wisdom in their domains, they lack both genuine and human wisdom with respect to the most important things (τὰ μέγιστα, 22 D 7)—that is, with respect to moral virtue. So though the craftsmen have some genuine wisdom whereas Socrates has none, his human wisdom (which covers at least the moral sphere but may be more extensive), which is not genuine wisdom at all, gets him closer to genuine wisdom about the most important things, which is more important than having genuine wisdom about less important things. See further below.

[58] Contrast Lesher, 'Socrates' Disavowal of Knowledge', 283.

[59] Perhaps Chaerephon went to the oracle because *he* thought Socrates was wise; it does not follow that the oracle agreed.

be richer or healthier than another without being rich or healthy, so one person can be wiser than another without being wise; one might just be closer to being wise than the other person is.

Nor does (T4) unambiguously represent the oracle as saying that Socrates is wise. Rather, the oracle is represented as saying that Socrates is wisest.[60] To say that he is wisest need not imply that he is wise.[61] Someone might be the healthiest or richest person around, without being healthy or rich; he might just be the closest to being healthy or rich. Similarly, someone might be the wisest person there is, without being wise; he might just come the closest to being wise. What Socrates learnt from the oracle is not that he has some wisdom after all. Rather, he learnt that he is closer to being wise than others are. He is closer to being wise than others are because, unlike them, he realizes that he lacks wisdom. This brings him closer to genuine wisdom for a reason already mentioned: it enables him to enquire

[60] Actually, it is not clear that Socrates says in (T4) that the oracle said that Socrates is wisest. For he is paraphrasing the oracle: it is *as if* it were saying that Socrates is wisest. However, in 21 B 6 he says the oracle claimed that he is wisest. This comes right after 21 A 6–7, in which Socrates says that the oracle said that no one was wiser than Socrates. One might wonder whether any difference is intended between the comparative and the superlative. Thanks to Brad Inwood for suggesting that there is no difference when, as here, the comparison is with all other members of a group: if one member of a group is wiser than all the others, that amounts to his being the wisest of them all. Even if Socrates should find someone who is at his cognitive level, they could be equal wisest: they would be the wisest of all; that is, they would be equally close to being wise. And (T4[b]) seems to leave open the possibility that others are at Socrates' cognitive level: for the oracle says that anyone who, like Socrates, realizes he is worthless in respect of wisdom (in an appropriately reflective way: see n. 48), is wisest. See also Reeve, *Socrates in the Apology*, 22. Though he differs from me in thinking that being wiser and wisest imply being wise, we agree that Socrates does not intend any difference between being wiser and wisest, and that both claims leave open the possibility that others (who, however, are not discovered in the *Apology*) are at the same cognitive level as Socrates.

[61] A scholium to Aristophanes' *Clouds* 144 cites the oracle as saying: 'Wise Sophocles, wiser Euripides, but Socrates is the wisest of men' (σοφὸς Σοφοκλῆς, σοφώτερος δ' Εὐριπίδης, ἀνδρῶν δὲ πάντων Σωκράτης σοφώτατος). (See Parke and Wormell, *The Delphic Oracle*, ii. 170, no. 420.) On this wording (in contrast to Plato's in the *Apology*), the oracle implies that Socrates is wise. For it says he is wiser than others, who are themselves said to be wise. Parke and Wormell argue that for chronological reasons the scholium is unlikely to be accurate, since Euripides might not have written any plays at the time when Chaerephon questioned the oracle. They give more credence to Plato's version than to others. The oracle is more often cited in a one-line, than in a two-line, version: ἀνδρῶν ἁπάντων Σωκράτης σοφώτατος; see e.g. D.L. 2. 37. (In Diogenes Laertius there is no δέ, which suggests he is not omitting a first line. However, in the two-line version cited above, there is a δέ.) The one-line version does not imply that Socrates is wise.

in a more open-minded way; he is therefore in a better position to acquire moral knowledge, and so virtue, than others are.[62]

We have now reached the following paradoxical conclusion: Socrates is closer to being wise than others are because, though he lacks all wisdom, he has human wisdom, which consists in his realizing that he lacks genuine wisdom. Yet he has said that the craftsmen have genuine wisdom in their domains. How can he be closer to being wise than others are, if he lacks all wisdom but the craftsmen have some wisdom? The answer, I think, is that the craftsmen he discusses are wise only in their respective domains: they are wise only *qua* craftsmen. What Socrates is interested in is being wise as such, or as a human being.[63] No one is wise in this way.[64] Though his human wisdom is not genuine wisdom, it gets him closer to being a wise person than the craftsmen's wisdom does. This explains why he says at 22 E that he is better off with his ignorance (*amathia*) than the craftsmen are with their wisdom. For the latter are not wise about the most important things (τὰ μέγιστα, 22 D 7). Nor is Socrates; but he is closer to being wise about them than the craftsmen are. This does not mean that he uses 'wise' in different senses or ways. At most, he acknowledges that one can in principle be wise about different things (about crafts, about moral virtue); and that being wise about some things matters more than being wise about others does.

So far I have argued that Socrates continues to believe that he lacks all genuine wisdom: that is why he says he is worthless in respect of wisdom. But he credits himself with something else: human wisdom. Let us now look at it. It consists, we are told, in his realization that he lacks wisdom. What exactly is involved in

---

[62] Even if saying that someone is wisest generally has the conversational implicature that the person is wise, the phrase does not *have* to be so understood. Perhaps Socrates initially took the suggestion that he is wisest, or wiser than others, to imply that he is wise: hence his initial surprise. He then came to understand that the oracle meant instead just that he was closer to being wise than others are. Thanks to Lesley Brown for this suggestion.

[63] Cf. *Rep.* 428 B 1 ff., where Socrates asks what *sophia* in the ideally just *polis* consists in: not, he says, in the *epistēmē* that carpenters or farmers have, but in a particular sort of *epistēmē* that only the guardians have. Similarly, a person is *sophos* (as a person, not as e.g. a carpenter), not in virtue of having any old *epistēmē*, but in virtue of having *epistēmē* of what is advantageous for each part of the soul and for the whole soul (442 C 5–8). Cf. Arist. *NE* 6. 7.

[64] Which is not to say that it is impossible to be wise as such or as a human being. Though no one, so far as Socrates knows or believes, is wise in this way, it does not follow that no one can be.

realizing that he lacks wisdom? One might argue that to realize something is to know it.[65] And, I have argued, to be worthless in respect of wisdom is to lack all wisdom, which, in turn, implies lacking at least a sort of knowledge. One might then conclude that Socrates' human wisdom consists in his knowing that he knows nothing.[66]

As against this, we should first note that even if there is a way in which we can represent Socrates as saying that he knows that he knows nothing, it is again misleading to do so. For, again, the English has just one word—'know'—where the Greek has two, this time forms of *gignōskein* and *sophia*. Hence, at the very least, the passage is not explicitly self-contradictory.

Nor do we need to take it to be implicitly contradictory. To be sure, Plato often uses *gignōskein* (*gnōsis*) for knowledge.[67] But even if he so uses it here, it need not imply wisdom: it can be knowledge of a lower-level sort. Since we can easily understand *gignōskein* in this way, and since doing so avoids contradiction, it would be reasonable to do so—if we take *gignōskein* to indicate knowledge here.

But it is not clear that *gignōskein* is being used for knowledge here. Plato sometimes uses *gignōskein* and its cognates for a cognitive condition that is weaker than knowledge.[68] If *gignōskein* is so used in (T4), then, in saying that he *egnōken* that he lacks *sophia*, Socrates does not mean that he *knows* that he knows nothing. He means that he *realizes*—where that falls short of knowing—that he lacks wisdom.

[65] So Brickhouse and Smith, *Plato's Socrates*, 33 n. 11. Vlastos, 'Socrates' Disavowal of Knowledge', 91, thinks Socrates has elenctic knowledge that he lacks certain knowledge. Cf. Kraut, *Socrates and the State*, 267–8, 271–3, though 271 also says that Socrates 'now *thinks* he has a certain form of wisdom' (emphasis added).

[66] Stokes, *Plato*: Apology, 19, considers something like this line of argument; like me, he rejects it.

[67] See, for example, the end of *Rep.* 5. I discuss this passage in 'Knowledge and Belief in *Republic* V' and in 'Knowledge and Belief in *Republic* V–VII', both in my *Plato on Knowledge and Forms*, 66–84 and 85–116 respectively.

[68] So also Stokes, *Plato*: Apology, 19. For example, at *Ap.* 25 D 9 and 33 D 3 *gignōskein* need not mean anything more than 'realize' or 'recognize'. Similarly, in the *Meno* the slave is said to recognize (*gignōskei*) what a square is like (82 B 9). I do not think Plato is attributing knowledge to him; rather, the slave has just a true belief about what a square is like. For he does not satisfy Plato's conditions for having knowledge: the slave's true belief is not tied down by an αἰτίας λογισμός. Cf. *Rep.* 375 E 3 (γνωρίμους) and 376 A 6 (γνώριμον), where dogs are said to be gentle to, and welcome, those they 'know'. Presumably dogs lack knowledge in the sense at issue here; the point is just that they recognize certain people. On Plato's use of *gnōrizein* and the cognate noun, see Lyons, *Structural Semantics*, 202; cf. 177 (d).

If we say this, it is then tempting to say that *suneidenai* is likewise used for less than knowledge in (T1) and (T3): there too, Socrates is *aware* that he is not *sophos* and does not *epistasthai* anything; but he does not claim to *know* this fact. Similarly, we saw that in (T2) he says just that when he does not know something, neither does he *think* he knows it. Socrates reiterates the same claim throughout: he is aware or realizes that he lacks wisdom, that is, a high-level knowledge most people lack (whereas others do not realize that they lack it). He need not be taken to say that he *knows*, even in a low-level way, that he lacks wisdom or a high-level kind of knowledge.

Just as there are two readings of (T1) and (T3[a]), so there are two readings of the last part of (T4): either Socrates knows, in a low-level way, that he lacks wisdom; or else he realizes, in a way that falls short of knowing, that he lacks wisdom. Either way, (T4) is not explicitly or implicitly self-contradictory any more than are the other passages we have explored. It is true that, on one reading, there is a sense in which Socrates can be taken to imply that he knows that he knows nothing: he knows (*egnōken*), in a low-level way, that he lacks high-level knowledge (*sophia*). As before, though, it would be misleading to say that he uses 'know' in two different ways or senses. Rather, he uses two different words—this time, forms of *gignōskein* and *sophia*—for two different cognitive conditions.[69] Once again, then, though a case can be made for taking Socrates to say that he knows that he knows nothing, doing so involves a controversial interpretation of his cognitive vocabulary. It is also misleading, given that Socrates uses different cognitive terms, where the English uses just one.

8. Conclusion

I began by noting that some people take Socrates to say that he knows that he knows nothing, whereas others deny that he says this. I have argued that there is something to be said on both sides. A case can be made for saying that there is a sense in which he claims to know that he knows nothing. For if *suneidenai* and *gignōskein* are used here for knowledge, then he claims to know that he lacks *sophia* and *epistēmē*. *Epistēmē* is often translated as 'knowledge'; however

---

[69] Contrast Vlastos, 'Socrates' Disavowal of Knowledge', 91.

it is translated, it is a kind of knowledge, as knowledge is conceived of here. And, though *sophia* is generally translated as 'wisdom', if someone is *sophos*, he has *epistēmē*, and so a kind of knowledge. And, as I have said, I see no decisive way of ruling out the view that *suneidenai* and *gignōskein* indicate knowledge here.

But even if they do, it is misleading to represent Socrates as saying that he knows that he knows nothing. For putting his point this way makes it sound as though he uses just one word, and we then have to figure out whether it is used in the same way or sense, or in different ways or senses. However, in the relevant passages Socrates uses *different* cognitive words for *different* cognitive conditions.[70] The English[71] introduces an air of paradox that is not present in the Greek. If *suneidenai* and *gignōskein* indicate knowledge, we should take Socrates to say, not that he knows that he knows nothing, but that he knows, in a low-level way, that he lacks wisdom (*sophia*), that is, a high-level kind of knowledge (*epistēmē*). This no longer sounds so paradoxical.[72]

But it is not clear that *suneidenai* and *gignōskein* indicate knowledge here; they might be used instead for a sort of awareness or realization that falls short of knowledge. On this reading, which I prefer, Socrates says, not that he knows that he knows nothing, but that he is aware, or realizes, that he lacks genuine wisdom.

Whichever of the two interpretations we favour, it takes considerable work to explain Socrates' cognitive stance. Among other things, we need to read the text in a holistic way, paying careful attention to his use of cognitive terms and to his general epistemological commitments. And in so far as there is dispute about the meanings of the relevant words, and about Socrates' implicit epistemological commitments, any attempt to explain his position is bound to be somewhat insecure.

Cornell University/Merton College, Oxford

---

[70] I suggested above that Socrates uses *eidenai* in more than one way in the *Apology*. But I am not convinced that, in the *Apology*, any of the other key cognitive terms we have considered is used in more than one way. Even if *eidenai* is used in more than one way, that does not help with our main concern: see the last paragraph of n. 40.   [71] Like the use of forms of *scire*: see n. 1.

[72] But one can raise serious questions here; and I take it that one point of the *Charmides* is to raise such questions. For example, one might ask whether one can really have low-level knowledge that one lacks high-level knowledge. Above, I sketched a way one might argue that one can. But accepting this argument requires accepting controversial epistemological views.

BIBLIOGRAPHY

Ackrill, J. L., 'Aristotle's Theory of Definition', in Berti (ed.), *Aristotle on Science*, 359–84.

Ahbel-Rappe, S., and Kamtekar, R. (eds.), *A Companion to Socrates* (Oxford, 2006).

Annas, J., 'Plato the Skeptic', in P. Vander Waerdt (ed.), *The Socratic Movement* (Ithaca, NY, 1994), 309–40.

Bastianini, G., and Sedley, D., text of and commentary on the Anonymous Commentary on the *Theaetetus*, in *Corpus dei papiri filosofici greci e latini*, vol. iii (Florence, 1995), 227–562.

Benson, H., *Socratic Wisdom* (New York, 2000).

Berti, E. (ed.), *Aristotle on Science* (Padua, 1981).

Beversluis, J., 'Does Socrates Commit the Socratic Fallacy?', *American Philosophical Quarterly*, 24 (1987), 211–33.

—— 'Socratic Definition', *American Philosophical Quarterly*, 11 (1974), 331–6.

Brickhouse T., and Smith, N., *Plato's Socrates* (Oxford, 1994).

Brittain, C., *Cicero, On Academic Scepticism* (Indianapolis, 2006).

Brunschwig, J., 'Le fragment DK 70 B 1 de Métrodore de Chio', in K. Algra, P. van der Horst, and D. Runia (eds.), *Polyhistor: Studies in the History and Historiography of Ancient Philosophy* (Leiden, 1996), 21–38.

Burnyeat, M. F., 'Antipater and Self-Refutation', in B. Inwood and J. Mansfeld (eds.), *Assent and Argument* (Leiden, 1997), 277–310.

—— 'Aristotle on Understanding Knowledge', in Berti (ed.), *Aristotle on Science* 97–139.

—— 'Enthymeme: Aristotle on the Rationality of Rhetoric', in A. Rorty (ed.), *Essays on Aristotle's Rhetoric* (Berkeley, 1996), 88–115.

—— 'Socrates and the Jury', *Aristotelian Society*, suppl. 54 (1980), 173–91.

Everson, S. (ed.), *Epistemology* (Companions to Ancient Thought, 1; Cambridge, 1990).

Fine, G., 'Knowledge and Belief in *Republic* V', in Fine, *Plato on Knowledge and Forms*, 66–84.

—— 'Knowledge and Belief in *Republic* V–VII', in Everson (ed.), *Epistemology*, 85–115; repr. with minor modifications in Fine, *Plato on Knowledge and Forms*, 85–116.

—— 'Knowledge and True Belief in the *Meno*', *Oxford Studies in Ancient Philosophy*, 27 (2004), 41–81.

—— *Plato on Knowledge and Forms: Selected Essays* (Oxford, 2003).

Hackforth, R. (trans. and comm.), *Phaedrus* (Cambridge, 1952).

Hankins, J., 'Socrates in the Italian Renaissance', in Ahbel-Rappe and Kamtekar (eds.), *A Companion to Socrates*, 337–52.

Irwin, T. (trans.), *Plato:* Gorgias (Oxford, 1979).

—— *Plato's Ethics* (Oxford, 1995).

Janko, R., 'Socrates the Freethinker', in Ahbel-Rappe and Kamtekar (eds.), *A Companion to Socrates*, 48–62.

Kirk, G. S., *Heraclitus: The Cosmic Fragments* (Cambridge, 1954).

Kraut, R., *Socrates and the State* (Princeton, 1984).

Lackey, J., 'Norms of Assertion', *Nous*, 41 (2007), 594–626.

Lesher, J., 'Socrates' Disavowal of Knowledge', *Journal of the History of Philosophy*, 25 (1987), 275–88.

Long, A., 'Wisdom in Heraclitus', *Oxford Studies in Ancient Philosophy* 33 (2007), 1–17.

Lyons, J., *Structural Semantics: An Analysis of Part of the Vocabulary of Plato* (Oxford, 1963).

Long, A. A., 'Socrates in Hellenistic Philosophy', *Classical Quarterly*, NS 38 (1988), 150–71; repr. in id., *Stoic Studies* (Cambridge, 1996), 1–34.

McGinn, C., 'The Concept of Knowledge', in P. A. French, T. E. Uehling, Jr., and H. K. Wettstein (eds.), *Causation and Causal Theories* (Midwest Studies in Philosophy, 9; Minneapolis, 1984), 529–54.

Parke H. W., and Wormell, D. E., *The Delphic Oracle* (2 vols.; Oxford, 1956).

Reeve, C. D. C., *Socrates in the* Apology (Indianapolis, 1989).

Riddell, J., *The* Apology *of Plato* (1877; repr. New York, 1973).

Rowe, C. J. (trans.), *Plato:* Phaedrus (Warminster, 1986).

Sedley, D., *The Midwife of Platonism: Text and Subtext in Plato's* Theaetetus (Oxford, 2004).

—— 'The *Theaetetus*: Three Interpretations', in C. Gill and M. M. McCabe (eds.), *Form and Argument in Late Plato* (Oxford, 2000), 79–103.

Stokes, M., *Plato:* Apology (Warminster, 1997).

—— 'Socrates' Mission', in B. S. Gower and M. Stokes (eds.), *Socratic Questions* (London, 1992), 26–81.

Tarrant, H., 'Socratic Method and Socratic Truth', in Ahbel-Rappe and Kamtekar (eds.), *A Companion to Socrates*, 254–72.

Taylor, C. C. W., *Socrates* (Oxford, 1998).

Vlastos, G., 'Socrates' Disavowal of Knowledge', *Philosophical Quarterly*, 35 (1985), 1–31, repr. in G. Fine (ed.), *Plato 1: Metaphysics and Epistemology* (Oxford, 1999), 64–92.

—— *Socrates, Ironist and Moral Philosopher* (Cambridge, 1991).

Westerink, L. G. (ed.), *Anonymous Prolegomena to the Philosophy of Plato* (Paris, 1990).

Williamson, T., 'Knowing and Asserting', *Philosophical Review*, 105 (1996), 489–523.

—— *Knowledge and its Limits* (Oxford, 2000).

Woodruff, P., 'Plato's Early Theory of Knowledge', in Everson (ed.), *Epistemology*, 60–84.

—— and Nehamas, A., translation of Plato's *Phaedrus*, in J. Cooper (ed.), *Plato: Complete Works* (Indianapolis, 1997).

PLATO ON THE POSSIBILITY
OF HEDONIC MISTAKES

MATTHEW EVANS

I

MOST of us—philosophers and non-philosophers alike—accept that at least some pleasures are appropriate targets of ethical criticism. Even hedonists typically concede that there is something bad about taking pleasure in certain states or events, such as the undeserved suffering of other people.[1] So it is not particularly surprising to find that Plato, the first philosopher to deal with this issue in any significant detail, holds a similar view. In three of his most celebrated dialogues—the *Gorgias*, the *Phaedo*, and the *Republic*—he gives lengthy arguments to the effect that part of what it is to be virtuous is to be pleased by the right sort of thing in the right sort of way.[2]

In the *Philebus*, however, he takes this idea in a dramatic new direction. He has Socrates insist, with great fanfare, that pleasures are to be criticized in precisely the same way that beliefs are (36 C–42 C). Indeed, he has Socrates go so far as to say that pleasures, like beliefs, are bad just in so far as, and just because, they are *false* (40 E 9–10).[3] This claim—which I shall call *the Grounding Thesis*—

© Matthew Evans 2008

I would like to thank David Barnett, Don Garrett, Jim Hankinson, Liz Harman, Terry Irwin, Larry Jost, Hyunseop Kim, Brian Leiter, Colin Marshall, Phillip Mitsis, Jessica Moss, John Richardson, Nishi Shah, Sharon Street, Paul Woodruff, and two anonymous *OSAP* referees for reading and criticizing earlier drafts of this paper. Many thanks also to the faculty and fellows at the Center for Human Values at Princeton, 2007–8, where much of this paper was written and revised. I am especially grateful to David Sosa and Steve White for triggering and sustaining my interest in this idea, and to Brad Inwood for generously editing the result.

---

[1] For a sophisticated recent attempt to reconcile this intuition with a fairly robust version of ethical hedonism, see F. Feldman, *Pleasure and the Good Life* (Oxford, 2004), 117–23.

[2] See *Gorg.* 492 D–500 A; *Phaedo* 64 D–67 B; and *Rep.* 580 D–588 A.

[3] Of the many commentators who grapple with Plato's treatment of pleasure in

Matthew Evans

is liable to strike most of us, at least initially, as misguided if not unintelligible. Even those who accept that pleasures and pains can be bearers of ethical value are not inclined to accept that the ethical value in question here is, or is grounded in, any sort of *semantic* or *representational* value.[4] Nor are they likely to accept that it is useful (or even possible) to assign such values to pleasures and pains in the first place. From the standpoint of today's common sense, then, Plato's thesis looks implausible at best.

But at least Plato himself seems to understand why it might look that way. For he has Socrates' hedonist respondent Protarchus raise the same sort of objection to it that we would be inclined to raise if we were in his shoes. The proximate target of this objection is an attempt on Socrates' part to cast the Grounding Thesis as a natural consequence of the argument that he and Protarchus have just worked through. This argument—which I shall call *the Anticipation Argument*—purports to establish *inter alia* that some pleasures (particularly the pleasures of anticipation) can fail to meet certain basic standards of accuracy, and to that extent can be appropriately assessed as false (37 A–40 E).[5] In this passage Socrates manages to

the *Philebus*, only one—J. C. Dybikowski—explicitly notes the significance of what Socrates says in this passage. 'The development of some such thesis', he writes, 'would appear to be the final object of an insistence on speaking of pleasures as false' (J. C. Dybikowski, 'False Pleasure and the *Philebus*' ['False Pleasure'], *Phronesis*, 15 (1970), 147–65 at 160–1). However, Dybikowski does not explore how Plato develops (or might develop) such a thesis, and it is this exploratory work that I intend to do here.

⁴ None of the arguments that will seriously concern me in this paper turns on the idea that a pleasure can be false in the non-semantic, non-representational sense of being unreal, untrustworthy, or inauthentic. Though this idea plays an important role in arguments from some earlier dialogues (e.g. *Rep.* 583 B–587 A) as well as several arguments from the *Philebus* itself (e.g. 42 C–50 C), Socrates repeatedly implies that it plays little or no role in the arguments I shall be examining here. See e.g. his comments at 37 A 11–B 3 and 40 D 7–10.

⁵ The Anticipation Argument is the first in a continuous series of four arguments, each of which is designed to show that pleasures can be false in some sense (36 C–50 C). The latter three, if I understand them correctly, hinge on the following three views respectively: (1) that a pleasure, when compared with pains or other pleasures, can appear to be greater than it really is (41 C–42 C); (2) that a mental state, because it is not a pain, can appear to be a pleasure even though it is not (42 C–44 B); and (3) that a mental state, because it is a single blended mixture of a more intense pleasure with a less intense pain, can appear to be a pleasure even though it is not (44 B–50 C). I shall not be addressing any of these three arguments in this paper, since it seems clear that none of them can support the claim that false pleasures are false in the same sort of way that false beliefs are. At best they can support the claim that certain mental states systematically generate false beliefs about whether,

wring two important concessions out of Protarchus: first, that bad people typically have false pleasures (40 c 1–3); and second, that pleasures can be false in the same sort of way that false beliefs are false (40 D 7–E 5). But when Socrates goes for a third concession, he runs into some stiff resistance:

SOCR. Now what about this? Can we say that what makes beliefs bad . . . is anything other than their being false [πονηρὰς δόξας . . . ἄλλως ἢ ψευδεῖς γιγνομένας ἔχομεν εἰπεῖν]?
PROT. No.
SOCR. Nor, I think, do we comprehend any way for *pleasures* to be bad except by *their* being false [οὐδ' ἡδονάς γ' οἶμαι κατανοοῦμεν ὡς ἄλλον τινὰ τρόπον εἰσὶν πονηραὶ πλὴν τῷ ψευδεῖς εἶναι].
PROT. Quite the contrary, Socrates! One would hardly hold that pleasures and pains are bad through falsehood; rather [one would hold that they are bad] through some other great and manifold badness they fall in with. (40 E 6–41 A 4)

Evidently Socrates thinks that the analogy between pleasure and belief—which he invokes repeatedly throughout the Anticipation Argument (36 c–40 E)—is tight enough to support the idea that what makes a pleasure bad, if it is bad, is nothing other than its being false. But Protarchus disagrees. In his view, Socrates is trying to extend the analogy further than has been justified by the argument. Though he is willing to accept that some pleasures are false, and even that pleasures can be false in the same sort of way that false beliefs are false, Protarchus is none the less emphatically *unwilling* to accept that bad pleasures, like bad beliefs, are bad *just because* they are false. The badness of bad pleasures, he insists, is grounded in their having some other feature that has yet to be discussed.

Socrates' response to this challenge is disappointing. Instead of facing it squarely, he tables the issue and turns his attention to a new and different sense in which pleasures and pains can be false (41 A 5–B 2). This is a shame, I think, because the concern Protarchus raises here is both highly intuitive and potentially devastating. As we have seen, the Grounding Thesis does seem implausible, and for roughly the same reason that Protarchus gives. If and when we submit a person's pleasures to evaluative scrutiny—pleasures of

and to what extent, they are pleasures. For a useful overview of these three arguments, see D. Frede, 'Disintegration and Restoration: Pleasure and Pain in Plato's *Philebus*' ['Disintegration'], in R. Kraut (ed.), *The Cambridge Companion to Plato* (Cambridge, 1992), 425–63.

anticipation included—we do not seem to base our assessment of them *as good or bad* on our assessment of them *as true or false*. As Protarchus suggests, the badness of bad pleasures (and the goodness of good pleasures) seems to consist in something altogether different from this.

To respond effectively to Protarchus' objection, Socrates needs to do more than just wave it away. He needs to explain why (and not merely assert that) his account of false pleasure can support the idea that what makes bad pleasures bad is their being false. Though it is clear from the text that he *does not* do this, my aim here is to figure out whether he *could*. I want to know whether Protarchus is really right to think that the account of false pleasure Socrates gives us in the Anticipation Argument—or anywhere else in the *Philebus*, for that matter—is too weak to vindicate the Grounding Thesis. This is a delicate and difficult issue, as it turns out, because there is a great deal of disagreement among commentators over how to interpret both the argument itself and the account of false pleasure that emerges out of it.[6] This disagreement is perhaps best characterized as a struggle between two competing schools of thought. According to one school—which I shall call *the Old School*—the Anticipation Argument entails that what makes a pleasure false is either its having false content or its sharing its content with some false belief.[7] If you are pleased (and believe) that the war is ending, for example, then on this view your pleasure is false if it is not the case that the war is ending. According to the other school—which I shall call *the New School*—the argument entails that what makes a

[6] There is a vast body of post-war scholarship on the Anticipation Argument. For the opening round of discussion, see B. Williams, 'Pleasure and Belief' ['Pleasure'], *Proceedings of the Aristotelian Society*, suppl. 33 (1959), 57–72; J. C. B. Gosling, 'False Pleasures: *Philebus* 35 C–41 B', *Phronesis*, 4 (1959), 44–54; A. Kenny, 'False Pleasures in the *Philebus*: A Reply to Mr. Gosling' ['False Pleasures'], *Phronesis*, 5 (1960), 45–52; and J. C. B. Gosling, 'Father Kenny on False Pleasures in Plato's *Philebus*', *Phronesis*, 6 (1961), 41–5. For the second round, see A. McLaughlin, 'A Note on False Pleasures in the *Philebus*', *Philosophical Quarterly*, 19 (1969), 57–61; Dybikowski, 'False Pleasure'; and T. Penner, 'False Anticipatory Pleasures: *Philebus* 36 A 3–41 A 6', *Phronesis*, 15 (1970), 166–78. Two especially influential recent treatments include J. C. B. Gosling and C. C. W. Taylor, *The Greeks on Pleasure* [*Greeks*] (Oxford, 1982), and D. Frede, 'Rumpelstiltskin's Pleasures: True and False Pleasures in Plato's *Philebus*', *Phronesis*, 30 (1985), 151–80. For an interesting survey, see F. Bravo, 'La critique contemporaine des faux plaisirs dans le *Philèbe*', in M. Dixsaut (ed.), *Contre Platon* (Paris, 1995), 235–70.

[7] For a sample of Old School arguments, see Gosling, 'False Pleasures'; Penner, 'False Anticipatory Pleasures'; and S. Delcomminette, 'False Pleasures, Appearance and Imagination in the *Philebus*' ['False Pleasures'], *Phronesis*, 48 (2003), 215–37.

pleasure false is its having content that is *bad*, or at least *not good*.[8] So if you are pleased that the war is ending, then on this view your pleasure is false if the war's ending would be a bad thing, or would not be a good thing.

It is against the backdrop of this exegetical dispute that my argument in this paper is best understood. In Section II I try to show that, strictly speaking, the Old School is right and the New School is wrong. For the Anticipation Argument makes sense as an argument, in my view, only if it proceeds on the assumption that an anticipatory pleasure is false if and because its content—that is, the anticipation on which it is based—is false. Then in Section III I argue that this is bad news for Plato and his friends, because the Old School account of false pleasure simply is not powerful enough, by itself, to protect the Grounding Thesis from Protarchus' objection. My primary finding, then, will be a negative one. But in Section IV—the last major section of the paper—I take a more positive line. First I show that Socrates, in an often overlooked part of the *Philebus* (54 E 1–55 A 11), sketches out a rudimentary version of the same sort of account that the New School (wrongly) claims to find in the Anticipation Argument. Then I argue that the account I find there provides Plato with the resources he needs to secure a certain limited victory over his opponents. Finally, I conclude the paper with a very brief assessment of Plato's overall view. As this assessment will suggest, I am convinced that this view merits further investigation. For it, unlike many competing views, has the power to capture some widely shared and deeply held intuitions about how pleasures are to be evaluated when they are understood as attitudes rather than sensations.

II

In order to establish that pleasures can be false in the same sort of way that false beliefs are false, Plato needs to establish first that pleasures are like beliefs in being what we now call *attitudes*. For it is only in virtue of being an attitude that a belief is capable of

---

[8] For a sample of New School arguments, see R. Hackforth, *Plato's Philebus* [*Philebus*] (Cambridge, 1972), 73; V. Harte, 'The *Philebus* on Pleasure: The Good, the Bad and the False', *Proceedings of the Aristotelian Society*, 104 (2004), 111–28; and D. Russell, *Plato on Pleasure and the Good Life* [*Plato on Pleasure*] (Oxford, 2005), 176–82.

being about something; and it is only in virtue of *being about* something that a belief is capable of being true or false.[9] This is why
anyone who wants to base an account of false pleasure on an analogy between pleasure and belief—as Plato clearly does—is thereby
committed to the view that at least some pleasures are attitudes.

Does Plato recognize this commitment? I believe he does.[10] For
at the outset of the Anticipation Argument he has Socrates draw
a careful distinction between the attitudes of belief or pleasure on
the one hand, and *the contents of* these attitudes on the other:

SOCR. Let's distinguish more clearly still what's just been said about pleasure and belief.[11] For *believing* is something in us, right [ἔστιν γάρ πού
τι δοξάζειν ἡμῖν]?

PROT. Yes.

SOCR. And *being pleased* [ἥδεσθαι]?

PROT. Yes.

SOCR. And *that which is believed* is also something, right [καὶ μὴν καὶ τὸ
δοξαζόμενόν ἐστί τι]?

PROT. Of course.

SOCR. And *that by which the one who is pleased is pleased* [καὶ τό γε ᾧ τὸ
ἡδόμενον ἥδεται]?

PROT. Certainly.   (37 A 1–10)

The evident purpose of this exchange is to establish that at least
some pleasures are, like beliefs, attitudes with contents. Just as it is
appropriate to ask of a given attitude of belief *what is believed*, so
it is appropriate to ask of a given attitude of pleasure *what pleases*.
And to give a correct answer to these questions is to specify the
contents of these attitudes.[12]

[9] As Victor Caston has argued, many ancient thinkers (including Plato) were well
aware that mental states such as belief and desire must have this property, which
Brentano later called 'intentionality'. See Caston, 'Towards a History of the Problem
of Intentionality among the Greeks', *Proceedings of the Boston Area Colloquium in
Ancient Philosophy*, 9 (1993), 213–60, and id., 'Connecting Traditions: Augustine
and the Greeks on Intentionality', in D. Perler (ed.), *Ancient and Medieval Theories
of Intentionality* (Leiden, 2001), 23–48.

[10] Most commentators are in agreement on this point. For a representative sample,
see Penner, 'False Anticipatory Pleasures', 172–8; Frede, 'Disintegration', 444–5;
T. Irwin, *Plato's Ethics [Ethics]*, (Oxford, 1995), 319–21; Delcomminette, 'False
Pleasures', 217–18; Harte, 'The *Philebus* on Pleasure', 112–18; and Russell, *Plato
on Pleasure*, 176–82. For a noteworthy dissent, see Gosling and Taylor, *Greeks*, 441.

[11] Socrates is referring here to what Protarchus has just said, which is that pleasures, unlike beliefs, cannot be false. This passage is preparing us for an argument
against that very claim.

[12] That Socrates acknowledges the distinction between attitude and content, par-

Once Socrates establishes that some pleasures are like beliefs in being attitudes, he claims that some of these pleasures 'occur with' (37 E 10–11) or 'follow upon' (38 B 9–10) false beliefs. His thought here seems to be that if a pleasure 'occurs with' or 'follows upon' a false belief, then that pleasure is false as well.[13] Protarchus resists this thought at first, claiming that in such a case 'we say that the *belief* is false . . . No one would call the *pleasure itself* false [τὴν δ' ἡδονὴν αὐτὴν οὐδεὶς ἄν ποτε προσείποι ψευδῆ]' (37 E 12–38 A 2). And at this point Socrates backs off a bit. Instead of pressing his suggestion that pleasures tied to false beliefs are themselves false, he takes up the issue of what makes a *belief* false. He begins by inviting Protarchus to consider cases in which certain beliefs are formed on the basis of perception. In such cases, he says, 'the *psychē* is like a

ticularly in the case of pleasure, is confirmed by the language he uses consistently, throughout the dialogue, to specify *what pleases us* when we take pleasure in something. He marks off the contents of these attitudes by using the dative without a preposition (e.g. 12 D 1–4 and 37 A 9); the dative with ἐπί (e.g. 37 E 5–7, 40 D 7–10, and 49 D 3–4); or the accusative with περί (e.g. 51 B 3–5, 51 E 1–2, and 54 D 4–7). In each case Socrates uses the construction to pick out *that about which* the person who is pleased is pleased. Cf. Penner, 'False Anticipatory Pleasures', 175, and Delcomminette, 'False Pleasures', 218–19. Like Penner, Delcomminette concludes that these constructions are intended to mark off the contents of attitudes. But Delcomminette seems to have a non-standard way of understanding what these contents are. He specifies 'the mere fact of taking pleasure' as a pleasure's 'form' and '*what is felt as pleasure*' or '[that] which makes me feel *this* or *that* pleasure' or 'the pleasure as it is *felt*' as a pleasure's content. I would agree with Delcomminette here if he were simply observing that pleasures are partially individuated by their contents. But I suspect that he is trying to say something more, namely, that the content of a pleasure just is its *qualitative feel*. I think this would be a mistake. For we should not assume at the outset of the discussion that (according to Plato) pleasures with different qualitative feels cannot have the same content, or that pleasures with the same qualitative feel cannot have different contents. The operative notion of content here, I think, is *that in which a pleasure is taken*, not (necessarily) *the way a pleasure feels*.

[13] As Norman Mooradian points out, this *does not* imply that the pleasures in question *just are* the beliefs 'with which' they arise; indeed, Socrates never suggests any such thing. See N. Mooradian, 'Converting Protarchus: Relativism and False Pleasures of Anticipation in Plato's *Philebus*', *Ancient Philosophy*, 16 (1996), 93–112 at 101–2. Cf. Penner, 'False Anticipatory Pleasures', 174. For a contrasting view, see D. Frede (trans. and comm.), *Plato: Philebus [Philebus]* (Indianapolis, 1993), 38 n. 2. But Mooradian goes on to suggest, wrongly in my view, that 'it is unlikely that Plato treats pleasure as intrinsically representational and hence capable of falsity in much the same manner as belief' (103). Why does Mooradian think this? Apparently he supposes that if pleasures have propositional content then they *are* beliefs: 'if one is willing to hold that certain pleasures . . . have propositional content, then one is accepting that they are judgments' (101). But if 'judgments' here is standing proxy for 'beliefs', then this claim is unmotivated. Mooradian has given us no good reason to think that Plato cannot hold *both* that some pleasure-attitude has the same content as some belief-attitude, *and* that these attitudes are not of the same type.

kind of book' (38 E 12–13), since the perceiving agent's experience, in effect, 'writes propositions [λόγοι] in the *psychē*. And when what it writes is true, true beliefs and true assertions come to be in our *psychē* as a result of this. But when the writer in us writes what is false, the result is the opposite of the truth' (39 A 3–7).[14] Socrates then adds that there is 'another craftsman' in the *psychē* who works alongside the writer: a 'painter [ζωγράφος]' who 'follows the writer and paints in the *psychē* pictures of the [written] propositions' (39 B 1–7).[15] And these pictures, he thinks, have the same truth conditions as the propositions they depict (39 C 4–5).

The opening moves of the Anticipation Argument flow directly from this account of perceptual belief. First Socrates gets Protarchus to agree that one's internal representations—whether they be discursive or pictorial—can be about the future and the past as well as the present (39 C 10–12). He then reminds Protarchus of a point made earlier (at 32 B 9–C 5): 'some pleasures of the *psychē* pre-occur [future] pleasures . . . in such a way that it is possible for us to be pre-pleased . . . about the future [ὥσθ' ἡμῖν συμβαίνει τὸ προχαίρειν . . . περὶ τὸν μέλλοντα χρόνον]' (39 D 2–5). The contents of these 'pre-pleasures', he says, are what we call 'hopes' (ἐλπίδες, 39 D 7–E 6). His argument then proceeds as follows:

SOCR. So in each of us there are propositions [λόγοι] which we call hopes?
PROT. Yes.
SOCR. And also the pictured images [τὰ φαντάσματα ἐζωγραφημένα] [of these propositions]. And one often sees an enormous amount of gold coming to oneself, along with its many consequent pleasures. Moreover one sees oneself in the picture enjoying oneself immensely [ἐνεζωγραφημένον αὐτὸν ἐφ' αὑτῷ χαίροντα σφόδρα καθορᾷ].
PROT. Indeed.
SOCR. Now should we say that the pictures good people have in them are for the most part true, since they are loved by the gods? And that the

[14] I translate λόγοι here as 'propositions' rather than 'sentences' because it is not clear that Socrates wants us to think of these psychologically inscribed items as natural language expressions. In fact, given what he says here about their relation to beliefs and assertions, it would seem that he wants them to serve as all-purpose truth-apt contents for anything from pictures and inscriptions to thoughts and speech-acts. The two examples he gives are 'that it is a man' (ὡς ἔστιν ἄνθρωπος) and 'that it is . . . a statue' (ὡς ἔστι . . . ἄγαλμα) (38 D 5–10).
[15] It is worth noting here that Plato's view about the relative priority of discursive content to pictorial content in the formation of perceptual beliefs is the converse of the consensus view today. Most of us now suppose that it is the writer who follows the painter, not the other way round.

pictures bad people have in them are the opposite? Or should we not say this?

PROT. We certainly should.

SOCR. So pictured pleasures are no less present in bad people, but these pleasures are somehow false [τοῖς κακοῖς ἡδοναί γε οὐδὲν ἧττον πάρεισιν ἐζωγραφημέναι, ψευδεῖς δὲ αὗταί που].

PROT. Right. (40 A 6–B 8)

This is the first time that Socrates gets Protarchus to concede that some pleasures are false. Yet it is hard to understand, at least initially, how this concession is warranted by the argument Socrates has just given. For consider the difference between (A) the pleasures that bad people *expect to experience*, and (B) the pleasures that bad people *experience by expecting to experience pleasures*. Since the only pleasures that Socrates calls false here are the 'pictured pleasures' or the 'pleasures within the picture [ἡδοναί . . . ἐζωγραφημέναι]', the argument as it stands picks out as false only A-pleasures, not B-pleasures. But A-pleasures are merely *expected* by bad people, not actually *experienced* by them. Thus Socrates cannot fairly claim to have shown, by this argument alone, that the bad person is often pleased in such a way that *this very pleasure* is false.

It would appear, then, that we have an interpretative dilemma on our hands. Either the argument is designed to establish that some *actually experienced* pleasures are false, or it is designed to establish that some *merely expected* pleasures are false. If the former, then the argument is grossly invalid. If the latter, then the argument yields an account of false pleasure that is plainly incapable of supporting the claim that false pleasures are analogous to false beliefs. For according to the account on offer here, false pleasures are false only in the sense that they are unreal or chimerical—mere figments of benighted hopes. Obviously Plato needs something stronger than this if he wants to give the Grounding Thesis a decent defence. He needs to say that a person can take pleasure in something such that *this very pleasure* is false, just as a person can believe something such that *this very belief* is false. Even if there is some reasonable sense of 'false' on which every pleasure that is expected to occur, but will not in fact occur, is false, this is not a sense of 'false' that Plato will be able to use here.

Though it is not entirely clear how we (as interpreters) should proceed at this point, I believe our best option is to grasp the dilemma's second horn and admit that the account on offer in this stretch of argument is largely useless.[16] To admit this much, however, is not (yet) to give up the game. For we can still insist that this stretch of argument is only the first part of the Anticipation Argument as a whole, and that there is a different and more useful account of false pleasure to be found in the argument's other part (or parts). On this approach, the first part of the argument can be reconstructed more or less as follows:

(A1) If a person internally pictures that p, then there is in that person an internal picture with the content that p. (39 B 3–C 2) [To say that a person *internally pictures that p* is just to say that the painter in his *psychē* depicts the proposition that p. And an *internal picture with the content that p* is just the product of a person's internally picturing that p.]

(A2) An internal picture with the content that p is false if and only if it is not the case that p. (39 C 4–5; 38 B 6–39 A 7)

(A3) The bad person hope-pictures that he will get rich and enjoy his riches. (40 A 3–12) [To say that a person *hope-pictures that p* is just to say (i) that he internally pictures

[16] This dilemma, in one form or another, has fuelled a long, nettlesome, and intricate debate among commentators. For a snapshot, see Gosling, 'False Pleasures'; Kenny, 'False Pleasures'; Dybikowski, 'False Pleasure'; and Penner, 'False Anticipatory Pleasures'. For an especially useful overview, see Gosling and Taylor, *Greeks*, 435–42. Since I cannot hope to adjudicate this debate comprehensively in this paper, I shall offer my own solution in a spirit of humility. But before I do I would like to comment briefly on an intriguing proposal advanced recently by Verity Harte. On her reading, Plato thinks that there is no precise distinction to be drawn between A-pleasures and B-pleasures after all, since every B-pleasure is *a proper part of* some A-pleasure. What Plato is advocating here, she thinks, 'is an account of an anticipatory pleasure viewed as an advance instalment of the pleasure depicted. This anticipatory pleasure is not a pleasure *in* the anticipated pleasure; it *is* (an advance instalment of) the anticipated pleasure . . . The pleasure anticipated is enjoyed, not in the sense that it is that in which pleasure is taken, but in the sense that it is the pleasure of which the anticipatory pleasure takes an advance instalment' (Harte, 'The *Philebus* on Pleasure', 124–5). One advantage of this reading—over and above its power to preserve the validity of the argument—is that it gives Plato a way to explain the qualitative similarity between A-pleasures and B-pleasures. But I suspect that it also saddles him with an indefensible position. For if the relevant A-pleasure will not in fact occur, as Harte herself suggests (121–2), then it is hard to see how the relevant B-pleasure could be an advance instalment of it. How could someone receive a non-zero advance instalment of *nothing*? If Plato replies that in this case the pleasure one expects to get is different from the pleasure one will not in fact get, then he must accept either that the pleasure one expects to get *just is* the pleasure one gets by expecting to get pleasure, or that one will in fact get the pleasure one expects to get. Neither alternative strikes me as coherent.

that p, and (ii) that the proposition that p is a proposition
to the effect that he will experience a certain pleasure.]

(A4) So there is in the bad person a hope-picture with the content that he will get rich and enjoy his riches. (A1, A3)

(A5) The bad person is hated by the gods. (39 E 10–40 A 1)

(A6) The hope-pictures in people who are hated by the gods are false. (40 B 2–4)

(A7) So the hope-pictures in the bad person are false. (A5, A6)

(A8) *The Figment Account.* If there is in a person a hope-picture with the content that he will experience a certain pleasure H, then (*a*) H is in him, and (*b*) if it is not the case that he will experience H, then H is false.

(A9) So there are false pleasures in the bad person. (40 B 6–7) (A2, A4, A7, A8)

Though this is a valid argument, the account of false pleasure
on offer in (A8) (that is, the Figment Account) and the conclusion
in (A9) are, as we have seen, much too anaemic to get Plato what
he needs. Yet there is good reason to doubt that the conclusion
in (A9) is the ultimate conclusion of the Anticipation Argument.
For in the exchange that directly follows (A9), Socrates gives a
characterization of false pleasure that differs markedly from the
Figment Account. He begins by getting Protarchus to agree that
every false belief—be it about the present, the past, or the future—
is false because its content is 'not what is, nor what was, nor what
will be [μὴ ἐπ' οὖσι δὲ μηδ' ἐπὶ γεγονόσι μηδὲ ἐπ' ἐσομένοις ἐνίοτε]'
(40 C 8–D 2). Then he presses hard, once again, on the proposed
analogy between pleasure and belief:

SOCR. Should we not give to . . . pleasures the corresponding feature?

PROT. How so?

SOCR. Whoever takes pleasure in anything at all in any way always genuinely takes pleasure, but sometimes not in things that are, nor in things that were, nor—perhaps most often—in things that will be.

PROT. That's necessarily so, Socrates.

SOCR. So wouldn't the same account [ὁ αὐτὸς λόγος] hold, about fear and anger and all things of this sort, that all such things are also sometimes false?

PROT. Certainly. (40 D 4–E 5)

On this account, pleasure and belief are alike in that one can take
pleasure in 'what is not' just as one can believe 'what is not'. Here

Socrates is apparently using what is sometimes called the 'veridical sense' of the verb 'to be' (εἶναι).[17] If so, then by 'what is not' he means something like 'what is not *the case*' or 'what is not *true*'. His claim, then, is that pleasures, fears, angers, and the rest are like beliefs in that they can have false content: just as *what is believed* can be false, so can *what scares*, *what angers*, and *what pleases*. And if having false content is sufficient to make an attitude of belief false, then—according to Socrates—having false content is *also* sufficient to make an attitude of *pleasure* false.[18] This new account, which I shall call *the Content Account*, can then be added as a further premiss in the argument:

> (A10) *The Content Account.* If a person experiences a pleasure with the content that *p*, then that pleasure is false if it is not the case that *p*. (40 D 4–E 5)

The Content Account leaves Socrates in a much-improved position. For the only thing he needs now is a premiss that is more or less implied by the earlier part of the argument, namely, that bad people often experience pleasures the contents of which are false hope-pictures. His first move in that direction occurs, I think, right after Protarchus concedes that the bad person's 'pictured pleasures' are false. Here Socrates makes a point of saying that 'bad people generally enjoy false pleasures [ψευδέσιν ἄρα ἡδοναῖς τὰ πολλὰ οἱ πονηροὶ χαίρουσιν]' (40 C 1). Since the 'false pleasures' he refers to here are presumably the 'pictured pleasures' that Protarchus has just conceded are false, Socrates seems to be adding the non-trivial claim that the bad person *takes pleasure in* the 'pictured pleasures' that are in him.[19] If so, then another premiss can be added to the argument:

[17] For discussion, see C. Kahn, 'Some Philosophical Uses of "to be" in Plato', *Phronesis*, 26 (1981), 119–27.

[18] Cf. Penner, 'False Anticipatory Pleasures'. Dorothea Frede resists this way of reading the argument, claiming that Socrates does not observe any distinction between the falsehood of content and the falsehood of attitude. In her view, 'the whole enjoyment provided by the soul's inner dialogue or the painter's work consists in nothing but the logoi or pictures in the soul' (Frede, 'Disintegration', 445–6; compare J. C. B Gosling (trans. and comm.), *Philebus* (Oxford, 1975), 217, and Gosling and Taylor, *Greeks*, 440–1). This view is mistaken, I think, since Plato—both here and elsewhere in the dialogue (e.g. 37 A–B, quoted above)—takes such care to distinguish between *being pleased* on the one hand and *what pleases* on the other. So I see no need to accuse him of confusion on this point.

[19] Gosling and Taylor are less sanguine about this way of interpreting the sentence in question. In their view, there is an important distinction to be drawn between

(A11) If the bad person has in him a hope-picture with the content that *p*, then he experiences a pleasure with the content that *p*. (40 C 1)

By making this claim Socrates effectively shifts the target of his attack from the bad person's *merely expected* pleasures to the bad person's *actually experienced* pleasures. And once he does that, the conclusion he wants follows fairly quickly:

(A12) So the bad person experiences a pleasure with the content that he will get rich and enjoy his riches. (A4, A11)

(A13) So the bad person experiences a false pleasure (40 E 2–5). (A2, A7, A10, A12)

If this reading is correct, then it manages to secure an important threefold result: first, that the Anticipation Argument is valid; second, that its ultimate conclusion is (A13), not (A9); and third, that there are two accounts of false pleasure at work in the argument, not just one. This third result is especially important because the second of the two accounts—that is, the Content Account—does not have the same fatal weaknesses as the first account does. For it allows Plato to support the idea that a person's actually experienced pleasures can be false in the same sort of way that a person's actually formed beliefs can be false.

And yet this interpretation—which I referred to earlier as the Old School interpretation—is still fairly unpopular among recent commentators, and it is worth pausing for a moment to understand why. Remember that, if the Old School is right, then 'false' in (A6) has no special evaluative meaning. When Socrates claims here that the bad person's hope-based pleasures are false, he is not saying

(i) a person's *enjoying the anticipation of experiencing* some future pleasure and (ii) a person's *being pleased that he will experience* some future pleasure. And they think that the case described by the sentence in question is a case of (i) and not (ii). Since they also think that only cases of (ii) have propositional content, they doubt that the case Plato gives us here can be read in the way I am suggesting. For their argument, see Gosling and Taylor, *Greeks*, 441. But whether or not there is an important distinction to be drawn between (i) and (ii), I am not persuaded that Plato is alive to it. From his various discussions of pleasure throughout the dialogue it is clear that his primary concern is to work through the consequences of thinking of hedonic phenomena in general—including the phenomena of enjoyment—as fundamentally *attitudinal* in nature. So I think it is safe to assume that when he writes that 'bad people *enjoy* false pleasures', he means that bad people *take hedonic attitudes towards* false pleasures. And this leaves plenty of conceptual space for him to ascribe content to those attitudes, more or less as I have just suggested.

anything about whether these hopes are worthless or inadequate or reprehensible; he is saying only that they will not come about. And it is precisely this alleged evaluative silence that makes many commentators uncomfortable. Dorothea Frede expresses this general discomfort rather well when she writes: 'It is not likely that Plato [at 40 B 2–4] is merely referring to the . . . Greek folk wisdom that those whom the gods love [or hate] are those who prosper [or suffer] in life. He must also be implying that the moral content of foolish pleasures is mistaken, so that they represent a skewed view of life.'[20] Frede's thought here, if I understand it correctly, is that the Anticipation Argument's classification of the bad person's hope-based pleasures as false must somehow outstrip the claim that these hopes *will not be realized*; it must encompass the additional claim that these hopes *express bad values*. Otherwise the explicitly established link between false hope and bad character would seem to have no rationale. Therefore, since the Content Account plainly fails to encompass this additional claim, it likewise fails to capture Plato's considered view of what makes a pleasure false. This, I take it, is the New School's animating thought.

Though there is something undeniably attractive about this thought, I believe that it carries the prohibitive cost of making the Anticipation Argument invalid. For if 'false' in (A6) has a special evaluative meaning, then clearly it does not have the same meaning as 'false' in (A2). In the (A2) text Socrates applies 'true' and 'false' to propositions such as 'it is a man' and 'it is a statue' (38 D 5–10). Here he gives no indication whatsoever that he expects these propositions to be assessed according to some non-veridical, evaluative standard. (Indeed, it would be extremely odd of him to use these particular propositions if that were his expectation.) So 'false' in (A2) plainly does not have any special evaluative meaning. And from this it follows that, if 'false' in (A6) *does* have some special evaluative meaning, then Plato is equivocating on 'false' and the inferences to (A9) and (A13) are (individually) invalid.

Since this cost is high indeed, I think we should try to stay out of the New School if we can. But in that case we will need to figure out how the Old School can make sense of the plainly non-accidental link that Plato wants to establish between false hope and

---

[20] See Frede, *Philebus*, 44. For a sample of broadly similar views, see Hackforth, *Philebus*, 73; Harte, 'The *Philebus* on Pleasure', 125; and Russell, *Plato on Pleasure*, 181–2.

bad character. We can do this, I believe, but only by attending carefully to the *strength* of that link. According to the New School, I take it, the falsehood of the bad person's hopes is *intrinsically* guaranteed by the badness of his character. On a view of this sort, the bad person's hopes would be false even if—*per impossibile*—there were no gods around to hate him. But must we agree that the link between false hope and bad character is as strong as this? I think not. For we can just as easily hold that the falsehood of the bad person's hopes is *extrinsically* guaranteed by the badness of his character. On this alternative view, it is not the case that the bad person's hopes would be false even if there were no gods around to hate him, because the role of the gods is precisely to ensure that the bad person's hopes will not be realized. This falls short of 'Greek folk wisdom', as I understand it, because the Greek folk think that the will of the gods is more or less whimsical, and obviously Plato does not. But he may well think that the gods, knowing what is best, intervene in the world frequently enough (or imbue the world with enough justice) to ensure that the hopes of the bad are generally thwarted.[21] If so, then the Old School interpreter can hold that the non-accidental link Plato wants to establish between false hope and bad character is secured not via his account of false pleasure, but via his theology. So it looks as though we do not have to join the New School to explain why Socrates brings bad people and gods into the argument.

But even if the Old School is right, and the Anticipation Argument is both valid and relevant, Plato still faces an enormous challenge. For it remains unclear whether he (or anyone else for that matter) can use the Content Account to mount an adequate defence of the Grounding Thesis. In fact there is good reason to suspect, as I shall argue shortly, that he cannot.

III

If Plato wants to use the Content Account to vindicate the Grounding Thesis, then he needs to show not only that pleasures can have false content, but also that a pleasure's having false content is what makes it bad, if it is bad. He has to show that pleasures are like

---

[21] For a persuasive defence of this suggestion, see Gosling and Taylor, *Greeks*, 442–3.

beliefs *in that way*. To appreciate what this requires, reflect for a moment on our everyday practice of assessing beliefs as false. Suppose you come to know that not-*p*, and then find out soon afterwards that I believe that *p*. When you kindly inform me that my belief is false, you are not just telling me that it is not the case that *p*; you are also *advising me not to believe* that *p*. You are suggesting that, all else equal, this belief of mine is a bad one to have and should be given up. This is the normative force that the term 'false' has when it is applied to beliefs with false content. What Plato needs to convince us of, then, is that 'false' has the same normative force when it is applied to *pleasures* with false content. He needs to show that pleasures with false content are worth rejecting in the same sort of way that beliefs with false content are.

Surprisingly, perhaps, he gives every indication of appreciating this explanatory burden. For he has Socrates linger over the distinction between attitude and content long enough to make it perfectly clear to Protarchus that the standards of assessment for attitudes do have normative force, and that meeting these standards is, for each attitude, just a matter of having the right sort of content. Consider the following exchange:

SOCR. If badness [πονηρία] is added to some [belief or pleasure], then in that case will we claim that a belief comes to be bad, or that a pleasure comes to be bad?

PROT. Of course.

SOCR. What if correctness [ὀρθότης] or incorrectness is added to one of them? Won't we say that a belief is correct if it has correctness, and that a pleasure [is correct if it has correctness]?

PROT. Necessarily.

SOCR. And if what is believed is mistaken, should we agree that the belief making the mistake at that time is incorrect, and is believing incorrectly [ἂν δέ γε ἁμαρτανόμενον τὸ δοξαζόμενον ᾖ, τὴν δόξαν τότε ἁμαρτάνουσάν γε οὐκ ὀρθὴν ὁμολογητέον οὐδ' ὀρθῶς δοξάζουσαν]?

PROT. Yes.

SOCR. But what if we observe that some pain or pleasure is making a mistake about that by which it is pained or pleased? [ἂν αὖ λύπην ἤ τινα ἡδονὴν περὶ τὸ ἐφ' ᾧ λυπεῖται ἢ τοὐναντίον ἁμαρτάνουσαν ἐφορῶμεν;] Shall we then call it 'correct' or 'good' or any other fine names?

PROT. That would be impossible, if in fact a pleasure makes a mistake.[22]

(37 D 2–E 9)

---

[22] It is worth noting that in this passage Socrates attributes the relevant mistakes to *the attitudes* rather than to *the agent*.

Here Socrates says (and Protarchus concedes) that a pleasure is bad if it is incorrect. He *does not* say (and Protarchus *does not* concede) that a pleasure is bad *if it has false content*. This is noteworthy because, if Socrates had made the latter claim, then he would have begged the question in advance against Protarchus. For although Protarchus is ultimately persuaded (by the Anticipation Argument) that some pleasures have false content, he is never persuaded that a pleasure's having false content is what makes it bad, if it is bad (41 A 1–4). To overcome Protarchus' resistance in a principled fashion, Socrates needs to argue (and not just assume in advance) that a pleasure is incorrect, and hence bad, if it has false content. So he needs to respect a distinction between the property of *being incorrect*—or *being false*, understood in this context as a property belonging exclusively to attitudes—and the property of *having false content*.[23]

But even if he respects this distinction, he still has a lot of work to do. For he still has to defend the Grounding Thesis, and that thesis looks pretty much indefensible when it is fleshed out by the Content Account:

The Grounding Thesis (Content Version)

(C1) If a pleasure is bad, then its content is false.

And:

(C2) If a pleasure's content is false, then it is bad *because* its content is false.

The problem is that (C1) is fairly obviously false. For it seems clear that not all of the pleasures that we (and Plato) would classify as bad have false content. Consider, for example, cases of malicious joy, in which someone takes pleasure in someone else's undeserved suffering. Plato condemns this sort of pleasure as 'unjust' (49 C 8–D 10), and rightly so; it is widely accepted (even by hedonists) that there is something bad about pleasures taken in such things. According to (C1), however, a malicious pleasure is bad only if the harm in which

---

[23] Compare Penner's observation that belief 'may mean something I do or tend to do, namely believing, or it may mean something believed by me . . . "True" and "false" apply primarily to the latter, but are applied derivatively to the former' ('False Anticipatory Pleasures', 169). As Penner rightly suggests, drawing the distinction between the property of *being false* (as applied to attitudes) and the property of *having false content* is crucial to the task of understanding what attitudes are.

it is taken is not actually occurring. And this is absurd by anyone's lights. Consider also the intense bodily pleasures associated with excessive indulgence in eating, drinking, or sex—pleasures that, according to Plato at any rate, should be avoided at all costs (45 A 4–E 7, 63 C 5–64 A 6). Either these pleasures have content or they do not. If they do not, then obviously they do not have false content; if they do, then presumably their content is true just in case the pleased agents are actually undergoing the relevant physiological changes.[24] But then the vast majority of bad bodily pleasures do not have false content.

Since (C1) is such a non-starter, the Content Version of the Grounding Thesis seems hopeless when taken in its entirety. On the other hand, (C1) is both more ambitious and less interesting than (C2); and (C2), if true, would support Plato's basic idea that a pleasure's being false is sufficient to make it bad. This idea by itself is striking, and deserves a closer look. For if Plato can manage to defend it, then perhaps he would be justified in claiming a certain limited victory over his opponents. Let us consider, then, whether (C2) fares any better than (C1).

No doubt there is something attractive about (C2). Part of what makes narrowly hedonistic theories of the good so hard to believe is that they are unable in principle to register the badness of pleasures that are based on falsehoods.[25] If you are pleased that the war is ending, for example, then your pleasure seems deficient somehow if, in fact, the war is just beginning. But what is it about this pleasure, exactly, that makes it deficient? One possibility is that it is based on a deficient *belief*. This seems to be what Terence Irwin thinks the Anticipation Argument is designed to impress upon us. 'In order to have false anticipatory pleasures,' he writes, 'we must suffer from . . . the cognitive defect that gives us the false anticipations. We are justified in preferring to be free of this defect.'[26] If we follow this suggestion, then we can attribute to Plato the view that

---

[24] The pleasure of drinking when thirsty, for example, would presumably have (roughly) the following content: *that my throat and belly are being filled with liquid.* For this, if anything, is what pleases the thirsty person when drinking.

[25] I take it that this is one of the lessons of Robert Nozick's famous 'experience machine' thought-experiment. See R. Nozick, *Anarchy, State, and Utopia* (New York, 1974), 42–5. For a useful overview of the issue, see S. Kagan, *Normative Ethics* (Boulder, Colo., 1997), 31–6.

[26] Irwin, *Ethics*, 330. For a prominent early attempt to develop an interpretation along similar lines, see Kenny, 'False Pleasures', 51–2. And for some interesting commentary on Kenny's proposal, see Gosling and Taylor, *Greeks*, 442.

pleasures with false content are bad because *the beliefs they take their content from* are bad. On this view, then, it is in virtue of being based on false beliefs that false pleasures are worthy of rejection.[27]

But this view, taken by itself, will not support (C2). To see why not, consider the difference between (i) the claim that a person's pleasure is bad if it takes its content from one of that person's false beliefs, and (ii) the claim that a person's pleasure is bad if it has false content. Though (i) is the view that Irwin attributes to Plato, (C2) is equivalent to (ii), and (ii) *is not* equivalent to (i). For it is possible (and indeed common) for a person to experience a pleasure such that the content of that pleasure, though false, is not the content of any of that person's beliefs. Consider, for example, the pleasures of imagination, such as those involved in daydreaming. These pleasures certainly have content, and their content is almost always false.[28] Yet their content is almost always not believed. The very possibility of these pleasures seems to show not only that (ii) is not equivalent to (i), but also that both (ii) and (C2) are false. For it is absurd to think that pleasures of imagination are bad simply because they have false content.

The most efficient way to deal with this problem, I take it, is to add a rider to the Content Account stipulating that a person's pleasure qualifies as false only if it shares its content with one of that person's false beliefs.[29] This adjustment may well reflect Plato's own considered view of the matter, since he has Socrates claim (in

---

[27] Its other merits aside, this view has the power to explain why so many pleasures seem just as sensitive to evidence as the beliefs on which they are based. If you believe that the war is ending, and take pleasure in this prospect, then if (and when) you are faced with subjectively sufficient evidence that the war is just beginning, your pleasure will seem to be just as worthy of rejection as your belief will. For some useful discussions of this phenomenon, see Williams, 'Pleasure', 66; Penner, 'False Anticipatory Pleasures', 167; and T. Penelhum, 'Pleasure and Falsity', *American Philosophical Quarterly*, 1 (1964), 81–91 at 84.

[28] Strangely, Irving Thalberg denies this. He writes: '*Pleasure in the thought of* [where this thought is not a belief] is not a counterexample to Plato's thesis, since mere *thoughts*, or unasserted propositions, are neither true nor false' ('False Pleasure', *Journal of Philosophy*, 59 (1962), 65–74 at 70). If Thalberg really means what he says here, then he holds that the proposition *George Bush is over a thousand years old* is not false unless someone asserts it. But that is absurd. If, on the other hand, he means that only attitudes of belief or acts of assertion are correct or incorrect in virtue of having true or false contents, then he is—apparently despite himself—contradicting Plato's thesis.

[29] This strategy is pursued most vigorously by Dorothea Frede. See Frede, 'Rumpelstiltskin's Pleasures', 173–5, and ead., *Philebus*, pp. xlvii–xlviii. For a broadly similar approach, see Delcomminette, 'False Pleasures', 220–9.

retrospect) that the Anticipation Argument, if sound, illustrates how 'false beliefs . . . infect pleasures with their own condition [αἱ δόξαι ψευδεῖς . . . ἡδονὰς ἅμα τοῦ παρ' αὐταῖς παθήματος ἀνεπίμπλασαν]' (42 A 7–9). On this approach, then, the Content Account should be replaced with:

The Belief Account

If a person experiences a pleasure with the content that p, then that pleasure is false if (1) it is not the case that p, *and* (2) he believes that p.

Unlike the Content Account, the Belief Account does not entail that the pleasures of imagination are systematically false. Better yet, the Belief Account can replace the Content Account in the Anticipation Argument without affecting its validity. For the role of the Content Account in that argument is simply to establish that the bad person's hope-pictures are false, and clearly the Belief Account can do this. Moreover, it is clear from the early stages of the argument that the bad person also *believes* the contents of his hope-pictures, so the Belief Account is consistent with all of the relevant premises. If we now go ahead and revise the Grounding Thesis by replacing the Content Account with the Belief Account, then we will end up with something like the following view instead:

The Grounding Thesis (*Belief Version*)

(B1) If a person's pleasure is bad, then the content of that plea-sure is both false and believed by that person.

And:

(B2) If the content of a person's pleasure is both false and be-lieved by that person, then that pleasure is bad *because* its content is both false and believed by that person.

This would seem to be an improvement on the Content Version. For although (B1) is false for roughly the same reasons that (C1) is, (B2)—unlike (C2)—is not falsified by the pleasures of imagina-tion. Moreover, (B2) seems to capture the intuition behind Irwin's original proposal far better than (C2) does. And best of all, (B2) seems true.

But once we remind ourselves of the work that Plato needs his account of false pleasure to do, I think we shall see that the Belief

Account is no more useful to him than the Content Account is, even if (B2) is true. Recall that Protarchus, by the end of the Anticipation Argument, is willing to concede that pleasures can be false in the same sort of way that false beliefs are false. What he is *not* willing to concede, however, is that pleasures are bad if and because they are false *in that way*. In other words, he is willing to concede:

The Similarity Claim

False pleasures are false in the same sort of way that false beliefs are false.

But then he is *not* willing to concede:

The Normative Claim

False pleasures are bad because they are false.

In order to defeat Protarchus' objection, then, Plato needs to provide an account of false pleasure that allows him to assert both the Similarity Claim and the Normative Claim at once. The problem with the Content Account, as we have seen, is that although it allows him to make the Similarity Claim, it does not allow him to make the Normative Claim. It allows him to say that pleasures, like beliefs, are false simply in virtue of having false content, but—given the pleasures of imagination—it does not allow him to say that false pleasures are bad because they are false.

Once we frame the challenge in this way, however, we can see that the Belief Account will fare just as poorly, and for a very similar reason. For although the Belief Account allows Plato to make the Normative Claim, it does not allow him to make the Similarity Claim. It allows him to say that false pleasures are bad because they are based on false beliefs, but it does not allow him to say that false pleasures are false in the same sort of way that false beliefs are false. This is because, as Socrates himself repeatedly points out, false beliefs are false simply in virtue of having false content; yet according to the Belief Account, *false pleasures are not* false simply in virtue of having false content. They are false *only also* in virtue of sharing their content with (some of) the pleased person's false beliefs. So if Plato replaces the Content Account with the Belief Account, then he merely exchanges one serious problem for another. Pleasures that are false according to the Content Account are not guaranteed to be bad, and pleasures that are false according to the Belief Account are not false in the same way that false beliefs are. Thus Plato's opponent is entitled to insist at this point that neither of the two accounts on offer succeeds in establishing that the same standards of evaluation apply equally to pleasures and beliefs alike.[30]

The problem with (B2), then, is not that it is false. For even if Plato is right to think (as I do) that pleasures based on false beliefs somehow share in the badness of these false beliefs, this by itself will not help him defeat his current adversary. It *will* help him defeat those (including many hedonists) who claim that the value of a pleasure is in no way compromised by its relations to other mental states. But Protarchus, in this particular dispute at least, is not claiming this. He is claiming only that pleasures and beliefs are not to be evaluated according to the same standards of normative correctness. And it seems clear, on reflection at least, that (B2) not only *fails to block* this claim, but actually *reinforces* it. For (B2) implies, as we have seen, that the evaluation of a person's pleasures asymmetrically depends on the evaluation of that person's beliefs. This is ironic, in a way, since the original point of the Grounding Thesis was to build up the analogy between pleasure and belief in such a way that asymmetries of just this sort could be avoided. Clearly the real problem with (B2) is not that it is false, but rather that it is ill-formed. The Belief Version of the Grounding Thesis simply does not engage properly with the underlying debate.

Does the joint failure of the two accounts discussed so far indicate that Plato's attempt to defend the Grounding Thesis is doomed to fail? Not if he can develop an account that will allow him—as these other accounts do not—to make both the Similarity Claim and the Normative Claim at once. And it is not difficult to see, at least in outline, what an account of this sort *should* look like. It should assign to all and only pleasures a distinct, belief-like role, such that a pleasure's failure in this role is both necessary and sufficient for that pleasure to be worth rejecting. Does Plato offer us such an account anywhere else in the *Philebus*? My answer to this question is positive, but qualified. Though he never explicitly labels it as such, and though he never explicitly argues for it, Plato provides—much

---

[30] Thus I concur with Gosling and Taylor's verdict that the Anticipation Argument's account of false pleasure does not 'provide an adequate justification of the attribution of falsehood to pleasure, as distinct from its attribution to belief' (*Greeks*, 452).

later in the dialogue—the sketch of an account of false pleasure that comes surprisingly close to doing exactly what he needs it to do.

IV

In the latter half of the *Philebus* Plato advances an argument that appears to hinge on the idea—familiar from the New School—that a pleasure is incorrect (and therefore bad) if it is taken in something that is not good. The argument as a whole, which I shall call the *Aiming Argument,* runs from 53 c 4 to 55 A 11. But the part of the argument that bears directly on the question of incorrect pleasure begins at 54 D 6. Here Socrates has just claimed that, because every pleasure is a 'becoming' (γένεσις), no pleasure should be included in the class of good things. (His thought, roughly put, is that no pleasure is a good, since every good is an end in itself, and since no becoming is an end in itself.) Socrates carries this conclusion over to the next part of the argument, which begins with his assertion that the esteemed author of the *Genesis Theory*—that is, the theory that every pleasure is a becoming—will 'laugh at' two groups of people: those who believe that pleasures are good (call them the *Believers*), and those who take pleasure in being pleased (call them the *Enjoyers*) (54 D 6–E 2).

At first blush, Socrates' talk of laughter here might not seem to add anything significant to the argument. But as I see it this passage has important substantive implications. For just a few pages earlier (at 48 A–50 D) Socrates provides a lengthy, technical, and somewhat bizarre excursus on the topic of 'the laughable' (τὸ γελοῖον). His focal claim here is that a person is laughable just in so far as he is in error about how well he is doing, especially with regard to looks or wealth or virtue (48 c 4–49 A 2). So when Socrates starts the second part of the Aiming Argument with talk of laughter, he seems to be inviting Protarchus (and us) to recall this earlier discussion, and to consider whether the Believers and the Enjoyers are making some sort of mistake about how well they are doing. With that earlier discussion in mind, let us take a closer look at the pivotal exchange:

SOCR. . . . It is clear that [the author of the Genesis Theory] will laugh at those who claim that pleasure is a good [τῶν φασκόντων ἡδονὴν ἀγαθὸν εἶναι].

PROT. Most definitely.

SOCR. And this same man will also laugh at those who find satisfaction in becomings [τῶν ἐν ταῖς γενέσεσιν ἀποτελουμένων].[31]

PROT.Why? And what sort of people do you mean?

SOCR. I mean those who, when curing hunger or thirst or anything that a becoming cures [ὅσα γένεσις ἐξιᾶται], rejoice on account of the becoming in so far as it is a pleasure [χαίρουσι διὰ τὴν γένεσιν ἅτε ἡδονῆς οὔσης αὐτῆς], and claim that they would not agree to live without thirsting and hungering and experiencing all the effects that follow upon [thirsting and hungering].[32]   (54 E 1–8)

Evidently Socrates thinks that the Enjoyers are making some sort of laughable mistake here. But it is not entirely clear what mistake he thinks they are making. As far as I can tell, the passage yields just three possible mistakes: (E1) their undergoing curative processes; (E2) their *enjoying* undergoing curative processes *in so far as these processes are pleasures*; or (E3) their *claiming that life is not worth living without* undergoing curative processes. Since it is hard to see how Socrates (or anyone else) could think that there is something objectionable about merely undergoing a curative process, (E1) seems not to be a live option. And the logical structure of the passage strongly suggests that the pleasure mentioned in (E2) is supposed to account (at least in part) for the claim mentioned in (E3). For it is apparently the Enjoyers' second-order pleasure— the pleasure they take *in being pleased*—that serves to explain their wholesale rejection of pleasureless lives. So the most basic mistake that Socrates attributes to the Enjoyers here seems to lie not in

---

[31] The sense of τῶν . . . ἀποτελουμένων is difficult to gauge. As R. Bury notes (*The* Philebus *of Plato* (Cambridge, 1897), 126), ἀποτελουμένων can be taken as a neuter, in which case the objects of ridicule would be the becomings themselves. But then the ὅσοι at 54 E 4 would have to be emended. Better to take ἀποτελουμένων as I have above. As for the verb, ἀποτελέω in the active typically means 'to complete' or 'to bring to an end' (as at *Rep.* 443 B 7) but Plato uses it in the *Gorgias* to mean something like 'to satisfy' or 'to fulfil' one's appetites or desires (503 C 7–D 1). Cf. Hackforth, *Philebus*, 107.

[32] Normally διά with the accusative and ἅτε with the genitive absolute have distinctly *causal* force. Thus Gosling translates: 'are delighted because of the relevant process, because it is a pleasure'. See Gosling, *Philebus*, 56. But the 'because' here must be understood as the kind of 'because' that picks out the *content* of the pleasure—the kind we find in the sentence 'I am pleased because I won the lottery'. For if we take the 'because' as strictly causal, then we can make no good sense of the idea that the Enjoyers are committing an error by taking pleasure in being pleased. This is why Frede's translation ('take delight in generation as a pleasure') is better: it emphasizes that what the Enjoyer enjoys *about* curative processes is *their being pleasures*. See Frede, *Philebus*, 65–6.

their belief that pleasureless lives are not worth living, but in the second-order pleasure that gives this belief its conviction.

What kind of mistake does Socrates think this is? Interpreted in the context of the Aiming Argument, the exchange strongly suggests that he sees it as a *mistake of evaluation*. After all, the Aiming Argument as a whole aims to settle the question whether any pleasure is good, and clearly the first part of the argument is designed to provide a negative answer to that question. So it makes sense to suppose that, from Plato's perspective at least, the Enjoyers described in the second part of the argument are committing the very same error that the first part of the argument *reveals as* an error, namely, that of taking pleasures to be good. Moreover, Socrates holds that people are laughable just in case they are mistakenly optimistic about how well they are doing. Since he plainly thinks that the Enjoyers are laughable, he presumably also thinks that they are mistakenly optimistic about how well they are doing by being pleased. And since it is something of a conceptual truth for Plato's Socrates that people do well just to the extent that they acquire or achieve goods, he presumably also thinks that the Enjoyers are laughable in so far as they are mistakenly optimistic about whether they are acquiring or achieving goods *simply by being pleased*. According to Socrates, then, part of what it is to take pleasure in being pleased is *to be mistakenly optimistic about the value of* being pleased. In his view, taking pleasure in something is a way of valuing it, and hedonic error (in general) is a kind of *evaluative* error.

As we have seen, however, Socrates appears to be interested in more than one kind of mistake in this passage. On the one hand we have the mistake of believing that pleasures are good, and on the other hand we have the mistake of taking pleasure in being pleased. Does Socrates see these mistakes as the same or different? If he sees them as the same, then he thinks that taking pleasure in something is just a way of believing that it is good. But in my view the text of the passage strongly suggests that he does not think this. For although he seems comfortable with the idea that all and only Believers are Enjoyers, he makes a point of distinguishing between them *as objects of the theorist's ridicule*. He seems to think that the laughable error involved in being a Believer is different from the laughable error involved in being an Enjoyer. And I suppose he would be right to think so. For it is one thing to criticize people for endorsing a certain claim about the value of being pleased, and it is quite another to criticize them for 'finding satisfaction' in being pleased. The former attributes a straightforward error of belief, but the latter attributes something more like an error of affect, desire, or intention. Since Socrates never proposes anywhere in the *Philebus* that taking pleasure in something is just a way of believing something, there is no compelling reason to think that the mistake he sees in the Enjoyers' pleasure is the same as the mistake he sees in the Believers' belief. On the contrary, the textual evidence suggests that for Socrates the Believers' *doxastic* error is fundamentally distinct from the Enjoyers' *hedonic* error.[33]

In any event we have good reason to think that, no matter which account of hedonic error Plato ultimately accepts, he also accepts (or should accept) a closely corresponding account of *false pleasure*. For what he wants most from his account of false pleasure, as we have seen, is a non-trivial way to specify that feature of every incorrect pleasure which makes it incorrect (and therefore bad). This is why, for Plato's purposes at least, any account that picks out a certain set of pleasures *as mistaken* will stand or fall with some (distinct) account that picks out *exactly the same* set of pleasures *as false*. So the account of false pleasure supported by the Aiming Argument will entail, very roughly, that what makes a pleasure false is not its having false content, nor its sharing its content with some false belief, but rather its having content that is *not good*. Here, then, is the suggested account:

The Value Account

If a person experiences a pleasure with the content that p, then that pleasure is false if it is not (or would not be) good that p.

Notice, however, that this account is very similar to (if not the same as) the one the New School has been attributing to Plato all along. Were we then too quick to embrace the Old School alternative? I believe not, though it is worth pausing for a moment to explain

---

[33] It is worth pointing out here that neither the Content Account nor the Belief Account has the power to explain the Enjoyers' error. Since the Enjoyers take pleasure in undergoing curative processes in so far as these processes are pleasures, and since these processes *really are* pleasures—according to Plato's preferred theory—the Content Account entails that the Enjoyers' second-order pleasures are true, not false. And since the Enjoyers presumably also *believe* that these processes are pleasures, the Belief Account yields the same verdict. What this suggests, then, is that neither of these accounts can explain the incorrectness of the Enjoyers' second-order pleasure as Plato himself understands it.

why. One good way to do this, I think, is to consider how the view we are entertaining here differs from the one advanced by Verity Harte in her outstanding recent defence of the New School.[34] As I understand it, Harte's view—which she credits in part to Sabina Lovibond—is that (according to the Anticipation Argument) pleasures are to be assessed as true or false depending only on whether their contents are *pleasant*, not on whether their contents are *true*. 'The falsity of a false pleasure', she writes, 'consists in the inadequacy of its view of what is pleasant, and not in the accuracy or otherwise of other descriptions or predictions.'[35] Now I take it that, in this context at least, to claim that the content of a pleasure is *pleasant* is not merely to claim (trivially) that this content is the content *of a pleasure*; it is to claim (substantively) that this content *merits being* the content of a pleasure. So if we can assume that a content is *good* just in case it merits being the content of a pleasure, then we can see that both Harte and I wish to attribute the Value Account to Plato.[36] But if Harte and I end up in the same place, we get there by very different routes. For remember that the disagreement between the Old School and the New School does not turn on whether the Value Account can be found anywhere in the *Philebus*; it turns on whether this account can be found *in the Anticipation Argument*. (The New School says yes, the Old School says no.) So it is perfectly consistent for an Old School interpreter (such as myself) to argue that the Value Account can indeed be found *in the Aiming Argument*.

Of course, one might claim that the New School has an advantage here in so far as it (unlike the Old School) gives Plato a uniform account of false pleasure from one argument to the other. I concede that this is an advantage, but its significance should not be over-

---

[34] Harte, 'The *Philebus* on Pleasure'.

[35] Ibid. 126, and see n. 16 above. Consider also Lovibond's claim that our calling someone's pleasure false is just a matter of 'refusing to accept the construction of [that person's] experience of the bad object as a pleasurable experience' (S. Lovibond, 'True and False Pleasures' ['True and False'], *Proceedings of the Aristotelian Society*, 90 (1990), 213–30 at 222).

[36] The case of Lovibond is not so clear. Unlike Harte, for example, she seems uncomfortable with the idea that Plato's account is consistent with the existence of attitude-independent facts about (i) whether a particular person is taking pleasure in something at a particular time, and (ii) whether the object of that pleasure is good. She repeatedly suggests that such facts must be somehow socially constructed ('True and False', 217–25). But if Lovibond means to be attributing that sort of account to Plato, then she and I disagree. For Plato's account, as I understand it, has no such implications.

stated. For in the course of this particular dialogue Plato proposes at least three (and at most six) different accounts of false pleasure, some of which are plainly incompatible with each other.[37] Indeed, it sometimes seems as if his overall strategy is to introduce as many new and different accounts of false pleasure as he can, perhaps in order to maximize the likelihood that one of them will stick. So we should not be especially surprised or embarrassed if we find that he advances one account in the Anticipation Argument and another, distinct account in the Aiming Argument. On balance, then, we still have good reason to stay out of the New School—even if New School interpreters are right to hold that Plato ultimately endorses the Value Account.

Though (as I have said) I think it is fair to attribute the Value Account to Plato on the basis of the Aiming Argument, I think it is equally fair to point out that Plato never gives this account anything like the careful development it deserves. In fact he never explicitly marks it off as an account of false pleasure in the first place. None the less, I think it would be worthwhile to consider in a more detailed fashion the impact this account would have on the Grounding Thesis:

> *The Grounding Thesis (Value Version)*
>
> (V1) If a pleasure is bad, then its content is not good.

And:

> (V2) If a pleasure's content is not good, then that pleasure is bad *because* its content is not good.

It seems obvious, almost immediately, that this new version of the Grounding Thesis can better withstand the objections that troubled the other two versions. Consider, for example, cases of malicious joy, which—as we have seen—provide decisive counter-examples to both (C1) and (B1). These pleasures seem bad whether or not they have false content, and *the reason why* they seem bad is precisely because they have *bad* content. So (V1) is actually *confirmed* by these examples. Bad bodily pleasures pose a more serious threat, since it is not clear that bad pleasures have content at all, let alone bad content. But even on this point Plato seems to have some interesting routes of escape. If his opponent insists that bad bodily pleasures have no

---

[37] See n. 5 above.

content, then he can respond by denying that these pleasures are bad *by being incorrect*, since only attitudes can be bad *in that way*. Then he can say that the Grounding Thesis is designed to apply exclusively to pleasures *understood as attitudes*. If his opponent claims instead that bad bodily pleasures do have content, then he can deny that the content of any bad bodily pleasure is good. And in defence of this denial he can say, first, that such pleasures are typically taken in intense physiological changes, and second, that these changes are not themselves good. Without pronouncing at the moment on Plato's largely negative evaluation of bodily pleasures, and of the body in general, we can at least see that and why (V1) is better than (C1) or (B1) at making his negative evaluation of these pleasures intelligible.

But there is a deeper and more serious objection to (V1) lurking here—one that emerges directly out of the intuition underlying the Belief Account. According to (B2), remember, a pleasure is bad if and because it is based on a false belief. And this seems true. But if (B2) is true, and if there are any pleasures that have good content but are based on false beliefs—such as those of the kind-hearted fool—then (V1) is false. This is a powerful objection, but I suspect that Plato can handle it. First he can claim, as before, that the Grounding Thesis is designed to capture only what makes pleasures bad *as attitudes*. Then he can add that the only properties of an attitude that are capable of making it bad in this way are *the kind of attitude it is* and *the content it has*. What makes a belief bad as an attitude, for example, consists entirely in its having content that no belief should have; by extension, then, what makes a pleasure bad as an attitude is its having content that no pleasure should have. And the pleasures of the kind-hearted fool, by this criterion, are not bad after all. For if the world did accord with the kind-hearted fool's beliefs, then his pleasures would be just as they should be. To be sure, these pleasures are bad, and what makes them bad is their entanglement with false beliefs; but they are not bad *as attitudes for that reason*. By adopting this strategy, I think, Plato can go some way towards defusing this line of objection.[38]

---

[38] This move can also help Plato deflect worries about whether the Value Version of the Grounding Thesis is consistent with the conclusion of the Aiming Argument. This conclusion, remember, is that no pleasure is good. Yet the Value Version suggests, at the very least, that pleasures with the right sort of content are better than pleasures with the wrong sort of content. Can Plato avoid saying that these better pleasures are good, if only in so far as they have the right sort of content? If he

If we turn our attention now to (V2), we shall see that it too can withstand many of the objections that its competitors cannot. First of all, (V2) handles the pleasures of imagination far better than (C2) does. For while (C2) entails the patently unacceptable claim that the pleasures of imagination are bad simply in virtue of having false content, (V2) does not. On the other hand, (V2) does entail the controversial claim that a given pleasure of imagination is bad if and because *what is imagined* is not good. And at this point Plato's opponent might object that even (V2) is too tyrannical, since most people are not committed to the realization of their fantasies, especially when they recognize that the content of their fantasies is worthless or bad.[39] But the line of thought behind this objection is at least debatable. Even if pleasures of this sort do no harm—and indeed, even if they *prevent* harm—they still constitute positive attitudes towards things that (at the very least) do not merit being the objects of such attitudes. So Plato can insist here, once again, that having the wrong sort of content is precisely what makes an attitude bad *as an attitude*. Since it is possible for pleasures to have good-making or bad-making features that outstrip their being bad *in that way*, the complete evaluation of a given hedonic attitude may well require more than an evaluation of its correctness as an attitude. Other things—such as its origins, its effects, its relations to other attitudes, and its place in the life of the person who takes it—might also need to be considered. But none of these other factors should affect our evaluation of it as an attitude. Or so Plato might argue.

Of course, one might wonder at this point why, if a pleasure's being false does not depend in any way on its having false content, we should agree to call it 'false' rather than, say, 'worthless' or 'bad'

makes the move I am recommending here, then he does not have to. He can say that the Aiming Argument is meant to show not that pleasures cannot be good *as attitudes*, but that pleasures, *precisely because* they can be good *only* as attitudes, cannot have the same sort of value that their contents (optimally) do. It is not that pleasures are not worth taking *at all*; it is that they are not worth taking *as ends in themselves, regardless of their contents*. According to the Aiming Argument, then, pleasures are *essentially aiming things*, and this is precisely why they do not qualify as things at which it is appropriate to aim. Clearly this is consistent with the idea that well-taken pleasures are good *as attitudes*. For a more extensive defence and discussion of this way of reading the Aiming Argument, see my 'Plato's Anti-Hedonism', *Proceedings of the Boston Area Colloquium in Ancient Philosophy* (forthcoming). Thanks to an anonymous referee for forcing me to confront this issue more explicitly.

[39] The idea here is that the *prima facie* badness of a pleasure that has bad or worthless content would be cancelled out by its not sharing its content with any of the pleased person's beliefs. Thanks to Jim Hankinson for pressing me on this point.

or simply 'incorrect'. The worry here is that our only rationale for thinking of incorrect *beliefs* as false is that their *content* is false; so even if we have good reason to accept that pleasures (like beliefs) can be correct or incorrect, we have no reason to accept that incorrect pleasures (like incorrect beliefs) are *false*. On this view, the Value Account is actually an implausible and unnecessary supplement to the Value Version of the Grounding Thesis. For we could at once accept the correctness conditions implied by the latter and reject the truth conditions spelt out by the former. (The most obvious evidence of this possibility is that the Value Version, unlike the other two versions, makes no use of the term 'false'.) What we seem to lack, then, is a compelling reason to think that the Value Account is anything more than a dubious and disposable feature of an otherwise attractive account of hedonic error.

Though this too is a powerful line of attack, I think Plato has the resources to make a strong stand against it. For he can claim, with some justification, that it is driven by the very thought that the Value Account is meant to challenge. This thought, remember, is that only attitudes of belief are *incorrect by being false*; other attitudes (such as those of pleasure, pain, fear, anger, and the rest) belong in a different category, since their being incorrect is not just a matter of their having false content. But surely this is exactly what the Value Account is pressing us to reconsider. It demands that we ask ourselves why we are inclined to carve up the attitudes in this particular way. If we respond that beliefs are the only attitudes whose conditions of attitudinal incorrectness provide conditions of propositional falsehood, then we beg the question against Plato's view. For according to the Value Version of the Grounding Thesis, a pleasure with the content *that p* is incorrect if and only if the proposition *that it would be good that p* is false. (Similar stories can be told about the other attitudes.) If we respond instead that beliefs are the only attitudes that have robust representational roles, then we beg the question again, but in a deeper way. For the very point of Plato's aggressively drawn analogy between pleasure and belief is *precisely to deny* that beliefs are the only attitudes that have robust representational roles. To endorse the Value Account is, in effect, to cast doubt on the idea that, of all of the attitudes we have, only our beliefs are responsible for getting (and keeping) us in touch with reality. Of course, one might continue to hold onto this idea, even in the face of Plato's suggestion, but to do so is just to restate

one's disagreement with that suggestion, not to offer any additional
reason to reject it.

Other strengths and weaknesses aside, the Value Account's most
striking pay-off is that it gives Plato a way to make both the Similarity Claim and the Normative Claim at once. It allows him to make
the Similarity Claim because it holds that pleasures, like beliefs, are
false in virtue of having *inappropriate* content (i.e. content that it is
inappropriate for an attitude of that kind to have); and it allows him
to make the Normative Claim because it holds that false pleasures
(i.e. pleasures with worthless or bad content) are bad because they
are false. Thus the Value Account has the potential to vindicate the
Grounding Thesis in a way that neither of the other two accounts
does. For it assigns to all and only pleasures a distinct, belief-like
role, such that a pleasure's failure in this role is both necessary
and sufficient for it to be worth rejecting. Thus the Value Version
of the Grounding Thesis is perhaps best understood as a combination of two connected ideas: first, the psychological thesis that
the correctness or incorrectness of a given pleasure is determined
by the value of its content; and second, the metaphysical thesis
that some contents are good and others are not.[40] On a view of this
sort, a person's pleasures are appropriate targets of ethical criticism
simply because they constitute our sensitivity (or lack thereof) to
genuine goodness: our taking pleasure in things is roughly equivalent to our perceiving (or misperceiving) their value.[41] And this

---

[40] In sections 184 and 186 of his commentary on the *Philebus*, the Neoplatonic
philosopher Damascius suggests, but does not argue, that this is indeed Plato's view.
According to Damascius, Plato recognizes two ways for a pleasure to be false: either
its content is 'not present' or its content is 'not good'. If it is not good, then the
pleasure is false *because pleasure aims at the good*: 'the love of the ugly, or of what is
not beautiful, is false, since it is a striving that seeks the beautiful' (L. G. Westerlink
(ed., trans., and comm.), *Damascius: Lectures on the Philebus* (Amsterdam, 1959),
86–8). Gosling sees that Plato's account *should* take this form: 'for any given state of
affairs, there is an appropriate reaction, and just as when we make a judgement we
are aiming at the right judgement about the thing, so when we react we are aiming
at the right reaction'. But then he goes on to say that this 'cannot be what Plato has
in mind' (Gosling, *Philebus*, 50). I agree with Gosling in part, since his attention
here is confined to the Anticipation Argument, but of course I disagree with his
overall assessment of Plato's view.

[41] As far as I know, Lovibond is the first commentator to pursue this line of
thought in a systematic way. 'The development of the capacity for value-perception',
she writes, 'just is . . . the elaboration and remodeling of the capacity for pleasure'
('True and False', 215). Penner does consider whether Plato sees pleasure as a kind
of perception, but does not consider whether he sees it as a *distinctively evaluative*
kind of perception. See Penner, 'False Anticipatory Pleasures', 171–2 n. 7.

seems to capture rather well some widely shared intuitions about what makes an attitude of pleasure commendable or questionable, at least when there is general agreement about the value or dis-value of its content. Thus the Value Account gives Plato a coherent and distinctive view about how the critical evaluation of pleasures works, and why it is justified.

V

If my reading is right so far, then in the end Plato gives us an account of false pleasure that comes surprisingly close to vindicating the Grounding Thesis. But there is a lingering concern that, even if this account is the best Plato can come up with, it is not entirely successful. One worry, as we have seen, is that this account—unlike the Content Account, say—is relatively sketchy and incomplete. Another, more substantive worry is that this account is simply not credible, for one or more of the various reasons I mentioned obliquely at the beginning of the paper. I would like to conclude now with a very brief discussion of what I take to be the best of these reasons.

The problem I am especially interested in is one that faces anyone who tries to defend the idea that pro-attitudes (such as pleasure) have the belief-like role of picking out things that are good. To see why this might be a problem, consider the following reasonable constraint on attitudes that have such roles:

The Representation Constraint

If an attitude A has the belief-like role of picking out things that have some property F, then, for any x, if x has F, it is not because A picks out x that x has F.

The thought behind the Representation Constraint is that the task of any attitude with a belief-like role is to *take* things the way they are, not to *make* things the way they are. If an attitude towards a thing is what makes that thing have a certain property, then that attitude cannot have the belief-like role of *picking out* that thing *as having* that property.

This is worrisome, from Plato's perspective at least, because it often seems as though attitudes of pleasure, when taken towards things, are precisely what make these things good, if anything does.

Suppose, for example, that I enjoy drinking cola X more than I enjoy drinking cola Y, because of the way they taste, and that this is my reason for believing—and defending in public—the claim that X is better than Y. If pressed, I might find it hard to deny that the pleasure I (and others) take (or would take) in drinking X is precisely *what makes* X better than Y, if anything does. How reasonable would it be for me to insist that, on the contrary, the pleasure that I (and others) take in drinking cola has the belief-like role of representing a property of goodness that, in virtue of inhering more in X than in Y, explains why I (and others) enjoy drinking X more than we enjoy drinking Y? This is not a rhetorical question, of course, but it does give some indication of how extreme the Grounding Thesis really is. Elsewhere I have argued that this thesis can, with significant qualifications, be given a decent defence.[42] Here I wish only to hold out the hope that, if there are any things that are not made good simply by being pleasant, then Plato's thesis can be fruitfully applied to whatever pleasures are taken in those things.

Still, one might suspect that there is little to be gained by agreeing with Plato that such pleasures are not merely incorrect, but also false. His view, as we have seen, is that the incorrectness of nearly every attitude is grounded in its failure to represent how things stand in an attitude-independent reality. For him, then, nearly every incorrect attitude is false. But it remains unclear whether he has given us any compelling reason to agree with him about this. Many philosophers today would be inclined to hold that most (if not all) of the non-doxastic attitudes—including those of pleasure and pain—provide clear counter-examples to Plato's view, either because these attitudes are not capable of being incorrect, or because little or no sense can be made of the idea that their being incorrect is just a matter of their being inaccurate.[43] Moreover, it is hard to see why we could not concede that such attitudes are to be evaluated (at least in part) on the basis of their contents, but then deny that this is because they have belief-like representational roles. So far, then, Plato's view awaits a more forceful defence. But even if we ultimately decide that it is unsustainable, we can still credit him with having illuminated quite powerfully the idea that all of our

---

[42] See my 'Plato's Anti-Hedonism'.

[43] For a succinct articulation of this complaint, see J. Searle, *Intentionality* (Cambridge, 1987), ch. 1.

attitudes—not just our beliefs—are charged with the critical task of getting things right.

New York University

BIBLIOGRAPHY

Bravo, F., 'La critique contemporaine des faux plaisirs dans le *Philèbe*', in M. Dixsaut (ed.), *Contre Platon* (Paris, 1995), 235–70.

Bury, R., *The* Philebus *of Plato* (Cambridge, 1897).

Caston, V., 'Connecting Traditions: Augustine and the Greeks on Intentionality', in D. Perler (ed.), *Ancient and Medieval Theories of Intentionality* (Leiden, 2001), 23–48.

—— 'Towards a History of the Problem of Intentionality among the Greeks', *Proceedings of the Boston Area Colloquium in Ancient Philosophy*, 9 (1993), 213–60.

Delcomminette, S., 'False Pleasures, Appearance and Imagination in the *Philebus*' ['False Pleasures'], *Phronesis*, 48 (2003), 215–37.

Dybikowski, J. C., 'False Pleasure and the *Philebus*' ['False Pleasure'], *Phronesis*, 15 (1970), 147–65.

Evans, M., 'Plato's Anti-Hedonism', *Proceedings of the Boston Area Colloquium in Ancient Philosophy* (forthcoming).

Feldman, F., *Pleasure and the Good Life* (Oxford, 2004).

Frede, D., 'Disintegration and Restoration: Pleasure and Pain in Plato's *Philebus*' ['Disintegration'], in R. Kraut (ed.), *The Cambridge Companion to Plato* (Cambridge, 1992), 425–63.

—— (trans. and comm.), *Plato:* Philebus [*Philebus*] (Indianapolis, 1993).

—— 'Rumpelstiltskin's Pleasures: True and False Pleasures in Plato's *Philebus*', *Phronesis*, 30 (1985), 151–80.

Gosling, J. C. B., 'False Pleasures: *Philebus* 35 C–41 B', *Phronesis*, 4 (1959), 44–54.

—— 'Father Kenny on False Pleasures in Plato's *Philebus*', *Phronesis*, 6 (1961), 41–5.

—— (trans. and comm.), *Philebus* (Oxford, 1975).

—— and Taylor, C. C. W., *The Greeks on Pleasure* [*Greeks*] (Oxford, 1982).

Hackforth, R., *Plato's* Philebus [*Philebus*] (Cambridge, 1972).

Harte, V., 'The *Philebus* on Pleasure: The Good, the Bad and the False', *Proceedings of the Aristotelian Society*, 104 (2004), 111–28.

Irwin, T., *Plato's Ethics* [*Ethics*] (Oxford, 1995).

Kagan, S., *Normative Ethics* (Boulder, Colo., 1997).

Kahn, C., 'Some Philosophical Uses of "to be" in Plato', *Phronesis*, 26 (1981), 119–27.

Kenny, A. 'False Pleasures in the *Philebus*: A Reply to Mr. Gosling' ['False Pleasures'], *Phronesis*, 5 (1960), 45–52.

Lovibond, S., 'True and False Pleasures' ['True and False'], *Proceedings of the Aristotelian Society*, 90 (1990), 213–30.

McLaughlin, A., 'A Note on False Pleasures in the *Philebus*', *Philosophical Quarterly*, 19 (1969), 57–61.

Mooradian, N., 'Converting Protarchus: Relativism and False Pleasures of Anticipation in Plato's *Philebus*', *Ancient Philosophy*, 16 (1996), 93–112.

Nozick, R., *Anarchy, State, and Utopia* (New York, 1974).

Penelhum, T., 'Pleasure and Falsity', *American Philosophical Quarterly*, 1 (1964), 81–91.

Penner, T., 'False Anticipatory Pleasures: *Philebus* 36 A 3–41 A 6', *Phronesis*, 15 (1970), 166–78.

Russell, D., *Plato on Pleasure and the Good Life* [*Plato on Pleasure*] (Oxford, 2005).

Searle, J., *Intentionality* (Cambridge, 1987).

Thalberg, I., 'False Pleasure', *Journal of Philosophy*, 59 (1962), 65–74.

Westerlink, L. G. (ed., trans., and comm.), *Damascius:* Lectures on the *Philebus* (Amsterdam, 1959).

Williams, B., 'Pleasure and Belief' ['Pleasure'], *Proceedings of the Aristotelian Society*, suppl. 33 (1959), 57–72.

THE SELF, THE SOUL, AND THE INDIVIDUAL IN THE CITY OF THE *LAWS*

MARIA MICHELA SASSI

THE question of the role played in Plato's *Laws* by his conception of the soul, and in particular by his understanding of psychological conflict, has experienced changing fortunes in Plato scholarship. In 1957 D. A. Rees noted that the question of the division of the soul in Plato's last work 'seems to have been on the whole neglected by scholars', while at the same time observing that the tripartite conception presented in the *Republic* plays a notably diminished role in the later dialogues—with the exception, of course, of the *Timaeus*. Indeed, Rees maintained that in the later dialogues one tends to find a conception of the soul as divided into only two elements, one rational and the other irrational, a conception which also appears to have been popular in discussions in the Academy.[1] Rees's reasoning was criticized a few years later by T. J. Saunders, who considered it highly unlikely that in the *Laws* Plato would abandon 'such a prominent and vivid feature of [his] thought' as the tripartite division of the soul, and argued that 'the bipartite analysis can never *exclude* the tripartite', as is shown by the coexistence of both conceptions in many of Plato's texts (see, for instance, *Rep.* 571 C–572 A and 589 D–E). Indeed, through a close reading of the *Laws* Saunders attempted to show that *thumos* continues to play an important role even in this, Plato's last treatment of psychological drives.[2]

[1] See D. A. Rees, 'Bipartition of the Soul in the Early Academy', *Journal of Hellenic Studies*, 77 (1957), 112–18. The popularity of this conception in the Academy is revealed in the *Magna Moralia* (1182ᵃ23 ff.), which attributes to Plato a division between λόγον ἔχον and ἄλογον elements of the soul, and this division is also recalled by Aristotle in *DA* 432ᵃ26.

[2] T. J. Saunders, 'The Structure of the Soul and the State in Plato's *Laws*' ['Structure'], *Eranos*, 60 (1962), 37–55 (quotations from pp. 38 and 37 respectively).

Saunders's proposal found little support, however, probably at least partly due to his relating it to a rather less plausible claim, namely, that the city of the *Laws*, like that of the *Republic*, has a tripartite structure analogous to that of the soul. Rees's thesis, on the other hand, has become generally accepted, without being subjected to much further debate, such that generally it has simply been taken for granted that the moral psychology of the *Laws* is based on a dichotomy between the rational and the irrational.[3] Recently, however, this consensus has been challenged by C. Bobonich, who has argued that in the *Laws* Plato intended to replace the idea of a division of the soul, which had created insurmountable logical difficulties in the *Republic*, with an entirely different moral psychology. According to Bobonich, this new theory no longer considers moral behaviour to be determined by the play of different, 'agent-like' components of the soul, but rather considers the soul as a single subject of many contrasting affections, ranging from elementary desires to rational calculations, which succumbs to or resists them *in its entirety*. Bobonich maintains that the key to this interpretation lies in the image of the man-puppet in the first book (644 D–645 A), which he believes to provide 'the clearest description of strict akratic action'. Bobonich interprets the strings that pull the puppet in different directions as representing not parts of the soul, but different mental states—opinions, desires, and emotions—among which the soul, as a single, indivisible agent, is to decide.[4]

In an article on *akrasia* in the *Laws*, Lloyd Gerson has observed that Bobonich's interpretation presents Plato as a Stoic, in the sense of one committed to the unity of the principle of action, but as a rather odd one, engaged in employing this unity to explain *akrasia*, which for the Stoics is a crux.[5] I would add that Bobonich's interpretation of the moral psychology of the *Laws* also seems not to

---

[3] For instance, in *Plato's Psychology* (Toronto, 1970), 145, T. M. Robinson writes that 'the familiar bipartition of soul into reason and impulse is taken for granted throughout'. W. W. Fortenbaugh, in *Aristotle on Emotion*, 2nd edn. (London, 2002), 23–5, appears to take a similar view, although he also rightly emphasizes that, for Plato as for Aristotle, emotions always have a cognitive content.

[4] C. Bobonich, 'Akrasia and Agency in Plato's *Laws* and *Republic*' ['Akrasia'], *Archiv für Geschichte der Philosophie*, 76 (1994), 3–36; id., *Plato's Utopia Recast: His Later Ethics and Politics* [*Utopia*] (Oxford, 2002), esp. 247–92.

[5] See L. Gerson, '*Akrasia* and the Divided Soul in Plato's *Laws*', in S. Scolnicov and L. Brisson (eds.), *Plato's Laws: From Theory to Practice* (Proceedings of the VI Symposium Platonicum, Selected Papers; Sankt Augustin, 2003), 149–53, repr. with revisions in Gerson, *Knowing Persons: A Study in Plato* (Oxford, 2003), 265–75.

escape the main impasse which he himself identifies in the *Republic*. As he admits, according to his interpretation, 'the person seems to be nothing more than the passive container of affections that pull against one another, or the passive spectator of these pulling forces'. But if we are therefore to consider the golden puppet-string of reason as an affection among other affections, of which the person is only a container or even a mere spectator, then how are we to explain those cases in which reason manages to control *akrasia*, by, to use the terms of the metaphor, exerting the strongest 'pull'? According to Bobonich, such cases can be explained only by appeal to the idea that a person can actively intervene in the process—in Bobonich's terms, we must accept that 'we can pull our own wires'.[6] Such a solution might sound reasonable, particularly given Plato's often neglected claim, in his description of the man-puppet, that the various affections (τὰ πάθη) are like puppet-strings 'inside us' (ἐν ἡμῖν . . . ἐνοῦσαι)—a claim which suggests that we are pulled *from within* in various directions, towards or away from virtue or vice. However, the idea that 'we can pull our own wires' would thus also seem to reintroduce precisely the *complexity* of the psychological agent which Bobonich had been concerned to reject.[7]

Since I share many of Gerson's criticisms of it, in the following I shall not discuss Bobonich's interpretation in detail. Nor shall I directly consider the development of Plato's political project from the *Republic* to the *Laws*, in relation to any corresponding evolution in his psychology. In this regard, I simply refer the reader to C. H. Kahn's admirably balanced discussion of Bobonich's interpretation, and particularly to Kahn's demonstration that the peculiarities of Plato's psychology in the *Laws* can be adequately explained by its different context, and thus without having to postulate any change in Plato's thinking about the soul—a change which, after all, is unlikely, given that the tripartite division of the soul is endorsed in the *Timaeus,* the composition of which may have

[6] Bobonich, *Utopia*, 266.

[7] Cf. ibid. 259: 'The *Laws* still recognizes complexity within the soul and a division between rational and non-rational aspects.' In 'Fil d'or et fils de fer: sur l'homme "marionnette" dans le livre I des *Lois* de Platon (644 c–645 a)', *Archives de philosophie*, 69 (2006), 461–73 at 461, J. Laurent, having followed Bobonich's interpretation, comes to a similar conclusion: 'c'est l'homme lui-même qui, par les décisions de l'âme, accepte ou refuse les tractions reçues de l'extérieur, dans un combat qui a lieu "en chacun de nous contre nous-mêmes"'.

partially coincided with that of the *Laws*.[8] Rather than consider
these questions, then, my purpose in this article is to determine
Plato's conception of the structure of the soul in the *Laws* by carefully examining the various references to it that can be found in
the text. This will entail, among other things, giving due attention
to the questions of the immortality of the soul and of metempsychosis, questions often marginalized, presumably because of the
difficulties that they raise for interpretations which attempt to contain Plato's moral reasoning within strict parameters of analysis. In
this regard, I intend to show that, whether one likes it or not, the
notion of the immortality and divinity of the soul provides a fundamental link between Plato's treatment of the self and his treatment
of the city.

1. A divided self

It is difficult to deny that the great idea that Plato introduces
into moral psychology in the *Republic*, namely, the idea of intra-
psychological *conflict*, is also present in the *Laws*. Indeed, throughout the text, the problem of the internal equilibrium of the community is treated by means of an analogy with power dynamics
within the soul, a strategy which recalls that of Socrates in *Republic* 4, when he proposes to illuminate the problem of justice in the
City by turning back to the individual (434 C–435 A). The notion
of a conflict between each individual's better and worse 'selves' is
expressed particularly clearly in the following passage at the very
beginning of the *Laws*:

ATHENIAN. And should a man consider himself with regard to himself
[αὐτῷ . . . πρὸς αὑτόν] as an enemy facing an enemy? Or can we put
things differently?
CLEINIAS. Stranger from Athens . . ., by rightly reducing the argument to
its essentials you have made it clearer, and thus you will discover more
easily the rightness of what we have just claimed, namely, that not only
is everyone the enemy of everyone else in public, but also in private each
man is his own enemy. . . . In this case as in others, Stranger, victory
over oneself is the first and best of all victories, and conversely to be
defeated by oneself is the most shameful and worst of defeats. This is

[8] C. H. Kahn, 'From *Republic* to *Laws*: A Discussion of Christopher Bobonich,
Plato's Utopia Recast', *Oxford Studies in Ancient Philosophy*, 26 (2004), 337–62.

to say that there is a war [πόλεμος] against ourselves [πρὸς ἡμᾶς αὐτούς]
within each of us.

ATHENIAN. So let us try and reverse the argument. Since each of us is
either victorious over himself or is defeated by himself, can we say or not
that the same is true of a house, a village, or a city?   (626 D 1–627 A 2)

Significantly, the terms employed here also recall another well-
known passage of *Republic* 4 (430 E–431 B), in which temperance
(σωφροσύνη) is defined as the ability to dominate (ἐγκράτεια) desires
and pleasures, and the idea of being 'stronger' or 'weaker' than oneself gives rise to a discussion of the presence in the soul of elements
with different values. In the *Republic*, of course, this discussion
prepares the way for Plato's argument for the division of the soul
into parts, among which there is an 'internal war' or στάσις (440 A).⁹

The definition of temperance as a 'victory over oneself' is present
throughout the first book of the *Laws*,¹⁰ providing the psychological
basis for the book's main theme, namely, the necessity that the in-
stitutions of the city train the young to resist pains and fears, just as
much as pleasures and desires (633 C–634 B; 635 C–D; 645 B; 647 C–
D). If in Plato's text—just as in our current, everyday language—
rational control is conceived of as a control 'over oneself', then this
probably reflects the assumption that the sphere of the passions is
the most individual and individualizing one, which must be controlled by taking a more objective perspective—one which lies, as it
were, 'outside oneself', in the network of intersubjective relationships. (One is tempted to suggest that this distinction resembles
Freud's distinction between the pleasure and reality principles.)
However that may be, both the 'parties' that fight over the soul
aspire to a total occupation of the territory—that is, to the title of
'the self'—although Plato, of course, insists that only the rational
element does so legitimately, since it is the 'best' element of the
soul (cf. *Rep.* 431 A–B).¹¹

When Plato defines virtue at the beginning of the second book

⁹ The contrast between two psychological principles, one tending to pleasure and
the other to moderation, and the use of the metaphor of government (ἀρχή) or power
(κράτος), is also present in *Gorg.* 491 D–E and *Phdr.* 237 D–238 A. In *Soph.* 228 B
wickedness is seen as the product of a discord (στάσις) or illness (νόσος) of the soul
divided between reason and the passions.
¹⁰ This theme often surfaces later in the text. See, for example, two instances in
the discussion of sexual habits in book 8, at 840 C 5 and 841 B 7.
¹¹ As regards the *Laws*, this point is grasped by R. F. Stalley, in *An Introduction
to Plato's* Laws (Oxford, 1983), 46.

of the *Laws*, he identifies it as a concord (συμφωνία) between parts of the soul which, according to his musical model, are conceived as elements of different 'pitch'. Indeed, this concord results from the passions' obedience to the dictates of reason. *Paideia* is therefore given the important function of acting on the young, with games and songs, at a stage of life in which reason is not yet formed, so as to predispose them to a future management of joy and pain that is correct—that is, consistent with wisdom. Discord (διαφωνία) between reason and the passions, on the other hand, constitutes the worst form of ignorance (ἀμαθία), or even a kind of folly or ἄνοια (653 A–C; 659 D–660 A; 689 A–D; 696 C).[12] Importantly, συμφωνία is conceived as a concord *with oneself* (see 691 A), just as when Socrates describes his own συμφωνία in the *Gorgias* (482 B). The 'best' element is thus conceived of as the 'truest' one, that which, when victorious, defines the moral subject *as such*. Moreover, throughout his work Plato's theory is characterized by the tension between a normative tendency to identify the individual with his intellect, his highest and most divine part, and the opposed tendency to recognize the complexity of the human soul, and the *Laws* is no exception in this regard (cf. *Phaedo* 115 C; *Alc. I* 113 C; *Rep.* 588 B ff.). There is no reason, then, not to consider the controversial image of the man-puppet as representing precisely this complexity—that is, as insisting on an internal tension, constitutive of human nature, between the superior impulse of reason and the confused multiplicity of emotional drives. The relevant passage reads as follows:

ATHENIAN. . . . . Let us suppose that each of us living beings is a puppet made by the gods, either for fun or for some serious purpose: this we do not know, but we do know that these affections [πάθη] that lie within us like sinews or strings pull us and, being opposed to one another, pull against each other, towards opposed actions: and here is the line that divides virtue from vice. Our argument holds that we should always follow only one of these pulling forces without ever giving it up, and thus resist the pull of the other sinews. This is the golden, sacred guide of rational calculation

---

[12] This contrast produces interesting effects in individuals of good character but bad habits (or the opposite). Such individuals express value judgements that conflict with their actual feelings—indeed, they may come even to feel pleasure in immoral dance movements, while simultaneously experiencing shame (αἰσχύνονται) when seen doing so by those who think wisely (φρονεῖν: 655 E–656 A, cf. 656 B). This psychological dynamic is similar to that which moves Leontius in the well-known episode of *Republic* 4 (439 E–440 A), for both cases concern a disagreement between ἐπιθυμία and reason. Notably, in the *Laws* the shame experienced is not claimed to be caused by θυμός, which is significant, as we shall see below.

that is called the public law of the city and that, being golden, is flexible, while the other cords are rigid and made of iron, and have the most varied forms [παντοδαποῖς εἴδεσιν]. (644 D–645 A)

Clearly, while the golden puppet-string symbolizes reason, the other puppet-strings, of less value but multiple and destabilizing, represent emotions. Despite being opposed to reason, however, emotions are not here conceived of as completely blind forces. A few lines earlier, the Athenian insists that, although the soul of each person must be considered as a single entity, it none the less has 'inside it' two 'opposing, non-intelligent [ἄφρονε] advisers', namely, pleasure and pain. The sensations of pleasure and pain thus act *internally* to the soul, and although they admittedly act without *phronēsis*,[13] they none the less always *advise*. They must, then, have some, albeit minimal, cognitive content, which, accompanied by a series of emotional correlates, motivates the soul to pursue objectives that are presented as pleasant and avoid those that are presented as unpleasant. Furthermore, the Athenian adds that the soul forms 'opinions' (*doxai*) regarding the future, and that such an opinion is generally called an 'expectation' and a 'confidence' when the expected object is pleasant, and a 'fear' when the expected object is unpleasant (644 C–D).[14] Such opinions are obviously 'instinctive' in a certain sense, since they can lead to action immediately, without being filtered by rational evaluation. Yet in this passage the term *doxa* none the less also refers to a basic level of interior representation of sensible reality.[15] As a *vox media*, the term also assumes a positive value in contexts in which Plato emphasizes the need for rational reflection on the data of opinion—for instance, in situations in which the disagreement (διαφωνία) between, on the

[13] Here we find that sense of φρόνησις as practical, calculating wisdom which becomes the cornerstone of Aristotle's ethics.

[14] Following J. Annas, *An Introduction to Plato's* Republic (Oxford, 1981), 142–52, I see no real difficulty in Plato's attribution in the *Republic* of a series of functions (the representation of objects, desires, etc.) to different parts of the soul, thus making of each part a *homunculus* in which a dynamic between reason and desire may be reproduced, and raising the problem of a regression *ad infinitum*. Indeed, it is precisely because they are conceived of as *homunculi* that the various parts have only some of the characteristics of the person whose behaviour they are to explain. Consequently, I maintain that in the *Laws* too, the division of the soul and the attribution of specific abilities to its irrational parts raise no genuine problems.

[15] Similarly, at 717 D Plato mentions the case of the father who yields to anger because he maintains (δοξάζει) that his son has offended him. See below, however, for a discussion of the role played by *thumos* in this case.

one hand, feelings of pain and pleasure and, on the other, 'opinion agreeing with reason' produces 'the greatest ignorance', he groups *doxa* with *epistēmē* and *logos* as faculties which by nature are to have command of the soul (689 A–B).

Noting that in 689 A–B pleasure and pain are defined as the 'multitude' or 'crowd' of the soul (τὸ πλῆθος τῆς ψυχῆς), Bobonich claims that they are therefore to be considered as an indistinct, as it were faceless, mass of affections, to which we can attribute neither opinions nor desires.[16] But this interpretation fails to take account of the claim, made in the same passage, that 'what feels pain and pleasure'—an expression which itself suggests a certain substantiality—occupies a position in the soul analogous to that which the people (δῆμος) and the crowd (πλῆθος) occupy in the city, and thus a very specific position, similar to that of the desiring element and the class of producers in the *Republic*. Moreover, it is precisely multiplicity, accompanied by disorder and elusiveness, that Plato treats as characteristic of the *epithumētikon* principle in contexts in which he clearly admits a division of the soul. One is reminded of his description, in the *Republic*, of the tripartite soul as an assemblage of a man (symbolizing reason), a lion (symbolizing *thumoeides*), and a wild beast, 'variegated and with many heads' of various different animals, and continually changing form (θηρίου ποικίλου καὶ πολυκεφάλου, 588 C 7–10, cf. τοῦ πολυκεφάλου θρέμματος, 589 B 1–2, and πολυειδὲς θρέμμα, 590 A 7). The multitude of desires is also described as a 'wild beast of many varied shapes' (τὸ παντο-δαπὸν θηρίον, 588 E 5), using an adjective which, significantly, one later finds also in the man-puppet passage, in the claim that the iron puppet-strings are susceptible to the most varied shapes (παν-τοδαποῖς εἴδεσιν). Finally, in the *Phaedrus* the distinction between the state of *sōphrosynē*, produced by the predominance of opinion acting with reason, and the state of *hubris*, produced when desire drives the individual irrationally (ἐπιθυμίας ἀλόγως ἑλκούσης) towards pleasures, is accompanied by the observation that the latter state actually has many names (πολυώνυμον), because it has many limbs (πολυμελές) and many forms (πολυειδές, 237 E–238 A).

These linguistic resonances suggest that there is a continuity between the psychology of the *Republic* and that of the *Laws*, at least in the sense that in the latter work too there is an idea of a contrast between different psychological components, well captured

---

[16] Bobonich, 'Akrasia', 27.

by the distinction between rational judgement and the irrationality of desire. However, despite this similarity to the *Republic*, the *Laws* also lacks a significant element of the theory presented there. For, while it is true that in the *Laws* one finds desire described as a many-shaped, animal element that is barely kept in check by the higher part of the soul, one does not also find indications of the intermediate psychological element, or the 'lion' so essential to the psychology of the *Republic*. In the *Laws*, no silver strings move the puppet, and this absence cannot be without significance, especially if we think of the importance, for Plato as for others from Hesiod onwards, of the notion of a hierarchy of metals, rich with symbolic associations—one thinks, for instance, of the 'gold and silver of the soul' mentioned at *Rep.* 416 E. I would suggest that the main innovation of the *Laws* lies in the fact that this intermediate psychological element, the *thumoeides*, is missing. It is worth considering this conceptual development and its possible motivations in more detail.

2. *Thumos* without *thumoeides*

In the *Republic* courage is presented as the virtue distinctive of the *thumoeides* part of the soul, with the function of 'safeguarding', among different pains and pleasures, the criterion of what is really to be feared and what is not (442 B–C). J. M. Cooper has shown that this conception owes much to the Homeric notion of *thumos* as relating primarily to self-assertion and the sense of offended dignity, a relation that Plato emphasizes and examines in some detail. Thus in the *Republic* competitiveness and self-esteem, along with the related pursuit of social approval, are considered to constitute a source of motivation as important as reason, on the one hand, and appetites, on the other.[17] However, such an autonomous psychological element appears to play only a minor role in the *Laws*, and, although some traces can be found of the tripartite division of the soul affirmed in the *Republic*, this division no longer provides the basic framework for the psychological argument, and does so even less for the political one.

In the text of the *Laws* there are numerous references to the love

[17] J. M. Cooper, 'Plato's Theory of Human Motivation', *History of Philosophy Quarterly*, 1 (1984), 3–24.

of victory (φιλονικία) and the love of honours (φιλοτιμία), which in the eighth and ninth books of the *Republic* are identified as the two main characteristics of a *thumoeidēs* personality. These references reflect the ambivalence which is attributed to *thumos* in the *Republic*, in that φιλονικία and φιλοτιμία are considered to be involved in the striving for virtue, or at least in healthy competitiveness (730 D 7; 731 A 2; 820 C 8; 907 B 10; 907 C 2), yet also as being negative dispositions in other cases (677 B 7; 796 A 5; 841 C 4; 870 C 5; 957 D 3), and especially if they are accompanied by a desire for riches—an association which perhaps hints at the tripartite conception (632 D 1; 841 C 4; 938 B 6, C 4). However, the same terms are also used in more neutral, commonplace senses (834 B 6; 834 C 4; 840 A 2; 860 D 9; 860 E 1; 935 C 1), and the contexts of these uses suggest that Plato no longer ascribes to φιλονικία and φιλοτιμία the crucial place in the definition of the individual personality that they have in the *Republic*.

The passages in which *thumos* itself is mentioned suggest similar conclusions. In particular, one finds a certain ambivalence in the uses of this term. In one important passage Plato mentions a 'noble *thumos*' which opposes injustices, yet emphasizes that it ought to be fully vented only in cases of entirely irremediable wrongdoing, and that the virtuous man must therefore be as mild as he is irascible (*thumoeidēs*) (731 B–D).[18] In another passage Plato claims that anger must also be controlled with regard to the young who deny the existence of the gods, and therefore they must be gently persuaded of their error rather than angrily scolded (888 A). Similarly, in another passage Plato accepts that someone who has met a violent death may rightly become enraged (*thumoutai*) at his assassin, to the point of wanting to torment him in revenge, but none the less insists that such a person is equally disturbed himself (ταραττόμενος . . . ταράττει, 865 D–E). In these passages, then, it would seem that Plato, while recognizing the motivations of 'just' anger, is none the less more concerned with the disturbing effects which this emotion may have if it is not controlled.[19]

---

[18] Other cases of rightful anger are considered at 927 C and D. However, Plato considers the anger that assails a father to the point of making him want (ἐπιθυμεῖν) to disown his son, whether rightly or wrongly, to be 'by no means welcome', and holds that such a decision must therefore be discussed and made by the whole family (929 A–B).

[19] At 900 A–B Plato expresses the fear that even believers in the existence of the gods might, indignant at the rewards and honours gained by the most unjust men,

Although Plato occasionally attributes to *thumos* a positive function, he more often presents it as one of many emotional states, like
erōs, hubris, amathia, philokerdeia, and *deilia* (649 D). Like *phobos,
hēdonē, lupē, phthonoi*, and *epithumiai*, *thumos* can exert a 'tyrannical
force' that inevitably leads to injustice and directly opposes the rule
of the 'opinion about what is best' (κρατοῦσα, 863 E–864 A). In other
words, in the *Laws thumos* is a passion on the same level as others,
and like them can be considered one of the iron strings that pull
the man-puppet in different directions, and always contrary to the
golden string. Indeed, it would seem that *thumos* is a particularly
destructive emotion, being more difficult to control than others because it is so difficult to 'sate'. For *thumos* involves a greedy pleasure
in sating (ἐμπίμπλάς) rage with 'bad food', making the soul run wild
and destroying the fruits of upbringing—whoever indulges in such
behaviour, Plato maintains, 'loses a great part of his magnanimity'
(μεγαλονοίας ἀπώλεσεν μέρη πολλά, 935 B). Plato even claims that a
bad natural tendency to anger can lead to madness (διὰ θυμοῦ κακὴν
φύσιν, 934 D), and that one can be so 'unable to control one's anger'
(ἀκρατὴς θυμοῦ) as to kill a parent in a mad fit of rage (869 A). He also
notes that a parent can fly into an excessive rage at a son who does
not show him the respect which he thinks he deserves—in this case,
Plato thinks it advisable that the son not argue with the parent, but
rather let him give vent to his rage, or, in the words of the text, 'fill
up' his *thumos* (717 D).[20] Furthermore, as is well known, for Plato
the loss of reason entails a lack of moral responsibility—indeed, it is
significant that in the discussion of involuntary crimes in the ninth
book, those committed in outbursts of anger are considered to be
the most excusable (866 D–867 B, and see also the following lines,
until 869 E, and 878 B).[21]

None the less, there remains a passage of the *Laws* which, not

be led by a completely irrational (ὑπὸ ἀλογίας) πάθος to deny that the gods concern
themselves with human affairs.

[20] Notably, the verb ἀποπίμπλημι, which here indicates the action of 'satisfying'
θυμός, is also used in the *Gorgias*, in relation to ἐπιθυμία and Callicles' description
of the superior man who must satisfy every desire that comes to his mind (492 A).
Note that it is the soul that tends to pleasures and desires (ἐπιθυμίαι) which demands
to be continually 'filled up', and is therefore afflicted by an 'incessant and insatiable
illness' (714 A), an image which seems to be taken from *Gorg.* 493 A ff.

[21] Plato has a different view of cases in which the crime is committed in an anger
that has been 'nursed' for a certain time, such that the act is premeditated and not
regretted, and thus resembles second-degree murder (866 E–867 A). Plato certainly
does not approve of the idea that 'revenge is a dish best served cold'.

without reason, many interpreters consider to show some signs of a continued commitment to the tripartite division of the soul. Here, three kinds of wrongdoing are clearly distinguished: that caused by yielding to pleasure, that caused by an impulse to anger, and that caused by a lack of knowledge of good and evil. In this passage one finds the following two statements in particular:

ATHENIAN. . . . . It is indeed clear that, regarding the soul, we say to each other or hear it said that anger is found in it as an aspect of its nature, whether it be an affection or a part [ἐν μὲν ἐν αὐτῇ τῆς φύσεως εἴτε τι πάθος εἴτε τι μέρος ὤν], an innate possession that is unruly and difficult to fight against [δύσερι καὶ δύσμαχον κτῆμα], which causes havoc through its irrational violence [ἀλογίστῳ βίᾳ]. . . . And we affirm that pleasure is not the same thing as anger, but we say that it rules with a contrary strength [ἐξ ἐναντίας . . . ῥώμης δυναστεύουσαν], and that by means of persuasion and violent deceit it does everything that its will desires. . . . And one would not be lying if one were to say that the third cause of wrongdoing is ignorance [ἄγνοιαν]. (863 B–C)

ATHENIAN. . . . having shown that there are three kinds of wrongdoing, it is important first of all to recall them to the memory. For us one kind [ἓν εἶδος] is that of pain, which we call anger or fear. . . . The second is that of pleasure and desires, the other, the third, which is distinct, is that of expectations and untrue opinion about the attainment of what is best. (864 B–C)

The rather hesitant expression with which *thumos* is presented here—'whether it be an affection or a part'—would appear to be an intentional reference to the theory affirmed in the *Republic* and is sufficiently vague for each interpreter to read his own view into it, whether this view be that in the *Laws thumos* is still considered as an autonomous psychological force or that there the idea of a division of the soul into 'parts' has been abandoned.[22] However, an alternative possibility is that this expression is intentionally vague, since rather than state his position regarding the number of parts of the soul, here Plato simply intends to raise the question of the definition of *thumos* in the specific context of a discussion of the causes of moral errors. For, with respect to *thumos*, the two passages make an important, yet perhaps still not adequately appreciated, claim— namely, that the forces of pleasure and anger are opposed to each other, since anger, like fear, is a kind (εἶδος) of pain. This claim notably prepares the way for Aristotle's definition of anger, in which

---

[22] Cf. Saunders, 'Structure', 38–9, for an example of the first approach, and Bobonich, 'Akrasia', 26, for an example of the second.

the relation to pain is essential—for him, the offended ego desires revenge precisely because of the pain produced by the wrong suffered.[23] With regard to Plato's moral psychology in the *Laws*, it is significant that the relation between anger and pain is discussed in a framework that remains fundamentally dichotomous. Although in Plato's image of the man-puppet there are many iron strings which pull the 'puppet' confusedly in all directions, in the passage on the three kinds of wrongdoing the careful distinguishing of crimes and punishments leads Plato to identify two basic orientations of emotions: one driving the individual towards pleasure and the other driving him away from pain, whether by fleeing it in fear or by angrily pursuing revenge. Crucially, however, both orientations belong to the most elementary level of individual behaviour, at which immediate desires prevail over rational judgement or escape it entirely. (That these elements are presented together at 732 E is significant: 'pleasures, pains, and desires [*epithumiai*] above all are part of human nature, and it is inevitable that every mortal being simply depends on them, as if suspended with the greatest anxieties'.) The impression that the passages at 863 B–C and 864 B–C reflect a commitment to the tripartite division of the soul is therefore misleading. Rather, the explanation of moral errors given in these passages appeals only to the distinction between the rational and the irrational, the first two kinds of error being explained as deriving from the prevalence of pleasure or pain over rational calculation, and the third being considered to be the result of total ignorance, such that no conflict with the rational arises at all.[24]

To summarize, then, although in the *Laws* Plato continues to attribute to *thumos* an important role in moral psychology, in this text his attention is focused more on its irrational and uncontrollable manifestations, which make it a decidedly unlikely candidate for that alliance (συμμαχία) with reason which is hinted at in both the *Republic* and the *Timaeus*. This downgrading of the role of *thumos* is a development of some importance, since it opens a gap between the rational and the irrational in Plato's psychology. While, admittedly, this development might be thought to open the way to interpretations like Bobonich's, in my opinion it is to be explained

---

[23] See *Rhet.* 2. 2, 1378ᵃ30; *DA* 1. 1, 403ᵃ30–1; *Pol.* 5. 10, 1312ᵇ32–4; *Top.* 4. 5, 125ᵇ29, 32, etc.; 6. 13, 151ᵃ15.

[24] Cf. 934 A, where fears, desires, envies, and fits of rage that are 'difficult to remedy' (and to be punished more severely than normal displays of anger) are attributed to folly (ἄνοια) and to ἀκράτεια concerning pains and pleasures.

differently, in so far as it rests not on a more optimistic project, but rather on an acutely pessimistic view of human capacities.[25] In the *Laws*, man is considered to possess a much more fragile psychological structure than he is in the *Republic*, because he is tormented by an internal, and now unmediated, struggle between reason and the passions. I shall attempt to substantiate this thesis further in the following, final section of my paper. Firstly, I shall attempt to show how, in the *Laws*, the regulatory force of the law is intended precisely to fill the gap between the rational and the irrational that is opened up by the reduced motivational role of *thumos*. Secondly, I shall argue that this move is part of a broader strategy aimed at the depersonalization of psychological conflict, and, indeed, that a primary aim of legislation is the repression of the *whole* plane of emotions. This plane is now considered as only a dangerous principle of individuation contrary to the perfect order of the ideal *polis*, to be ruled according to the rationality of the city and the cosmos.

3. The individual's relation to *nomos*

In numerous passages of the *Laws*, *nomos* is clearly treated as the expression of a supreme principle of rationality. It is defined as the 'regulation of reason' (τὴν τοῦ νοῦ διανομήν, 714 A), and as reasoning (*logismos*) regarding pleasures and pains that 'is called "law" when it becomes the common opinion of the city' (δόγμα πόλεως κοινόν, 644 D; cf. 636 D, 663 B–C). The law aims primarily at imbuing souls with a healthy moderation (*sōphrosynē*) regarding desires which would destroy the city if taken to excess, and its spirit must therefore pervade the entire *paideia* (835 E–836 A, cf. 643 C–644 A), while it shows its repressive side—albeit reluctantly on the part of the legislator—to those who do not allow themselves to be moulded by their upbringing, and therefore risk becoming completely wicked (880 E, cf. 853 D).[26]

[25] Here my interpretation is similar to that of E. R. Dodds in 'Plato and the Irrational Soul', ch. 7 of *The Greeks and the Irrational* [*Greeks*] (Berkeley and Los Angeles, 1951).

[26] In the *Laws* Plato's general definition of παιδεία emphasizes its etymological link with παῖς and identifies its purpose as the instilling of virtue, by means of practices intended to form correct habits in individuals not yet endowed with reason (see 643 C–644 B and 653 A–C). Interestingly, the educative process is here described as a process by which psychological energy (ἔρως) is directed away from the most

The subject of the rationality that finds expression in the law is a god conceived of as a 'measure of all things', and whoever wishes to be dear to the gods must try to make himself similar to them in all respects (716 A, 716 C). Man must therefore aspire to the 'intermediate' state that characterizes the life of the gods and gives it its uniform serenity (792 D), and in particular to their ability never to be overcome by pleasures and pains—which implies, notably, that they never suffer psychological *conflicts* (902 B). Although a favourable nature and correct upbringing can render man 'the most divine and gentle animal', without such a nature or upbringing man may become 'the wildest animal that the earth can produce' (766 A), thus diverging from the divine to the maximum degree. The latter possibility reflects the same pessimistic anthropology which colours the image of the man-puppet, in which man, a toy created by the gods (803 C, cf. 804 A–B), is literally to cling (ἐχόμενος) to his creator by clinging to the golden, 'sacred' puppet-string of reason (645 A).[27] Whoever refuses to acknowledge the need for divine guidance, taking pride in his own individual beauty, wealth, or prestige, is left to himself and 'begins to jump around causing general chaos' (716 A–B). Such physical agitation reflects a psychological disorder with which every animal is born, as infants' restlessness and crying shows. Man, however, differs from other animals in being able gradually to escape this disorder by developing his rationality, thanks to the ability to perceive the orderliness and disorderliness of movements—an ability which, along with rhythm and harmony, the gods endowed him with (653 D–654 A; 664 E–665 A; 672 C–D; 673 C–D).[28]

Here, therefore, the ideal of human nature involves a transition from animality to the divine which leaves no room for any virtuous management of the lower elements of the soul. The ideal of

elementary pleasures and desires, and towards 'high' objectives (643 C–D). Here as at 783 A a 'hydraulic' model is at work, a model which Plato often adopts to illustrate psychological dynamics. I discuss this model in 'Eros come energia psichica: Platone e i flussi dell'anima', in M. Migliori, L. M. Napolitano Valditara, and A. Fermani (eds.), *Interiorità e anima: la psychè in Platone* [*Interiorità*] (Milan, 2007), 275–92.

[27] The term ἀγωγή used in the man-puppet passage to indicate the 'pull' of the golden string—which is 'also called the common law of the city'—is also used at 659 D, where παιδεία is defined as the ability to pull (ὁλκή τε καὶ ἀγωγή) the young boy towards a correct control of pleasures, as determined by the law.

[28] This idea is, of course, based on the discussion in the *Timaeus* of the benefits of listening to and playing music for the correction of irrational movements of the soul joined to the body (*Tim.* 44 A–C; 47 C–D; 80 B).

οἰκειοπραγία endorsed in the *Republic* thus finds no place in the city of the *Laws*. In particular, as we have seen, in the *Laws* there is no trace of that positive competitiveness and self-esteem associated with *thumos* which according to both the *Republic* and the *Timaeus* (70 A) is to assist in the battle against the raging appetites. In the *Laws*, human beings are considered to be *naturally* incapable of governing themselves autonomously without falling into *hubris* and injustice, and it is therefore the gods and daemons, as perfect models of moderation and intelligence, who are to be our 'allies' (σύμμαχοι) in the 'battle' against evils (713 C–E; 906 A–B).

It must be admitted that even in the *Republic* passages can be found which suggest a similar view. Indeed, in one passage of book 9 we read that 'it is better to be ruled by a divine, intelligent element, especially if one has it in oneself as one's own', and that, if this is not possible, then a higher principle must be imposed from the outside so as to homogenize all citizens by subjecting them to it, in a process in which *nomos* is σύμμαχος (590 D). However, in the *Republic* Plato still intended, or at least hoped, that *men* would sit at the top of the hierarchy and govern the *polis*, while in the *Laws* precisely this hope is lacking. And if at one point in the *Laws* it is admitted that *either* a god *or* some enlightened individual who has grasped the divine pull of reason may make the city accept this as a law (645 A), in another passage the law is claimed to be only a 'second best' (δεύτερον) necessary to prevent private interests prevailing over the common good, because a *nous* with the right to govern must be 'authentic and free by nature', and such a *nous* 'does not exist anywhere, except perhaps in small measure' (875 A–D).[29]

In basing the effectiveness of the law on its universality and impersonality, Plato draws on elements of the conception of *nomos* which were already developed in Greek, and particularly Athenian, culture. However, this cannot be said for the ideas regarding the law which Plato develops *a parte post*—that is, for his ideas regarding the law's relation to those who are subject to it. One notes, not without a certain apprehension, that in the name of the good order of the city the laws of Magnesia intrude upon not only the sphere of the family and the home—including its most private rooms—but

[29] See also 713 E, where it is claimed that a city governed by a 'mortal', rather than a god, will inevitably suffer ills. Such statements raise certain questions regarding the status of the legislators who mediate between *nous* and the city, and particularly the first legislator, and regarding the precise epistemological status of the laws of Magnesia. However, these questions are beyond the scope of the present article.

also that of the soul and of the individual. Thus, while drawing on a culturally prevalent notion of citizenship, which tended to identify individual freedom with citizenship, Plato gives it an unusual form: in order that the city may 'live well, just like a single man' (καθάπερ ἕνα ἄνθρωπον, 829 A), Plato considers it necessary to subordinate to it not only private material interests and the passions, but even citizens' perceptions.

At the core of Plato's thought here is the idea, at once psychological and epistemological, that the greatest of all evils is innate (ἔμφυτον) in the soul of most men, such that every man tends to be morally lenient towards himself, and makes no effort to escape this (ἀποφυγὴν οὐδεμίαν μηχανᾶται, 731 D–E). This evil is self-love, the individual's focus on himself and his own particular interests, which ensures that he is unable to have a correct view of what is truly right (731 E–732 B; on δίκαιον as a criterion cf. 859 E). Such self-love finds expression above all in the desire (*erōs*) for riches, because this is necessary—as is frequently noted in the *Republic*— to satisfy the individual's insatiable animal appetites (*aplēstia*) for food, drink, and sex. If the citizen's soul is 'hanging' as if by a string (κρεμαμένη) towards the care of his own private possessions, then he will inevitably care only about them, and not for the common good (831 C). The laws respond to this danger in two ways: firstly, by strictly regulating the distribution of land, which remains common property (740 A ff., cf. 923 A–B), and, secondly, by removing greed (φιλοχρηματία) and narrow-mindedness (ἀνελευθερία) from souls themselves (747 B) through the more subtle means of education and their preambles.[30]

Furthermore, one reads in book 1 that the principal task of the legislator is 'to scrutinize and supervise' joys, pains, desires, erotic passions, fears, and fits of rage, by approving of actions which conform with justice and disapproving of those that do not, in all interpersonal relations and in all circumstances of illness, war, and poverty. The legislator is thus to define with the greatest possible precision every detail of each individual's life, in every interpersonal relation of his life, from his youth until his old age, and even in the grave, through the regulation of wills and funerals (631 D–

---

[30] In the preamble to the law on impiety, a fundamental exhortation is that each individual see his own particular sphere as part of a whole which the deity takes care of as a whole (903 B–E, cf. 905 B). The law itself prohibits private cults established with the aim of requesting special favours (909 D ff.).

632 D). This programme is then elaborated in detail—indeed, even obsessively—in the rest of the text. For example, much considera-tion is given to *paideia* and the ways in which it is to work on the sensations and feelings of children from birth, and even in the mother's womb (788 A ff., and in particular 789 E, 790 B). There is also an extremely detailed set of laws on marriage, aimed at repress-ing any sexual disorder, as well as ensuring that the sexual impulse is always subjected to the end of procreation (771 E ff.). This repres-sive attitude towards *erōs* is based on the idea, which Plato argues for in the *Timaeus*, that sexual immoderation is an illness (νόσος, νόσημα) of the soul with a precise physical cause (86 B–E). Hunger and thirst are also, like sexual desire, elementary needs that must be directed *beyond* immediate satisfactions, 'illnesses' to be cured by means of fear, the law, and true reason, and also with the help of the Muses (782 D–783 A).[31]

Plato admits that the regulations regarding the family might seem 'severe'. These extend even to imposing spouses on individual citi-zens at great personal sacrifice, such as when one is required to marry a physically or mentally disabled relative for hereditary rea-sons. Plato concedes that, being primarily concerned with the com-mon interest, the legislator may not always be fully aware of all of the details of citizens' private lives (ἴδιαι συμφοραί) and that he also must allow for more complex decision-making procedures when necessary (925 D ff.). But this is the only exception made in a ge-neral panorama of subjection of every private possession, whether material or psychological, to an ideal of *homogenization* of citizen-ship.[32] Thus not only appetites, but also the potentially positive release of *thumos*, are suppressed. This is particularly notable in the military context, in which absolute obedience must be given

---

[31] The reference here is clearly to the educative function attributed to artistic representation, and particularly music, in the *Laws*. The idea of moral evil as an illness to be cured (cf. also 714 A; 853 D; 854 C) is linked to a conception inherited from the *Gorgias* of politics as a τέχνη of therapy for the soul, to be based on a thorough knowledge of different natures and dispositions (650 B).

[32] It is significant that Plato also applies the vocabulary of possession used for material goods (κτάομαι, κτῆμα) to all intellectual and moral qualities, in most cases to emphasize the superiority of the latter over the former (834 B; 840 A; 863 B; 913 B) on the grounds that, 'of all the good we possess, the most divine (though it is not as divine as the gods) is the soul, because it is the most intimate' (726 A, cf. 727 E). But, like ownership of the land, the virtues of the soul must be shared with others (730 E–731 A), and once again here the soul's individuality does not seem to be given much importance. Furthermore, like every living being, man is in his turn the κτῆμα of the gods (902 B; 906 A).

to the commander and every personal initiative banished. On this, one reads the following:

ATHENIAN. . . . the most important thing is that no one, whether man or woman, ever be left without a commander, that, whether in serious occupations or in play, no one's soul develops attitudes that would lead him to act alone, on his own initiative, and that each rather lives, in every circumstance of war and peace, with his gaze always fixed on [βλέποντα] his commander, following him, and allowing himself to be guided by him in even the simplest things. . . . In short, through habits a soul must be instructed to neither know nor be able to do anything separately from the others, and everyone's life must be as united [ἀθρόον] and common [κοινόν] to all as possible. (942 A–C)

Here it is notable that the soldiers of a garrison are all to *look* in a single direction, towards the commander, so as to be able to receive and carry out his orders as a unit. In the process of making everyone similar, indeed, not only the objects of and the reasons for joy and pain, but even acts of perception are to be made common.[33] Another passage reads as follows:

ATHENIAN. The ideal city and constitution and the best laws are to be found where the whole city most puts into practice the ancient saying that the goods of friends are really shared . . . This can happen if what is called 'private' is completely removed from life, by whatever means and everywhere, and one does as much as possible to make somehow shared [κοινά] also those things that are private [ἴδια] by nature, such as the eyes, ears, and hands, so that they would seem to see, hear, and act collectively, and as far as is possible everyone approves and disapproves unanimously, feeling pleasure and pain at the same things. (739 B–D)

The ideal of absolute subjection to the law—or, equivalently, to the divine—is therefore to be achieved by minimizing, and even eliminating, everything of a 'private' nature. Since, according to Plato, to submit to the rule of the gods means to conform with 'what is immortal in us' (713 E), it follows that 'what is immortal in us' is at most contingently related to our 'private' person: that is, to that unique combination of physical and psychological characteristics that makes each member of the human species an *individual*. Indeed, at only one point in the *Laws* does Plato refer unequi-

[33] When Plato claims that the city 'perceives' (758 D) or 'has *nous*' (919 C), these expressions are more than mere *façons de parler*. In particular, the function of the 'head' of city, in which both *nous* and the most important senses lie, is concentrated in the Nocturnal Council (cf. 961 C–D; 962 C–D; 964 D–965 A).

vocally to *personal* immortality, and there he is concerned merely with the 'immortality' human beings achieve 'naturally', through procreation (721 B–C).[34] It will therefore be useful to conclude my discussion by considering the notion of the immortality of the soul in so far as it relates to the question of the notion of 'person' in Plato's thought. In thus leaving the field of moral psychology and entering into certain aspects of Plato's metaphysics, I shall take my bearings from the interpretation recently proposed by Lloyd Gerson in *Knowing Persons*. It goes without saying, of course, that I do not intend to provide a thorough discussion of Gerson's interesting interpretation, but simply to use elements of it to make certain points regarding the *Laws*.

Gerson identifies and analyses in many of Plato's dialogues the tension to which I have referred above—namely, that between a notion of the subject as a soul united with the body, and therefore sharing the body's appetitive and emotional drives, and a notion which identifies the subject with reason alone, a cognitive capacity which operates independently of the sensible world. In this regard, Gerson introduces an extremely useful distinction between an 'embodied' and a 'disembodied' person, the former being a corporeal subject and the latter being a subject that, by exercising the capacity for self-reflection which characterizes it, recognizes its identity with the Forms. In these terms, the arguments for the immortality of the soul in the *Phaedo*, the *Phaedrus*, and *Republic* 10 are intended to show that the 'embodied' person is an imperfect version of the ideal, 'disembodied' person.

The conception of the person in the *Laws* would seem to fit quite easily into this framework. The soul's superiority to the body is claimed by appeal to a certain set of ideas which directly recall the *Phaedo* (66 D ff.; 81 E ff.), including the idea of life in the world beyond as a life shared with the gods, in which one enjoys with them the greatest goods (726 A ff., in particular 727 D), the idea that the union of soul and body is 'no better' than their separation (828 D), and the idea of death as the least of evils (854 E). In a passage of book 12, in the context of a discussion of why corpses ought not to be laid out for more than three days, the 'true self' is explicitly identified as

---

[34] This passage is considered in two particularly interesting discussions, in G. R. Carone, 'Mind and Body in Late Plato', *Archiv für Geschichte der Philosophie*, 87 (2005), 227–69 at 260, and B. Centrone, 'L'immortalità personale: un'altra nobile menzogna?', in Migliori *et al.* (eds.), *Interiorità*, 35–50 at 38.

the soul which departs for Hades to face divine judgement, having left behind the mortal remains, the mere 'semblance', of the body. Here one reads the following:

ATHENIAN. It is necessary to trust the legislator also when he says that the soul is superior to the body in all respects, and that in life itself what makes each one of us what he is is nothing other than the soul, whereas the body is a semblance [ἰνδαλλόμενον] which follows us around, and that it is quite right to say that the bodies of the dead are images [εἴδωλα] of the deceased, and that what each of us really is, that which is called our 'immortal soul', departs to the other gods to give an account of itself. (959 A–B)[35]

But while the text of the *Laws* would thus seem merely to echo Plato's discussion elsewhere, it actually has a more complicated story to tell. If we consider Plato's tales of the hereafter to be a 'serious', if not therefore necessarily 'realistic',[36] portrait of the meaning of a fully rational life, then we must attend to a particularly important aspect—namely, that, once separated from the body, a soul which proceeds to be judged by the gods of the underworld is not considered to have acquired *ipso facto* a state of absolute purity. As I have already mentioned, in one passage Plato claims that a man who has been violently murdered may feel both fear and anger towards his assassin, and attempt to take revenge on him in the hereafter (865 E–866 A). Furthermore, the souls of the deceased continue to 'care about' human affairs and, being naturally concerned for their children in particular, feel benevolent towards whoever respects them and hostile towards whoever neglects them (927 A–B). The soul therefore takes to Hades feelings and passions experienced in its 'embodied' life. Moreover, it also arrives in Hades with the responsibilities of all its past actions, and deserves exemplary punishment if judged guilty (881 A–B).[37] Rewards and punishments are assigned in the course of different reincarnations—indeed, in

[35] What is buried is a mere 'lump of flesh', a 'soulless altar', for which it is not worth spending much on funeral rituals (959 C–D).

[36] Personally, I see no grounds for denying that Plato believed in the reincarnation of souls, but my argument holds even assuming that the eschatological myths have a merely symbolic value, and therefore that, for example, in the *Laws* Hades represents merely a 'state of mind', as Dodds puts it (*Greeks*, 221).

[37] According to the myth presented in the *Gorgias* (523 A–524 A), Zeus decrees that men arrive dead in Hades in order that their souls may undergo judgement 'naked'. Here the soul's separation from the body is understood as a removal of the social mask that would obscure the judges' view. Without the outer ornament of the roles played in social life, the judges are able better to observe, even in the souls of rulers, both the natural characteristics and the passions felt in the course of

Laws 10 there is an account of reincarnations that recalls the account in *Republic* 10 and shares essential features with it, including the idea that a soul's future life is decided according to both the gods' concerns regarding the law of cosmic justice[38] and the wishes of the soul itself. The passage reads as follows:

ATHENIAN. Since the soul, combined now with one body, now with another, is always subject to every kind of change, whether due to itself or other souls, there remains no other task for the player of *petteia* than to move each improved character [ἦθος] to a better place and each worsened one to a worse place, as is appropriate in each case, so that each will have the destiny that he deserves. . . . And regarding all this he has worked out which home and even which places each part must change and inhabit, according to its quality, while leaving to the will of each of us the determination of more specific events. Indeed, what we become generally corresponds roughly with what we desire and the quality of our souls. . . . All that contains the soul changes, having within itself the cause of change, and as it changes it moves according to the order and law of destiny; if it changes in the smaller aspects of character it moves less along the surface of an area, while if it changes more and towards greater injustice, it moves downwards, towards those places which are called lower, and which—as they show by giving them names such as Hades—men greatly fear and have nightmares about, both when they are alive and once they are separated from their bodies. When a soul is particularly full of vice or virtue, due to the strong influence of its will and the people whom it has frequented, if it becomes divine by uniting itself with divine virtue, then it is transferred to a higher place, being carried to some superior place along a sacred path; when the opposite happens, it is sent to live its life in the opposite places. (903 D–904 E)

Admittedly, these souls are 'disembodied'. Yet they are clearly *complex* souls none the less, rich with desires and passions developed together with the bodies which they occupied in their past lives. Some elements of a soul's previous embodied life can even survive when it takes on a new body, in the form of retribution—for instance, those souls which have stained themselves by committing murder are destined to die at others' hands, and those who have killed their mothers will even be reborn in a female body, so as to

various experiences, since the signs of wickedness remain imprinted in the form of wounds and scars (524 D–525 A). Cf. A. Fussi, 'The Myth of the Last Judgment in the *Gorgias*', *Review of Metaphysics*, 54 (March 2001), 529–52.

[38] In reference to this Dodds coined the phrase 'law of spiritual gravitation' (*Greeks*, 221).

be killed in their turn by their children (870 D–E; 872 E). In short, it must be admitted that, for Plato, the soul of a dead person—despite its no longer having any direct association with a body—is still involved in the world of sensible affections, as long as it is condemned to be reincarnated.[39] Only when it finally manages to escape from the cycle of reincarnation, by purifying itself, can a soul be said to have achieved identity, being perfectly aware of its own cognitive state and of its affinity with the Forms. But since every individual feature of the soul's past existences is thus definitively left behind, at this point one can no longer speak of personal immortality.

In conclusion, the ideal which Plato consistently endorses and develops in the *Laws* is one of a city which, like the ideal soul, is perfectly at peace with its inner conflicts. The law is presented as a remedy for the destabilizing influence of the sensations and emotions which make every human being an individual, before he is a citizen. The authoritarian aspect of this remedy may worry contemporary readers, but Plato supports it with his presupposition regarding the extreme weakness of human nature. In particular, the law imposes that rational regulation which each man potentially possesses within himself in so far as he is a divine creature, but which only a 'small stock of men' (918 C) is able to exercise. In short, the price that Plato asks us to pay for political order is the suppression of our 'worse', yet more human, selves.

Università di Pisa

BIBLIOGRAPHY

Annas, J., *An Introduction to Plato's* Republic (Oxford, 1981).

Bobonich, C., 'Akrasia and Agency in Plato's *Laws* and *Republic*' ['Akrasia'], *Archiv für Geschichte der Philosophie*, 76 (1994), 3–36.

—— *Plato's Utopia Recast: His Later Ethics and Politics* [*Utopia*] (Oxford, 2002).

Carone, G. R., 'Mind and Body in Late Plato', *Archiv für Geschichte der Philosophie*, 87 (2005), 227–69.

Centrone, B., 'L'immortalità personale: un'altra nobile menzogna?', in Migliori *et al.* (eds.), *Interiorità*, 35–50.

[39] This point was well understood by W. K. C. Guthrie in 'Plato's Views on the Nature of the Soul', in *Recherches sur la tradition platonicienne* (Entretiens sur l'Antiquité Classique, 3; Vandœuvres and Geneva, 1955), 3–22.

Cooper, J. M., 'Plato's Theory of Human Motivation', *History of Philosophy Quarterly*, 1 (1984), 3–24.

Dodds, E. R., *The Greeks and the Irrational* [*Greeks*] (Berkeley and Los Angeles, 1951).

Fortenbaugh, W. W., *Aristotle on Emotion*, 2nd edn. (London, 2002).

Fussi, A., 'The Myth of the Last Judgment in the *Gorgias*', *Review of Metaphysics*, 54 (March 2001), 529–52.

Gerson, L., '*Akrasia* and the Divided Soul in Plato's *Laws*', in S. Scolnicov and L. Brisson (eds.), *Plato's* Laws: *From Theory to Practice* (Proceedings of the VI Symposium Platonicum, Selected Papers; Sankt Augustin, 2003), 149–53; repr. with revisions in Gerson, *Knowing Persons: A Study in Plato* (Oxford, 2003), 265–75.

Guthrie, W. K. C., 'Plato's Views on the Nature of the Soul', in *Recherches sur la tradition platonicienne* (Entretiens sur l'Antiquité Classique, 3; Vandœuvres and Geneva, 1955), 3–22.

Kahn, C. H., 'From *Republic* to *Laws*: A Discussion of Christopher Bobonich, *Plato's Utopia Recast*', *Oxford Studies in Ancient Philosophy*, 26 (2004), 337–62.

Laurent, J., 'Fil d'or et fils de fer: sur l'homme "marionnette" dans le livre I des *Lois* de Platon (644 C–645 A)', *Archives de philosophie*, 69 (2006), 461–73.

Migliori, M., Napolitano Valditara, L. M., and Fermani, A. (eds.), *Interiorità e anima: la psychè in Platone* [*Interiorità*] (Milan, 2007).

Rees, D. A., 'Bipartition of the Soul in the Early Academy', *Journal of Hellenic Studies*, 77 (1957), 112–18.

Robinson, T. M., *Plato's Psychology* (Toronto, 1970).

Sassi, M. M., 'Eros come energia psichica: Platone e i flussi dell'anima', in Migliori *et al.* (eds.), *Interiorità*, 275–92.

Saunders, T. J., 'The Structure of the Soul and the State in Plato's *Laws*' ['Structure'], *Eranos*, 60 (1962), 37–55.

Stalley, R. F., *An Introduction to Plato's* Laws (Oxford, 1983).

'AS IF WE WERE INVESTIGATING SNUBNESS': ARISTOTLE ON THE PROSPECTS FOR A SINGLE SCIENCE OF NATURE

JAMES G. LENNOX

1. Introduction

SINCE it has been determined in how many ways nature is spoken of, we need next to study in what way the mathematician differs from the natural scientist (for natural bodies too have planes, solids, lines, and points, things which the mathematician investigates). (*Phys.* 2. 2, 193^{b}22–5)

So opens the second chapter of *Physics* 2.[1] Aristotle seems to be saying that the distinction made in the previous chapter between nature understood as the underlying matter of a natural thing and as the shape and form of a natural thing implies that the next question to clear up is how the *mathēmatikos* and *physikos* differ from

© James G. Lennox 2008

This paper began as a presentation to a Werkmeister conference in March 2003 honouring Russ Dancy. I thank Michael Ruse for the opportunity to take part in that wonderful event. I thank Myles Burnyeat, John Cooper, Mary Louise Gill, Deborah Modrak, and Steve Strange for helpful questions and comments on that occasion. I am also grateful for invitations to present these ideas from the Departments of Philosophy at the University of Texas, Austin, Ohio University, the University of Pisa, the University of Bologna's Institute of Advanced Studies, which also provided support for work on them, and the Department of Philosophy at Concordia University. Most recently I presented some of these ideas to a seminar on Aristotle's conception of natural science in my department, co-taught with Allan Gotthelf. I am thankful to the participants in that seminar and members of previous audiences for many hours of fruitful discussion and challenging questions. I thank Zvi Biener, Andrea Falcon, Devin Henry, Brad Inwood, Monte Johnson, Kelly Jones, Larry Jost, Sean Kelsey, Stephen Menn, Diana Quarantotto, and Alan Silverman for helpful discussion and written comments on various drafts. Finally, I thank the new editor of *Oxford Studies*, Brad Inwood, for pressing me to clarify and elaborate on a number of points.

[1] The chapters are a Renaissance invention, of course, but in this case, while the argument is continuous with the lines that precede it, the chapter division reflects a clearly marked transition.

one another. It is difficult to see why this is a natural, or even a reasonable, topic to take up at this point in the argument, however. The differences between mathematical study and natural study are interesting and we know they interested Aristotle; but such demarcation questions, if they belong anywhere within this work, would seem to belong in the first chapter or two of *Physics* I (presuming, as I do, that our first two books are a unit). Yet the chapter not only opens with such a discussion; this opening sentence states that this is exactly where this discussion should be.[2]

Without a compelling answer to this question, moreover, a strong case could be made that the discussion of this topic, running from 193^{b}22 to 194^{a}12, is an intrusion. Chapter 1 presents the case for reducing the study of nature to the study of underlying material constituents, and then defends the view that natural things have two natures, based in their matter and form,[3] and that the study

---

[2] Ross tries to make the connection this way: 'The previous chapter has revealed that φύσις has two main senses, "matter" and "form". In the present chapter Aristotle discusses the attitude of φυσική to these elements and distinguishes it from μαθηματική. . . . Physics studies forms as involving matter for their embodiment; mathematics studies them in abstraction from such embodiment' (W. D. Ross (ed. and comm.), *Aristotle's* Physics [Ross] (Oxford, 1936), 506). Note that Ross does not explain why this subject should come up here, and he misreports Aristotle's argument in an instructive way. Here Aristotle stresses that mathematics does *not* study natural forms in abstraction; rather, it studies certain proper attributes of natural things. This is an *instructive* misrepresentation of the argument because, as I shall discuss below, it is a fair representation of the way in which Aristotle discusses mathematical abstraction in the *Posterior Analytics*. Charlton does not comment directly on why this topic is discussed here (W. Charlton (trans. and comm.), *Aristotle: Physics I, II*, rev. edn. [Charlton] (Oxford, 1992), 93). Simplicius (*In Phys.* 290. 1–8 Diels) looks forward from the chapter's opening question without asking why Aristotle thinks the immediately preceding discussion necessitates it. Philoponus (*In Phys.* 218. 19–219. 8 Vitelli) and Mansion (A. Mansion, *Introduction à la Physique aristotélicienne* [Mansion] (Louvain and Paris, 1946), 122–4) see Aristotle as embarking on the task of differentiating natural science from the other two theoretical sciences. This, I think, gets at an important part of the truth, but still does not face the question of why this discussion is here, and why Aristotle says this is the proper place for this discussion.

[3] I say 'based in' because the connection between a natural being's matter and form and its own source of change is not quite as direct as is often assumed; Aristotle repeatedly says natural things are things with natures, and that what distinguishes things with natures from other things is the presence of a source of change in themselves (192^{b}13–16, 18–23, 32–3); and at 193^{a}29–31 he distinguishes two ways in which people refer to nature, as the primary underlying matter and as the shape and form in things that have their own source of change. The two natures are thus kept conceptually distinct from the inherent source of change, a subtlety that is also found in the lexical entry on φύσις, *Metaphysics* Δ 4. This would make sense if, as is suggested by Allan Gotthelf ('Aristotle's Conception of Final Causality',

of form should somehow take precedence over the study of matter. If we were to remove the discussion of the differences between the mathematician and the natural philosopher, the argument would then resume with Aristotle saying: 'Since, then, nature is in two ways, the matter and the form . . .', and using an *aporia* that is a direct consequence of that duality to set up a discussion of how to investigate these two natures in a unified way ($194^{a}12$– 23). A digression on how the mathematician and the natural investigator differ from one another appears to interrupt the flow of argument.

I shall argue that this is no digression and that it is critically important that Aristotle clarify the differences between the *mathēmatikos* and the *physikos* before he proceeds to discuss the question of how one science is to study two natures; and that the discussion from the beginning of book 2 to the end of our second chapter is a single, complex argument. I begin by outlining the thesis to be defended.

In *Physics* 2. 1 Aristotle introduces a distinction between a nature rooted in the underlying subject and matter, and a nature rooted in shape and form, telling us at one point that the form he is referring to is not separable other than in *logos* ($193^{b}5$). This having been done, the possibility of a serious misunderstanding of his proposal for the investigation of nature arises. Given his views about mathematical objects, it would be natural for his audience to imagine that Aristotle is proposing a bifurcation of the investigation of nature between the mathematician and the natural philosopher, the *physikos* who searches for the fundamental material constituents of things. The mathematician will study form; the *physikos* will, as he always has, study matter. Not only will this seem a perfectly natural suggestion given the variety of options available prior to Aristotle's alternative; I shall argue that certain passages in the *Posterior Analytics* could easily be taken, by an audience familiar with current discussion in the Academy, to be pointing in precisely this direction.

The chapter begins, then, by stating two reasons why this is a reasonable expectation for his audience to have—and then proceeds to argue vigorously against it. Aristotle will insist that, as he

in A. Gotthelf and J. G. Lennox (eds.), *Philosophical Issues in Aristotle's Biology* (Cambridge, 1987), 204–42 at 226 n. 51), natures are 'internalized potential-pairs'; for in this case it is not the matter and the form that are the natures but the potentials, the sources of change, possessed in virtue of the matter and form.

understands them, formal natures will not be studied by mathematicians—even those engaged in 'the more natural of the mathematical studies', i.e. astronomy, optics, and harmonics. Yet some easy ways of drawing the boundaries between mathematics and natural science are closed to him, since unlike Plato he does not believe that mathematicians study a different realm of objects from natural scientists. Nevertheless, while the ontological source of natural and mathematical concepts is the same, Aristotle insists that the processes by which we form and define them are different.

If this account of the aims of the first part of this chapter is roughly correct, it provides a very attractive way of seeing the unity of the chapter as well. For immediately after concluding the discussion of the differences between mathematical and natural investigation, Aristotle refers back to the claim that natural objects are 'spoken of just like snub nose, but not like concavity' (194^a6–7). The fact that there are two natures, he says, might well lead one to puzzle about which one the *physikos* is to investigate. This concern about whether two natures can be investigated by a single science is still on the table and perhaps in a heightened form; for the first half of the chapter has taken an initially attractive alternative for the study of the formal nature—mathematics—*off* the table. Moreover, as Aristotle immediately goes on to say, earlier *physikoi* studied only the matter of natural things. The first half of the chapter has raised the question of who is to study natural form, given that it is not the mathematician, and has forced on Aristotle's audience the *aporia* that shapes the remainder of the chapter, the *aporia* of whether the formal and material natures can be the subject of a single investigation. It motivates us to take seriously his concern about whether a unified study of nature is possible.

Seen in this light, the chapter is closely connected to the methodological discussion at the beginning of *De anima* I. 1 (403^a22–$^b19$); to the discussion of the differences between mathematical and natural *episteme* in *Metaphysics E* 1 (1025^b18–1026^a16); and to a number of other passages that discuss the 'snub-like' nature of the objects of natural investigation.

2. Making the case

To make the case for this reading, I need to begin with some details about the first chapter of *Physics* 2; and a couple of those details require a brief reminder of the closing lines of *Physics* 1:

> As for the starting-point in virtue of the form [τῆς κατὰ τὸ εἶδος ἀρχῆς], to determine with precision whether there is one or many, and of what sort or sorts it is, is a function of first philosophy; so let us reserve this topic for the appropriate occasion. But we will speak about forms of natural and perishable things[4] in the discussions to follow. That there are starting-points, however, and what and how many in number they are, we may thus assume to be determined. Let us now proceed, beginning again from another starting-point. (192ª34–ᵇ4)

By the end of 1. 7 Aristotle is prepared to say that the starting-points of natural change are three, and that form and underlying subject are the two fundamental ones (the third being privation of form). But the question of whether form or underlying subject has a *better* claim to be called οὐσία is still on the table (191ª19–22; cf. 2. 1, 193ª9–10). Furthermore, in these closing chapters of book 1 Aristotle occasionally substitutes 'matter' for 'under-lying subject' (190ᵇ26, 192ª31–3), but here 'underlying subject' (ὑποκείμενον) refers at times to the material constituent of a com-posite (e.g. the bronze of a goblet) and at times to the composite subject underlying its attributes (e.g. the cultured human being). Whatever Aristotle may have in mind by postponing to first phi-

---

⁴ The majority of manuscripts, reflected in Bekker's printed text, have περὶ τῶν φυσικῶν καὶ τῶν φθαρτῶν εἰδῶν. Ross follows MS E, perhaps also the text read by the Greek commentators, which omits the second article and thus suggests taking the first with εἶδος. Since Aristotle does not believe that natural forms are generated (*Metaph.* Z 8, 1033ᵇ5–9, ᵇ16–21; Z 9, 1034ᵇ7–10) and the same arguments that lead to that conclusion should lead to the conclusion that they are not perishable, a reading that avoids attributing to Aristotle a belief in perishable forms is desirable, and there are two ways of doing so. One is to read the text as printed by Bekker and translate 'concerning forms of natural and perishable things', taking the genitive plural of εἶδος to be governed by περί and taking the adjectives φυσικόν and φθαρτόν substantivally. If one follows Ross, it is still reasonable, given Aristotle's Greek, to treat the adjectives as substantives, even in the absence of definite articles. Moreover, since Aristotle believes that there are both perishable and eternal natural things, the καί should not be rendered as 'i.e.', as it is in the Hardie and Gaye translation (R. P. Hardie and R. K. Gaye (trans.), *Physica*, in W. D. Ross (ed.), *Works of Aristotle Translated into English*, vol. ii (Oxford, 1930). The addition of 'perishable' here is probably intended to delimit the class of natural forms to those about to be discussed in book 2.

losophy[5] a discussion of whether there is one or more than one 'starting-point in virtue of the form' and what it is (or they are), it seems clear that the point of mentioning such a discussion here is to differentiate it from the discussion of forms to come, which will be restricted to 'forms of natural and perishable things'. As we proceed to book 2, then, what can be taken as settled is *that* there are three starting-points of natural change, the two primary being the underlying subject of change and the form towards which the change proceeds. Little has yet been said, however, about what it is to be a natural being, whether one or both of these starting-points constitutes the nature of a natural thing, whether one has priority over the other, or whether these principles of change are also causes of natural change.

While book 2 does, then, make a fresh start, it also moves swiftly to deal with a number of questions opened up by the conclusions of book 1.[6] It assumes that nature is a cause of certain *beings*, lists them, provides a definition of nature,[7] and uses that definition to differentiate natural from other beings. Less than a Bekker column into the discussion, he proclaims he has told us what nature is and what we mean by 'due to nature' and 'according to nature'. He derides the attempt to answer the 'whether it is' enquiry about nature—the investigation of nature is one of those where one must begin by assuming not only the significance of the term 'nature', but also that there is such a thing. One could 'prove' *that* there are natures, he says, only by starting from premises less secure than the conclusion to be proved (193^a3-9). However, the precise nature and substantial being of natural things remain, he reminds us, a topic up for grabs.[8]

---

[5] Though that it may have to do with the sense or senses in which forms can be separate is suggested by the last lines of *Phys.* 2. 2, 194^b14-15.

[6] On the question of the independence of books 1 and 2, see Ross, introduction, 4–6. In most of our manuscripts there is no connecting particle (though in MS E there is a clear attempt to tie the closing remark of book 1, about an upcoming fresh start, to the beginning of book 2, by inserting a γάρ). Ross, 499, argues that the easiest way to make sense of the ancient lists of Aristotle's works is to suppose that book 1 was originally independent.

[7] Charlton's translation of the clause beginning ὡς οὔσης τῆς φύσεως as a new sentence, opening with 'This suggests . . .', misconstrues the ὡς (Charlton, 23). There is nothing tentative about the point Aristotle is making, which is that the artefacts being discussed have a nature only in so far as they are made of elements which do. The definition of nature as an inherent source of change or rest is already assumed at 192^b14-15.

[8] The issue here—what is it about natural things that constitutes their 'nature

The first answer canvassed is that the nature and οὐσία of natural things is 'the primary constituent in each thing, in itself without structure' (193ᵃ10–11).⁹ The criterion that provides this answer with its initial plausibility is *persistence*:

. . . this seems to show that the disposition of parts customary for beds and the artistry ⟨that goes into them⟩ belong only by virtue of concurrence, and that the substantial being is that which persists uninterruptedly while being affected in these ways. (193ᵃ14–17)

On this view one or a number of the elements is the entire οὐσία, everything else either being an affection, a state, or a disposition of it/them (193ᵃ24–6).

Nature is also said to be the shape and the form that accords with the *logos* (ἡ μορφὴ καὶ τὸ εἶδος κατὰ τὸν λόγον) of the natural thing. Here he insists, by analogy with art, that what is flesh or bone potentially—absent the form identified by the defining account of flesh or bone—neither has its own nature nor exists by nature (193ᵃ31–ᵇ3). These two purported natures are at 193ᵃ28–30 and 193ᵇ3–5, given exactly parallel articulations:

Material Nature: The primary underlying matter in each of those things having a source of movement and change in themselves.

Formal Nature: The shape and form of those things having a source of movement in themselves.

But the account of Formal Nature adds one, critical, note:

So in another way nature might be the shape and form of things having a source of movement in themselves—*but form not separable other than in account.*¹⁰ (193ᵇ3–5)

and οὐσία'—is not precisely the question said to be still on the table in 191ᵃ19–22, namely the question of whether the form or the underlying subject has a better claim to the title οὐσία. But once you start with the assumptions that there are natural things and that their nature is the cause of their being the natural things they are, the questions are very closely related. Moreover, he has just put the case for the underlying subject, and is about to put the case for form.

⁹ When he summarizes the view before going on to consider form, the summary statement is 'the primary underlying matter in each of those things which have a source of movement and change in themselves'. This is critically reworded in his own voice—the substitution of 'underlying matter' for 'the primary constituent', the inclusion of the definition of nature in the statement, and the neutrality with respect to the question of whether the underlying matter might be *a* or *the* source of change.

¹⁰ I am reading κατά in κατὰ τὸν λόγον as signalling the manner in which the form

Up to this point, then, two candidates for the nature of natural things have been identified and a case made for each.[11] The remainder of the chapter provides three grounds for the priority of form.[12]

These three arguments are very different, but each points to nature as form more than as underlying matter. The first appeals to our referential practices: when we speak of 'elm' or 'elephant', we are referring to *actual* trees and pachyderms. The unstated implication is that an elm or an elephant is *actually* such in virtue of its form more than its matter. The second argument refers us back to an earlier defence of the view that underlying matter is nature, a defence that takes as an indication of a thing's nature what arises out of the thing. Suppose you start with the assumption that both artefacts and natural things are composites of matter and form, and you are asking which of these components has a better claim to the title of the nature of the thing. In the case of artefacts, if anything meets the above standard it is their matter. But in the case of at least some natural things, Aristotle argues, it is the *form* that meets the standard. That is, it is not just the material that arises from a living thing, but another living thing, one in form with the parent.[13] The third argument appeals to an alleged derivative 'process' use of the

is separable—'being separable in account' is to be contrasted with being separable in being, and the separation in question is separation from the thing of which it is the nature. It does not follow from the fact that the form has the sort of separability that an account has that one can give an account of the form that makes no reference to matter or change.

   [11] This is in line with S. Waterlow, *Nature, Change and Agency in Aristotle's Physics: A Philosophical Study* (Oxford, 1982), 57–8; it is odd, however, that she translates 193^{b}6–7 as 'Shape and form is nature *rather than* matter', since his repeated claim that there are two natures, form and matter, seems to require that we read μᾶλλον with the genitive here as 'more than'. Waterlow does not discuss chapter 2, a chapter that seems almost entirely motivated by the problem created once one acknowledges that every natural thing has both a material and a formal nature.

   [12] The different arguments are signalled grammatically by the particles γάρ (^{b}7), ἔτι (^{b}8), ἔτι δ' (^{b}12).

   [13] All the manuscripts read τέχνη at 193^{b}11. The evidence from the commentators that Ross gives for substituting φύσις for τέχνη is weak, and I think the passage makes tolerable sense without it. So Philoponus: 'For if the fact that what arises from the bed is not a bed but the matter of the bed, wood, means that matter is nature [in those artefact cases], then the fact that what arises from a man is a man and not the matter of man [in those natural cases] clearly means that form is nature; for this is what arises, as the matter does in the case of bed' (210. 5–9 Vitelli, trans. Lacey: A. R. Lacey (trans.), *John Philoponus, On Aristotle, Physics 2* [Philoponus] (London, 1993)).

term 'nature', and insists that this derivative sense is parasitic on the term's primary reference being to the *result* of the process so called.[14] Once again, it is assumed that the result is what it is in virtue of its form. None of these arguments is intended to convince you that the form is a nature of natural things, but only that if you agree that both matter and form are natures of natural things, then form is more the nature of a natural thing than matter is.

The discussion ends with an echo of the conclusion of book 1, since it reminds us that there was a sense in which the principles of natural things were two and a sense in which they were three. At the end of book 1 we were told:

It is clear that there must be something to underlie the opposites, and that the opposites must be two in number. Yet in another way that is not necessary. One of the opposites, by its absence or presence, will suffice to effect the change. (191ª4–7, trans. Charlton)

While 2. 1 concludes:

But shape and nature are spoken of in two ways, for even privation is a form in a way. But whether or not there is a lack and an opposite with respect to simple generation, we must consider later. (193ᵇ18–21)

3. The problem

What up to this point would necessitate that we immediately turn to the question of the relationship between the investigator of mathematics and the investigator of nature? The answer to that question must be approached by putting the question in context. Aristotle's treatises, whether thought of as transcripts of a series of lectures or more as 'textbooks', have a narrative structure, one which aims to start with what is familiar to the audience and move them gradually towards an increasingly sophisticated understanding of the subject being investigated. In this case Aristotle is addressing an audience that, broadly speaking, knows variants of only two models for the theoretical investigation of nature—that represented by Democritus and Empedocles, on the one hand; and that represented by

---

[14] English does the same thing with 'nature'. It would be quite 'natural' to refer to the process of development from egg to pupa to chrysalis to butterfly as 'nature at work'. But if asked about *which* nature is at work, we would surely say the nature of the butterfly.

Plato, mathematically minded members of the Academy, and perhaps certain Pythagoreans, on the other. For reasons to be discussed shortly, I am also going to suppose that his audience may have already studied 'analytics', as represented by the *Prior* and *Posterior Analytics*. If this is a fair representation of the background that Aristotle's audience brings to these texts (or lectures), then there are compelling reasons for Aristotle to take up the question of the differences between the mathematician and natural scientist at precisely this moment. I shall outline my reasons for saying this, and then provide a reading of 193ᵇ22–194ᵃ12 that strongly suggests this is precisely what motivates the passage.

Up to this point in the argument, Aristotle's defence of his own theory of nature has developed a case against the all-sufficiency of the underlying matter of a natural thing as its nature; and in favour of the natural scientist investigating, in addition to matter, another aspect of natural things, variously referred to as shape ($\mu o \rho \phi \acute{\eta}$), form ($\epsilon \hat{\iota} \delta o s$), or figure ($\sigma \chi \hat{\eta} \mu a$), as being another, and indeed perhaps a better, candidate for the nature of natural things. In his three arguments for giving priority to form as the nature of things there are hints of the account of form to come—but, I shall argue, only if you already know and understand what is coming. Otherwise, you are simply told that what a thing actually is, what it is when it is an $o \mathring{v} \sigma \acute{\iota} a$, should count as nature in the strongest sense of the term, and that it is the thing's shape ($\mu o \rho \phi \acute{\eta}$), form ($\epsilon \hat{\iota} \delta o s$), or figure ($\sigma \chi \hat{\eta} \mu a$) that determines what a thing actually is.[15]

As I noted in setting up the problem posed by this discussion (pp. 151 and 155 above), when introducing nature as form to his readers Aristotle remarks, without explanation, that the form he is considering is 'not separable other than in account [$o \mathring{v} \chi \omega \rho \iota \sigma \tau \grave{o} v$ $\mathring{o} v \mathring{a} \lambda \lambda$' $\mathring{\eta}$ $\kappa a \tau \grave{a}$ $\tau \grave{o} v$ $\lambda \acute{o} \gamma o v$]'. As Ross notes,[16] by adding this brief clause Aristotle is reminding (or alerting) his readers that the $\epsilon \hat{\iota} \delta o s$ he is discussing is not that of Plato's middle dialogues. But an important ambiguity lurks in this brief aside. For in chapter 2 (at 193ᵇ34) the properties studied by mathematicians are features of natural things, but are *separable in thought*. So, while this aside might steer a reader or listener away from the assumption that

---

[15] To be precise, the phrases used in chapter 1 are: $\mu o \rho \phi \grave{\eta}$ $\kappa a \grave{\iota}$ $\epsilon \hat{\iota} \delta o s$ at 193ᵃ30–1, ᵇ4; $\mu o \rho \phi \acute{\eta}$ at 193ᵇ11, 18, 19; $\epsilon \hat{\iota} \delta o s$ at 193ᵃ35, ᵇ1; $\sigma \chi \hat{\eta} \mu a$ at 193ᵇ9. Twice the reference to $\epsilon \hat{\iota} \delta o s$ specifies that he is thinking of $\tau \grave{o}$ $\epsilon \hat{\iota} \delta o s$ $\tau \grave{o}$ $\kappa a \tau \grave{a}$ $\tau \grave{o} v$ $\lambda \acute{o} \gamma o v$ (193ᵃ31, ᵇ1–2).

[16] Ross, 504, ad 193ᵇ4–5.

the formal natures investigated by the *physikos* are ontologically separate, it might encourage him to think that they may be most properly investigated by a distinct, mathematical science.

Aristotle is, then, rejecting full-blown materialism and is endorsing form as an alternative candidate for the nature of a natural body—a candidate there is good reason to think will be given priority over matter. The form to be investigated by natural science will not be ontologically 'separate', however, but an aspect of natural bodies variously referred to as their shape, figure, and form.[17] Guided only by what is said in chapter 1 about that option, a member of Aristotle's audience would, I suggest, have an obvious thought. Investigating nature is a hybrid project, involving the traditional *physikos* investigating the underlying subject and matter of natural things, and the mathematician investigating their shape, figure, or form. And the following passage from the *Posterior Analytics*, with which I am supposing members of his audience would be familiar, might well encourage them to think along these lines, though I do not think it forces one to do so:

The reason why differs from the fact in another way, in so far as each is studied by a different science. Such are those studies related to each other so that the one falls under the other, e.g. optical investigations are related to geometry, mechanical investigations to solid geometry, harmonic investigations to arithmetic, and the making of observations to astronomy. Some of these sciences are practically synonymous, as with mathematical and nautical astronomy, and mathematical and acoustic harmonics.[18] For here it is for the observers [τῶν αἰσθητικῶν][19] to know the fact, and for the mathematicians to know the reason why. For they possess demonstrations

---

[17] A likely source working in the Pythagorean tradition who might encourage Aristotle's audience to think in this direction is Archytas. In a recent paper Myles Burnyeat, noting that Diogenes Laertius (2. 25) attributes three books *On the Philosophy of Archytas* to Aristotle, points to similarities in the wording of certain fragments of Archytas and Aristotle's description of the subordinate sciences in *Post. An.* 1. 7–13 (M. F. Burnyeat, 'Archytas and Optics' [Optics], *Science in Context*, 18/1 (2005), 35–53 at 42). Cf. C. A. Huffman, *Archytas of Tarentum: Pythagorean, Philosopher and Mathematician King* (Cambridge, 2005), ch. 1.

[18] It is interesting to compare this passage with *Philebus* 57 A–E. Socrates there makes the point that though it is important to distinguish the 'exact' and 'philosophical' use of numbers and measurement from that of the non-philosopher, they often and confusingly go by the same name: 'there are two arts of numbering and two arts of measuring, and plenty of other kindred arts which are similarly paired as twins, though they share a single name' (54 D 5–6, trans. Hackforth).

[19] This is an unusual use of αἰσθητικός, which Aristotle typically uses substantively to refer to bodily organs, capacities of the soul, or to animals with such organs or capacities. It has been variously translated 'observers' (Ross), 'empirical observers'

of the causes, and in many cases do not know the fact, even as those who are studying the universal in many cases do not know some of the particulars because of a lack of investigation. These [investigations] are those which, while they are somehow different with respect to substantial being [οὐσίαν], make use of forms [κέχρηται τοῖς εἴδεσιν].[20] For the mathematical investigations are concerned with forms [περὶ εἴδη]; that is, they are not investigations of a certain underlying subject [καθ' ὑποκειμένου]; for even if geometrical investigations are of a certain subject, they are nevertheless not of that subject *qua* that subject. (78ᵇ36–79ᵃ11)

Slightly later, at 79ᵃ11–13, in a discussion of the hierarchy of optical investigations, Aristotle explicitly identifies the *physikos* as the one who investigates the facts and the optical scientist (using the term either in an unqualified way or with reference to mathematical optics) as the one who is concerned to know the reason why.

The focus of the last two sentences is on the 'mixed' or 'subordinate' sciences, in which features of natural phenomena studied by the student of nature are explained by appeal to arguments developed within geometry, stereometry, or arithmetic. In understand-

(Mure), 'empirical scientists' (Barnes), and 'osservatori' (Mignucci). Sir Thomas Heath (*Mathematics in Aristotle* (Oxford, 1949), 59), in an attempt to capture something of its usual force, renders it 'the business of perception'; but this (*a*) ignores the plural and (*b*) forces a most inelegant contrast with 'the mathematicians'. So reluctantly I follow Ross. The idea being conveyed is that the facts in need of explanation are acquired by investigators who rely on their perceptive capacities.

[20] There are a number of decisions that need to be made in reading the Greek here. The reference of ταῦτα at 79ᵃ7 is unclear. I take it to be picking up on the general subject under discussion, namely the different sorts of mathematical investigations being discussed. The reason most translators do not go this route is the participial clause that suggests the subject must be 'somehow different in respect of οὐσία', apparently an odd thing to say about mathematical investigations. On the other hand, if one supposes that Aristotle is *not* discussing investigations but rather the objects being investigated, it is hard to make any sense of his assertion that the subject being discussed 'makes use of forms'. Aristotle's reasoning is much easier to understand if one takes the subject to be as I have suggested. And branches of mathematics can 'differ in respect of οὐσία' if one takes οὐσία here to refer to the underlying subject, a reading supported by 79ᵃ8–10, as I discuss below. The other important decision concerns the interpretation of εἶδος in this passage. Burnyeat has argued that the *Posterior Analytics*, along with the rest of the *Organon*, eschews the matter/form distinction at the core of his natural philosophy (M. F. Burnyeat, *A Map of* Metaphysics Zeta (Pittsburgh, 2001), 8, 87). But here εἶδος appears to have the sense it has when Aristotle treats it, in *Physics* 2. 1, as interchangeable with μορφή or σχῆμα. It clearly is not being used here to refer to Platonic forms (as it is at 77ᵃ5), yet it *does* refer to items that can be present in a subject but considered apart from being in a subject. As Burnyeat notes ('Optics', 42), the phrase κέχρηται τοῖς εἴδεσιν here finds a close parallel at *Rep.* 510 D 5, where Plato is discussing the use of visible shapes by geometers.

ing the meaning of οὐσία here it is helpful to look forward to *Post. An.* 1. 27. There, in the context of giving grounds for one science being more exact or precise (ἀκριβεστέρα) than another, Aristotle distinguishes 'unit' from 'point' by saying that the unit is an οὐσία without position and the point is an οὐσία with position. In this context, then, οὐσία refers to the primary subject of the science, even if that subject is as 'insubstantial' as a point or unit. This very brief later chapter helps with the interpretation of 1. 13 in another respect as well. For it also claims that one science is more exact than another if the one is *not* καθ᾽ ὑποκειμένου while the other *is* καθ᾽ ὑποκειμένου (87ᵃ32–4)—precisely the distinction Aristotle introduces in 1. 13 to explicate the idea of a science 'concerned with forms'.

These discussions in the *Posterior Analytics* are, then, suggestive of a way of viewing the relationship between the mathematical and natural sciences. In *Post. An.* 1. 13 and 27 the investigations that are somehow different in respect of οὐσία, but make use of forms, are the subordinate sciences, such as astronomy, optics, or harmonics. Being different in respect of οὐσία may refer to differences between them and their respective mathematical foundations—geometry, stereometry, arithmetic—or it may refer to a difference among them in the subject-matter to which mathematics is being applied, i.e. to acoustical, visual, mechanical, or celestial subjects. In either case, the next sentence aims to explicate these ideas, as the γάρ indicates. These sciences *use* forms (i.e. shapes, figures, ratios) in so far as they are based on mathematical sciences, which, Aristotle tells us, are *about* forms.[21] The mathematical sciences are not, however, about forms predicated of a subject, for even if those forms in fact belong to some subject or other, geometry does not study them as such.

These passages in the *Posterior Analytics* can easily send the following message: the traditional *physikos* has been demoted; he is the under-labourer of the mathematician. And even if we allow for the fact that geometric forms are 'of a subject', geometers do not study them *as* belonging to a particular subject.[22] That is the job

---

[21] The fact that harmonics is among the sciences being discussed suggests that we should take the reference to εἶδη at least broadly enough to include ratios and proportions (recall that Aristotle's first example of the formal cause in *Phys.* 2. 3, 194ᵇ26–9, is the ratio 2 : 1). On the other hand, Aristotle's thoughts may be primarily focused on geometry, as the substitution of τὰ γεωμετρικά for τὰ μαθήματα at 79ᵃ9 suggests.

[22] *Metaph. B* (998ᵃ7–19) and *M* (1076ᵃ32–ᵇ10) describe a position in the philosophy

of those sciences that take their *propter quid* from mathematics and apply it to the *quia* discovered in the investigation of nature.

I do not want to be misunderstood here—there are ample examples in the *Posterior Analytics* of Aristotle discussing natural phenomena that are not amenable to such an understanding of natural investigation and which cry out for the sort of natural investigation towards which Aristotle is aiming.[23] I am pointing to this passage about the 'mixed' or 'subaltern' or 'subordinate' sciences to suggest an obvious and natural response to Aristotle's critique of materialist natural philosophy and his defence of the priority of form in the study of nature in the opening pages of *Physics* 2. The natural response among those who see the fundamental alternatives as between some traditional *physikē* as described in the *Phaedo* or in *Physics* 1,[24] on the one hand, and some form of Platonism or, to use Julia Annas's term, 'partial platonism',[25] on the other, would be to imagine that Aristotle is recommending that all natural study

of mathematics whereby the mathematicals are neither separate objects intermediate between forms and sensibles nor merely attributes of natural bodies, but are rather ontologically distinct objects in some way embedded within perceptual objects. Aristotle rejects this as having ontologically impossible implications, and it may well be among the positions he wants to distance himself from here. Thanks to my colleague Helen Cullyer for pointing this out to me.

[23] Thus the standard examples used during the discussion of how definition and demonstration are related in *Post. An.* 2. 1–10 are eclipses (e.g. 90ᵃ15–17, 25–30, 93ᵃ23, 30–1, 37–8, 93ᵇ5–7, 98ᵇ17–22) and thunder (93ᵃ22–3, 93ᵇ7–12, 94ᵃ3–5); in 2. 13, in discussing division as an aid to hunting the essence, he notes that whole-winged/split-winged is not an appropriate division of animal but only of *winged* animal (96ᵇ35–97ᵃ6); and in 2. 14 the discussion of constructing problems for demonstration uses only biological examples, including some requiring detailed biological knowledge such as that animals with few upper front teeth and horns also have multiple stomachs and that certain cephalopods have rudimentary skeletal structures (98ᵃ1–23). Finally, in the discussion of how to move from problems to demonstrative explanations the examples include periodic flooding (98ᵃ31), rainbows (98ᵃ28), leaf-shedding (98ᵃ35–ᵇ16, 98ᵇ36–8, 99ᵃ23–9), and longevity in quadrupeds (99ᵇ5–7). In these chapters a mathematical and a natural example are occasionally used together to illustrate the same point (e.g. 99ᵃ16–28).

[24] See the discussion of 'that wisdom they call περὶ φύσεως ἱστορία' at *Phaedo* 96 A–98 B 5; and the contrast with the Eleatics Aristotle has just finished discussing implied by the opening words of *Physics* 1. 4: ὡς δ' οἱ φυσικοὶ λέγουσι . . . In both cases the intended reference is to a group that seek material-level explanations and eschew teleology.

[25] See J. Annas, *Aristotle: Metaphysics M, N* (Oxford, 1976), 137–9. She argues that the first section of *Metaphysics M* 2 is an attack on a view, which might be neo-Pythagorean, which takes the objects studied by mathematics to be distinct constituents of the world apart from, yet 'within', the changing physical objects of our experience.

be modelled on astronomy or optics, as outlined in *Post. An.* 1. 13. The *physikos* as traditionally understood provides us with an account of natural objects as bodies constituted of various materials and looks to the mathematician to provide a formal account of these natural objects. The mathematician studies forms in abstraction; the *physikos* studies the matter and underlying subject and (perhaps) also makes use of the results of the mathematician in a study of the forms of natural things. Perhaps certain attributes will be explained by reference to their formal, mathematical structure and others by reference to the materials from which they are constituted.

Before beginning to develop his own understanding of how the natural scientist investigates both matter and form, Aristotle must disabuse his readers of this understanding of the study of nature. That is why *Physics* 2. 2 opens by claiming that the results of the discussion of the various referents of 'nature' in chapter 1 require that we next consider the ways in which the natural scientist and the mathematician differ. Once we understand those differences, one way of imagining how the two natures will be investigated, one that calls into question the unity of such an investigation,[26] will be blocked, and the way will be open for a radically different approach to the investigation of nature.

4. Blocking demotion

Up to this point I have been arguing that, on a plausible construal of Aristotle's audience as he begins his 'fresh start' in *Physics* 2. 1, his delineation of two ways in which nature is spoken leaves room for a serious misunderstanding of the science of nature he is proposing. That misunderstanding derives from a mistaken view about the relationship between mathematics and natural science, a view that one might be encouraged to believe by certain key passages in the *Posterior Analytics*. At this point Aristotle needs to clear up the question of how the modes of investigation of the mathematician and the natural scientist differ in order to foreclose that misunder-

---

[26] Recall that the general topic of *Posterior Analytics* 1. 13 is how knowledge of the fact and of the reason why differ. The subordinate sciences are discussed because they present the special problem of knowledge produced when the fact and the reason why are investigated by different sciences; cf. 78^b34–9.

standing. Mathematics, it will turn out, is not suited to investigating 'forms of natural and perishable things'.

It is of some interest, and of some importance, that this chapter not only begins by asking about the difference between the mathematician and the natural scientist—it *closes* by distinguishing the way in which form is investigated by the natural philosopher and by the first philosopher:

But it is the work of first philosophy to determine the character of the separable and what it is.[27] (194^{b}14–15)

That is, one overarching purpose of the chapter is to situate the study of *natural* form with respect to theoretical sciences.[28] And the key question will be how form, as the 'prior' nature of natural things, is to be investigated if it is *not* to be investigated by mathematics or metaphysics. Since, in the first chapter of *Physics* 2, Aristotle makes no clear distinction between shape, form, and figure, and allows that the form studied by the natural scientist is separable from its underlying subject κατὰ τὸν λόγον, his audience will view the thought that it is to be investigated by mathematics (or, depending on the character of its separability, first philosophy) as a real possibility.

We are now ready to return to the opening lines of *Physics* 2. 2, which present an *aporia* intended to make this possibility even more vivid:

Since it has been determined in how many ways nature is spoken of,[29] we need next to study in what way the mathematician differs from the natural

---

[27] The conjunction 'and' here harbours a troubling ambiguity. Aristotle may be saying that it is a task of first philosophy to investigate the manner in which the separable exists and what the separable is; or he may be distinguishing the question of how the separable exists and how 'the what is it' exists, the latter being shorthand for the topic assigned to first philosophy at *Phys.* 1. 9, 192^{a}34–6. Recalling that this paragraph opens by asking about the limitations of the natural scientist's knowledge 'of form and what something is', and answers by indicating a limited sort of separability for natural form, I am inclined to the second alternative, keeping in mind, however, that they are intimately related questions. Waterfield's translation favours the first alternative: 'Questions remain—in what sense is anything separable? What is it that is separable?—but it is the job of first philosophy to answer them' (R. Waterfield (trans., with introduction and notes by D. Bostock), *Aristotle: Physics* [Waterfield] (Oxford, 1996), 38).

[28] A point stressed by Mansion, 122–43; Simplicius and Philoponus consider the opening of *Physics* 2. 2 to be aimed at situating natural science among the theoretical sciences, yet they provide no motivation for this topic being taken up here. See n. 2 above.

[29] The λ group of manuscripts and Philoponus read λέγεται after ἡ φύσις. But

scientist (for natural bodies also have planes, solids, lines, and points, things which the mathematician investigates). Moreover, is astronomy different from or a part of natural science? For it would be odd if it were up to the natural scientist to know what the sun or the moon is, but to know none of their proper attributes, especially since those who discuss nature apparently also discuss the figure of the moon and sun, as well as whether the earth and the cosmos are spherical in form or not. (193^{b}22–30)[30]

The need to take up this issue is a consequence of the argument in chapter 1 that there are both formal and material natures, along with the absence of any clarification of what an investigation of formal natures will look like. This lack of clarification leaves open the possibility that it will be the subject of a distinct, perhaps mathematical, science. The above passage now heightens the concern by immediately blocking one response—namely, that the things that mathematicians study are *not* features of natural things. This answer will not do, Aristotle insists, because the things mathematicians investigate *are* features of natural things—not only that, but natural scientists actually study at least some of those features.

The above passage suggests that two distinct questions are being asked. The first raises a concern about whether, given that the items studied by mathematicians (points, lines, etc.) are present in the very objects studied by the *physikos*, there is a difference between them. The second is a more specific question about whether astronomy, in particular, is different from or part of natural science. The second question is not motivated solely by Aristotle's reflections on his predecessors. *De caelo* 2. 4, 286^{b}10, announces its aim to prove that 'it is necessary for heaven to have a spherical figure [σχῆμα . . . σφαιροειδές]', and 2. 14, 297^{a}8, claims it will prove the same conclusion regarding the earth.[31] The relation of astronomy

whichever text one reads, I take it that Aristotle has given us a core definition of nature (source of change and stability in the thing itself), has identified two distinct natures (underlying matter and form), and has provided arguments for giving priority to nature as form.

[30] In a rich and valuable study of this text, Ian Mueller has made a convincing case for reading ἔτι ἤ at 193^{b}25, which is found in all the manuscripts, as opposed to ἔτι εἰ ἤ adopted by Ross following a suggestion by Susemihl. As well as a penetrating treatment of the interpretations of this passage provided by Ross, Simplicius, Thomas Aquinas, and Averroes, Mueller gives a thorough analysis of the history of the printed texts and translations of 193^{b}22–194^{a}12 (I. Mueller, 'Physics and Astronomy: Aristotle's *Physics* II. 2. 193^{b}22–194^{a}12' [Mueller], *Arabic Sciences and Philosophy*, 16 (2006), 175–206.

[31] As Simplicius stresses: *In Phys.* 290. 20–4 Diels.

to natural science is raised as a *distinct* question because later in the chapter Aristotle will draw a clear, though subtle, distinction between 'the more natural of the mathematical sciences', including astronomy (194ª7–8), and the mathematical sciences *tout court*. In the end, though closely related, the answer to the question of how the *geometer* differs from the natural scientist is quite different from the answer to the question of whether *astronomy* is part of natural science or not.[32]

What is interesting about this opening passage is that the problems that are raised for differentiating mathematics and natural science are problems generated by Aristotle's own philosophy of mathematics and his cosmological practice. For that reason, variants of a Platonic or Pythagorean answer to the question are not available; the problem is urgent because the view that is taken to generate it is the view that the mathematician and the natural scientist are enquiring about features of the very same objects. It is part of the task of natural science to know what things like the sun and moon are. But it would be odd to suppose that it should know what these heavenly bodies are, but not know their proper attributes—one of the primary tasks of a science, on the *Analytics* model, is to prove that the proper attributes of a kind must belong to that kind from a knowledge of the kind's essence. Not only do other natural philosophers study things like the *figure* (σχῆμα) of the sun and moon, and ask questions about whether the earth or the whole cosmos has the *form* of a sphere (σφαιροειδής)— Aristotle himself aims to answer these questions in the *De caelo*. The worry expressed here arises from Aristotle's own theory and practice.

Given the examples that are used, one might expect Aristotle to be focused on the 'second' question, that of whether astronomy is a part of natural science or not; but in fact he begins to develop his positive answer by developing his views on the ways in which the natural scientist and the 'pure' mathematician differ, returning to astronomy when considering 'the more natural of the mathematical sciences'.

Aristotle insists that though the mathematician and the natural

[32] Note, however, that in the pairing of mathematical and observational investigations at *Post. An.* 1. 13, 78ᵇ35–9, astronomy is on the side of geometry, stereometry, and arithmetic. Similarly, 1. 14 opens by claiming that the mathematical sciences demonstrate through the first figure, and cites arithmetic, geometry, *and optics* as evidence (79ª18–21).

scientist may investigate the same objects, the ways in which they investigate these objects are fundamentally different:

> The mathematician also makes a study of these things, *but does not treat each as a limit of a natural body; nor does he study these attributes as being attributed to such bodies.* And for that reason he separates; for each of these attributes can be separated from change by thought and it makes no difference, nor does falsity arise in separating them. (193ᵇ31–5)

What he accepts from the *aporia* that suggests mathematics can in some way be identified with natural science is as critical as what he rejects. While he rejects the idea that the mathematician studies these features *as* attributes, specifically limits or boundaries, of natural substances, he nevertheless accepts the view that they *are*, ontologically, *attributes of natural bodies.* In contrast to the discussion in the *Posterior Analytics* we looked at earlier, however, he is careful *not* to make use of the language of form as a description of the relation of mathematical properties to their natural bearers—they are limits of bodies, which are among their attributes (συμβεβηκότα).³³ His positive response thus has two important features. First, he is stressing that the mathematician makes use of a special sort of *cognitive separation* in his study of certain attributes of natural body; second, he carefully avoids referring to what is cognitively separated as the form of a natural body.³⁴

A brief return to *De caelo* 2. 14 is useful here. It presents an extended argument that the earth is 'by nature spherical'—and I take 'by nature' seriously. The arguments are *natural* arguments, arguing that the earth must be spherical from premises about natural place and the tendencies of the natural elements to move towards those places. Once, however, during this argument, he refers to 'statements derived from the mathematicians concerned with astronomy' (297ᵃ3–4) in support of his argument, stressing that he is borrowing from another science. So our *Physics* passage should not be thought to argue that the *physikos* cannot provide explanations of attributes such as the spherical shape of the earth. What

---

³³ Not that this language would be inappropriate in all contexts—in a purely mathematical context where the language of intelligible matter might be acceptable, talking about the form of a triangle would not, perhaps, be out of place. But here we are discussing the proper way to study formal natures, or natural forms.

³⁴ On the crucial role of the *qua*-operator as a predicate filter in this cognitive separation, see J. Lear, 'Aristotle's Philosophy of Mathematics', *Philosophical Review*, 91 (1982), 161–92.

he could *not* do, on Aristotle's view, is use proofs that start with premisses about spheres as such to explain certain other attributes of the earth that it has because it is a sphere—*that* would be a task for the astronomer.

It is, I think, revealing of the motives lying behind our passage in *Physics* 2. 2 that the transition to comparing the way the natural scientist studies these attributes with the way the mathematician does is effected by pointing out the problems of 'those who speak of the ideas':

Yet it escapes the notice of those who speak of the ideas that they too are doing this; for they separate natural things, which are less separable than mathematical properties. (193^{b}35–194^{a}1)

The fact that the 'friends of ideas' consider natural forms[35] in separation shows us that it has escaped their notice that they are merely separating the objects of study *in thought from change*—if they realized this is what they were doing, they would realize that, while it is possible to do so in the case of mathematical attributes, you cannot separate natural forms from change without introducing serious errors, since these are capacities of natural bodies to function in various ways:[36]

[35] Aristotle refers to these 'friends of the ideas' as mistakenly separating τὰ φυσικά; but since they are assumed to be 'speaking about ideas', I take it that what they are mistakenly separating are natural forms (which after all in their view would be what natural things really are, if they really are anything). Ross claims that Aristotle is charging the Platonists with 'doing improperly with regard to τὰ φυσικά what mathematicians do rightly with regard to τὰ μαθηματικά, not charging them as he often does with asserting ontological separation for Forms' (Ross, 506–7, ad 193^{b}22–35; cf. Bostock's note in Waterfield, 239–40; and P. Pellegrin (trans. and comm.), *Aristote: Physique* [Pellegrin] (Paris, 2000), 123). But Aristotle's charge against these Platonists is rather that they fail to recognize what mathematicians are actually doing, and their attempt to separate 'naturals' is evidence of that failure. If they did realize that there was a special form of cognitive separation peculiar to mathematics, they would not make the mistake they do. And the reason why they do not realize what is going on in mathematics might well be that they think of mathematics not as based on a cognitive separation, but on a cognition of separables.

[36] In this paragraph I assume answers to two questions: what does τοῦτο at 193^{b}35 refer to? and why does Aristotle say only that τὰ φυσικά are *less separable* than τὰ μαθηματικά? I take it that what the Platonists do not understand is that in mathematics separation is the result of an act of cognition, not a mere recognition of the actual separate existence of mathematicals; it is that separation is a 'doing' that they miss. On the other hand, natural forms are only *less* separable because they are, in their own way, separable. Cf. 193^{b}3–5 and 194^{b}12. As I shall discuss shortly, I see Aristotle articulating two distinct kinds of 'abstraction' here, one appropriate for mathematics and another for natural science.

And this[37] would become clear if one were to attempt to state the definitions of these things and their attributes. For on the one hand it will be possible to give definitions of odd, even, straight, curved, and again of number, line, and figure, without change, but not of flesh, bone, and man—these things are spoken of just like snub nose, but not like concavity. (194[a]1–7)

The error of treating natural things as *equally* separable is revealed once you attend to the differences in the way concepts in the two domains are defined. The cognitive isolation involved in mathematical concept formation is an isolation of certain attributes of physical objects from change, while change is at the very heart of the science of nature. Thus in framing a definition of unit or odd in arithmetic, or line or triangle in geometry, it is as if they are eternal and immutable. But the objects investigated by natural science are essentially material bodies with their own capacities for change. To leave that out of account would be to fail to understand them at all.

This is the theme that ties this discussion to what immediately follows, and I shall return to it shortly. But it is important that we do not leave the discussion of how the natural scientists and the mathematicians differ without considering the *other* evidence that Aristotle insists points to the error of the Platonists, namely the investigations of optics, harmonics, and astronomy, the 'subordinate' sciences. Considering them returns us to the second question with which Aristotle began, whether or not astronomy is a part of natural science:

And this is also clear with respect to the more natural of the mathematical sciences,[38] e.g. optics, harmonics, and astronomy, for they are in a way the reverse of geometry. For while geometry investigates natural line, but not

---

[37] Again the precise reference of τοῦτο is not obvious. I am taking it to refer to the general idea that natural forms are less separable than the attributes separated in thought by mathematicians (cf. Pellegrin, 123 n. 4).

[38] τὰ φυσικώτερα τῶν μαθημάτων. J. Barnes (trans. and comm.), *Aristotle: Posterior Analytics*, rev. edn. (Oxford, 1993), 159, erroneously cites this passage and a number of others as saying the opposite, that these are 'the more mathematical of the natural sciences'. And as Mueller notes (Mueller, 178) while Ross translates correctly, in his commentary he makes the same error (Ross, 507). A more subtle mistake is made in the translations of Charlton ('those branches of mathematics that come nearest to the study of nature') and Waterfield ('the branches of mathematics that are closest to natural science'). Translating the comparative as if it were making a point about proximity misses Aristotle's point: these special mathematical investigations use a distinct *method*, considering certain mathematical lines *as natural*. These recent translators, along with Pellegrin ('les parties plus physique des mathématiques'), also treat optics, harmonics, and astronomy as 'branches' or 'parts' of mathematics. There is nothing in the Greek that requires that—'the more natural of the mathematical

as natural, optics studies mathematical line, however not as mathematical but as natural. (194ᵃ7–12)

What is meant by the claim that these sciences reverse the proce-dure in geometry, and why would this fact help to make the error of the Platonists clear? I take the point to be this: since ontologically speaking lines are limits of body, the geometer is, in a qualified sense, investigating natural lines. But since, for example, the properties of a curve are what they are regardless of whether it is the curve of a nose, a mollusc shell, a shoreline, or an astronomical body, one can cognitively isolate curvature from the natural contexts in which it is found, and investigate it and its properties independently of those contexts. In optics, on the other hand, you may base your proofs on geometrical propositions and constructions having to do with arcs and tangents of a semicircle or circle, that is, with those very mathematical properties of curvature; but you then must specify those arcs and tangents and semicircles as features of a particular kind of natural phenomenon.[39] Phenomena such as eclipses and rainbows cannot be discussed without such a specification, which will introduce premises regarding movement and relative spatial position. Comparing geometry with optics once again reveals the error of the friends of ideas, who think that in these studies too you can separate without loss.[40] Again, Aristotle carefully avoids the suggestion of *Post. An.* I. 13 that these subordinate sciences study the mathematical *form* as the *form* of a natural subject. But how these 'more natural of the mathematical sciences' are to be distin-guished from natural science is by no means clear at this point.

Introducing at this juncture the idea that the objects to be inves-tigated by natural science are defined 'like snub nose' rather than like 'concavity' is revealing in two respects that I will attempt to bring out during the discussion of the second, constructive part of the chapter in the next section. This concept, along with the nominalized adjective 'the snub' and the abstract noun 'snubness'

sciences' does not impose a view about how these sciences are related to geometry and arithmetic.

[39] Compare the argument against the separation of the objects of astronomy, optics, and harmonics at *Metaph.* M 2, 1077ᵃ1–8, which concludes with the thought that consistency must force the Platonists to accept natural objects such as animals that are separate from the perceptual ones.

[40] Indeed, Plato's attitude in the *Republic*, only slightly modified in *Phileb.* 57 ff., is that you gain in understanding by such separation, in view of the lack of exactness introduced by attempting to number and measure in the realm of becoming.

introduced in the very next sentence, plays both a negative and a positive role in the Aristotelian corpus. The philosophical literature on Aristotle's views about essence and definition focuses almost exclusively on its negative role of pointing to certain problems that arise when one seeks to model definitions of substances on those of *per se* attributes such as straight and curved, in which the subject (line) must appear in the definition. In *Metaphysics E* 1 and here in *Physics* 2. 2, however, 'the snub' is used as a model for how natural objects, in contradistinction from the objects of mathematics, are to be defined.[41] How these two sorts of passage are to be understood relative to one another is the topic for another occasion; but I will here suggest that even in *Physics* 2. 2 Aristotle uses it both to point out a unique feature about natural definitions and to point to a way in which this model can foster misunderstanding.

5. The unity problem

To sum up the discussion to this point: according to the interpretation of 193^{b}22–194^{a}12 on offer, Aristotle is ruling out one reasonable expectation an audience might have about how to investigate nature once presented with the idea that natural objects have two natures, the primary one being their configuration, shape, or form. Nature understood as the form of a natural object will *not* be investigated by mathematics. The mathematician cognitively isolates certain attributes from the very changes that natural science seeks to understand. Not even in the case of the 'more natural of the mathematical sciences' is it their role to study natural form. Rather, those sciences are restricted to explaining certain mathematical attributes of natural objects and processes by reference to more fundamental mathematical properties.

However, while the idea of a hybrid science of nature with mathematics investigating formal natures has been rejected, no positive picture has been presented to take its place. It is clear from the very

---

[41] There are interesting discussions of 'the snub' in D. M. Balme, 'Aristotle's Biology is not Essentialist' [Balme], in Gotthelf and Lennox (eds.), *Philosophical Issues in Aristotle's Biology*, 291–312; M. Ferejohn, 'The Definition of Generated Composites in Aristotle's *Metaphysics*' [Ferejohn], in T. Scaltsas, D. Charles, and M. L. Gill (eds.), *Unity, Identity, and Explanation in Aristotle's Metaphysics* (Oxford, 1994), 291–318; and M. L. Gill, *Aristotle on Substance: The Paradox of Unity* [Gill] (Princeton, 1989).

next lines that it is the task of the remainder of the chapter to do just that. This passage deftly imports the one positive suggestion from the first part of the chapter and uses it to raise the key problem still on the table:

> Since nature is in two ways, the form and the matter, we should study it as if we were investigating what snubness is; we should study such things neither without matter nor according to matter. For indeed someone might very well raise a problem about this investigation: since there are two natures, about which is it for the natural scientist to study? Should he study the composite of both? But still, if he studies the composite of both, he also studies each one. So then, is it for the same or for a different science to know each nature? ($194^{a}12-18$)

Recall that Aristotle thinks that the error of the Platonists becomes clear when you compare definitions of concepts such as concavity, with those of, say, flesh or bone. The latter are referred to in the way that snub noses are, rather than in the way that curvature is. He now ties the thought that natural things have two natures to that very way of differentiating natural from mathematical investigation. His only hint here, however, about what such investigations are like is that they are carried out neither without matter nor simply in accordance with matter ($194^{a}12-15$).[42] However the investigation of these two natures is to be carried out, it will not be by means of the kind of separation practised appropriately by mathematicians.

The precise form of this methodological recommendation provides us with some additional interpretative clues. The model investigation is a τί ἐστι investigation περί σιμότητος. The object of investigation is not 'snub nose', which suggests a property predicated of a subject, but the abstract property 'snubness', and we are aiming to understand its essence.[43] This suggests that natural science will study universals that will refer to natural objects *as* material/formal unities. One cannot aim to know what natural things are *qua* natural by cognitively isolating their form

---

[42] For the force of 'not without matter', compare *DA* 3. 4, $429^{b}13-14$: ἡ γὰρ σὰρξ οὐκ ἄνευ τῆς ὕλης, ἀλλ' ὥσπερ τὸ σιμόν, τόδε ἐν τῷδε; cf. *Metaph. E* 1, $1026^{a}6$.

[43] I think this passage speaks against the statement in Gill, 114–15, that 'the essence of snubness is simply concavity'. Gill recognizes that what Aristotle says in what I have referred to as the 'positive' discussions of snubness runs counter to the implication of the *aporia* in Z 5. I of course am arguing that Aristotle is aware of the limitations of 'snubness' as a model for the unity of a natural composite.

from matter and change—snubness is necessarily concave flesh and bone.[44]

While 'snubness' is a fine model for making this point (since it is both an abstract noun and refers to a composite), it fails to solve the key problem that now needs to be solved, the problem of the nature of the unity of such composites. Before turning to Aristotle's solution, it is worth considering the limitations of 'snubness' as a model for the object of natural investigation.[45]

Aristotle sometimes claims that if we were to state what snubness is it might be something like 'concavity in a nose' or 'concavity in flesh and bone'. Defined in this way, he notes, the property of 'snubness' has certain affinities to the second sort of *per se* attribute discussed in *Post. An.* 1. 4, of which 'odd' and 'even' or 'male' and 'female' are good examples.[46] A number may be odd or even, but in defining 'odd' or 'even' you must mention 'number', and in defining male and female you must mention animal. Likewise, not every nose is snub, but in defining snubness you must mention nose.

To this point, the parallel is instructive. However, the proposed definition reduces snubness to the concavity of a certain sort of matter, or material part. If that is what snubness is, however, it is strikingly different from 'odd' or 'male'. For there are an indefinite number of concave things that are not noses, and a variety of noses that are not concave. It seems that 'the snub' refers to a contingent relationship between a certain geometric shape and certain materials. And thus the question of whether the two natures Aristotle has introduced his audience to have the requisite unity to be studied by a unified science of nature is still pressing.

Moreover—to anticipate the model of the unity of a natural object that Aristotle will soon begin to sketch—snubness fails to capture the most important fact about natural unity for Aristotle, its dynamic character. It is often noted, but as often ignored, that when Aristotle stresses the differences between mathematical and natural abstractions, it is typically by stressing that the mathematician studies his objects in separation from *change*, while the natural scientist

---

[44] This is stressed at *DA* I. I, 403ᵃ25, with the pregnant phrase λόγοι ἔνυλοι, which pointedly puts matter in the adjectival position.

[45] For insightful discussion of Aristotle's use of this example to raise puzzles about definitions of natural substances in *Metaphysics Z*, see Balme, 306–12; Ferejohn, 291–318; Gill, 114–16.

[46] The *aporia* is clearly stated at *Metaph. Z* 5, 1030ᵇ14–28.

cannot, in the nature of his investigation, do that.[47] Snubness is a good model for concepts that refer to unities of shape in material; but if the unity one aims to capture is that of capacity and activity, or of body and soul, it leaves much to be desired.

This explains an initially puzzling feature of this second part of *Physics* 2. 2, that an *aporia* about which of the two natures the natural scientist should study is raised *after* the snubness model has been endorsed. The fact that you are to investigate the matter but not restrict yourself to it does not settle the question of whether it is also up to the same science to study form; that will all depend on the nature of the relationship between matter and form. As he goes on to say, even if you are convinced that the objects studied by the natural scientist are matter/form composites, it remains an open question whether the natural scientist is to investigate both *components*. That will depend on the precise nature of their relationship. After all, the problem that drove the discussion up to this point was that the mathematician and the natural scientist begin their investigations with the same composites, and the very existence of mathematics proves that you need not study a composite *qua* composite.

This *aporia* is still on the table, then, because no positive account of how to investigate objects with both formal and material natures has been offered, and the option of conceiving it as some sort of amalgam of a mathematical and a natural study has been ruled out. The 'two sciences' option is still a possibility. Aristotle seeks to overcome it by focusing on the way in which natural form and natural matter are related.[48]

---

[47] 193[b]33–5 claims that what the mathematician does is separate by thought from change (χωριστὰ . . . τῇ νοήσει κινήσεως), and that this makes no difference from the standpoint of truth and falsehood; 194[a]1–7 contrasts the definitions given by mathematicians and natural scientists in the same terms, the former stating definitions without reference to change, the latter with reference to change; cf. *Metaph.* E 1, 1026[a]3.

[48] An interesting question, raised in comments on an earlier draft by Devin Henry, is what sort of investigator it might be, if not a mathematician. Pellegrin, 124 n. 4, following Philoponus, thinks the issue is whether it is one natural science or two. This, I think, cannot be right. Aristotle nowhere suggests that there is more than one science of nature. But the *De anima* offers a clear alternative, during a discussion of the very same issue in the context of the investigation of the affections common to body and soul, and the other science considered there is referred to as dialectic. The suggestion he is countering is that the natural scientist studies the bodily side and the dialectician the formal side. Since it is clear that Aristotle's central concern in articulating an account of natural science is to ensure that it can provide a full understanding of living things, it is reasonable to see these two discussions as closely related.

Confirmation for this reading comes from the very first thing he says after raising the *aporia*:

> Now if we turn to our predecessors, it would seem that the natural scientist should study the matter (for Empedocles and Democritus touched only to a tiny extent on the form and the essence) . . . (*Phys.* 2. 2, 194ᵃ21–3)

That he chooses these predecessors, and mentions that they touch slightly on form and essence, is revealing when seen in the light of his expansion of this thought in *De partibus animalium* 1. 1. Regarding Democritus, we are there told:

> If it were by virtue of configuration [σχῆμα] that each of the animals and their parts is what it is, Democritus might be speaking correctly. . . . Yet though the configuration of a corpse has the same shape [μορφή] [as a human being], it is nevertheless *not* a human being. (640ᵇ29–35)

When Democritus does nod in the direction of form, he takes his cue from mathematics and discusses configuration. Aristotle, on the other hand, insists that Democritus fails to speak correctly because in order to give an account of the essence of an animal or its parts, you must identify its (or their) capacities to function (641ᵃ1–6).

Empedocles makes precisely the same mistake:

> For [formal] nature is a starting-point more than matter. Even Empedocles occasionally stumbles on this, led by the truth itself, and is forced to say that the being [οὐσία] and the nature [φύσις] is the ratio [λόγος], e.g. when he says what bone is. He does not say it is some one of the elements, or two or three, or all of them, but rather that it is a ratio of their mixture. (642ᵃ17–21)

Logos can refer to various things in Aristotle, of course, but I think it is pretty clear what he has in mind here. Even if one translates it as 'account', the account that Aristotle has in mind here is one that specifies a precise quantitative ratio, a *harmonia*, among the elements.[49] Thus Empedocles too, in his stumbling attempts to move beyond a purely material account of nature, stumbles towards mathematics.

Aristotle looks for inspiration in another direction. Earlier, I in-

---

[49] Cf. Simpl. *In Phys.* 300. 21 Diels (=Empedocles 31 B 96 DK): 'And kindly earth received in its broad melting-pots two parts of the glitter of Nestis out of eight, and four of Hephaestus; and they became white bones, marvellously joined by the gluing of Harmonia.'

terrupted him in mid-sentence in order to pause over his comment
about Democritus and Empedocles; the sentence continues:

> . . . however, if art imitates nature, and it is the task of the same science
> to know both the form and the matter up to a certain point (e.g. of the
> doctor to know health and also bile and phlegm, in which health resides;
> and likewise of the builder to know the form of the house and the matter,
> that it is bricks and timber; and in the same way too in the other cases),
> it would also be the task of natural science to know both natures. (*Phys.*
> 2. 2, 194ᵃ21–7)

This passage harbours a number of puzzles; the first is rarely com-
mented on, but unless dealt with renders the argument one large
petitio. The goal, specified conditionally, is to defend the thesis that
it is up to natural science to know both the formal and material
nature. But the protasis of the conditional seems to assume from
the start that it is the task of the same science to know the form and
the matter, from which one could infer directly that it is the job
of one science of nature to study the formal and material nature.
It would seem, then, that the reference of ἐπιστήμη at 194ᵃ22 must
initially be restricted to the realm of τέχνη, as indeed is implied
by the examples that are used to defend his claim—that medicine
studies both health and bodily humours and that housebuilding
studies the form of a house as well as bricks and wood. With that
restriction, we can take the argument to be: if art imitates nature,
and the student of the arts investigates and seeks to know both the
form and the matter of his art, then the student of nature must seek
to know both the form and the matter of natural things.

So spelt out, however, a second puzzling aspect of this conditional argument reveals itself. There is indeed a parallel that Aristotle often notes between art and nature, understood as the sources
and causes of artistic and natural objects respectively—indeed this
was a key feature of his development of the concept of nature as
an internal source of change in chapter 1 (cf. 192ᵇ13–33). Art is a
source of coming to be of its product, but the source is in the artist,
not in the product; nature is a source of change within the natural
thing itself. In the current passage, however, the focus is not on art
as a *cause* of health or a house, but on art as *a kind of knowledge*
possessed by the artist. But here the parallel, on which the adage
'art imitates nature' depends, breaks down. The sense in which art
imitates nature is that the artist imposes formal structure on mate-

rials in a goal-directed manner, just as the nature of a natural thing does. But while the artist is at once the repository of the requisite artistic knowledge and the agent of artistic production, the natural scientist is only a knower of natural change, not its causal source. That is why, as we know from *Metaphysics E* 1, natural science is theoretical, while arts such as medicine and housebuilding are practical. Thus while the supposed major premiss of this argument is that art imitates nature, the feature of the arts to which he draws our attention—that the craftsman knows both form and matter up to a point—is *not* an imitation of nature (which does not know anything) but an imitation of, if anything, the natural scientist.[50]

Now it is possible that this is a highly compressed argument that, if expanded, might go something like this. 'I have made the case that there are two natures, and the issue now on the table is whether there is a single science of nature that studies them both. Since art imitates nature, perhaps we can gain insight into this question by looking at the arts. Now in the arts we can see that, as in nature, there is both a formal and a material aspect to its objects. But that does not lead to two distinct areas of knowledge, one of the formal aspect and one of the material aspect. Rather it appears that, for the doctor to do his job, he needs to have knowledge of both. If that is correct, then it will be for the natural scientist to know both natures as well.' However, it must be conceded that the argument Aristotle actually gives us trades critically on an unmentioned ambiguity in the notion that art imitates nature.[51]

With that in mind, I would like to suggest that this conditional argument is not intended to convince us of its conclusion so much as to point us towards the domain of artistic production for insight into how it might be that there could be a unified understanding of a composite of matter and form. That is, I see this somewhat puzzling, conditional argument as setting up the immediately following argument, one that is not conditional and that depends heavily on some detailed discussion of craft knowledge. It is in that discussion

---

[50] However, one of the crafts used as an example is medicine, which brings us quite close to natural science: the doctor, that is, both enquires what health—a capacity of the organism to function properly—is and what bile and phlegm are since health depends on them.

[51] There are also puzzles regarding the phrase εἰδέναι τὸ εἶδος καὶ τὴν ὕλην μέχρι του. Is it only matter that is to be known 'up to a point', as Ross (508, ad 194ᵃ23) claims, or both matter and form? And in either case, does Aristotle anywhere tell us up to *what* point? The answer to the second question is yes, he apparently does at 194ᵇ9–10, and I shall return to the first question when I consider his answer.

that Aristotle begins to present the case for a revolutionary concept of the unity of natural science, a case that it will take the rest of book 2 to complete:

> Further, it is the task of the same [science?] to know that for the sake of which and the end as well as what is for the sake of these; and nature is an end and for the sake of which (for among those things of which there is some end of continuous change, this final thing is also that for the sake of which [the change occurred]) . . . (*Phys.* 2. 2, 194^{a}27–30)

After a comical aside, Aristotle goes into some detail about the various sorts of knowledge that are involved in craftsmanship, using an example familiar to readers of Plato's *Cratylus*.[52] The 'art imitates nature' adage has guided Aristotle's audience to the idea that we might gain insight by looking at art as to how form and matter are unified in such a way that they can be known by one science. He then asserts, but does not argue for, the claim that if the objects of study are teleologically organized, that is, if the objects of study undergo changes that proceed continuously to a goal, then it will be for the same science to study both the goal and what is 'for the sake of' that goal. He also asserts without argument that the nature of a natural object is a goal, a 'that for the sake of which'. It follows, then, that if natural science studies *that* nature, it must *also* study what is for the sake of that nature.[53]

Aristotle does not at this point provide an argument to convince his audience that nature is a domain that is teleologically organized; that is the explicitly stated aim of *Physics* 2. 8. With that in mind, Aristotle's next move is reasonable. He is going to lay out a familiar, teleological picture of craft production and the knowledge involved in it, and by way of two disanalogies between art and nature, sketch the radical idea that matter and form are unified in natural substances in a way that allows them to be studied by one

---

[52] See *Crat.* 390 B 11–C 1: 'SOCR. And who will direct the shipwright? HERM. The pilot'; 390 D 1–3: 'SOCR. Then the work of the carpenter is to make a rudder, and the pilot has to direct him, if the rudder is to be well made. HERM. True.' This example is one of many used to drive home the point that it is the user of a craft product who knows the appropriate form and materials (cf. 390 B 1–11) for producing his instrument and therefore must direct the craftsman. Compare *Phys.* 2. 2, 194^{b}5–7: 'The pilot knows and prescribes what the form for a rudder is, and the carpenter knows out of what sort of wood and by what changes it will be made.'

[53] Cf. D. Quarantotto, *Causa finale, sostanza, essenza in Aristotele* (Naples, 2005). Quarantotto's discussion of *Phys.* 2. 2 (165–77) is the only one I have encountered that sees a connection between the two sections of the chapter, and indeed her discussion is complementary to the argument I am presenting here.

science—unified by virtue of the form being that for the sake of which the matter comes to be and is. I say 'sketch', because this core idea of Aristotle's *Physics* is nowhere in chapter 2 stated with the clarity and elegance of its expression in this summary statement of chapter 8:

And since the nature [of a thing] is twofold, on the one hand as matter and on the other as form, and the nature as form is an end, while other things are for the sake of the end, this [nature as form] would be the cause for-the-sake-of-which. (199ᵃ30–2; cf. 200ᵃ7–15, ᵃ32–ᵇ8)[54]

The craft model will aid his audience in taking a first step towards understanding the teleological unity of natural science; but it is only in chapters 7–9 that the full picture is presented clearly.

It would take us too far afield to explore the discussion of craft production here in detail. I want to extract only two points from it, both points about the greater unity of natural objects compared with craft objects. First, craftsmen not only make their objects by informing matter in a goal-directed way—they also make their matter.[55] While he does not elaborate, Aristotle insists this is not the case with nature, where the matter is already present. Second, the objects of craft, at least in one obvious sense, are produced for the sake of the beneficiary, which, Aristotle reminds us, is only one of two ways in which the expression τὸ οὗ ἕνεκα is used.[56] This passage implies that it is in the other sense, as *the goal for which* of a change rather than as its beneficiary, that nature is τὸ οὗ ἕνεκα.

To this point, then, most of the lessons we are to draw from examining craftsmanship are by way of contrasts. Because there is a craft involved in making the matter, there may in fact be a distinction between the knowledge involved in making the matter

---

[54] The compression of Aristotle's Greek is impossible to capture in English: καὶ ἐπεὶ ἡ φύσις διττή, ἡ μέν ὡς ὕλη ἡ δ ὡς μορφή, τέλος δ αὕτη, τοῦ τέλους δὲ ἕνεκα τἆλλα, αὕτη ἂν εἴη ἡ αἰτία, ἡ οὗ ἕνεκα.

[55] We need not go into the details, but Aristotle rightly distinguishes between crafts where the material used is made from scratch (for example, bronze is a manufactured alloy of copper and tin) and those where it is rendered workable (as when timber is hewn into lumber). Ross's note on the passage (509–10) is quite helpful.

[56] Without explaining what these two ways are he refers readers to *On Philosophy* (194ᵃ35–6), a lost work widely attested in the doxographical tradition. The distinction is very briefly elaborated on at *DA* 2. 4, 415ᵇ2–3, and *Metaph.* Λ 7, 1072ᵇ2–4; it is discussed in detail in W. Kullmann, 'Different Conceptions of the Final Cause in Aristotle', in A. Gotthelf (ed.), *Aristotle on Nature and Living Things* (Pittsburgh and Bristol, 1985), 169–75.

and the knowledge of the form required for directing production—
though nothing Aristotle says suggests there is more than one craft
involved in, say, building a ship. Moreover, because the crafts aim
at bringing about results for human benefit, there is at least one
way of answering the question 'what is it for?' of a craft product
that does not identify the form to be produced.

Which brings us to the final question to be faced in this chapter—
up to *what* point is it for the natural scientist to know the form and
'what-it-is' of things (194^b9-10)?[57] Recall that the entire discussion
of whether there could be a unified understanding of both the
formal and material nature was framed as a conditional of precisely
this form: 'But if art imitates nature, and it is for the same science
to know the form and the matter up to a point . . .' (194^a21-3). When
we last visited those lines, I postponed the question of whether
the scope of 'up to a point' ranged over knowledge of the matter
alone or over both the form and the matter, except to note that Ross
was inclined towards the first option. One reason for his inclination
could well be that at first sight the passage we are about to look at
appears to be about a third question different from either of those,
namely: 'Up to what point should the natural philosopher study
the form?' There would then, on Ross's suggested reading of the
first passage, be a pleasing balance: the first conditionally endorses
studying matter up to a point, the second equally conditionally
endorses studying form up to a point. It is now time to explain why
this apparently reasonable reading cannot be correct.

The clue to the correct understanding of both passages lies in
the apparent non sequitur formed by the question posed and the
answer given:

Up to what point, then, should the student of nature know the form and the
what-it-is? Perhaps just as a doctor knows sinew and a sculptor bronze, up
to the point of knowing what each is for, and about that which is separable
in form but in matter. (194^b10-13)

The question that is posed concerns the extent of the natural scientist's knowledge of *form*, but initially it looks as if the answer
concerns the extent to which the natural scientist should know
things analogous to a craftsman's knowledge of his *matter*. But notice Aristotle's full answer: the craftsman and the natural scientist

---

[57] The text is disputed. For a good discussion of the issues and some of the
options see Ross, 510–11, ad 194^b10-13.

need to know what the relevant matter is *for*. And what is the matter for? It is for its goal, τὸ οὖ ἕνεκα. That, however, is a certain sort of knowledge of the formal nature. It is, indeed, knowledge of the form, up to a point; but also of the matter, as present and organized for the sake of the form.

Aristotle's answer, then, takes us directly back to the teleological model of unity—'it is for the same science to know that for the sake of which and the end as well as what is for the sake of these'. It is up to the natural scientist to investigate form in so far as form is identified with *the goal of certain materials* (and again we are told to look to crafts such as medicine or carpentry for a model of how this works).[58] By framing the answer in the way that he does, Aristotle underscores the way in which the teleological unity of matter and form leads to an *epistemological* unity—one enquires into natural form by asking, about things like flesh and bone, 'What are they for?' Such teleological unification is characterized clearly at *PA* 2. 1, 646[b]14–25:

And since the actions and movements present both in animals as a whole and their non-uniform parts are complex, it is necessary for their components to have distinct potentials; for softness is useful for some things, hardness for others; certain things must have elasticity, others flexibility. Thus while in the uniform parts such potentials are distributed part by part (one of them is soft while another is hard, one moist, another dry, one pliant, another brittle), in the non-uniform parts they are distributed to many and are conjoined with each other; for a different potential is useful to the hand for pressing and for grasping.[59]

What makes it necessary that a hand is composed of flesh, bone, and muscle distributed in a certain way is the complex activity for which hands are constructed.

[58] Thus we return to Ross's note suggesting that the μέχρι του at 194[a]23 'is probably meant to qualify only the knowledge of the matter, since any science should know completely the form or essence of the things studied by it' (Ross, 508). In the light of Aristotle's remarks at the end of book 1, about a 'source according to form' that needs to be considered by first philosophy, and the claim there that the discussion to follow immediately will be restricted to 'forms of natural and perishable things', it is reasonable to take Aristotle to be restricting the knowledge of form here to what a natural scientist can say about it. Moreover, the second use of μέχρι του is clearly suggesting a limitation on the natural scientist's knowledge of form (contrary to Ross's note), but one which implies as well a limitation on his knowledge of matter. So I think we must read the first passage as I have suggested earlier, with μέχρι του ranging over both form and matter.

[59] J. G. Lennox (trans. and comm.), *Aristotle: On the Parts of Animals I–IV [PA]* (Oxford, 2001), ad loc.

That may or may not be all there is to say about form, however. In the last lines of this sketch of how a science of two natures might be unified, Aristotle returns to the question of separability. After saying that the *physikos* should study form just as a doctor studies the form of sinews by asking what they are for, he adds: 'and about things which are separable in form, yet are in matter' (194^b12–13). This expression is *prima facie* odd. For the things he appears to be discussing are natural forms, and it is odd to say that forms are separable in form. However, the immediate focus is on the idea that the natural scientist is to know what natural things are in the way that the doctor is to know that for the sake of which a bodily part is as it is. The thought, then, is that one can think of the biological function formally, but it is always the function of some material body.[60] The thought goes back to the idea that the Aristotelian conception of natural science is that it studies things that are 'not without matter, but not in accordance with matter'. 'Separable in form but in matter', in other words, is the positive way of saying 'not without matter, but not in accordance with matter'. The nature of this 'separability in form' or 'in account', however, and how it differs from the 'separability in thought from change' that Aristotle grants to mathematical attributes, is not explored here. There is much more to be said about this issue, and much more that *is* said in *Metaphysics Z–H*.[61] That, I take it, is why this is knowledge of form (and matter) only up to a point, and why, however one reads them, the last lines of *Physics* 2. 2 point to issues concerning separability that are to be taken up by first philosophy.

Aristotle does not justify his focus on the crafts in these initial steps towards a teleologically unified science of nature, but I can provide a conjecture that has some initial plausibility. He wants to move us away from the idea that natural form is to be thought

---

[60] Ross, 510, ad 194^b10–13, glosses over the problem but reaches the same interpretation. The parallels between this closing section of *Physics* 2. 2 and *DA* 1. 1, 403^a25–$^b19$, are extensive and worth exploring in depth. Both take seriously the question of whether the formal and material components of a composite are to be studied by a single science or not; and both discussions revolve around questions about the nature of the separability of the objects to be investigated by the natural scientist, the mathematician, and the first philosopher (cf. 403^b9–19), as if trying to ensure a place for a distinctive, and unified, theoretical science of nature.

[61] Moreover, it is instructive to consider the differences between the discussion of living functions in the *De anima* in comparison with works such as *De partibus animalium*, *De incessu animalium*, or *De respiratione*. There are ways of discussing living form that, while acknowledging its material basis, abstract significantly from it.

of as mathematical structure, so easily separable in thought from material embodiments, towards the idea that natural form is to be thought of as the functional capacity that is the source of unity of the natural thing's materials—to identify their proper function is to explain why certain materials are present rather than others, and why they are organized in the way they are. The shift takes place, as many commentators have noted, within a comfortably Platonic environment, reminiscent of *Gorgias* or *Cratylus*;[62] and yet by the end of *Physics* 2 that environment has been transformed into something utterly alien to a Platonic investigator of nature.[63]

6. Conclusion

In *Phaedo* Socrates sees two values in the Anaxagorean natural science he imagined; the first is that it will be able to explain, by reference to the good, why it is that organisms are configured as they are and behave as they do, when they do. The other is that it can give a similar explanation for the configuration of the earth and the cosmos. Plato presents, in the *Timaeus*, a teleological science of the created cosmos wherein mathematical structure, in the form of harmony, proportion, and geometric figure, is the model of how to implement the good in matter, starting with the heavens and implemented all the way through to accounts of flesh and bone.[64]

Aristotle is developing a teleological science of nature as well.

---

[62] For the parallels in the *Cratylus* see n. 53 above. Cf. *Gorg.* 503 E–504 A: 'Look, for example, if you will, at painters, builders, shipwrights, and all other craftsmen—any of them you choose—and see how each one disposes each element he contributes in a fixed order, and compels one to fit and harmonize with the other until he has combined the whole into something well ordered and regulated.'

[63] Sean Kelsey, in commenting on an early draft of this paper, urged the view that *Laws* 10 should be seen as an important background here as well (cf. S. Kelsey, 'Aristotle's Definition of Nature', *Oxford Studies in Ancient Philosophy*, 25 (2003), 59–87 at 84–6). I have no doubt that the ideas found in *Laws* 10, e.g. at 892 A–B, express a view to which Aristotle is self-consciously offering an alternative. But I believe that alternative is already explicit in the *Timaeus*, a dialogue to which Aristotle refers constantly and repeatedly in his natural works, while the *Laws* is referred to only in his political and ethical works, and to my knowledge book 10 is never explicitly referred to.

[64] On which see T. K. Johansen, *Plato's Natural Philosophy* (Cambridge, 2004), chs. 4–5; J. G. Lennox, 'Plato's Unnatural Teleology', in D. J. O'Meara (ed.), *Platonic Investigations* (Washington, 1985), 195–218; D. Sedley, 'Teleology and Myth in the *Phaedo*', in J. J. Clearly and D. C. Shartin (eds.), *Proceedings of the Boston Area Colloquium in Ancient Philosophy, Volume V (1989)* (Lanham, Md., 1991), 359–83.

But it is one that moves the study of life to centre stage. The study of form, as that for the sake of which matter is organized as it is, is not a mathematical study, but a study of function in relation to instrument. I have argued that *Physics* 2. 1 is addressed to an audience that may hear of a study of nature that distinguishes nature as matter from nature as form and imagine a natural science looking like a subordinate mathematical science of the sort described in *Posterior Analytics* 1. 13, one involving the mathematical study of form and an 'observational' study of matter. It is to subvert those expectations and convert that audience to a different idea of natural investigation that Aristotle constructs the argument of *Physics* 2. 2 as he does.

In the process, the concept of matter as a relational concept is quietly introduced. This will be of central importance to the success of this new science of nature. Aristotle's explanatory study of the parts of animals begins, as we saw, by defending layers of teleological explanation; simple bodies combined in a certain way so that the flesh will have the appropriate capacities; uniform bodies combined in certain ways so that non-uniform organs can perform their complex functions.[65] At least in the case of the living world, teleological unity goes all the way down. In practice, it leads to recommendations such as the following:

> The central reason why previous thinkers have not discussed these things [respiration] well *is their lack of experience with the internal parts and their failure to grasp that nature produces them all for the sake of something*; for had they been seeking that for the sake of which breathing belongs to animals, and had they been investigating this with respect to the parts, e.g. gills and lung, the cause would have quickly been discovered. (*Resp.* 3, 471^{b}23–9)

Thinkers in the seventeenth century, such as Galileo and Newton, by viewing all of nature as a great, divinely designed mechanism, envisioned a future in which all of natural philosophy would take on the character of a hierarchy of subordinate mathematical sciences, with a mathematical mechanics at its core. Astronomy was already being viewed as celestial mechanics, and a similar reduction of optics and harmonics was under way. The Cartesians clearly had hopes that anatomy and physiology would rapidly fall into line, though biology to this day is unified by its interest in functional adaptation, even when those adaptations are at the molecular level. What

---

[65] *PA* 2. 1, 646^{a}24–647^{a}3, part of which is translated and discussed above, p. 181.

is now the second chapter of the second book of Aristotle's *Physics* is, I have argued, addressed to an audience that had similar expectations, encouraged perhaps by Platonic and Pythagorean views about how a science of nature that takes form seriously should be organized, or by Aristotle's account of the subordinate mathematical sciences in the *Posterior Analytics*. That audience, as it turned out, was in for a surprise.

University of Pittsburgh

BIBLIOGRAPHY

Annas, J., *Aristotle* Metaphysics *M, N* (Oxford, 1976).

Aquinas, Thomas, *Commentary on the* Posterior Analytics, trans. F. R. Larcher, OP (Albany, NY, 1970).

Balme, D. M., 'Aristotle's Biology is Not Essentialist' [Balme], in Gotthelf and Lennox (eds.), *Philosophical Issues in Aristotle's Biology*, 291–312.

Barnes, J. (trans. and comm.), *Aristotle:* Posterior Analytics, rev. edn. (Oxford, 1993).

Bekker, I. (ed.), *Aristotelis opera*, vol. i (Berlin, 1831; repr. 1970).

Burnyeat, M. F., *A Map of* Metaphysics *Zeta* (Pittsburgh, 2001).

—— 'Archytas and Optics' ['Optics'], *Science in Context*, 18/1 (2005), 35–53.

Charlton, W. (trans. and comm.), *Aristotle:* Physics *I, II*, rev. edn. [Charlton] (Oxford, 1992).

Ferejohn, M., 'The Definition of Generated Composites in Aristotle's Metaphysics' [Ferejohn], in T. Scaltsas, D. Charles, and M. L. Gill (eds.), *Unity, Identity, and Explanation in Aristotle's Metaphysics* (Oxford, 1994), 291–318.

Gill, M. L., *Aristotle on Substance: The Paradox of Unity* [Gill] (Princeton, 1989).

Gotthelf, A., 'Aristotle's Conception of Final Causality', in Gotthelf and Lennox (eds.), *Philosophical Issues in Aristotle's Biology*, 204–42.

—— and Lennox, J. G. (eds.), *Philosophical Issues in Aristotle's Biology* (Cambridge, 1987).

Hackforth, R. (trans.), *Plato:* Philebus (Cambridge, 1972).

Hardie, R. P., and Gaye, R. K. (trans.), *Aristotle:* Physica, in W. D. Ross (ed.), *The Works of Aristotle Translated into English*, vol. ii (Oxford, 1930).

Heath, T., *Mathematics in Aristotle* (Oxford, 1949).

Huffman, C. A., *Archytas of Tarentum: Pythagorean, Philosopher and Mathematician King* (Cambridge, 2005).

Johansen, T. K., *Plato's Natural Philosophy* (Cambridge, 2004).

Kelsey, S., 'Aristotle's Definition of Nature', *Oxford Studies in Ancient Philosophy*, 25 (2003), 59–87.

Kullmann, W., 'Different Conceptions of the Final Cause in Aristotle', in A. Gotthelf (ed.), *Aristotle on Nature and Living Things* (Pittsburgh and Bristol, 1985), 169–75.

Lacey, A. R. (trans.), *John Philoponus, On Aristotle, Physics 2* [Philoponus] (London, 1993).

Lear, J., 'Aristotle's Philosophy of Mathematics', *Philosophical Review*, 91 (1982), 161–92.

Lennox, J. G. (trans. and comm.), *Aristotle: On the Parts of Animals I–IV* (Oxford, 2001).

—— 'Plato's Unnatural Teleology', in D. J. O'Meara (ed.), *Platonic Investigations* (Washington, 1985), 195–218.

Mansion, A., *Introduction à la Physique aristotélicienne* [Mansion] (Louvain and Paris, 1946).

Mignucci, M. (trans.), *Aristotele: Analytici secondi* (Bari, 2007).

Mueller, I., 'Physics and Astronomy: Aristotle's *Physics* II. 2. $193^{b}22$–$194^{a}12$' [Mueller], *Arabic Sciences and Philosophy*, 16 (2006) 175–206.

Pellegrin, P. (trans. and comm.), *Aristote: Physique* [Pellegrin] (Paris, 2000).

Quarantotto, D., *Causa finale, sostanza, essenza in Aristotele* (Naples, 2005).

Ross, W. D. (ed.), *Aristotle's Prior and Posterior Analytics* (Oxford, 1949).

—— (ed. and comm.), *Aristotle's Physics* [Ross] (Oxford, 1936).

Sedley, D., 'Teleology and Myth in the *Phaedo*', in J. J. Cleary and D. C. Shartin (eds.), *Proceedings of the Boston Area Colloquium in Ancient Philosophy, Volume V (1989)* (Lanham, Md., 1991), 359–83.

Waterfield, R. (trans., with introduction and notes by D. Bostock), *Aristotle: Physics* [Waterfield] (Oxford, 1996).

Waterlow, S., *Nature, Change, and Agency in Aristotle's Physics: A Philosophical Study* (Oxford, 1982).

ARISTOTLE'S NOTION OF PRIORITY IN NATURE AND SUBSTANCE

MICHAIL M. PERAMATZIS

1. Introduction

In *Metaph.* Δ 11, 1019[a]1–4, Aristotle introduces his notion of priority in nature and substance (which for brevity's sake I shall call 'ontological priority') and sets it out in terms of the following independence claim:

> [IC] *A* is ontologically prior to *B* just in case *A can be* [εἶναι] *without B* but *B cannot be without A*.

Virtually all important commentators on the *Metaphysics* construe [IC] or other equivalent claims made elsewhere in the corpus in what Kit Fine calls 'the existential-modal' way of understanding the notion of ontological independence:[1]

> [PIE] *A* is ontologically prior to *B* if and only if *A can exist* without *B existing* but not the other way about. Or equivalently: *B cannot exist* unless *A exists* but not conversely [Priority in Existence].[2]

In what follows I shall question and, in large measure, undermine

© Michail M. Peramatzis 2008

I would like to thank David Charles and Lindsay Judson for their invaluable criticisms, objections, and suggestions. Thanks are also due to Brad Inwood and an anonymous referee of *Oxford Studies in Ancient Philosophy*. Any mistakes made in the present paper are, of course, solely due to me.

[1] K. Fine, 'Ontological Dependence' ['Dependence'], *Proceedings of the Aristotelian Society*, 95 (1995), 269–90 at 271. Fine notes that Aristotle's account of ontological priority too is couched in similar terms (270). This remark, however, is not intended as an interpretational proposal.

[2] Cf. e.g. W. D. Ross (ed. and comm.), *Aristotle's* Metaphysics [*Metaphysics*] (2 vols.; Oxford, 1924), i. 318, or C. Kirwan (trans. and comm.), *Aristotle's* Metaphysics, *Books Γ, Δ, and E* [*Γ, Δ, & E*] (Oxford, 1971), 155–6. Similarly, Stephen Makin (trans. and comm.), *Aristotle:* Metaphysics, *Book Θ* [*Θ*] (Oxford, 2006), 192, holds that 'in *Met. Δ* 11 Aristotle explains priority in nature and substance in terms

this line of interpretation. It is not my primary concern in this paper to examine in detail whether or not the modal notions of necessity or possibility are a fundamental or indispensable part of Aristotle's account of priority.[3] By contrast, I shall criticize the alleged existential aspect of his view. Some of the problems arising from favouring [PIE] as an interpretation of his notion of ontological priority run as follows:

(*a*) Aristotle himself understands Platonist ontological priority in the manner of [PIE], as asymmetric existential independence of Forms from all their sensible instances. Indeed, he frequently criticizes and condemns the Platonist position that Forms can exist without any sensibles existing but not conversely. Assuming that his own preferred candidates for primary substancehood, his substantial forms, satisfy the criterion of ontological priority, it would be implausible to hold that they are ontologically prior in the manner of [PIE], in the very same Platonist fashion which Aristotle finds problematic.

(*b*) Under the existential construal, the examples offered in several crucial places of the *Metaphysics* (e.g. *Δ* 11, *Z* 10, and *Θ* 8) turn out to be misleading or incorrect. For in some cases the putative prior items cannot actually exist without the posterior ones existing. In other cases, while ontological priority requires an asymmetric ontological independence relation, prior and posterior items can (or cannot) exist independently of each other (non-symmetrically).

of existential independence'. Charlotte Witt (*Ways of Being: Potentiality and Actuality in Aristotle's Metaphysics* [*Ways*] (Ithaca, NY, 2003), 81; see also 13, 77–8, and 138 n. 2) construes *Metaphysics Δ* 11 in the existential manner too: 'if A is prior in being to B, then A can exist without B, but B cannot exist without A' (79). A similar approach is followed by Christos Panayides ('Aristotle on the Priority of Actuality in Substance' ['Priority'], *Ancient Philosophy*, 19 (1999), 327–44 at 329), who argues that *Metaphysics Δ* 11—together with *Cat.* 12, 14ᵃ30–5, and *Metaph.* *M* 2, 1077ᵇ1–9—clearly explicates priority in substance in terms of asymmetric existential independence. Lynne Spellman's view (*Substance and Separation in Aristotle* [*Separation*] (Cambridge, 1995), 83–99) constitutes an exception to this interpretative rule: she takes Aristotelian forms to be satisfying the criterion of separateness in being, which she understands as the ontological correlate of separation in account. My interpretation of Aristotelian ontological priority as asymmetric independence in 'being what something is' resembles, in some respects, her idea (see esp. pp. 86–8). She does not, however, set out this idea in the same direction or as fully as I do. I shall not discuss her views further as my paper is concerned not with separation but with priority.

   [3] Most commentators understand Aristotle's view in the modal manner. I shall make a few brief remarks about this issue towards the end of sect. 7.

(*c*) Assuming that substantial forms must (as primary substances) fulfil the requirement of ontological priority, they must be ontologically independent of (for example) the particular composites they en-form (but not conversely). Given [PIE], however, forms straightforwardly fail to satisfy this criterion: for they cannot exist without any en-formed composites existing.

(*d*) More importantly, essences or forms are not even the kinds of entity which could exist independently of particular composites or certain types of matter. For, quite generally, essences are not themselves independently existing objects but (essential) ways or modes of being for certain objects. Further, forms in Aristotle's sublunary world are entities which are essentially or necessarily (either sort of modality will suffice for present purposes) en-mattered or which essentially or necessarily en-form particular composites. If so, they cannot exist without the relevant types of matter or without the corresponding en-formed composites existing.

Because of these and further, related problems to be discussed below, I shall argue in favour of the following alternative understanding of Aristotle's notion of ontological priority:

[PIB] A is ontologically prior to B if and only if A can be what it is independently of B being what it is, while the converse is not the case [Priority in Being what something is].

This non-existential notion of ontological priority is inspired by, and is similar to, Kit Fine's own understanding of ontological dependence and independence.[4] It is the ontological correlate of definitional priority. Aristotle himself holds that A is prior to B in account or definition just in case (the definition of) A is included in the definition of B (but not conversely).[5] The idea behind [PIB], then, is that, just as some items are defined without others but not conversely, so too some entities are what they are without others being what they are but not conversely.

---

[4] Fine clarifies his account of ontological dependence as follows: 'The notion of one object depending upon another is therefore the real counterpart to the nominal notion of one term being definable in terms of another' ('Dependence', 275). He also acknowledges the Aristotelian origins of this idea, which he traces back to the *Top.* 6. 4 and *Metaph. Z* 1, 1028ᵃ35–6 ('Dependence', 275–6).

[5] Cf. e.g. *Metaph. Z* 1, 1028ᵃ35–6, or *M* 2, 1077ᵇ3–4. The problem of whether an item is defined in terms of another item's *name alone* or in terms of another item's *whole definition* is not pertinent to my present concerns. *Metaph. Z* 1, 1028ᵃ35–6, seems to support the second option.

The advantages of [PIB] over [PIE] but also its general conceptual merits could be summarized as follows:

(*a*) While it closely parallels the nominal or linguistic notion of asymmetric independence in account or definition, the notion of [PIB] is a distinctly ontological sense of priority. For it captures the intuition that what some items are is part of what other items are, while the converse is not the case. This is particularly important in Aristotle's overall metaphysical picture as it supports the claim of forms to primary substancehood. Armed with the notion of [PIB], Aristotle can argue that essences or forms are not merely linguistic items in terms of which other items are defined or simply our ways of explaining certain types of objects, features, or phenomena. Rather, they are fundamental parts of the fabric of the world, real-world entities which make ontologically dependent items what they are. Equivalently, essences or forms are the most important or fundamental parts of what other, derivative entities are, while the converse does not hold good.

(*b*) In this understanding of [PIB] as the ontological counterpart to definitional priority, *x*'s essence or form is not any old type of entity referred to in *x*'s *definiens*. As I just noted, the entities which satisfy [PIB] are not any or all items mentioned in a putative definition of *x* but only the ones which are crucial to *x*'s being what it is, the ones that make *x* what it is. Thus, for instance, in some views of definition, the defining formulae of certain types of composite include mention of their matter or their *genus*. In the present understanding of [PIB], this need not entail that *genera* or certain types of matter are ontologically prior to composites. For, arguably, these items are not the most important part of what it is to be the relevant types of composite as they do *not* make composites of these types what they are. Rather, it would be the corresponding essences or forms which satisfy [PIB] as they play the relevant fundamental ontological role.

(*c*) In *Metaphysics Δ* 11 and in the wider context of book *Δ* but also outside this context (e.g. *Z* 10 and *Θ* 8), the arguments advanced to underpin ontological priority and the examples given to clarify this notion work successfully only against the background of [PIB].

(*d*) This non-existential notion of priority underwrites a useful ontological independence criterion for primary substancehood. For, while forms are not the type of item which could fulfil the existential version of this criterion, they are prior to composites in being what they are and can serve as primary substances.

In what follows I shall argue, first, that the formulation put for-ward at *Metaph. Δ* 11, 1019ᵃ3–4, taken by itself, is neutral or open as it can be understood either as [PIE] or as [PIB]. This open formulation, it could be claimed, supports a weak thesis about Aristotle's notion of ontological priority along the following lines:

> [WT] The discussion of *Metaphysics Δ* 11 suggests that Aristotle's view of ontological priority does not require the existential construal as the only possible interpretation. It may well be that Aristotle left conceptual space for [PIB] too; or that he took [PIE] as applying only to some items, with [PIB] applying to others; or that he did not clearly distinguish between the two, although his arguments and examples presuppose both.

My own thesis, however, is bolder than [WT]. It can be formulated in terms of the following two claims:

> [BT]₁ The discussion of *Metaphysics Δ* 11, plus some related considerations from the wider context of *Metaphysics Δ*, imply that Aristotle's notion of ontological priority works successfully if understood as asymmetric independence in being what something is. By contrast, this notion raises serious, indeed insuperable, difficulties if construed in the existential fashion.
>
> [BT]₂ Outside the context of *Metaphysics Δ*, many of Aristotle's arguments and examples seem to work well if ontological priority is [PIB], while [PIE] renders Aristotle's views false and his examples misleading or unsuccessful.

My discussion will focus on *Metaphysics Z* 10 and *Θ* 8, where [PIB] proves to be significant in the difficult cases and 'recalcitrant' examples of prior and posterior items offered in these chapters.

2. The 'neutral' or 'open' formulation of [IC]: *Metaph. Δ* 11, 1019ᵃ1–4

In *Metaph. Δ* 11, 1019ᵃ1–4, Aristotle explicates ontological priority in terms of asymmetric ontological independence. This resembles an argument offered in the *Eudemian Ethics*, 1217ᵇ10–15, where Platonic Forms are thought to be existentially prior to or independent of their sensible instances but not conversely.[6] An initial difference between the Aristotelian account and (what Aristotle takes to be) the Platonist view seems to be that, while Platonists take priority to consist in the Forms' existential independence from sensibles, Aristotle's formulation of priority in *Metaphysics* Δ 11 leaves open the question of whether the independence at issue is existential or of some other type. Indeed, if taken by itself, the open formulation of ontological priority suggests that this type of Aristotelian priority may be either [PIE] or [PIB]. If taken together with Aristotle's overall argument and related examples, however, the formulation of ontological priority works successfully only if the existential approach is rejected and replaced by an interpretation in terms of being what something is.

Priority in nature or in substance is discussed in the following passage:

Some things are called prior and posterior in this way, while others are called so in nature and substance, those for which it is possible to be without other things, but not the latter without them; this division was used by Plato. (*Metaph.* Δ 11, 1019ᵃ1–4, trans. Kirwan, modified)

It is clear that at 1019ᵃ3–4 the formulation of [IC]—the claim that *A* is ontologically prior to *B* just in case *A can be* (εἶναι) *without B* but *B cannot be without A*—is, by itself, open as to what the exact ontological relation between *A* and *B* is. For εἶναι may be taken either existentially or as meaning 'to be what something is'.[7] If so,

---

[6] The connection between priority and separation which is put forward in the *Eudemian Ethics* passage is absent from *Metaphysics* Δ 11. Gail Fine ('Separation', *Oxford Studies in Ancient Philosophy*, 2 (1984), 31–87 at 35–6 and 38) maintains that separation and ontological priority are closely related: *A* is ontologically prior to *B* iff *A* is ontologically separate from *B* but not conversely. However, she understands ontological priority in the existential manner. For the competing account, see D. Morrison, 'Separation in Aristotle's Metaphysics' ['Separation'], *Oxford Studies in Ancient Philosophy*, 3 (1985), 125–57 at 130–6. Spellman (*Separation*, 93) argues convincingly (against Morrison) that *Aristotelian* separation is clearly connected with priority, although she disassociates ontological priority from *Platonist* separation, which she takes to be the Forms' numerical distinctness from sensibles.

[7] J. Cleary (*Aristotle on the Many Senses of Priority* [*Senses*] (Carbondale, Ill., 1988), 45) does not notice this openness of the 'being without' formula as between existence and 'being what it is'. Moreover, he later construes Δ 11's priority formula in the existential way (48). However, he holds (50) that 'existence' (or 'being') has many senses. As he says, 'the trouble with using 'existence' as a translation

A can be ontologically prior to *B* either in existence, [PIE], or in being what it is, [PIB].[8]

If this is correct, Aristotelian ontological priority may be something distinct from or more liberal than Platonist existential priority.[9] More importantly, there is reason to think that Aristotelian

of εἶναι is that it gives a false impression of univocity and so tends to mislead us in interpreting Aristotle'. For this reason, he claims, it is preferable to talk about 'being' and 'modes of being' rather than 'existence'. His formulations, however, are put in terms of 'existing without'.

[8] To avoid a 'premature' objection, the following clarification is in order. In the first instance, εἶναι is open between its existential and its *predicative* uses. However, the merely predicative use (which is 'being thus-and-so' but not straightforwardly 'being what something is') would yield philosophically uninteresting results if applied to the notion of ontological priority: what would the significance be in claiming that (for example) *A* can be white without *B* being white or, for that matter, without *B* sitting, being sun-tanned etc.? Second, why would priority in 'being thus-and-so' constitute a type of priority *in nature* or *in substance*? Third, priority in 'being thus-and-so' would, presumably, be included under the type of priority that *attributes* of prior items possess, a case already treated at 1018ᵇ37–1019ᵃ1: ἔτι πρότερα λέγεται τὰ τῶν προτέρων πάθη, οἷον εὐθύτης λειότητος· τὸ μὲν γὰρ γραμμῆς καθ' αὑτὴν πάθος τὸ δὲ ἐπιφανείας. Note, however, that even in this case the prior items are not accidental attributes of any old type but belong to the relevant subjects *per se*. In the light of these considerations, it is preferable not to understand [PIB] in the merely predicative manner. If 'being thus-and-so' is equivalent to 'being ―――', where the gap could be occupied even by essential predicates, this predicative use of εἶναι includes the 'being what something is' formula too (see sect. 3). If so, it is more plausible to take [PIB] in the philosophically important sense of '*A*'s being what it is without *B* being what it is', rather than in the general predicative sense of '*A*'s being thus-and-so without *B* being thus-and-so'.

[9] In his comments on *Metaphysics* Θ 8, Panayides ('Priority', 327–8) challenges the view that priority in substance is asymmetric ontological independence and favours Aquinas' and Ross's interpretations, which explicate priority in substance in terms of completion or perfection and degrees of reality or substantiality of an entity (330–1). However, Panayides thinks that ontological independence is nothing other than *existential* independence. In this respect, his criticism does not affect my view, which does not take priority in substance to be the same as existential independence. More importantly, my interpretation accommodates the argument put forward by Aristotle in *Metaphysics* Δ 11, where priority in substance (or in nature) clearly is asymmetric ontological (but not existential) independence. Thus, for instance, Panayides argues that *Phys.* 6. 7, 260ᵇ15–19, sharply distinguishes ontological priority (which he equates with existential independence) from priority in substance: τὸ γὰρ πρῶτον . . . ἂν λέγοιτο πλεοναχῶς. λέγεται δὲ πρότερον οὗ τε μὴ ὄντος οὐκ ἔσται τἆλλα, ἐκεῖνο δὲ ἄνευ τῶν ἄλλων, καὶ τὸ τῷ χρόνῳ, καὶ τὸ κατ' οὐσίαν. If so, he concludes, priority in substance cannot be ontological (=existential) independence (336–7). My view is invulnerable to this line of criticism, given that my notion of ontological priority is not one of existential independence. Panayides, however, cannot explain why *Metaphysics* Δ 11 uses the term 'priority in substance' for the notion of ontological independence (viz. *A* can be without *B* but not conversely), which—in his view of *Physics* 6. 7—is sharply distinct from priority in

ontological priority is not Platonist *existential* priority. When Aristotle discusses Platonist priority, he does not use the term εἶναι (as he does here), which is open between [PIE] and [PIB]. He rather uses the stronger term ἀναιρεῖσθαι, which implies destruction, annihilation, or going out of *existence*. At *EE* 1217ᵇ10–12 he claims that, if a Platonic Form *X* is thus destroyed, its sensible instances are destroyed too.[10] Similarly, at *Metaph. Δ* 8, 1017ᵇ18–21, if mathematical objects or number are 'eliminated', all things are eliminated too, for the defining parts of all things are mathematical objects or number.[11] These locutions suggest that Aristotle's account of Platonist priority is one which ascribes asymmetric existential independence to Forms. But Aristotelian priority need not be taken in this narrow way. Aristotle's formulation of [IC] favours a more liberal *ontological* claim of priority, one which could be read either as [PIE] or as [PIB].[12]

If one understands Aristotelian priority in this manner, it is not difficult to see why Aristotle notes at 1019ª4 that Plato used this distinction (between ontologically prior and posterior things) without criticizing him. Aristotle takes this distinction to be useful when construed (as in the previous paragraph) more liberally than the strictly existential approach allows. Indeed, if one agrees with Aristotle that Plato used the priority relation, one will have to admit that even Plato himself could have conceived ontological priority either

substance. By contrast, as I shall argue, my interpretation can unify *Metaphysics* *Δ* 11 and *Θ* 8 without equating priority in substance (or in nature) with existential independence.

[10] The Greek phrase is ἀναιρουμένου γὰρ τοῦ μετεχομένου ἀναιρεῖσθαι καὶ τὰ μετέχοντα τῆς ἰδέας, ἃ λέγεται τῷ μετέχειν ἐκείνης.

[11] With regard to mathematical objects it is said: ὧν ἀναιρουμένων ἀναιρεῖται τὸ ὅλον; for number: ἀναιρουμένου τε γὰρ οὐδὲν εἶναι, καὶ ὁρίζειν πάντα.

[12] Stephen Makin ('What Does Aristotle Mean by Priority in Substance?' ['Priority'], *Oxford Studies in Ancient Philosophy*, 24 (2003), 209–38 at 217–21) argues that priority in nature and substance is asymmetric existential independence. Thus, he is not sensitive to the openness of εἶναι as between existence and 'being what it is'. For this reason he understands ontological priority in potentiality and actuality as existential independence by invoking considerations about generation and destruction. Moreover, he applies this construal of *Δ* 11 to *Θ* 8: he thinks that actuality is ontologically prior to potentiality (1049ᵇ10–11; 1050ª4 ff.) in the sense of existential independence which he traces in *Δ* 11. The difference between his account and mine will become clearer when I discuss *Θ* 8 in sect. 6.2: in *Θ* 8 existential priority cannot work, even if one introduces premisses concerning generation and destruction from *Δ* 11, as Makin does. Furthermore, taking *Δ* 11's ontological priority as [PIB], instead of [PIE], gives better results (or so I shall argue) in the contexts of both *Δ* 11 and *Θ* 8.

as [PIE] or as [PIB]. A possible place where the priority criterion is used by Plato might be the following passage:[13]

Thus, we should also say that the things which are known not only owe to the Good their being known, but also have their being and/or their substance [καὶ τὸ εἶναί τε καὶ τὴν οὐσίαν] in virtue of it, although the Good is not substance, but surpasses substance to a great extent in seniority and potency. (*Rep.* 509 B 6–10, my translation)

Plato thinks that the Form of the Good is prior to all other Forms in seniority or rank and potency (ὑπερέχοντος πρεσβείᾳ καὶ δυνάμει). Not only does it make all other Forms knowable; it also provides them with their being (τὸ εἶναι) and/or their substance (τὴν οὐσίαν).[14] The latter claim seems to correspond to Aristotle's notion of ontological priority. That the Form of the Good is not itself an οὐσία but is far beyond οὐσία, is a further, separate claim which need not at present concern us. The important point is that Plato's priority thesis is compatible with either [PIE] or [PIB]. Moreover, the argument offered in this passage could be understood as employing not the existential but the 'being what it is' notion of εἶναι. Thus, the Form of the Good may be responsible *for making the rest of the Forms what they are* (but not conversely), without the rest of the Forms being dependent upon the Form of the Good *for their existence.* Understood in this way, the Platonist notion of ontological priority could and should be endorsed by Aristotle. But his use of Platonist priority is determined by two factors. First, given his use of εἶναι at *Δ* 11, 1019ᵃ3, as opposed to that of ἀναιρεῖσθαι at *Δ* 8, 1017ᵇ18–21, or *EE* 1217ᵇ10–12, the formulation of the priority claim should be open between [PIE] and [PIB].[15] Second, since he denies that there

---

[13] Cleary, *Senses*, 45–6, compares Aristotle's reference to Plato's priority distinction with the Platonic method of division in the *Sophist* and the *Politicus*. In that context, genera are thought to be prior to species, because a certain species implies a certain genus but not conversely (for example, if there is a man, then there is an animal; but it is not the case that, if there is an animal, then there is a man). I prefer to compare this part of *Metaphysics Δ* 11 with the *Republic*, a Platonic work which clearly argues that the Form of the Good is superior in power and seniority to other Forms. This claim is directly relevant to the question of what οὐσία or primary reality is and so is connected with Aristotle's own discussion in *Metaphysics Δ* 11. Cleary's own references (46) to *Metaph. B* 5 and *Δ* 8 concerning the priority of number over point, of point over line, etc. are closely connected with the notion of priority discussed in the *Republic*.

[14] I am not assuming that τὸ εἶναί and τὴν οὐσίαν necessarily designate separate notions. The present argument works even if these two terms constitute a virtual hendiadys.

[15] To be sure, even the Platonist notion of priority might be taken neutrally

are any Platonic Forms, the *relata* of this type of ontological priority
cannot be the Form of the Good and all other Forms, contrary to
the claims made in the passage just quoted from the *Republic*.[16]

3. More on the distinction between existing and being what something is

Some might object that the distinction between the notions of existing and 'being what something is' is not an admissible move
to make. This objection has a *conceptual* and an *exegetical* aspect
which can be treated separately from each other. That the distinction between existence and 'being what something is' is conceptually plausible becomes clearer on the basis of Kit Fine's observation
about the difficulties that arise when one identifies the two notions:

> For it does not seem right to identify the 'being' of an object, its being
> what it is, with its existence. In one respect, existence is too weak; for there
> is more to what an object is than its mere existence. In another respect,
> existence is too strong; for what an object is, its nature, need not include
> existence as a part.[17]

This argument suggests that the notion of 'being what something
is' can be explicated independently of the notion of existence. If so,
the notion of ontological priority could be coherently distinguished
into priority in existence and priority in 'being what it is'.

between [PIE] and [PIB]. If so, in describing Platonist priority as [PIE], Aristotle
is perhaps misreading the Platonist position in a critical, even polemical, spirit.

[16] Cleary, *Senses*, 45, thinks that 'it is perhaps a little surprising to find Aristotle
apparently accepting a Platonic criterion for what is prior with respect to substance
(κατὰ οὐσίαν), especially in one of the books of the *Met*.'. But, as I shall argue,
Aristotle may be accepting the formulation of the criterion without agreeing with
Plato on *what* satisfies this criterion. Cleary himself solves this problem by claiming
(48) that, in introducing the subjecthood criterion at 1019ᵃ5–6, Aristotle keeps the
Platonist priority criterion formula ('being without') but now this is not satisfied by
Platonic Forms but by different things. For it is not Platonic Forms but particular
objects or primary substances of the *Categories* which are *Δ* 11's subjects. In my
interpretation I prefer to leave this point open: there is no reason, in *Δ* 11's context,
to favour the primacy of particular substances in the manner of the *Categories*.
The priority criterion plus the subjecthood requirement should make substance
ontologically prior, independently of whether it may be a particular substance or a
substantial form. If so, it is better to think that Aristotle uses the same Platonist
formulation of the criterion but contends that different items satisfy it; for he rejects
certain other Platonist tenets but also introduces theses of his own.

[17] Fine, 'Dependence', 274.

A consideration which suggests not only that this last distinction is conceptually legitimate but also that the notion of priority in 'being what something is' fares better than existential priority is that the latter has temporal implications which should not affect purely ontological types of priority. For instance, a thinker (especially someone holding distinctly Aristotelian views) may wish to claim that a completed house is, in some relevant ontological sense, prior to (for example) the bricks which constitute it. However, if one adopts the existential approach, one has to explain in what way the completed house could exist without the bricks existing, while the latter could not exist without the former. This seems to be a difficult task, given that the bricks can or do exist *before* the completed house exists: hence, the former seem capable of existing without the latter existing but the converse does not hold good. Further, there is not even a *prima facie* plausible reason why the bricks' *temporally* prior existence should determine whether the house is *ontologically* prior. It seems, then, that the existential construal invokes considerations of temporal priority which are either irrelevant or yield incorrect results.

The objection under discussion involves a further radical challenge. A brief but sharp way to put forward this challenge runs as follows. Assuming that the notions of existing and being what something is are distinguished and that ontological priority is accordingly understood either as [PIE] or [PIB], it still seems that items which fail to satisfy the former cannot qualify for the latter or/and conversely. If so, these two notions of priority cannot be properly demarcated independently of each other and, hence, the distinction may be groundless. Thus, for instance, my view entails that a form *F* is what it is independently of the composites it enforms being what they are but not conversely. This, it could be claimed, implies that, even if all composite *F*s cease to exist, *F* still is what it is independently of the existence of composite substances. However, the objector would argue, if there are no composite *F*s, *F* itself cannot even exist, let alone continue to be what it is.

My reply is that this objection is telling only if one assumes that the concept of 'being what something is' is essentially dependent upon the notion of existence. By contrast, my account questions and, in some measure, undermines this assumption. It may even be the case that, by *metaphysical* necessity, for a form *F* to be what it is, *F must exist*. And similarly, by metaphysical necessity, *F cannot exist* independently of (perhaps) *at least one* composite *F existing*. What follows from these two claims is only that, for a form *F* to be what it is, it is metaphysically necessary that at least one composite *F* exist. Yet by no means does this entail that *what it is to be F* consists in at least one composite *F*'s *existing*. This is the deeper motivation for my view, which argues that the notion of 'being what something is' could be explicated independently of the notion of existence. If this is correct, ontological priority can be successfully understood as [PIB], without invoking the notion of existence. Indeed, the notion of being what something is, as employed by [PIB], has the additional merit of emphasizing the purely *ontological* aspect of the priority at issue, an aspect which should not be contaminated by considerations such as the objection just raised. Contrary to the existential approach, the notion of [PIB] is not corroded by *temporal* considerations (such as the ones noted in the house-bricks example) or *numerical*, as it were, facts: how many existing composite *F*s are needed for a form *F* to exist? All such concerns are ostracized from the account of [PIB] as irrelevant to the issue of how an item qualifies as an *ontologically* basic entity.

The exegetical question of whether and in what way Aristotle himself clearly distinguished between existing and 'being what something is' is extremely important.[18] It cannot, however, be settled on the basis of *Metaphysics Δ* 11 alone. There is some evidence that the distinction is drawn elsewhere in the corpus but not in *Metaphysics Δ* 11. For instance, in the *Posterior Analytics* (2. 1, 89ᵇ32–5; 2. 2, 89ᵇ38, 89ᵇ39–90ᵃ1, 90ᵃ2–5, 32–4) Aristotle thinks that ἔστι can be used either *simpliciter* (without any predicates: ἁπλῶς καὶ μὴ τῶν ὑπαρχόντων τι) or qualifiedly (as having predicates: τὸ ὅτι ἢ εἰ ἔστιν . . . τὸ ἐπὶ μέρους; τῶν ὑπαρχόντων). The first use is exemplified by statements such as 'God is' or 'Centaur is not', which clearly have existential meaning. The second is found in claims such as '*A* is white' or 'The moon is suffering eclipse'. This second use of ἔστι as 'being thus-and-so', even if primarily predicative, includes the 'being what something is' formula too: for 'being thus-and-so' entails that ἔστι is used with a place-holder which can be filled in by predicates of any kind, even essential ones. If these two different

---

[18] There are three possible answers to this question: (1) Aristotle did not properly draw the distinction between existence and 'being what it is' *anywhere* in the corpus; (2) he did distinguish them *both* elsewhere *and* in *Metaphysics Δ* 11; (3) he made the distinction *elsewhere but not* in *Δ* 11. My argument will not be committed to any of these three alternatives.

uses of ἔστι correspond to distinct ontological notions of existing and being what something is, it is plausible to think that, at the conceptual level too, Aristotle drew the distinction between these two notions.

Moreover, quite apart from the different uses of the verb ἔστι, Aristotle argues, at *Post. An.* 2. 8, 93ᵃ14–28, that one can have *some* grasp of 'what X is' before (or independently of) establishing the existence of X (where X is a kind).[19] Similarly, at *Post. An.* 2. 2, 72ᵃ18–24, he argues that, in the context of demonstrative sciences, one needs to assume as principles both 'what it is' (τί ἐστι) or definitions (ὁρισμός) and 'that it is' (τὸ εἶναι) or hypotheses (ὑπόθεσις). These points seem to presuppose that the notions of existing and 'being what it is' are distinct: if there were no clear distinction between them, one could not have any grasp of 'what it is' before (or independently of) knowing 'that it is'; nor would one need to assume both but just one of them. The distinction seems to be drawn explicitly at 72ᵃ23–4: 'for what the unit is and that the unit is are not the same [τὸ γὰρ τί ἐστι μονὰς καὶ τὸ εἶναι μονάδα οὐ ταὐτόν].

I shall not discuss in detail these passages from the *Posterior Analytics*, as they present some difficulties which are not relevant to my present concerns. More importantly, it is not clear whether and in what measure the *Posterior Analytics* engage with the ontological issues discussed in the *Metaphysics*. It may well be that the *Analytics* are concerned with merely linguistic, predicative, or at most epistemological problems without circumscribing, or committing Aristotle to, definite metaphysical positions. It would constitute a separate project to study Aristotle's explication of and arguments for the distinction between existing and being what it is. Nevertheless, this task lies outside the scope of the present paper. It is perhaps more important to answer, not the questions of whether, where, and in what way Aristotle drew this distinction, but rather why he did not do so in the *Metaphysics*, where the notion of ontological priority plays a significant role as a criterion for primary substancehood. Again, this is not an issue which could be satisfactorily settled in a few brief remarks. One way of tackling the question might in-

---

[19] This seems to hold good at least according to some views: see e.g. D. Charles, *Aristotle on Meaning and Essence* (Oxford, 2000), 23–56; also id., 'Some Comments on Prof. Enrico Berti's "Being and Essence in Contemporary Interpretations of Aristotle"', in A. Bottani, M. Carrara, and P. Giaretta (eds.), *Individuals, Essence and Identity: Themes of Analytic Metaphysics* (Dordrecht and London, 2002), 109–26 at 114–24.

volve the idea that Aristotle's levels of discussion vary from one treatise to another or even within a single work and are layered in ways which may rule out certain otherwise pertinent or important considerations from the treatment of a topic. In particular, the intricacies of the semantics of εἶναι and the corresponding distinction between the concepts of existence and being thus-and-so constitute important problems in their own right but may not be congenial to the level of discussion or the type of argument advanced in certain parts of the *Metaphysics*. Perhaps these are issues which fall under the subject-matter of 'logical' works such as the *Analytics*.

Metaphysics Δ 11 does not, however, explicitly draw the distinction between existing and being what something is. For this reason, my argument is based on the following, non-committal claim: at *Metaph. Δ* 11, 1019ᵃ3–4, Aristotle uses εἶναι in his formulation of ontological priority in a way which is neutral or open between existence and 'being what it is' (independently of whether he clearly makes this conceptual distinction anywhere or not). However—I shall also argue—his further distinctions and examples (both in *Metaphysics Δ* 11 and elsewhere) work successfully if the εἶναι employed in his formulations is understood non-existentially. Indeed, his notion of ontological priority yields philosophically significant results only if taken as [PIB].

4. Evidence for favouring [PIB] in *Metaphysics Δ* 11

My view of *Metaphysics Δ* 11 is that the notion of [PIB] successfully accommodates the discussion in this chapter, while [PIE] faces serious problems, if it does not completely fail (see [BT]ᵢ in Section 1). My argument for this thesis is twofold:

(i) While the notions of subjecthood, potential and actual being, as introduced in *Δ* 11 and set out in the wider context of *Metaphysics Δ*, render [PIE] problematic, they work well in the framework of [PIB].

(ii) The distinctions drawn in *Metaphysics Δ* 11 between priority in respect of potential being or destruction and priority in respect of actual being or generation and the examples offered to clarify these distinctions clearly favour [PIB] as an understanding of the relevant types of ontological priority. By contrast, [PIE] does not seem to work satisfactorily.

4.1. *Ways of being and ways of being ontologically prior*

A question that is fundamental to understanding ontological priority as [PIB] is which items are prior in 'being what they are' and which are posterior to, or dependent upon, the former in this ontological but non-existential mode. A first, albeit general and somewhat vague, answer to this question would be that Aristotelian substances are ontologically prior in 'being what they are' to certain dependent items. A similar answer is given in the following passage from *Metaphysics Δ* 11:

> But since there are many ways of being, firstly, the subject is prior and for that reason substance is prior; but, secondly, in a different way potential and actual beings [are prior]; for some things are prior in potentiality, while others in actuality. (*Metaph. Δ* 11, 1019ᵃ4–8, trans. Kirwan, modified)

First, Aristotle emphasizes that there are many ways of being. The two ways of being mentioned in this passage have already been introduced in the wider context of *Metaphysics Δ* (subjecthood is treated at *Δ* 7, 1017ᵃ19–30, and *Δ* 8, 1017ᵇ13–14, 23–4, while potential and actual being are discussed at *Δ* 7, 1017ᵃ35–ᵇ9).[20] In *Δ* 7, 1017ᵃ19–22, Aristotle distinguishes between accidental and *per se* being and seems to suggest that only genuine subjects can be *per se* beings:

> Those things which are said to be *per accidens* are said so either because both belong to the same being [for example, both *just* and *musician* belong to a man; cf. 1017ᵃ15–16]; or because that [accident] belongs to a being [for example, *musician* belongs to a man; cf. 1017ᵃ13–15]; or because this being is [or exists], to which the accident belongs, and of which this [the accident] is predicated [for example, *not-white*, something which might be taken to be a *non-being*, is nevertheless said to be, because it belongs to something which *is* or *exists*; cf. 1017ᵃ18–19]. (My translation)

In all three cases, accidents are called 'beings' because they belong to a subject which, presumably, is a genuine, *per se*, being. Moreover, at 1017ᵃ22–7 the different categories are introduced as ways of *per se* being, while substance (the category signifying τί ἐστι)

---

[20] Cleary, *Senses*, 45–8, makes no reference to *Δ* 7 in connection with *Δ* 11's 'many different ways of being'.

is distinguished from non-substance categories. If one takes these two points together with the prominence given to the subjecthood criterion in $\varDelta$ 8 ($1017^{b}13-14$, $23-4$), one can explain why subjects and substances are held to be ontologically prior at $\varDelta$ 11, $1019^{a}4-6$. Further, one can specify the items which are posterior to them. Substances are ontologically prior because they are *per se* beings and ultimate subjects, to which other items belong. Further, non-substance items which belong to substances are accidental beings and so are ontologically posterior to and dependent upon substance.

It is important to note that, on this general model, essences or Aristotelian substantial forms seem to fulfil the criterion of onto-logical priority, while particular composite substances cannot do so. First, it is clear that particular composites cannot satisfy [PIE] relative to their non-substance attributes, such as the ones men-tioned in the passage from *Metaphysics* $\varDelta$ 7 just quoted. For in-stance, Socrates can exist without being walking and have another attribute instead of *being walking* but, similarly, *being walking* can exist without Socrates' existing and be an attribute of another sub-stance (e.g. Callias). Taking Socrates' walking as a particularized property which cannot exist apart from him does not solve the problem: for it is not clear whether Aristotle accepts and how he construes particularized properties.[21] Further, just as Socrates' ex-isting is necessary for the existence of some accidental attribute or other, so too the existence of the latter is necessary for Socrates'

---

[21] Even if we allow particularized non-substance properties in the ontological picture of Aristotle's *Metaphysics*, it is not obvious why they *must* belong to one particular bearer *rather than another*. Why, that is to say, a peculiar property of being walking—even if specified down to the smallest detail—cannot exist independently of Socrates' existing, as the very same particularized attribute of being walking which, however, belongs to (for example) Callias. The claim that this attribute of being walking cannot exist without Socrates' existing just because it is Socrates' own particularized property is not a satisfactory answer. More importantly, this answer does not address the further crucial question of why this attribute of being walking *cannot* belong to any other particular substance *instead of Socrates*: for the claim that this is so because this attribute belongs to Socrates alone seems, once more, to beg the question. The basic difficulty, at this juncture, is that, while particularized non-substance properties must belong to one particular bearer, there is no reason to deny that they could belong to one particular bearer instead of another. One might reply that (for example) Socrates' peculiar property of being walking cannot even be specified or referred to without mentioning the proper name or a definite description of Socrates. This, however, may merely reflect the linguistic or epistemic limitations of our ways of describing or referring to putative particularized properties. It need not imply anything about the existence conditions or the nature of these properties themselves.

existing: for he cannot exist independently of all his determinate accidental attributes. Similarly, although he can exist without some or other determinate accidental attributes (for example, he can exist as weighing 71 kg. instead of weighing 70 kg. or as being tanned instead of being pale), he cannot exist without any determinable ones, such as *having weight* or *having complexion* etc.[22] It seems, then, that particular substances cannot be prior to their non-substance attributes in the sense that they could *exist* without them existing but not conversely.

Second, particular composite substances cannot even be prior in 'being what they are' to their non-substance attributes. If one thought that a particular substance, *A*, is ontologically prior to its non-substance attributes, *B*s, in that *A* is what it is independently of any given one or even all of *B*s being what they are, one would be unable to preserve the requisite asymmetry. For *B*s also are what they are independently of *A* being what it is: just as Socrates is what he is (a man) independently of white being what it is (a certain type of colour), so too being white is what it is independently of Socrates' being what he is.[23]

----

[22] For these problems, see M. Burnyeat *et al.*, *Notes on Z* [*Z*] (Oxford, 1979), 4–5, and D. Bostock (trans. and comm.), *Aristotle: Metaphysics Books Z and H* [*Z & H*] (Oxford, 1994), 58–60. The last two points suggest that Aristotle's particular substances are not bare particulars from which all attributes can be removed. According to some commentators (W. Charlton, *Aristotle's Physics I, II* (Oxford, 1970), 136–8; M. L. Gill, *Aristotle on Substance: The Paradox of Unity* [*Substance*] (Princeton, 1989), 26–31; T. Maudlin 'Substances and Space–Time: What Aristotle Would Have Said to Einstein', *Studies in the History and Philosophy of Science*, 21 (1990), 531–61 at 532 and 534–6), the claim that one cannot 'strip away' all attributes from a subject seems to be argued in *Metaphysics Z* 3. Aristotle's ontological independence requirement cannot violate *Z* 3's provisos, for otherwise the absurdity of prime matter would follow. This absurdity is not unrelated to the impossibility of bare particulars. Maudlin (538–9) claims that Aristotle's *reductio* argument in *Z* 3 shows that both prime matter and bare particulars are 'the twin monstrosities of metaphysics'. In *Z* 3 Aristotle's argument is primarily directed against prime matter but it can equally well apply to bare particulars. The basic claim of his argument, which makes both prime matter and bare particulars impossible, is that there are some attributes which are essential for the existence and being of a subject: not all attributes can be removed from it.

[23] If one held that particular substances are ontologically prior in 'being what they are' to their particularized non-substance properties, one would encounter the following difficulty: why should a peculiar property of (for example) being white depend upon Socrates' being what he is for its being the particular whiteness it is? It would be unsatisfactory to answer that this is so because this particular whiteness belongs to Socrates alone or because our way of specifying or referring to it involves (even necessarily) the proper name or a definite description of Socrates. One would need to offer a more basic reason why this particular whiteness itself is not, or even

In the light of these considerations, one is forced to conclude that priority cannot apply to particular substances relative to their non-substance attributes if conceived as capacity for being—either existing or being what it is—without them but not conversely. If so, particular substances cannot, it appears, satisfy any ontological priority requirement in the manner of [IC].[24]

cannot be, the particular whiteness it is independently of Socrates' being what he is. I do not need to answer questions of this sort as I see no reason to invoke talk of particularized non-substance properties in discussing the *Metaphysics*.

[24] These considerations suggest that the *Categories'* criteria of primacy for particular substances are problematic in the context of the *Metaphysics*. For this reason, I have restricted my treatment of ontological priority only to the *Metaphysics*, where the claim that form is the primary substance seems more promising. In the *Categories* the fundamental thesis which grounds the primacy of particular substances is that they neither are said of nor are in anything (any given one or all taken collectively?) as a subject. By contrast, other things (any given one or all taken together?) either are said of or are in particular substances (or both) as subjects (*Cat.* 2, 1^{b}3–6; 5, 2^{a}12–14; 2^{a}34–^{b}5; 2^{b}15–17). This fundamental thesis of subjecthood seems to explain the ontological priority or independence of particular substances: because they are basic subjects of this type, it is impossible for anything else (any given one or all of the rest?) to be, if they are not (2^{b}5–6; cf. ^{b}6–6c). There are two ways in which to understand this ontological independence claim. (*a*) Asymmetrically, by adding the rider 'but not conversely': if particular substances are not, it is impossible for anything else to be, but if anything else (assuming a weak distributive scope) is not, it is possible for particular substances to be. However, my arguments above imply that particular substances cannot unproblematically be ontologically independent *in this asymmetric manner*, either in existence or in being what they are. (*b*) Symmetrically: just as anything else cannot be, if particular substances are not, so too particular substances cannot be, if the rest (assuming a strong collective scope) are not. In this case, one could argue that the priority of particular substances is akin to the fifth type of priority in *Cat.* 12, 14^{b}10–23. This type of priority holds between items which reciprocally or symmetrically imply each other's being: if x is, then y is; and if y is, then x is. However, there is a further asymmetric causal relation between the *relata* such that (for example) x's being is the cause of y's being but not conversely. The idea, then, would be that, although particular substances and the rest of things reciprocally imply each other's being, yet particular substances' being grounds or explains, in some way, everything else's being. However promising this construal may appear, it involves serious difficulties. (i) What is caused by particular substances and in what way: the existence of everything else by their own existence or the 'being what it is' of everything else by their own 'being what they are'? (ii) What is the notion of cause at work in this type of ontological priority? (iii) As I noted above, there are scope issues in all the formulations of independence claims put forward in the *Categories*. In this case, however, this problem is even more urgent: is it *all collectively* or *any given one* of the rest of entities that particular substances are causally responsible for? (iv) Where in the *Categories*, if at all, could one find any theoretical resources to cash out this type of priority by answering any of the above questions? For example, is one allowed to bring in the *Physics'* account of the four causes to tackle question (ii) above? These questions show that the view of the *Categories* raises special problems of its own. To avoid these problems, it is preferable to restrict our discussion to the *Metaphysics*. In this work Aristotle him-

Essences or substantial forms, by contrast, cannot be 'stripped away' from a subject, for without them the subject itself would vanish. For example, Socrates (a putative subject) cannot continue to be what he is if his essence or form is 'taken away' from him.[25] Thus, after dying, Socrates is no more a human being (or the human being he is prior to his death) but, perhaps, just a corpse (or Socrates' dead body). If so, although particular substances are genuine substances of some type, they are not asymmetrically independent of their essences or forms in being what they are. This is part of the reason why the *Categories'* notion of subjecthood as applied to particular substances may not be prominent, adequate, or successful as a requirement for primary substancehood in the *Metaphysics*.

An essence or form could, however, qualify as a certain type of subject, *per se* being, and primary substance in that it is what it is independently of all composites it en-forms being what they are. Indeed, the locution 'what it is' (τί ἐστι) at *Metaph. Δ* 7, 1017ᵃ25, as applied to the category of substance seems to refer not to particular composite substances but to essences. If so, the suggestion appears to be that essences are not accidental but *per se* beings and so are ontologically prior in the manner of *Δ* 11. Thus, *Metaphysics Δ* seems not merely to remain open between [PIE] and [PIB] but strongly to undermine [PIE] in favour of [PIB]. Let me spell this out.

First, an essence or form *F* is not even the kind of entity which could exist independently of the objects whose essence or form it is. In so far as *F* is an essence, it is not itself an *object* but an essential *way of being* for the objects whose essence it is. This, I think, is part of the reason why Aristotle uses the technical term 'what-it-is-*for-something*-to-be-*F*' or similar locutions for essence (e.g. *Metaph. Z* 4, 1029ᵇ20: τί ἦν εἶναι ἑκάστῳ). Thus, *F* is not the type of entity that could exist independently of other items or in its own right, let alone in the asymmetric fashion of [PIE]. Moreover, in the Aristotelian sublunary world a substantial form is necessarily

self seems to refine or even to undermine the centrality of the *Categories'* notion of subjecthood as a criterion for primary substancehood or as ground for the ontological primacy of particular substances. For in the *Metaphysics*, it appears, he qualifies the notion of subjecthood in terms of thisness, separateness, and priority, or even favours these last three criteria over subjecthood; see e.g. *Metaph. Z* 3, 1029ᵃ5–10, 26–30. Cf. also Gill, *Substance*, 31.

[25] This holds true independently of what the essence of Socrates is (e.g. *being a human being* or *having a certain type of soul* or whatever) and of whether his essence is universal or particular.

or even essentially an entity which en-forms certain types of matter or certain types of composite. If so, an entity of this sort could not exist independently of certain types of matter or, more to the present point, without the composites it en-forms existing, especially if this independence relation is understood asymmetrically as [PIE] requires. Thus, consistently with my view of *Metaphysics Δ* 11, an essence or form *F cannot exist* if there exist no particular composite substances en-formed by *F*.

Second, as primary substance, an essence or form *F* must cover the requirement of ontological priority, even if not in its existential version. Indeed, *F* can satisfy this requirement if it is understood in terms of [PIB]: for *F* is what it is independently of all composite *F*s being what they are but not conversely. In other words, *F* makes particular substances (the entities in which *F* exists) what they are (but not conversely) and so *F* is ontologically prior to them: *what a particular substance is* depends on *what its essence or form is* but the converse is not the case. This, to be sure, does not entail that particular substances are non-substance or accidental entities in the manner of *Δ* 7's examples (*being musical* or *being white*). It implies only that they are posterior to or dependent upon their essences or forms for their being what they are.

Δ 11's second way of being (1019ᵃ6–7) is that of potential and actual being. At *Δ* 7, 1017ᵃ35–ᵇ9, Aristotle has already drawn this distinction with the help of some examples: something is said *to be* ɸ'ing (e.g. to be seeing, to be knowing or to be resting) both when it *actually* ɸ's and when it *can* ɸ. Accordingly, the distinction is between *being potentially* and *being actually* ɸ or between *what is potentially* and *what is actually* ɸ. This point is significant for present purposes. For it clearly suggests that Aristotle thinks of potential and actual beings not as items which *exist potentially or actually* but which *potentially or actually are what they are*. This is further evidence in favour of my bolder position, [BT]₁. The wider context of *Metaphysics Δ* is not simply congenial to the distinction between existing and 'being what something is'; rather, it positively introduces and works with the notion of 'being what something is'. In effect, this last point, if applied to *Δ* 11's discussion of priority, favours the notion of [PIB].

One can, on the basis of these considerations, explain Aristotle's distinction between the following two types of ontological priority:

Type (a): one of the most central ways of being is being a subject and so subjects are ontologically prior in the manner of [IC]. However, since substances must, in a way, fulfil a criterion of subjecthood, it follows that substances are ontologically prior to certain items in the manner of [IC].[26] But which are these items supposed to be? This question remains unanswered in the present context. As I suggested above, the allusion to the subjecthood requirement and the wider context of *Metaphysics Δ* 7–8 seem to favour the claim of essences or forms to being ontologically prior (in the manner of [PIB]) to particular composite substances. However, this is not unproblematic. For instance, the scope of [IC] as applied to essences or forms is not clearly determined: are they ontologically prior in 'being what they are' to *all* composites they en-form or *only to some*?[27]

Type (b): the second type of ontological priority follows from another way in which εἶναι is said. Since ontological priority is asymmetric independence with respect to εἶναι and there are potential and actual ways of εἶναι (just as *Δ* 7, 1017ᵃ35–ᵇ9, argues), it follows that things are also ontologically prior or posterior to one another in respect of potential or actual being.

4.2. *Priority in respect of potential being or destruction and actual being or generation*

An initial difference between type (a) and type (b) ontological priority is that type (a) is an asymmetric ontological independence *requirement for substancehood*, while type (b) is distinguished into two asymmetric independence relations:

(b1) priority in respect of potential being;
(b2) priority in respect of actual being.

. . . for some things are prior in potentiality, while others in actuality, as, for instance, half of a line [is prior] in potentiality to the whole line, and

---

[26] That substances must satisfy the subjecthood requirement is clear from *Metaph. H* 1 (1042ᵃ26 ff.), *Δ* 8 (1017ᵇ13–14, 23–4), and *Z* 3 (1028ᵇ36–1029ᵃ2). *Z* 3 also suggests that substances must satisfy this criterion under the constraints of *thisness, separateness*, and *priority* (1029ᵃ2–10, 27–30).

[27] Even if one successfully argued in favour of the wide scope, still the term 'all' would be ambiguous as between its collective and distributive senses. Because these pressing questions are not addressed in *Metaphysics Δ* 11, I shall leave them aside for further study. However, I shall make a few brief comments upon the scope issue in sect. 7.

the part to the whole, and matter to substance, but posterior in actuality; for when the whole is dissolved, they will be in actuality. In a certain way, then, all things called prior and posterior are said to be so in respect of these last; for it is possible for some to be without the others in respect of coming to be, as, for instance, the whole in relation to its parts, while for others in respect of destruction, as, for instance, the part in relation to the whole. Similarly in the other cases too. (*Metaph. Δ* 11, 1019ᵃ7–14, trans. Kirwan, slightly modified)[28]

I shall structure my discussion of the distinctions and examples of this passage by categorizing the different types of priority into the following two groups:

(i) priority of type (*a*), type (*b*2), and in respect of generation or coming-to-be;
(ii) priority of type (*b*1) and in respect of destruction or passing-away.

My assumption is that each of these two groups can be treated uniformly since the examples offered to clarify the different priority relations in each group are the same. The basic idea, then, is that using the same examples of prior and posterior items implies that the distinct priority relations yield equivalent results and, hence, can be treated together. It should be noted, however, that this approach does not make the relevant types of priority identical with each other: although equivalent in that they are exemplified by the same *relata*, the types of priority in each of the above two groups are not the same. One could, perhaps, put forward a related claim at the semantic level: while the corresponding relational terms (e.g. 'prior in potential being' and 'prior in passing-away') have the same reference, they do not have the same meaning.[29]

First, type (*a*) and type (*b*2) priority seem to yield the same results and, hence, to be equivalent in the sense just specified. Given the priority of substance (type (*a*)) and that in respect of actual being (type (*b*2)), substance items (such as whole lines, wholes in

---

[28] In the appendix I shall discuss in some detail the textual and interpretative issues arising from this passage and *Metaph. Δ* 11, 1019ᵃ1–14, as a whole.

[29] Compare this case with the following example: although both 'Socrates' and 'Plato's teacher' have the same reference, they are not identical expressions as the former is a proper name, the latter a definite description. Similarly, although both 'prior in respect of potential being' and 'prior in respect of passing-away' refer to (for example) parts relative to wholes or segments relative to lines, they do not have the same meaning.

general, and substances) are ontologically prior to non-substance items (such as segments of lines, parts of wholes, and matter). In effect, both criteria—type (*a*) and type (*b2*) priority—seem to be satisfied by substance. If so, these two types of ontological priority could function equivalently *as substancehood requirements*.

Ontological priority of type (*b1*), by contrast, reverses the relation between substance and non-substance items. Given this criterion of ontological priority in respect of potential being, segments, parts, and matter are held to be ontologically prior to whole lines, wholes in general, and substance respectively. This implies that—whatever its other merits—type (*b1*) ontological priority is *not* a successful substancehood requirement as it renders substance items posterior to non-substance ones.

Second, at 1019ᵃ12–14 Aristotle's examples for ontological priority in respect of generation and destruction agree with those offered for priority in respect of actual being (*b2*) and potential being (*b1*) respectively: in respect of generation (just as in respect of actual being) the whole is prior to the part, while in respect of destruction (just as in respect of potential being) the part is prior to the whole. This entails that type (*b1*) ontological priority is equivalent to priority in respect of destruction, while type (*b2*) is equivalent to priority in respect of generation. Further, since type (*a*) ontological priority (that of subjects-substances) seems equivalent to (*b2*) (in respect of actual being), while the latter yields the same results as priority in generation, it would follow that type (*a*) priority is equivalent to that in respect of generation.

The main problem, however, is to shed some light on Aristotle's specific examples, rather than merely bringing in line his abstract distinctions. In particular, the question is whether and in what way each of the items used as examples qualifies for the specified sorts of priority relative to the other items mentioned in these examples. At this juncture, my account of [PIB], the ontological parallel of definitional priority, seems helpful. It is plausible to assume that items such as half-a-line (a *segment* which is half a whole line) and a human body (a type of *matter* en-formed by the form of human being) are definitionally dependent upon items such as a *whole line* and the form of human being (a *substance* example) respectively. Given that type (*a*) ontological priority of substance over non-substance items is the ontological counterpart to this last, definitional type of priority, it is reasonable to think that:

(1) What it is to be half-a-line depends on what it is to be a whole line but not conversely.

And:

(2) What it is to be a human body depends on what it is to be (the form of) a human being but not conversely.

Clearly, the existential construal cannot straightforwardly accommodate these examples of asymmetric independence: for, just as no (en-formed) human body can exist without the form of human being existing in and en-forming it, so too the form of human being cannot exist without any (en-formed) human body existing. The mathematical example seems even more problematic: while half-a-line can exist without a whole line existing, a whole line cannot exist without one of its halves existing. For without it, a whole line ceases to exist as such and gives its place to a remaining half-segment.

Moreover, as suggested above, type (*a*) ontological priority seems equivalent to priority in respect of actual being (*b*2) and in respect of generation. The characterizations 'actual being' and 'generation' can plausibly be conceived as qualifying the way in which the prior and posterior items are what they are. In particular, as fully functional (actual) beings or as beings at the later or final stages of coming-to-be (hence, nearer to completion or 'perfection'), the whole line and the form of human being (fully realized in an appropriate type of body) are ontologically prior to half-a-line and a human body respectively, precisely in respect of actual being or generation:

(1′) What it is to be a *complete* or 'proper' half-a-line depends on what it is to be a *complete*, 'proper', or 'perfect' whole line but not conversely.

And:

(2′) What it is to be a *fully functional* human body depends on what it is to be a *fully functional* human being, one in which the relevant form is fully realized, but not conversely.

It should be emphasized that the characterizations 'complete', 'proper', 'perfect', etc. in (1′) and 'dissolved', 'truncated', etc. in (3) below are not intended to assimilate the mathematical cases to the biological ones. There is a sharp difference between the two types of case. At the same time, however, there is an analogy between them. Just as there are some complete or fully functional instances of biological kinds, similarly there are some paradigmatic or fully fledged tokens of mathematical types of entity. For example, a particular breadth- and depth-less line (a length) could be such an instance of the mathematical type of line. Further, just as there are some non-complete or not fully functional instances of biological kinds, so too there are some 'lesser' examples of mathematical types of entity. For example, a bronze circle would be a less than paradigmatic instance of the mathematical type of circle.

If these considerations are correct, the important substancehood criterion of type (*a*) ontological priority can be aligned not only with type (*b*2) priority (in respect of actual being) but also with priority in respect of generation. More importantly, all three relations can be successfully set out on the basis of the notion of [PIB], without invoking any problematic claims of independent existence. The existential construal is problematic for reasons similar to those mentioned above. First, it does not yield the desirable asymmetric independence relations: a fully functional human body cannot exist without the form of a human existing in and fully en-forming it *and conversely*. Second, the existential approach gets some of the examples in incorrect priority order: while a whole line cannot exist without one of its halves existing, half-a-line can exist without a whole line existing. More importantly, the existential construal can accommodate the characterizations 'in respect of actual being' or 'coming-to-be' only in an artificial and *ad hoc* fashion: how is one to understand the claim that (for example) a whole line can exist actually without half-a-line existing actually but not conversely, without turning it into an instance of empty scholastic jargon? If, by contrast, this claim were to be explicated in the plausible manner of (1′) and (2′), it would be misleading or incorrect also to invoke the notion of existence.

Ontological priority in respect of potential being, (*b*1), and priority in respect of destruction, however, seem to require that some items should be prior or posterior to others only as incomplete (potential) beings or as products of some type of passing-away. Candidate types of passing-away could be (for example) the complete dissolution of a thing into its parts or the detachment of a part from a whole. Thus:

(3) What it is to be a *dissolved* or *truncated* line (of a certain type) depends on what it is to be a *remaining* or *detached* half-segment (of the relevant type) but not conversely.

And:

(4) What it is to be a human being which has *passed away* or has been *maimed* depends on what it is to be a *remaining* body or *cut-off* bodily part (of the relevant type) but not conversely.

Just as a *dead* human being is *defined* in terms of a remaining body of a certain type (e.g. a corpse), so too at the *ontological* level what it is to be this type of human being which has passed away depends on what it is to be this type of remnant matter. As Aristotle remarks at 1019ᵃ10–11, when a whole or a complete and fully en-formed thing (a line, a whole, or a substance) dissolves into its parts or passes away, the relevant remaining potential being (a segment, a part, matter) *actually* is the potential being or non-functional remnant it is said to be (διαλυθέντος γὰρ κατ᾽ ἐντελέχειαν ἔσται). If so, it is ontologically prior to the whole (which is no longer what it is to be a complete, fully functional whole) in respect of incomplete, potential, being or, more relevantly, in respect of passing-away.[30] By contrast, the existential approach once more seems unsuccessful. First, similarly to the previous cases, it cannot yield the requisite asymmetry. If one held firm to the existential construal of priority in respect of potential being or passing-away, one would have to claim that a remnant body (e.g. Socrates' corpse) can exist without the corresponding dead human (dead Socrates) existing or ever having existed (but not conversely). The first option looks unpromising: for Socrates' corpse and dead Socrates reciprocally imply each other's existence. The second option is obviously false:

---

[30] An alternative (but equivalent) formulation would run as follows: after the dissolution of the whole into its parts or the detachment of a part, the relevant remnant or detached part is prior *in actual being* to the whole in that the former *actually* or *completely* is a remnant or non-functional part, while the latter depends for its being what it is upon the actual remnant or cut-off part being what it is. In this last formulation, however, we are dealing with an extremely attenuated notion of actual being in respect of which certain items are ontologically prior to others: for it is products of mutilation or of other types of passing-away which are taken as ontologically prior to other items *in respect of actual being*. For this reason, I prefer the first formulation: after mutilation, dissolution, or passing-away, detached parts, remnants, etc. are *actualized as detached parts or remnants* etc. and so are prior to other items in respect of potential being or, more to the point, in respect of passing-away.

Socrates' corpse cannot exist without dead Socrates ever having existed. To give a further example: just as a detached bodily part can exist (as non-functional or detached) independently of the mutilated human, so too a mutilated human can exist (as maimed or not fully functional) independently of the detached part. Second, the claim that half-a-line can exist potentially without the whole line existing potentially but not conversely does not seem to convey any satisfactory meaning, unless it is understood in the fashion of (3) and (4). But if so, it is preferable to employ the notion of [PIB] rather than [PIE].

What, however, is the precise ontological status of certain types of matter or material parts which are prior to the whole in respect of passing-away or potential being? For instance, after the death of a complete and functional human (a substance), his or her body is an actual, independent, but non-functional body or corpse (mere matter), not an actual and functional *human* body. Hence, it is ontologically prior in that what it is to be a *dead* or 'destroyed' human being (one which has passed away) depends on what it is to be a corpse but not conversely. To be more precise: non-en-formed matter of substances which have passed away and, quite generally, parts of wholes which have perished are ontologically prior (in respect of passing-away or potential being) only as material stuffs which sustain the corresponding fully en-formed material parts of the complete and functional wholes before the latter's passing-away.[31] Strictly speaking, after a human being has passed away, it is not his or her fully en-formed and functional *human* body which is ontologically prior to him or her in respect of passing-away but the material stuffs which constitute the human body of the fully functional living human being (prior to his or her death).[32]

---

[31] Cleary's position (*Senses*, 50) on the διαλυθέντος at 1019ª10 is similar to mine: 'material parts of a living whole cannot "be" (in the sense of having substantial form) without the whole and, hence, they are posterior in this sense of actuality. But when the whole is dissolved they are actualized *as* material parts (which is a different sense of "being"). . . . The point is that, *after* the dissolution of the whole, the material parts will no longer be the matter of *that* substance; just as the severed finger is no longer informed by the life principle that is called ψυχή' (emphasis original). On my view, after the dissolution of the living whole, what remains is the matter which sustains the bodily part or the whole body of that substance prior to its dissolution. This remnant is actual as non-functional remaining matter of that substance but not actual as en-formed and functional bodily part or body (proximate matter) of that substance.

[32] I shall come back to this point in sect. 6.1, in my discussion of some of the examples offered in *Metaphysics Z* 10.

5. Interim conclusions

The moral to be drawn from the discussion of *Metaphysics Δ* 11, 1019^{a}1–14, as a whole is that, while Aristotle's notion of ontological priority works successfully as [PIB], it raises serious or even insurmountable difficulties if construed as [PIE].

Second, given that [PIB] is the ontological correlate of definitional priority, Aristotle's remarks about priority in respect of potential being or passing-away and in respect of actual being or coming-to-be become more plausible. Just as *Metaph. Δ* 7, 1017^{a}35 ff., suggests, potential or actual beings are *not* items which *potentially or actually exist* but which *potentially or actually are what they are*. If so, ontological priority in respect of potential or actual being is best formulated in terms of [PIB], a notion which entails that the qualifications 'potential' and 'actual being' modify the ways in which the prior or posterior items *are what they are*. Thus, there is no need to introduce any unnatural assumptions about *degrees* or *modes of existence*.

Third, the notion of [PIB], as opposed to that of [PIE], could serve as a criterion which respects the claim of essences or substantial forms to primary substancehood. A substantial form *F* cannot exist if there are no particular composites which are en-formed by *F*. If so, ontological priority, understood as [PIE], cannot be satisfied by forms and, hence, cannot render them the primary substances of the *Metaphysics*. This is so, unless one holds (perhaps somewhat desperately) that forms can exist as abstract items or thoughts, independently of all particular composites existing. Alternatively, a resolute proponent of [PIE] might think that, while a form cannot exist independently of *all* particular composites it en-forms *taken together*, it can exist without *any given one* of them existing. In either way, however, the plausibility of [PIE] as a criterion for primary substancehood is significantly diminished. By contrast, [PIB] seems capable of functioning as a successful requirement for the primary substancehood of forms, without rendering them mind-dependent items or seriously restricting the scope of their independence. Just as a form is defined independently of all the particular composites it en-forms (but not conversely), so too what it is to be this type of form is independent of all those particular composites being what they are (but not conversely).

6. Test cases for [PIB]

6.1. *Right–acute angles* (Metaphysics *Z 10*)

To support my second bold thesis, [BT]₂, I shall seek to show that [PIB] is a notion which is employed, even if not directly explicated, by Aristotle even outside the context of *Metaphysics Δ* 11. To do so, I shall first examine some relevant parts of *Metaphysics Z* 10. My argument is restricted to explaining the priority relations that Aristotle posits in these contexts and to understanding them through the notion of [PIB], which seems to work better than [PIE]. In *Z* 10 Aristotle explores the priority relations between form (and its parts), matter (and its parts), and composite:

> Further, if the parts are prior to the whole, then since an acute angle is part of a right angle, and since a finger is part of a [certain type of] animal, the acute angle will be prior to the right angle, and the finger to the man. But the reverse appears to be the case; for with respect to the account the former are defined in terms of the latter, and the latter are prior in that they are [τῷ εἶναι] without the former. (1034^{b}28–32, trans. Bostock, modified)

> The parts of the formula, into which the formula is divided, are prior—some of them or all of them; and the formula of the right angle is not divided into the formula of the acute, but that of the acute into that of the right; for one who defines the acute uses the right angle; for the acute is less than the right. And, similarly, in the case of the circle and the semicircle; for the semicircle is defined through the circle and the finger through the whole; for finger is such-and-such a part of man. Thus those parts that are material, and into which a thing is divided as into its matter, are posterior; but those that are parts of the formula and of the substance which accords with the formula, are prior—some or all of them. Now, since the soul of animals (for this is the substance of the animate) is the substance which accords with the formula, i.e. the form and what-it-is-to-be such a body (at least, if each part is properly defined, it cannot be defined without its function, which it cannot have without sense perception), it follows that the parts of the soul are prior—some or all of them—to the whole compound animal, and similarly in the particular cases, while the body and its parts are posterior to this substance, and it is not this substance [the one according to the account: e.g. the soul of animals, 1035^{b}14–16] but the compound whole that is divided into these bodily parts as into its matter. (1035^{b}4–22, trans. Bostock, modified)

The argument advanced in the first passage seeks to refute the view that parts, quite generally, are prior to the whole. The type of priority is not initially specified as either definitional or ontological but lines 1034ᵇ31–2 seem to require both. The central claim which denies that parts are prior to the whole is formulated at 1034ᵇ30–2: while an acute angle is part of a right angle and a finger is part of a human, a right angle and a human are prior to an acute angle and a finger respectively, both in account and in 'being without them'. This claim indicates the correct priority relations and clearly shows that both definitional ($\tau\hat{\omega}$ $\lambda\acute{o}\gamma\omega$) and ontological ($\kappa\alpha\grave{\iota}$ $\tau\hat{\omega}$ $\epsilon\hat{\iota}\nu\alpha\iota$) priority are intended. Aristotle, however, does not specify the kinds of whole or the kinds of part he is dealing with. The second passage suggests that his argument applies to whole forms (and their parts), for they (and some or all of their parts) are prior to material parts (1035ᵇ4–6, 11–14). Thus, forms must be prior to material parts both definitionally and ontologically. It is clear from 1034ᵇ31 that forms are definitionally prior to material parts in that the latter are defined in terms of the former: an acute is defined as an angle which is less than a right one, a finger is defined as such-and-such a part of a human etc. (1035ᵇ6–11). However, it is not clear how forms are *ontologically* prior to material parts.

The claim that a right angle is ontologically prior to an acute has caused many problems to commentators. Their difficulty arises because they construe this type of ontological priority relation in the existential way. Hence, they see Aristotle as making an obvious mistake: a right angle may be defined independently of an acute (and not conversely) but cannot exist as such without an acute angle existing as one of its parts. For, if one of its parts were detached, a right angle would not exist but would, presumably, be replaced by a remaining acute angle. Conversely, there is no reason to deny that an acute angle could exist without a right angle existing.[33] However, there is no need to understand Aristotle's explication of ontological priority at 1034ᵇ31–2 in this existential way:[34] *A* is said to be

---

[33] Cf. Ross, *Metaphysics*, ii. 196; Bostock, *Z & H*, 146. My interpretation resembles a suggestion made by Burnyeat *et al.*, *Z*, 80, under (i): 'the acute could exist without the right but would not be *acute*, as goalposts can exist without footballs but are not yet *goalposts*; this seems to assimilate the acute case to the finger case' (emphasis original). My interpretation differs from this view in that I understand ontological priority on the basis of—and as the ontological counterpart to—the notion of definitional priority which is employed by Aristotle at 1034ᵇ30–1 and 1035ᵇ6–11.

[34] M. V. Wedin, *Aristotle's Theory of Substance: The* Categories *and* Metaphysics

ontologically prior to *B* just in case *A is without B* (τῷ εἶναι ἄνευ ἀλλήλων). Just like [IC] in *Metaphysics* Δ 11, this claim is neutral as between [PIE] and [PIB]. Indeed, [PIB] liberates Aristotle from the mistake that commentators ascribe to him. A right angle is what it is without an acute being what it is but not conversely. This holds true because of the connection between definitional and ontological considerations: just as a right angle is defined independently of an acute but not conversely, so too the former is what it is independently of the latter being what it is but not conversely.

One objection to my view might be that the existential construal appears to work in the finger–human case: a human can exist independently of his or her finger existing but a finger cannot exist (as a fully functional finger) without a human existing. Why should Aristotle here introduce the notion of [PIB], instead of that of [PIE], as I took him to be doing? An initial answer is that [PIB] works successfully in the acute–right angle case, while [PIE] does not. More importantly, [PIE] seems unsuccessful even in the finger–human example as it does not render the ontological priority relation asymmetric. A fully functional, complete human cannot exist (as such) without his or her finger existing: for without his or her finger, he or she would not be complete but mutilated. And conversely, a fully functional finger cannot exist (as such) if detached from a human. Further, just as a mutilated human can exist (as such) without his or her detached finger, so too his or her detached and non-functional finger can exist (as such) without the corresponding maimed human. Thus, the notion of [PIE] is problematic independently of our example of choice.

In both cases of the finger–human example just discussed I added the qualifications 'fully functional' or 'complete' and 'detached' or 'non-functional'. This serves as a way of connecting the discussion of *Metaphysics Z* 10 with Δ 11's distinction between priority in respect of actual being or coming-to-be and in respect of potential being or passing-away. Consistently with Δ 11, the example offered at *Z* 10, 1034^{b}30 and 1035^{b}11, entails that a whole, complete, and

---

Zeta (Oxford, 2000), 301–2, takes the acute–right angle case as an instance of existential independence and so faces the above difficulties. His formulation runs as follows:

x is defined in terms of *y* & *x* cannot exist without *y* ↔ *y* is prior to *x*.

In the second conjunct of the left-hand side of the bi-conditional, the existential condition cannot be satisfied by forms. Hence, I propose to modify this conjunct into '*x* cannot be what it is without *y* being what it is'.

fully functional human is prior to a fully functional finger in respect of actual being or coming-to-be: for, given my account of [PIB], what it is to be a complete, fully functional finger depends on what it is to be a complete, fully functional human—one which is at later or completion stages of the process of coming-to-be a human—but not conversely.

The example given at *Z* 10, 1035^{b}22–5, by contrast, implies that a detached, non-functional finger is, *in a way*, prior to a maimed human being:

> And it is not this substance [the form, the one according to the account: e.g. the soul of animals, 1035^{b}14–16] but the whole that is divided into these bodily parts as into its matter—and these bodily parts are prior to the whole in a way, but not in another (for they cannot even be, if separated [from the whole]; for it is not a finger in any and every state that is the finger of the animal, but a dead finger is so only homonymously). (1035^{b}21–5, trans. Bostock, modified)

It seems clear that material parts are ontologically prior to a whole composite substance in respect of potential being or passing-away, in the manner specified in my discussion of *Metaphysics Δ* 11 (Section 4.2): for what it is to be a mutilated human of a certain type depends on what it is to be a detached bodily part of the relevant type (e.g. a cut-off finger), one which is the end product of the corresponding process of truncation or passing-away. The converse, though, is not the case: for, just as a maimed human is defined in terms of the relevant end product of the corresponding process of mutilation—as (for example) one who lacks his or her detached finger—but not conversely, similarly his or her being a mutilated human depends on that detached bodily part, its being the type of cut-off part it is, *but not conversely*.

Apart from establishing the connection with *Metaph. Δ* 11, 1019^a 6–14, my qualifications 'detached', 'cut-off', etc. bring out the idea that a detached bodily part, such as a cut-off finger, is not complete or properly functional. Further, because it is non-functional or dead, calling it 'finger' is only a homonymous characterization. Indeed, this is Aristotle's point at 1035^{b}21–5: when a bodily part of a whole composite substance is detached, it ceases to be an en-formed and functional part of the composite. It becomes a product of mutilation and is called (for example) 'finger' only homonymously (1035^{b}25). In the examples of *Metaphysics Z* 10, after a circle's or a human's passing-away or after maiming a circle or a human, the remaining or the detached items are called 'semicircle' or 'finger' only homonymously. They have the same *names* as a complete semicircle or a fully functional finger respectively but do not satisfy the same *definitions* as the latter. For what they are cannot even be what it is to be a proper or functional part of the complete or functional wholes (Z 10, 1035ᵇ23: οὐδὲ γὰρ εἶναι δύναται). The one is only homonymously a semicircle; in reality it is just (for example) a remaining arc.³⁵ Similarly, the other is called 'finger' only homonymously, for it really is only a lump of flesh, bones, etc.³⁶ If, however, they

---

³⁵ As I noted in sect. 4.2, the characterizations 'proper', 'functional', 'complete', etc. or their opposites do not presuppose that mathematical and biological cases are equivalent. They suggest only that there is an analogy between the two types of case. Aristotle himself argues that certain instances of mathematical entities are not proper and so are called what they are called in name only. For example, a particular perceptible triangle or a bronze circle are not proper or perfect instances of the mathematical types of triangle or circle. For this reason, presumably, he claims, in the very context of *Metaphysics* Z 10, at 1035ᵇ1–3, that a particular circle is called 'circle' only homonymously to a circle which unqualifiedly satisfies the definition of a mathematical circle (ὁμωνύμως γὰρ λέγεται κύκλος ὅ τε ἁπλῶς λεγόμενος καὶ ὁ καθ' ἕκαστα): for there are no names peculiar to such 'imperfect' or 'lesser' mathematical particulars (διὰ τὸ μὴ εἶναι ἴδιον ὄνομα τοῖς καθ' ἕκαστον). This last claim does not, I think, imply that there are no proper names, demonstratives, or similar linguistic devices to refer to mathematical particulars of this sort. Rather, the idea is that, apart from items such as 'circle', there are no general or common names—descriptions or characterizations—peculiar to them.

³⁶ Some might object that the term δάκτυλος need not be defined in terms of the form of a human being. Similarly, it is not necessary that what it is to be a finger depends on what it is to be (the form of) a human being. The reason, it could be argued, is that (for example) in *HA* 498ᵃ31–ᵇ4 Aristotle uses the term δάκτυλος for the toes or fingers of beasts such as seals. If so, a δάκτυλος could be defined independently of a human being. Moreover, at the parallel ontological level, what it is to be a finger need not depend on what it is to be (the form of) a human being. This is a weak objection. First, it does not envisage the possibility that Aristotle may be using certain terms analogically or by similarity, perhaps because he lacks more precise terms or terms peculiar to certain bodily parts of beasts. Indeed, at 498ᵃ32 (ὥσπερ πεπηρωμένον τετράπουν), ᵃ33 (τοὺς πόδας ὁμοίους χερσίν), and ᵇ3–4 (παραπλήσιοι ταῖς τῶν ἰχθύων οὐραῖς) he clearly uses certain terms (such as τετράπουν, χερσίν, and οὐραῖς) on the basis of analogy with or similarity to (ὥσπερ, ὁμοίους, παραπλήσιοι) the cases of quadrupeds, bipeds, and fish. All these non-standard, similarity- or analogy-based uses may suggest that Aristotle intends simply to draw the analogy or emphasize the similarity at issue. Or they may imply that he lacks precise terms or appropriate descriptions for some bodily parts of certain types of animal. They do not, however, entail that just because (for example) seals' extremities are called δάκτυλοι, they are of the same type as human fingers. More importantly, at the ontological level, this objection is not sensitive to the idea that the type of finger under discussion at *HA* 498ᵃ34 is just not a human finger. This is the reason why its being what it does not, presumably, depend on what it is to be a human being. It does not follow from this, though, that there is no type of finger which depends, for its being the sort of

were called 'semicircle' or 'finger' non-homonymously or properly, they would satisfy the relevant definitions. In that case, because these definitions are formulated in terms of the whole circle and the whole human respectively, the semicircle and the finger, their being what they are, would be ontologically dependent upon what it is to be circle and human respectively, just as they are dependent upon the latter in account or definition. In the present, *post-mortem* or *post-mutilationem*, cases, however, a *dissolved* or *truncated* circle or a *maimed* human are defined in terms of the relevant types of *detached* semicircle or finger respectively—as (for example) a circle which lacks one of its halves or as a human who has lost his or her finger—but not conversely. At the parallel ontological level, then, what it is to be a *dissolved* or *truncated* circle or a *maimed* human depends on what it is to be the relevant type of *detached* semicircle or finger respectively—the end products of the corresponding processes of mutilation or passing-away—but not conversely. For this reason, as I argued in the previous paragraph, the material remnants or remaining corporeal parts (potential beings) are ontologically prior to the wholes (which have passed away) in respect of potential being or passing-away.[37]

finger it is, upon what it is to be (the form of) a human being. Aristotle's examples in *Metaphysics Z* 10 are consistent with this idea. At some places he claims that a finger is definitionally and ontologically posterior to an animal or a whole animal (1034^{b}29; 1035^{b}10–11, 22, 24). The terms 'animal' or 'whole animal' are, it appears, intended to mean 'a certain type of animal or whole animal': for he goes on to add that (for example) a human being is prior to his or her finger (1034^{b}30; 1035^{b}11). This also suggests that in these parts of *Metaphysics Z* 10 he is offering as an example the human type of finger which is definitionally and ontologically dependent upon the form of a human being.

   [37] The problem of reconciling *Metaphysics Δ* 11 and *Z* 10 is treated in some detail by Kirwan, *Γ, Δ, & E*, 155–6. In *Δ* 11, 1019^{a}10–11, Aristotle holds that a part is in actuality and is prior to the whole after the latter's dissolution. However, in *Z* 10, 1035^{b}23–5, he claims that, if a man's finger is detached, the finger 'cannot be' and is called a 'finger' only homonymously. If so, after a man passes away, his or her finger is not a finger in actuality or an independent functional part. How, then, can it be said that, after passing-away, a part (such as a finger) 'will be *in actuality*' or 'is prior to the whole (such as a human) in respect of passing-away', as *Δ* 11, 1019^{a}10–14, states? On my view of *Δ* 11, Aristotle does not claim that, after (or in respect of) passing-away, a segment of a line, a part of a whole, or the matter of a composite substance are independent, actual, and functional (or quasi-functional, in the geometrical case of a line and its segment) parts of a line, a whole, or a composite substance respectively but only *actual non-functional material remnants*. These are just the material (or quasi-material, in the geometrical case) stuffs which constitute or sustain the corresponding functional material parts of a complete and functional whole, such as a line, a whole, or a substance. For example, a segment

A further objection to my interpretation is that at Z 10, 1034^{b}31–2, Aristotle uses the phrase ἄνευ ἀλλήλων, which suggests that prior and posterior items may be independent of *each other* (non-symmetrically). In my view, however, this independence relation should be asymmetric: it should include the rider 'but not conversely'. Clearly, this objection threatens not only my interpretation but also the existential one. For the relation of ontological priority must be asymmetric, independently of whether it is [PIE] or [PIB]. Following a suggestion in the literature, a first response to this objection would be that ἄνευ ἀλλήλων reflects the first question which one usually asks concerning independence relations between two items: can two given items *be without each other?* The answer to such questions need not be affirmative in a way which makes the priority relation non-symmetric. One may answer that the one can be without the other but not conversely.[38] More importantly, a passage in the *Eudemian Ethics*, 1240^{b}38–1241^{a}14, suggests that the phrase ἄνευ ἀλλήλων need not be construed non-symmetrically. In that context, Aristotle discusses how friendship is related to concord (ὁμόνοια) and goodwill (εὔνοια, 1241^{a}1–3). He contends that for some thinkers friendship, concord, and goodwill are the same thing (εἶναι ταὐτά), while for others they cannot be without each other (οὐκ ἄνευ ἀλλήλων). With respect to goodwill, Aristotle seems to favour the second view, as he maintains that it is not the same as friendship but is not altogether different from it (^{a}3–4). Hence, he takes it that friendship and goodwill cannot be ἄνευ ἀλλήλων. But at ^{a}12–13, where he draws his conclusions concerning the relation between these two notions, he claims that, while every friend is good-willed, not every good-willed person is a friend. This suggests that, in a way, friendship cannot be without goodwill, while the latter can be without the former, although the two notions have been said not to be ἄνευ ἀλλήλων. While this is not a compelling argument, it seems to indicate that the phrase ἄνευ ἀλλήλων does not necessarily make an independence relation non-symmetric. If

---

is what is left of a line, a remnant of the original line. A part of a whole—e.g. a branch of a tree—is not a functional part of a tree after the latter's perishing but only a cut-off twig or a lump of timber. The matter of a composite substance, after the latter's passing-away, is not the proximate functional matter of this composite but a piece of non-functional matter (which is no longer en-formed by the form of this composite).

[38] See Burnyeat *et al.*, *Z*, 80.

so, it is more plausible to take the priority claim at Z 10, 1034^{b}31–2, as asymmetric, although Aristotle uses this controversial phrase.

Another, more serious, objection to my view is that the phrase τῷ εἶναι ἄνευ ἀλλήλων at 1034^{b}31–2 supports a strong ontological type of priority only in the finger–human case but not in abstract or mathematical cases. In these latter cases, such as that of the acute–right angle, only definitional priority is applicable. Since the case of forms resembles these abstract cases, forms are not prior in any ontological way but only in definition. This objection could be generalized into a global challenge to my view: what, if any, are the reasons for thinking that [PIB] is a substantive type of ontological priority rather than a disguised or inflated version of merely definitional priority?

An initial response to this objection is to accept its first premiss but deny its second. The fact that certain mathematical objects are definitionally and ontologically prior to others (e.g. a right angle to an acute, a point to a line, etc.) does not make them ontologically *primary* and independent of physical bodies. Nor does it make them substances in the manner of Aristotelian substantial forms. Even so, the fact that Aristotle uses the phrase τῷ εἶναι ἄνευ ἀλλήλων strongly suggests that he wishes to introduce ontological considerations on the basis of definitional theses. Further, in Z 10's overall context and on the basis of 1035^{b}4–21 cited above, it seems that the present discussion deals with the priority of substantial forms over certain items. Aristotle's aim, then, is to show that forms are both definitionally and ontologically primary. Even if mathematical objects cannot qualify for strict ontological primacy and substance-hood, the target of this example is to elucidate a point concerning substantial forms: the latter must be prior *both definitionally and ontologically* if they are to qualify as genuine substances.

To answer the globalized version of this objection and show that [PIB] is not just priority in definition, it is important to explain why the case of Aristotelian substantial forms is neither similar to nor the same as that of mathematical objects. The reason is that mathematical entities are not ontologically fundamental, real-world items but abstractions in thought. Thus, they do not make any real-world objects what they are. Nor are they basic constituents of what these objects are. It is true that mathematical entities are defined independently of natural bodies (and conversely). They do not, however, exist independently of all natural bodies; nor are they basic parts of what it is to be any natural body. Indeed, they exist and are what they are *in virtue of* the existence and being of the natural bodies from which they are abstracted in the first place. Hence, they cannot be ontologically primary and substances in the way in which substantial forms are. By contrast, substantial forms, as primary substances, are not abstractions in thought but fundamental parts of the furniture of reality: they make particular objects what they are by constituting basic parts of what it is to be these objects. For this reason, they must satisfy the ontological criterion of priority—over and above the definitional one—*relative to* the particular composites they en-form.

The second passage cited above from *Metaphysics* Z 10 indicates that Aristotle takes substantial forms not merely as abstract or linguistic items but as fundamental, real-world entities. This implies that in the case of forms he seeks to establish ontological priority over and above definitional priority. That definitional priority applies to forms in relation to material parts is clear from 1035^b4–12. The argument advanced at 1035^b13 ff. also seems to underpin the *ontological* priority of forms over material parts and composites.[39] First, Aristotle contends that there is a substance, the form, which corresponds to the account or formula and which is prior to the composites whose substance or form it is (1035^b13–15; 18–21). This clearly favours the idea of a correspondence between the definitional and the ontological levels: the phrase ἡ κατὰ τὸν λόγον οὐσία ($^b13$, 15) suggests that what occurs at the linguistic or definitional level is the parallel of what there is at the level of reality.

Second, this type of substance which corresponds to the account is, in the case of living beings, their soul (1035^b14–16). Souls, however, are not merely linguistic or definitional items but real-world organizing principles which make living beings what they are (1035^b16: τὸ εἶδος καὶ τὸ τί ἦν εἶναι τῷ τοιῷδε σώματι). This implies that—in addition to definitional priority—forms satisfy an ontological type of priority, [PIB], relative to animate beings. If this is correct, the type of priority and posteriority under discussion (1035^b18–19, 20–1) must be ontological: for Aristotle should be interested not only in definitional relations (1035^b16–18) but

---

[39] Aristotle clearly argues that forms are definitionally and ontologically prior to both universal and particular composites: the phrase τοῦ συνόλου ζῴου at 1035^b19 seems to refer to universal composites (cf. $^b27$–30), while καὶ καθ' ἕκαστον δὴ ὁμοίως at $^b19$–20 refers to particular ones (cf. $^b30$–1).

also in relations between living composites and their souls (^{b}18–21). The bracketed claims at ^{b}16–18 cannot imply that Aristotle is concerned only with definitional considerations, as the latter could not account for the relevant ontological relations between living beings and their souls. Rather, these parenthetical remarks suggest that ontological theses can be understood on the basis of parallel definitional claims. If so, there must be an ontological correlate of definitional priority, that is to say, [PIB], which makes forms qualify as genuine substances and not merely as definitional or linguistic items. This sort of priority of a form over the types of matter and composite it en-forms is ontological, in that the former makes the latter what they are (^{b}16). Without a form, matter and material parts are only incomplete, potential beings but not fully functional, actual composite substances or functional parts thereof.[40] Further, a composite, its being what it is, includes as a part what the relevant type of form is but the converse is not the case.

The notion of [PIB] does not face the problems implicit in the existential construal of the cases of right–acute angles and form–composites.[41] Apart from this exegetical virtue, however, my view

---

[40] As I argued in sect. 4.1, a form in the Aristotelian sublunary world could not be ontologically prior to matter *in existence*: in this case, only [PIB] will suffice.

[41] There are subsidiary problems which make *Z* 10's overall argument particularly difficult in its details. (1) Why does Aristotle claim that '*some or all* of the parts of the form' are prior to matter and material parts and to composites and their bodily parts (1035^{b}6, 14, 19)? As Burnyeat *et al.* note (*Z*, 82–5), this issue may be connected with concerns about the priority relations between the form, its formal constituents, and the composite having the relevant form. Some parts of the form may not be definitionally and ontologically prior to the composite, while others may be so. For example, at *Z* 12, 1038^{a}18–21, only the last *differentia* is said to be the essence of a thing and its definition. If so, only the last *differentia* is definitionally and ontologically prior to the composite. By contrast, at 1038^{a}5–9 the genus is said not to exist over and above the species or to exist only as a type of underlying matter which supports the species. If so, the genus, a putative part of the account and the form, either is not prior to the composite (for it does not exist alongside the species) or, strictly speaking, is not even a formal but only a quasi-material part. (2) How should one read the bracketed text at 1035^{b}16–18? Is *each part* of the animal ultimately dependent upon the function of or capacity for sense perception or only *each animal as a whole*? At 1035^{b}16–17 Ross reads with the manuscripts ἕκαστον γοῦν τὸ μέρος ἐὰν ὁρίζηται καλῶς, while Jaeger reads ἕκαστον γοῦν, [τὸ μέρος] ἐὰν ὁρίζηται καλῶς. On the first reading, in order to define each *part* of the whole composite substance, one must mention its function and ultimately its capacity for sense perception. But it is not clear that all bodily parts are defined in terms of sense perception. On the second reading, each *animate being*, presumably each animal, is defined in terms of its functions and ultimately in terms of sense perception: for, in Aristotle's view, what distinguishes animals from lower living organisms (such as plants) is their capacity for sense perception. But, again, why should the phrase τῶν

has a further, conceptual advantage. Not only is the notion of priority 'in being what something is' clearly distinct from the criterion of definitional priority. More importantly, it underwrites this criterion by supporting a real, as opposed to nominal or linguistic, notion of definitional priority. Definitional priority cannot, by itself, demarcate 'real' from 'nominal' definitions (e.g. definitions of non-existents). A human being is defined as (for example) an animal with a certain type of soul, while a goat-stag is defined as the offspring of goat and stag. On the criterion of definitional priority alone, just as the notion of a soul of a certain type is prior to that of a human, the notion of a goat-and-stag-offspring is prior to that of a goat-stag. It should not follow from this, however, that a goat-stag is the type of entity that has a real definition or is en-formed by any real-world substantial form. The notion of [PIB] serves as a way of blocking this type of inference. For what guarantees the 'reality' of definitions of certain kinds of object is that the items referred to in the *definiens* are real-world entities which make the defined objects what they are. Equivalently: the defining features referred to in real definitions, their being what they are, are ontologically basic parts of what it is to be the types of object defined. This does not hold good in the case of merely nominal definitions as the defining formulae need not correspond to any real-world entities which make any objects what they are.

The bedrock underlying the notion of [PIB], then, is that forms are primary substances, ontologically fundamental real-world entities. For this reason, forms are the referents of real *definientia*, that is to say, (non-propositional) linguistic items included in the defining formulae of certain types of object. Similarly, forms—their *being the way they are*, as opposed to their *mere existence*—constitute the truth-makers, as it were, of the (propositional) real definitions of certain types of object. These last two claims underwrite the facts that real *definientia* are successfully referring linguistic items and real definitions are 'true' or correct. Correspondingly, as primary substances, forms should fulfil a substantive criterion of asymmetric ontological independence from the relevant dependent objects.

ζῷων at 1035^{b}14 pick up only animals and not living organisms in general, including plants? After all, in this passage, the only distinctive feature of ζῷα is not that they are capable of sense perception but that they possess a soul (^{b}14–16). But all living organisms have a soul: even plants have a nutritive soul. At any rate, my argument in favour of [PIB] is relatively distinct from questions (1) and (2) and remains roughly intact, no matter how one may answer them.

This criterion, [PIB], underpins the notion of definitional priority as priority in real definition.

There is a further consideration which implies not only that forms themselves, as fundamental real-world entities, determine which definitions are correct but also that the notion of [PIB] supports 'real' definitional priority. It is not any and every defining formula or part thereof which successfully refers to a basic, real-world form. Nor is it any and every type of definitionally prior item which satisfies [PIB] and turns out to be primary substance. Thus, for instance, some putative *definientia* may be referring to ontologically non-fundamental entities. Or some definitionally prior items may not be integral to what the posterior items basically are. Some definers or definitional practices may favour formulae which mention certain types of matter, wider *genera*, merely necessary features, extra- or non-essential items which belong to the things defined. It does not follow, however, that these items are real-world substantial forms or ontologically prior to the things defined. Indeed, it is the other way about: because they make derivative objects what they are—by constituting fundamental parts of what these dependent objects are—certain real-world entities are substantial forms of, and ontologically prior to, these objects. *A fortiori* they are mentioned in those things' definitions and are prior to them in real definition. Even if definitions constitute our main route to gaining epistemic access to substantial forms, nevertheless, real-world objects, their being what they are, do not include as parts such definitional, linguistic items but the ontological counterparts of these items. In the light of this, it becomes clear why [PIB] is distinct from definitional priority and why a form, as genuine substance, is not only definitionally but more importantly ontologically (in 'being what it is') prior to the composites it en-forms.

6.2. *Form as actuality—matter as potentiality* (Metaphysics Θ 8)

The importance of [PIB] is also clear in the context of *Metaphysics* Θ 8. My aim is not to explore all the claims made in this long and difficult chapter or to understand all cases where actuality is said to be ontologically ($τῇ$ $οὐσίᾳ$) prior to potentiality. Thus, I shall leave out for further study Aristotle's examples of capacity possession and its exercise (1050^a10-14), capacities and their exercise quite generally ($^a23-^b2$), and eternal actualities ($^b6$ ff.). My interpretation in terms of [PIB] could, I think, work better than [PIE] in such cases too. My central aim, however, is to understand the relation between forms in complete composites and the corresponding incomplete, potential beings (e.g. adult–child, human–seed) and, more importantly, between form as actuality and matter as potentiality.

That the distinctions drawn in *Metaphysics* Δ 11 are, in some measure, present in Θ 8 is clear from Θ 8's opening sentence (1049ᵇ4–5): priority is said in many different ways, the ways which 'we have distinguished earlier', presumably in Δ 11's context.[42] At any rate, Θ 8 takes actuality to be prior to potentiality in account, in substance, and, in a certain way, in time too (ᵇ10–12). For brevity's sake, I shall leave out the definitional and temporal types of priority, which are relatively unproblematic (ᵇ12–17; ᵇ17–1050ᵃ3).[43] My aim is to show how my understanding of [PIB] can account for the claim that actuality is ontologically (τῇ οὐσίᾳ) prior to potentiality, a claim which is the focus of the following passage:

Further, [actuality is prior to potentiality] in substance too, first because things which are posterior in generation are prior in form and in substance (e.g. adult to child, and human to seed; for the former already have the form, while the latter do not), and because everything which is in the process of becoming moves towards the principle and the end [τέλος] (for 'that for the sake of which' [τὸ οὗ ἕνεκα] is the principle, and becoming is for the sake of the end), and actuality is the end, and potentiality is acquired for the sake of this. . . . Further, matter is in potentiality, because it may go to the form; but when it is in actuality, then it is in the form . . . For the function [or the work: ἔργον] is the end, while the actuality is the function [or the work]—and for this reason the name 'actuality' [ἐνέργεια] is used in accordance with the function [ἔργον]—and it [actuality] strives towards the complete reality [ἐντελέχειαν]. (1050ᵃ4–10, 15–16, 21–3, my translation)[44]

---

[42] Makin, Θ, 182, also takes the reference to Δ 11 to be obvious.

[43] I agree with Witt (*Ways*, 79) and Makin (Θ, 192) that, while the notions of definitional and temporal priority are straightforward or fairly clear, ontological priority stands in need of clarification.

[44] I leave out the examples offered at 1050ᵃ10–14, for they are not directly germane to my present concerns, as they deal with capacity possession and exercise. Similarly, I have not translated ᵃ16–21, which is a generalization to the cases where the end is a kind of change (teaching and learning), because my argument is primarily about substances. Such 'non-substance' cases can also be understood as making more concrete the claim put forward at ᵃ9–10 that potentiality (e.g. capacity possession in the examples) is for the sake of the end, the actuality (e.g. capacity exercise). My account of [PIB] seems to apply to such cases too. For example, a person's seeing (capacity exercise) cannot exist without his or her sight (capacity possession, a type of potentiality). But his or her seeing, its being what it is, makes his or her sight what

This argument rests on two basic assumptions which are closely interconnected:

(1) What is temporally posterior in generation is prior in form and in substance (premiss; 1050ª4–5).[45]

(2) Everything which is in the process of coming-to-be (γιγνό-μενον) moves towards its principle and final end (premiss; 1050ª7–8).

The cases of an adult and a human in relation to a child and a seed respectively are offered as examples of (1). The former are cases of actuality and as such are ontologically prior to the latter, which are cases of potentiality (1050ª5–7). Similarly, a form as actuality is ontologically prior to matter, a type of potentiality (ª15–16).

Aristotle's explanation of and examples for (1) rest on the fact that beings in earlier phases of generation are not complete and do not possess the form (1050ª6–7). This view, taken together with (2), introduces a rich conceptual framework of teleology:[46]

it is but not conversely: for the latter is what it is for the sake of the former being what it is, while the converse does not hold good (1050ª10–13). These are cases where the result or the final cause is not over and above (παρά) the exercise itself, but is immanent in the employment of a capacity (ª23–5; ª34–ᵇ2). By contrast, in cases of production the result is something over and above the capacity exercise: for example, a house exists even if/when there is no housebuilding (capacity exercise, a type of actuality). Further, this housebuilding activity is ontologically dependent upon the form or τέλος of a house (as the latter en-forms the completed house, the end result of housebuilding): what it is to be the relevant activity depends on what it is to be a form or τέλος of a certain type. Even so, however, the relevant activity is ontologically prior to the potentiality of the corresponding type: for what it is to be this type of capacity (e.g. the capacity of housebuilding) depends on what it is to be the relevant type of activity (e.g. housebuilding). This corresponds to the definitional relations between the two items: a capacity of a certain type is defined in terms of, or as a capacity for, exercising the relevant type of activity. Although, in cases of production, the end result (e.g. the completed house) is the teleological bedrock and is ontologically prior to the relevant activity, yet this activity is ontologically and teleologically prior to the capacity or potentiality. For the activity is directly dependent upon the end result or τέλος, while the capacity only indirectly, via the activity itself. This, I think, is the point of the remark made at 1050ª27–8: the completed house (fully en-formed by the form of a house) is the ultimate teleological principle (ἔνθα μὲν τέλος), while the activity of housebuilding (even if posterior to the completed house) is teleologically prior to the relevant capacity (ἔνθα δὲ μᾶλλον τέλος τῆς δυνάμεως). I have benefited from discussions with David Charles on this point.

[45] This assumption is also present at *Metaph.* M 2, 1077ª26–7, where it is argued that bodies more clearly are substances rather than mathematical objects (1077ª24–31). In M 2 the basis for this assumption is the claim that a body is a complete and structured whole as it comes to have a soul or form (1077ª28–9).

[46] Cleary (*Senses*, 59), Witt (*Ways*, 78), and Makin (Θ, 194) also notice the te-

(*a*) What is temporally prior in the generation process has not yet accomplished its final cause, that for the sake of which it is: for it does not yet possess the form in completeness.

(*b*) What is temporally posterior or last in the generation process is complete and possesses the relevant form: it has accomplished its final end.

Since, in such cases, the form and the final cause are the principles, it follows that the items falling under the scope of (*b*) are ontologically prior to those under (*a*). Yet Aristotle introduces some further premisses to support the conclusion that actuality is ontologically prior to potentiality:

(3) The working or functional being is the final cause (premiss; 1050ᵃ21).

(4) Actuality is the working or functional being (premiss; ᵃ22).

(5) Actuality is the final cause (from (3) and (4); ᵃ9).

(6) The principle is that for the sake of which things are in the process of generation (premiss; ᵃ8).

(7) In the generation process that for the sake of which things are is the final cause (premiss; ᵃ8–9).

(8) The principle is the final cause (from (6) and (7)).

(9) Actuality is the principle, that for the sake of which there is potentiality (from (5) and (8); ᵃ9–10).

(10) Therefore, as principle, actuality is ontologically prior to potentiality (from (9)).

This argument, it can be claimed, rests on unduly abstract and unsupported premisses.[47] To understand Aristotle's view, one should account for the particular examples of ontological priority: adult over child, human over seed, and form over matter.

Most commentators have understood these examples on the basis of the existential construal of the ontological priority relation. In their view, an adult can somehow exist independently of, or without, the relevant type of child having existed, a human can exist inde-

leological perspective of Θ 8's argument. However, they do not realize that their existential construal of the priority relation creates problems if applied to Aristotle's examples.

[47] It could even be objected that this argument is nothing more than 'School Metaphysics'; see R. M. Dancy, 'Aristotle and the Priority of Actuality' ['Priority'], in S. Knuuttila (ed.), *Reforging the Great Chain of Being* (Dordrecht, 1980), 73–115 at 92.

pendently of, or without, the relevant type of seed having existed, and so on. However, since these claims seem straightforwardly false, other interpreters have put forward different proposals to make the examples intelligible.

Stephen Makin, for instance, argues that teleological considerations about generation and its privileged stages make the examples perspicuous. Generation has a privileged stage, that of completeness (e.g. adult, human, possession of form), while all earlier stages are ontologically dependent upon that stage. If so, beings at earlier stages cannot exist without beings at the completeness stage existing in that the former are for the sake of the latter. The fact that something might go wrong—in which case a being at the completeness stage will never exist, although a being at an earlier stage has existed—does not imply existential dependence of the former upon the latter but just means that the generation process has been interrupted or interfered with. But interruptions of or interferences with the generation process are cases of destruction, and destruction cannot yield a being at the completeness stage. For this reason, in cases of destruction the privileged stage of generation never occurs. Yet, if all goes well, generation will yield a being at the completeness stage, which is existentially independent of beings at earlier stages.[48] But why take destruction processes in this way? Is it not more plausible to think that the destruction process at issue is one that affects a being which already is in complete existence? For instance, the case of infanticide, which interrupts the generation process and prevents an adult from existing, is not, strictly speaking, the passing-away of an adult but the passing-away of a child. One would expect that destruction, an adult's passing-away, should take place after an adult has come into full, complete being. Only if one takes destruction in a non-standard way can the existential construal make some sense.

Charlotte Witt argues that (for example) young Sally is not existentially dependent upon a particular τέλος (her future self, Sally

---

[48] See Makin, 'Priority', 226–7 and 230; cf. id., Θ, 193–5, where his view is formulated as follows: '[RE] Fs are prior in substance to Gs so long as there is some process which in *normal* conditions results in Fs rather than Gs; whereas the way to get Gs rather than Fs is to *interfere with*, *interrupt* or *hinder* that process' (Θ, 195, emphasis original). In my view, the main weaknesses of [RE] are the existential construal of the independence relation between Fs and Gs and the anomalous way of understanding destruction as subordinate to generation.

the adult) but upon 'the type or species which she will realize'.[49]
On her view, the end or actuality in question is not the individual
or (as she calls it) the token that Sally will become but the species.
However, young Sally and Sally the adult are cases of potentiality and actuality respectively, and as such Sally the adult must be
ontologically prior to young Sally. Ontological priority of actuality
over potentiality holds both at the token and at the type levels *for
the same reason*. Witt could argue, to be sure, that Sally the adult is
ontologically prior to young Sally, while insisting that this priority
relation obtains *on account of* the fact that the type or species will
exist in Sally the adult. However, combining the token and type
levels in this manner still does not yield the desired results. How
can the species exist in Sally the adult without Sally the adult ever
existing? In this case, it appears that the species' existing in Sally
the adult is dependent upon young Sally's having existed. For if
young Sally goes out of existence, the species will never exist in
Sally the adult. The fact that the species has existed in Sally's own
parents or will exist in other adults seems irrelevant, as in this particular case the actuality (Sally the adult) is existentially dependent
upon the potentiality (young Sally).[50]

[49] C. Witt, 'The Priority of Actuality' ['Priority'], in T. Scaltsas, D. Charles, and
M. L. Gill (eds.), *Unity, Identity, and Explanation in Aristotle's* Metaphysics (Oxford, 1994), 215–28 at 224 (and in general 222 ff.). Cf. ead., *Ways*, 85: 'although the
boy exists for the sake of the man, the boy is ontologically dependent on the type
or species he will realize, rather than the token or individual he might become. . . .
[T]he end or actuality in question is the species—in our example, the human species.
Aristotelian species, in turn, are ontologically dependent on the existence of their
individual members. Ultimately, then, the boy in our example is ontologically dependent on the existence of human beings.' Notably, in all her formulations Witt
takes ontological priority and dependence in the existential manner; see *Ways*, 13,
77–8, 79, 81, 138 n. 2.

[50] Witt would reply that young Sally's existence *as an immature human being*
depends on the existence of the species, which, in turn, depends on the actual
existence of any one presently existing human being *as a complete human being*. If
so, young Sally's existing as an immature human being ultimately depends upon
the existence of any one actually existing human being as a complete human being
(this seems to be the point of her claim that type-actualities are prior to token-
potentialities). However, the jargon of 'existing as' employed in this version of
Witt's view seems to make good sense only if understood in terms of the notion of
being what something is: for it is not the 'existing as' but the 'being what it is' of an
immature human being that depends on the 'being what it is' (and not the 'existing
as') of a complete human being. But if so, it is preferable completely to avoid talk
of existence and develop an interpretation in terms of [PIB]. Indeed, Witt herself
(*Ways*, 84) notes the problematic character of the existential construal as applied
to the examples of *Metaphysics* Θ 8: 'it is hard to see how the boy is ontologically
dependent on the man, since the man—and the man's form—*does not now exist*'

It is clear that the accounts just mentioned have a common weakness: they cannot explain how a being at a later or completion stage of a generation process can exist independently of, or without, a being existing or having existed at an earlier stage. It should be noted, however, that this difficulty does not consist merely in the following claim:

(1) It is necessary that there should exist or have existed *some immature entity or other* of type A, if there is going to exist or there exists a complete entity of type B.

This claim would allow that (for example) an adult man's existence depends on the existence of a werewolf boy who would transform into an adult man when drinking his first alcoholic beverage at the age of 21. Rather, the difficulty in question encapsulates more serious worries about the existence of certain types of entities as results of generation processes:

(2) As a mature or complete result of a certain type of generation process, G, an entity of type A cannot exist without the corresponding immature or incomplete entity of the appropriate type B having already existed at an earlier stage of G.

This, it appears, is one of Aristotle's points in introducing natural, end-directed processes of coming-to-be. As I argued in Section 3, the deeper reason for the difficulty stemming from (2) is that the existential construal inevitably carries with it temporal connotations which make it difficult for it to accommodate Θ 8's examples. But *temporal* considerations either yield incorrect results or are not relevant to the *ontological* type of priority which actuality possesses

(emphasis added). It is noteworthy that, at certain points, Witt's argument seems to approximate my view of [PIB]: 'if being human did not actually exist, then the boy could not be potentially human, or, in other words, he would not exist, where "exist" means *exist as what he is*. But the reverse ontological dependency does not hold' (*Ways*, 85, emphasis original). Similarly, she thinks that the relation between a potential being A and an actual being B is one of ontological dependence, in so far as what it is to be A is being potentially B (*Ways*, 83). However, her main thesis is formulated in terms of the problematic existential construal: she argues that potential beings, such as the child in our example, are existentially dependent on the *existence* of actual beings, such as being human (*Ways*, 85). Panayides, 'Priority', 334, criticizes Witt's existential construal on similar grounds: he argues that it is implausible to think that young Sally is ontologically dependent on Sally the adult, since young Sally 'exists now, whereas the adult Sally is not now in existence. In fact, she may never exist.'

over potentiality. Priority in time is a distinct type of priority which is treated in its own right by Aristotle (1049ᵇ17–1050ᵃ3): it does not, indeed should not, have any significant consequences for ontological priority.

Further, the existential construal seems to be undermined by Aristotle's teleological argument and his remarks on generation processes. Teleology and generation allow us to invoke the notion of hypothetical necessity from *Physics* 2. 9. Regardless of problematic details, it is clear that, in generation processes, matter is hypothetically necessary for a form to exist in a complete composite. For example, if a saw and its function (e.g. cutting) are going to exist, it is necessary that some type of matter appropriate for cutting (e.g. a proper type of metal such as iron) should exist and be the material nature of this saw. This is so, although a saw is not for the sake of (for example) the iron but the iron is for the sake of a saw (200ᵃ12–13, 24–9). This suggests that there is a relation of *existential* dependence of form upon matter, although the *teleological* dependence is the other way about (200ᵃ7–10, 19–22).[51]

Aristotle's examples in *Metaphysics* Θ 8 are, admittedly, different from those offered in *Physics* 2. 9: while a type of metal appropriate for cutting is the *proximate* matter of a saw (the matter constituting a fully functional saw), a child or a seed of the relevant types *do not*

---

[51] The mathematical cases (*Phys.* 2. 9, 200ᵃ15–30) bear some similarities to natural generation and craft production cases. If the straight line is thus-and-so (principle or premiss of a proof), the triangle *must* have a sum of internal angles equal to two right angles (=2R; theorem or conclusion of a proof). Conversely, if the triangle has 2R, the straight line *must* be thus-and-so (200ᵃ18–19). This corresponds to the relation of existential interdependence between form and composites in cases of natural generation and craft production: the form or τέλος of a house cannot exist if no enmattered houses exist, while an en-mattered house cannot exist without the form of a house existing in and en-forming it. In mathematics, however, the interdependence relation seems to entail the following claim: given inferential validity, the conclusion of a proof cannot be true if the premisses are not true *and conversely*. This is a type of *syllogistic* or *logical* interdependence (ᵃ21–4: μὴ ὄντος τοῦ συμπεράσματος ἡ ἀρχὴ οὐκ ἔσται; ἀρχὴ . . . τοῦ λογισμοῦ). In cases of natural generation and craft production, the ontological-teleological priority of a form-τέλος over matter corresponds to the *explanatory* priority of the demonstrative premisses-principles over the conclusion of mathematical proofs: it is *because of* the fact that the straight line is thus-and-so that the triangle has 2R *but not conversely* (ᵃ16–18). I leave out the mathematical cases from the main body of my argument, for in such cases the considerations from teleology and generation processes (which are central in *Metaphysics* Θ 8) cannot, strictly speaking, apply. However, the argument I just offered suggests that there are correspondences between the two cases in the manner of *Phys.* 2. 9, 200ᵃ15–30. Further, the notion of [PIB] can accommodate these correspondences between the mathematical and the natural generation or craft production cases.

materially constitute an adult or a human respectively. Rather, they are immature entities at earlier phases of the process of coming-to-be. However, it would be sufficient for present purposes if the two types of case shared the relevant important features which would render them hypothetically necessary for the corresponding forms to exist. Indeed, just as a type of metal appropriate for cutting must exist if a saw is to exist, so too an immature entity of the proper type must exist at an earlier stage of the generation process if a mature entity of the relevant type is to exist at a later or completion stage of this process. Aristotle himself seems to conceive of the two types of case as sufficiently similar in all relevant respects as he offers the example of matter as potentiality and form as actuality at Θ 8, 1050ª15–16. In this example, the potentiality is indeed the matter which constitutes or embodies the relevant type of form, the actuality. Since this is provided as a further (ἔτι: 1050ª15) example of the ontological primacy of actuality over potentiality, it follows that the previous examples too are similar as cases of actualities which are ontologically prior to corresponding potentialities. Conversely, in *Physics* 2. 9, there is no reason to rule out the possibility that (for example) a type of metal appropriate for cutting is hypothetically necessary for a saw to exist in so far as it is the corresponding type of not-fully processed material at earlier stages of the relevant *production process*, a material which *does not yet constitute* a fully functional saw.

On the assumption, then, that one can apply the claims of *Physics* 2. 9 to the examples of *Metaphysics* Θ 8, one can derive the following results:

(1) If an adult, a human, or a form *exists* or *is going to exist* at later or completion stages of certain types of generation process, the relevant types of child, seed, or matter *must exist* or *will have to exist* (respectively) at earlier stages of these processes.

This claim is based on the formulations at *Phys.* 2. 9, 200ª19–20, where Aristotle clearly takes hypothetical necessity to apply to cases of generation process, just like those in *Metaphysics* Θ 8. Now, on the existential construal of the notion of ontological priority, it must be true that:

(2) The relevant types of child, seed, or matter *do not exist* or *will not exist* at earlier stages of these processes.

But:

> (3) An adult, a human, or a form *can exist* or *will be able to exist* at later or completion stages of these processes, independently of the existence of the items in (2) respectively.

But the conjunction of (1) with (2) yields (by *modus tollens*) the following result:

> (4) An adult, a human, or a form *cannot exist* or *will not be able to exist* at later or completion stages of these processes.

Claim (4) contradicts (3), which reflects the existential construal of ontological priority. It turns out that an adult, a human, and a form are existentially dependent upon the existence of the relevant types of child, seed, and matter respectively.[52] Therefore, on the existential approach, actuality is not ontologically (τῇ οὐσίᾳ) prior to potentiality. For this reason, I think, [PIE] does not work successfully in *Metaphysics* Θ 8.

At this juncture, [PIB], once again, seems helpful. Although an adult, a human, and a form are existentially dependent upon the existence of the relevant types of child, seed, and matter respectively, yet they are what they are independently of the relevant types of child, seed, or matter being what they are. Indeed, the dependence works the other way about: the relevant types of child, seed, or matter, their being what they are, are ontologically dependent upon what it is to be an adult, a human, or a form respectively. At this point, considerations concerning generation, teleology, and hypothetical necessity are relevant. The fact that in generation processes the realization of a form in complete composites and so the exis-

---

[52] A possible objection might run as follows: how could the appropriate types of child or seed (potential beings) be identified without the relevant types of forms of an adult or a human (actual beings)? If these potential beings could not be identified without the corresponding actual ones, how could the latter be existentially dependent on the former? In that case, it appears, potential beings would effectively depend upon actual beings for their identity. However, I am not here claiming that a child or a seed of the relevant type is entirely non-enformed and unidentifiable. Rather, they are en-formed *as a child* or *as a seed* (respectively) and so can be identified on the basis of the corresponding 'lower-level' forms. The fact that these lower-level forms depend upon the forms of an adult or a human (respectively) for their being what they are is a further, separate issue. This issue is related to my wider thesis about the ontological priority of forms over matter (in 'being what it is') at earlier stages of a generation process. Nevertheless, this wider thesis does not entail that matter at earlier stages is an entirely form-less and so unidentifiable lump of material stuffs.

tence of a form in them depend (by hypothetical necessity) upon the existence of an appropriate type of matter does not entail that a form is *because* or *for the sake of* this type of matter (*Phys.* 2. 9, 200ᵃ9–10; cf. 26–7: οὐ διὰ ταῦτά ἐστι τὸ τέλος ἀλλ᾽ ἢ ὡς ὕλην, οὐδ᾽ ἔσται διὰ ταῦτα).

What it is to be an appropriate type of matter, by contrast, depends on what it is to be the relevant τέλος, the form to be realized. For a type of matter must be thus-and-so for the sake of the relevant type of form being thus-and-so. Therefore, a child, a seed, or an appropriate type of matter, their being what they are, respectively depends upon what it is to be an adult, a human, or a form of the relevant type. For the former 'move towards' the realization of the latter (1050ᵃ7–8). By contrast, what an adult, a human or a form is does not, in the corresponding way, depend upon what a child, a seed, or an appropriate type of matter is. For the former are the τέλη, the final causes which make the latter what they are but not conversely. This need not entail that any kinds of child, seed, or matter will suffice for an adult, a human, or a form of the relevant types to be what they are. But the range of appropriate types of child, seed, or matter is ontologically dependent upon what it is to be an adult, a human, or a form of the corresponding types respectively.

One possible objection runs as follows: although the view I have outlined seems to establish the correct kind of ontological priority of actuality, form, and substance over potentiality and matter, it does not show how a form can be prior in 'being what it is' to the *composite substances* it en-forms. However, given the priority relations between the different types of substance in *Metaphysics* Z 10 (1035ᵇ4–6, 11–14, 18–22), it is clear that this objection cannot be decisive. A form is ontologically prior both to matter (and its parts) and to composites (and their bodily parts). In *Metaphysics* Θ 8 these priority claims are implicitly present: since composites cannot be complete or realize their relevant τέλος if they do not possess their form, it follows that they are ontologically posterior to it. For, if they do not possess their form, they are on a par with matter and so are substances only in potentiality. However, a form's ontological priority over composites cannot be [PIE]: a form cannot exist if no en-mattered composites exist, while en-mattered composites cannot exist independently of their form. Nevertheless, a form satisfies [PIB]: it is what it is independently of the composites it en-forms being what they are but not conversely.

To overcome the difficulties resulting from Aristotle's examples in *Metaphysics* Θ 8, some commentators adopt what Stephen Makin calls a 'splitting' strategy: they argue that the notion of [PIE] is present only in the second part of the chapter, the one dealing with eternal actualities (1050^{b}6 ff.), but not in the first teleological section (1050^{a}4–^{b}6). However, so understood, the chapter's overall argument loses its uniformity.[53] Others adopt a 'non-splitting' strategy and think that the same type of ontological priority is present throughout *Metaphysics* Θ 8. However, they employ the existential construal. Hence, in order to understand Aristotle's examples on the basis of [PIE], they either develop complex theories with several unnatural assumptions about generation and destruction or restrict the existential priority claim to one between type-actualities and token-potentialities.[54]

My interpretation of *Metaphysics* Θ 8 has the following advantages. First, it adopts a 'non-splitting' strategy and applies the same, *ontological*, type of priority in both parts of the chapter. The difference between my approach and that of other 'non-splitting' theorists is that, on my view, ontological priority is best interpreted as [PIB]. Second, my account is conceptually simple and straightforward as it does not involve giving a convoluted account of either Aristotle's claims or his examples. It makes substance, form, and actuality ontologically prior in 'being what it is' to matter, potentiality, and composites, without invoking problematic claims about existence. Third, it links Θ 8's assumptions concerning teleology and generation with teleology and hypothetical necessity in generation processes in *Phys.* 2. 9, 199^{b}34–200^{a}30. In this manner, one can make sense not only of the *existential* dependence of form, substance, and actuality upon matter, potentiality, and composites but also of the ontological priority, understood as [PIB], of the former over the latter. If so, one can see a uniform account at work in these different parts of Aristotle's doctrine. In the light of all these considerations, it seems that the notion of [PIB] is not only

[53] Makin, 'Priority', 235–7, points out that the 'splitting' approach is followed by Ross, *Metaphysics*, ii. 262–5; Dancy, 'Priority', 88–9; M. F. Burnyeat *et al.*, *Notes on Eta and Theta* (Oxford, 1984), 133–4 and 144. He also argues that this approach undermines Θ 8's uniformity of argument.

[54] A 'non-splitting' strategy is followed by Makin ('Priority', 237). Makin himself (ibid.) thinks that Witt (see her 'Priority') endorses a 'non-splitting' strategy too. As I noted, however, both develop their 'non-splitting' strategies in terms of the problematic existential construal.

significant and clear but also consistent with and true to Aristotle's claims and examples.

7. Conclusion: further problems and some suggestions

It appears that my account of the ontological criterion of [PIB] offers a unified approach to *Metaphysics Δ* 11, *Z* 10, and *Θ* 8. The motivation behind this account is the fact that one should be sensitive to the different ways in which different items may qualify for ontological priority. In particular, a form cannot be existentially prior to the items Aristotle thinks it is (matter and composites). However, it must be ontologically prior in some way if it is to be a genuine substance. The notion of [PIB] provides the required solution to this puzzle. By contrast, it seems impossible straightforwardly to accommodate the examples given in *Metaphysics Δ* 11, *Z* 10, and *Θ* 8 on the basis of the existential construal of [IC].

A further important feature of the present account is that it posits that there is a 'match' between the levels of definition and reality. Just as the definition of an essence or form, *F*, is the account of what it is to be *F*, so too ontological priority in the sense of [PIB] is the *real* counterpart to definitional priority. The crucial notion behind definitional priority is that of being defined as or being understood in terms of some more basic concept, a notion formally represented by the relation of inclusion of (the definition of) a certain item in another item's definition. The idea underlying [PIB] is that an ontologically basic entity is the fundamental part of what it is to be a dependent or posterior entity: for it makes an entity of this type what it is. Schematically speaking, my interpretation introduces the idea of an ontological hierarchy every level of which corresponds to the relevant level of a parallel definitional or conceptual hierarchy. The items which are 'higher up in rank' are prior to, or independent of, those 'lower down' both in definition and in 'being what they are' but the converse is not the case.

It is no necessary part of views of this sort to place more importance on either of the two orders: one could argue for the parallel between definitional and ontological priority without also favouring the one or the other as more basic.[55] I argued, however, that

---

[55] Similarly, Kit Fine remarks that one can accept the connection between the definitional and ontological levels 'without assuming that the account of dependence

Aristotle would presumably hold that the ontological order is more fundamental than the definitional one: a definition is only an account of a form, a linguistic item that gains its importance because of its corresponding or referring to an ontologically primary entity, a form. A form is *what makes things what they are* and so it determines what the correct account is, the account which specifies *what the thing in question is*. If so, it appears, the notion of ontological priority has, at least in Aristotle's view, a better claim to being basic rather than definitional priority.

One might object to my formulation of the priority claim 'on suspicion of scope vagueness'. I argued that a form *F* is ontologically prior to the composite *F*s it en-forms. This formulation, however, does not specify whether *F* is prior to *all* or *some* composite *F*s. One could reply that it is implausible to take some composite *F*s as posterior, others as prior. Thus, the claim would be that *F* is prior to *all* composite *F*s. Even so, however, the wide scope is ambiguous between the collective ('*for all taken together* . . .') and the distributive ('take *any given one* . . .') senses. I avoided tackling this scope issue as it is directly dependent upon one's approach to the debate of 'universal vs. particular form'. Thus, if one argues in favour of particular forms, one faces no scope problems: a particular form is ontologically prior only to one composite substance, the one it exclusively en-forms. By contrast, if each form is universal, it could be ontologically prior either to all or some of its composite instances, in which case the discussion of the scope issue is urgent. To bypass the 'universal vs. particular form' controversy, I opted for the following neutral formulation: a form *F* is ontologically prior to *the composite Fs it en-forms*. If *F* is particular, the class of composite *F*s it en-forms cannot have more than one member and *F* is ontologically prior only to that one composite *F*. If, by contrast, *F* is universal, the class of composite *F*s it en-forms may have more than one member and the scope issue remains open.

The deeper reason for avoiding the question of whether forms are universal or particular and adopting a neutral stance on the scope issue is simple. The question of a form's ontological priority over composite substances should not be sensitive to one's approach to the problem of whether forms are particular or universal. Ontological priority is a criterion of ontological independence of some type,

in terms of understanding [or definition] is somehow more basic than the account in terms of essence' ('Dependence', 275).

one which must be fulfilled by forms, if indeed they are to qualify as primary substances. But forms should qualify for primary substancehood no matter whether they are universal or particular. Consequently, the notion of ontological priority is to be understood independently of a form's universality or particularity. This is so, despite the fact that the latter notions may, in some measure, influence some subsidiary aspect of the notion of ontological priority, such as the precise formulation of its scope.

A more important type of objection might stem from my comparison between Aristotle's account of ontological priority and Kit Fine's view of ontological dependence. My interpretation of Aristotelian priority complies with what Kit Fine calls 'the definitional approach to dependence':[56] priority in 'being what something is' is the ontological parallel of priority in account or definition. In this way, one can avoid the difficulties arising from the existential construal of ontological priority claims. Nevertheless, Kit Fine's account has a further important component: he understands ontological dependence without invoking any modal notions of necessity or possibility. Indeed, he argues that these modal notions render the account of ontological dependence vulnerable to knock-down counter-examples.[57] Aristotle's formulation of [IC] at *Metaphysics* Δ 11, 1019^{a}3–4, however, brings in such modal notions: A is ontologically prior to B if and only if A *can* be without B being but not conversely. Equivalently: B is ontologically posterior to A just in case, *necessarily*, A is if B is (while *it is possible* that B is not, if A is). Hence, even if Aristotle's view could avoid the difficulties which undermine the existential construal, it would still face the problems that any modal account of ontological priority has to overcome.

My interpretation of Aristotle's view followed his own varied formulations. Although in *Metaphysics* Δ 11 he seems to adopt the modal approach, by no means is this his uniform practice in the *Metaphysics*. Indeed, his claims appear divided in this respect:

[56] See Fine, 'Dependence', 275.

[57] Fine, 'Dependence', 271–2. For example, in modal-existential accounts of ontological dependence, an item, A, turns out to be ontologically dependent upon its singleton set, {A}: for, necessarily, {A} exists if A exists. Our intuition, however, is that the relation of ontological dependence holds the other way about: it is the singleton, {A}, which ontologically depends on its member, A. Worse still, the modal-existential model seems to entail that the existence of any kind of entity depends on the existence of necessary existents such as numbers. Kit Fine's example ('Dependence', 271) is as follows: 'given that [the number] 2 necessarily exists, it is necessarily the case that 2 exists if Socrates does'.

while in some passages he holds that ontologically prior items simply *are* (what they are) without others being (what they are) but not conversely, at other places he remarks that the former *can* be without the latter but the latter *cannot* be without the former. Even in formulating definitional priority, Aristotle sometimes claims that the prior items *can* be defined or understood without the posterior ones (but not conversely) and sometimes that the former *are* defined or grasped without the latter (but not conversely). In my view, it is not vital to determine whether the relevant passages favour modal or non-modal accounts.[58] Rather, it is preferable to specify what, if any, aspects of Aristotle's view—or of my interpretation of his view—could underpin the claim that the Aristotelian account is not open to the objections raised by Kit Fine against the modal construal. Indeed, it appears that the modal component of the Aristotelian view can be taken as clearly derivative or secondary, even if not entirely dispensable. Thus, it is not an important part of this view to claim that some items *can* or *cannot* be (or be defined) without others. As I emphasized at the beginning of this section, the basic ideas underlying ontological and definitional priority are (respectively) that a fundamental entity makes some dependent entities what they are, and that a basic concept defines some derivative concepts. If so, no modal notions of possibility or necessity are *required* to enter Aristotle's account of ontological or definitional priority. This is so, even if in some passages these

---

[58] The following passages, it appears, describe ontological or definitional priority in non-modal terms. *Metaph.* Z 10, 1034ᵇ30–2: τῷ λόγῳ γὰρ λέγονται ἐξ ἐκείνων, καὶ τῷ εἶναι δὲ ἄνευ ἀλλήλων πρότερα; M 2, 1077ᵇ2–4: τῇ μὲν γὰρ οὐσίᾳ πρότερα ὅσα χωριζόμενα τῷ εἶναι ὑπερβάλλει, τῷ λόγῳ δὲ ὅσων οἱ λόγοι ἐκ τῶν λόγων; Δ 8, 1017ᵇ17–21: ἔτι ὅσα μόρια ἐνυπάρχοντά ἐστιν ἐν τοῖς τοιούτοις ὁρίζοντά τε καὶ τόδε τι σημαίνοντα, ὧν ἀναιρουμένων ἀναιρεῖται τὸ ὅλον, οἷον ἐπιπέδου σῶμα, ὡς φασί τινες, καὶ ἐπίπεδον γραμμῆς· καὶ ὅλως ὁ ἀριθμὸς δοκεῖ εἶναί τισι τοιοῦτος (ἀναιρουμένου τε γὰρ οὐδὲν εἶναι, καὶ ὁρίζειν πάντα); Δ 11, 1018ᵇ34–6: καὶ κατὰ τὸν λόγον δὲ τὸ συμβεβηκὸς τοῦ ὅλου πρότερον, οἷον τὸ μουσικὸν τοῦ μουσικοῦ ἀνθρώπου· οὐ γὰρ ἔσται ὁ λόγος ὅλος ἄνευ τοῦ μέρους; contrast, however, the immediately subsequent claim at 1018ᵇ36–7, which involves modal notions: καίτοι οὐκ ἐνδέχεται μουσικὸν εἶναι μὴ ὄντος μουσικοῦ τινός. By contrast, ontological and definitional priorities are spelt out in modal terms in the following passages. *Metaph.* Z 10, 1035ᵇ22–5: τοῦ μὲν οὖν συνόλου πρότερα ταῦτ' ἔστιν ὡς, ἔστι δ' ὡς οὔ (οὐδὲ γὰρ εἶναι δύναται χωριζόμενα· οὐ γὰρ ὁ πάντως ἔχων δάκτυλος ζῴου, ἀλλ' ὁμώνυμος ὁ τεθνεώς) (contrast the non-modal claim made in the same chapter at 1034ᵇ30–2, quoted above); Δ 11, 1019ᵃ3–4: ὅσα ἐνδέχεται εἶναι ἄνευ ἄλλων, ἐκεῖνα δὲ ἄνευ ἐκείνων μή; Z 1, 1028ᵃ35–6: ἀνάγκη γὰρ ἐν τῷ ἑκάστου λόγῳ τὸν τῆς οὐσίας ἐνυπάρχειν. At *Metaph.* Z 5, 1030ᵇ23–6, we encounter both modal and non-modal ways of clarifying definitional priority: ταῦτα δ' ἐστὶν ἐν ὅσοις ὑπάρχει ἢ ὁ λόγος ἢ τοὔνομα οὗ ἐστι τοῦτο τὸ πάθος, καὶ μὴ ἐνδέχεται δηλῶσαι χωρίς, ὥσπερ τὸ λευκὸν ἄνευ τοῦ ἀνθρώπου ἐνδέχεται ἀλλ' οὐ τὸ θῆλυ ἄνευ τοῦ ζῴου.

modal notions do *in fact* play some explanatory role in setting out ontological or definitional priority.[59]

What is important, in effect, is to determine what is conceptually basic in Aristotle's theory. Judging by this standard, it seems that, in my interpretation, ontological and definitional priorities are fundamentally determined by considerations about what is *a part of* a thing's essence, its being what it is, and its defining account respectively. It is in virtue of these considerations that certain modal claims are put forward: it is because Y's essence or definition includes as a part X (where X is either a basic entity or a basic concept respectively) but not conversely that X *can* be or *can* be defined without Y but Y *cannot* be or *cannot* be defined without X. If so, such modal claims are secondary or derivative: for they depend on the basic notions of being a part of an entity's what-it-is or a concept's definition respectively. This seems consistent not only with Kit Fine's approach to ontological independence but also with his more fundamental account of essence. As he argues, the concept of necessity is 'inappropriate for understanding the concept of essence', although any essentialist claim (of the form 'x *essentially* is F') will entail some necessary truth. For the latter type of truth is not primary or basic, since it is true in virtue of an object's identity, its being what it is, but not the other way about.[60] Indeed, some of Aristotle's own formulations seem to favour this view of essence by taking the notions of being a part of an entity's essence or a concept's definition as basic and as the source of any relevant modal claims. Thus, for instance, in the context of clarifying a certain type of *per se* attribute, Aristotle writes:

These are those [attributes] in which there occurs either the account or the name of that of which they are attributes, and it is not possible to explicate such things without this, as, for example, the white may be explicated without the man, but the female cannot be explicated without the animal. (*Metaph. Z* 5, 1030^{b}23–6, trans. Bostock, slightly modified)

[59] In this respect my interpretation is different from and preferable to Makin's approach, which—alongside the problematic existential construal—takes the modal element to be basic in Aristotle's account of ontological priority and crucial for understanding this account as applied to (for example) *Metaphysics Θ* 8. Makin argues that 'in order to establish a conclusion about priority in substance we have to think about possibilities—whether it is *possible* for there to be Fs without Gs or not' (Θ, 193, emphasis original).

[60] See K. Fine, 'Essence and Modality', in *Logic and Language* (Philosophical Perspectives, 8, ed. J. Tomberlin; Atascadero, Calif., 1994), 1–16 at 8–9.

This passage, arguably, *grounds the modal claim* that the definition of (for example) 'being female' *cannot* be formulated without mentioning (the definition of) 'animal' (but not conversely) *on the definitional-essentialist claim* that the definition of the former *includes as a component* the name or the account of the latter. This last objection, then, just like the difficulties discussed earlier, does not constitute a serious or insuperable challenge to my view, which remains a philosophically and exegetically advantageous position.

Christ Church, Oxford

APPENDIX
Textual and Interpretative Issues in *Metaph. Δ* 11, 1019ᵃ1–14

[i] τὰ μὲν δὴ οὕτω λέγεται πρότερα καὶ ὕστερα, τὰ δὲ κατὰ φύσιν καὶ οὐσίαν, ὅσα ἐνδέχεται εἶναι ἄνευ ἄλλων, ἐκεῖνα δὲ ἄνευ ἐκείνων μή· ᾗ διαιρέσει ἐχρήσατο Πλάτων. (1019ᵃ1–4)

I take the notion of ontological priority to be introduced by the phrase τὰ δὲ κατὰ φύσιν καὶ οὐσίαν [λέγεται πρότερα καὶ ὕστερα] at 1019ᵃ2–3. This notion is explicated by the claim ὅσα ἐνδέχεται εἶναι ἄνευ ἄλλων, ἐκεῖνα δὲ ἄνευ ἐκείνων μή made at ᵃ3–4, which I labelled as [IC].

[ii] ἐπεὶ δὲ τὸ εἶναι πολλαχῶς, πρῶτον μὲν τὸ ὑποκείμενον πρότερον, διὸ ἡ οὐσία πρότερον, ἔπειτα ἄλλως τὰ κατὰ δύναμιν καὶ κατ' ἐντελέχειαν· . . . (1019ᵃ4–7)

In [i] the notion of ontological priority is understood in terms of [IC], while [IC] includes εἶναι as a crucial constituent. Thus, since ᵃ4–5 introduces the familiar Aristotelian claim that τὸ εἶναι πολλαχῶς [sc. λέγεται similarly to the λέγεται at ᵃ2?], it follows that ontological priority and [IC] are distinguished according to the relevant ways of εἶναι: εἶναι as subject and εἶναι as potential and actual being. If so, Aristotle can introduce the three corresponding types of priority: type (*a*) of subjects; (*b*1) in respect of potential being; and (*b*2) in respect of actual being.

Cleary (*Senses*, 47) argues (*contra* Ross, who thinks that ᵃ4–6 just introduces the distinction between subject/substance and non-substance categories) that the διό at 1019ᵃ5 shows that Aristotle argues *from* the priority criterion to the priority of subjects and from this to the priority of substance. I rather think that Aristotle's fundamental assumption is the multiplicity of the ways of εἶναι. On this assumption, plus the notion of ontological priority and [IC], Aristotle derives the type of ontological priority that belongs to subjects. However, since substances must be subjects of some type, he then infers the notion of ontological priority of substances.

[iii] τὰ μὲν γὰρ κατὰ δύναμιν πρότερά ἐστι τὰ δὲ κατὰ ἐντελέχειαν, οἷον κατὰ δύναμιν μὲν ἡ ἡμίσεια τῆς ὅλης καὶ τὸ μόριον τοῦ ὅλου καὶ ἡ ὕλη τῆς οὐσίας, κατ᾽ ἐντελέχειαν δ᾽ ὕστερον· διαλυθέντος γὰρ κατ᾽ ἐντελέχειαν ἔσται. (1019ᵃ7–11)

The participle διαλυθέντος at ᵃ10 is in the genitive singular and refers back to the examples in the same grammatical case at ᵃ9–10: τῆς ὅλης, τοῦ ὅλου, and τῆς οὐσίας. Accordingly, the subject of κατ᾽ ἐντελέχειαν ἔσται at ᵃ10–11 must be an understood ταῦτα which refers back to the nominatives ἡ ἡμίσεια, τὸ μόριον, and ἡ ὕλη.

There is no need to understand or supply πρότερα after κατ᾽ ἐντελέχειαν ἔσται at ᵃ10–11. However, even if one did so, my interpretation would not face any difficulties. Without πρότερα, my interpretation implies that 'they', the remnants or cut-off parts, are *actualized as remnants* or *cut-off parts*, after the passing-away of a complete whole; if so, they are ontologically prior to a whole *in respect of potential* or *incomplete being*. With an understood πρότερα, my view entails that 'they' are prior in respect of actual being to a whole *as actual remnants* or *cut-off parts*. As I noted, however, the second option, even if possible, seems far-fetched: it is effectively equivalent to the first option but unorthodox in expression.

[iv] τρόπον δή τινα πάντα τὰ πρότερον καὶ ὕστερον λεγόμενα κατὰ ταῦτα λέγεται· τὰ μὲν γὰρ κατὰ γένεσιν ἐνδέχεται ἄνευ τῶν ἑτέρων εἶναι, οἷον τὸ ὅλον τῶν μορίων, τὰ δὲ κατὰ φθοράν, οἷον τὸ μόριον τοῦ ὅλου. ὁμοίως δὲ καὶ τἆλλα. (1019ᵃ11–14)

I agree with Cleary (*Senses*, 47) that, in order to understand this section, one should first remove the brackets which Ross and Jaeger add at ᵃ4 before ἐπεί and at ᵃ11 after ἔσται. A first reason for this suggestion is that the example at ᵃ13–14, τὸ ὅλον τῶν μορίων and τὸ μόριον τοῦ ὅλου, is identical with one of the examples mentioned in the bracketed text (ᵃ9). Second, Aristotle maintains that things are prior or posterior to one another κατὰ γένεσιν and κατὰ φθοράν (ᵃ12; ᵃ13–14). But passing-away is also mentioned in Ross's and Jaeger's bracketed text (ᵃ10: διαλυθέντος). These two points suggest that Δ 11's conclusion in [iv] is closely connected (at least) with [iii], the last section of their bracketed text. If so, one should delete the brackets and seek to understand [iv] in the light of [iii].

I take πάντα τὰ πρότερον καὶ ὕστερον λεγόμενα at ᵃ11–12 as referring back only to τὰ κατὰ φύσιν καὶ οὐσίαν [πρότερα καὶ ὕστερα] at ᵃ2–3. The main reason for this is that the type of priority mentioned at ᵃ11–12 is set out at ᵃ12–14 in terms of the claim ἐνδέχεται ἄνευ . . . εἶναι, which is clearly equivalent to [IC] at ᵃ3–4. Hence, just as at ᵃ3–4 [IC] clarifies the ontological type of priority (κατὰ φύσιν καὶ οὐσίαν), so too at ᵃ12–14 it explicates πάντα τὰ πρότερον καὶ ὕστερον λεγόμενα as an ontological type of priority. If so, πάντα τὰ πρότερον καὶ ὕστερον λεγόμενα refers back only to priority κατὰ φύσιν καὶ οὐσίαν at ᵃ2–3 but not to all types of Δ 11's priority. If the reference were to *Metaphysics* Δ 11 as a whole, the claim would be that all types of Δ 11's priority can be reduced to or expressed in terms of ontological priority. This, however, would be an overambitious claim in need of some clarification, something which Aristotle does not offer in this context.

Ross (*Metaphysics*, i. 318), by contrast, takes πάντα τὰ πρότερον καὶ ὕστερον λεγόμενα as implying that 'all senses of "prior" can be reduced to that named in line 3, ὅσα ἐνδέχεται εἶναι ἄνευ ἄλλων, ἐκεῖνα δὲ ἄνευ ἐκείνων μή'. Similarly, Kirwan (*Γ, Δ, & E*, 156) holds that the aim of [iv] is to reduce all types of Δ 11's priority to priority in respect of 'these last' (in nature-substance or in potentiality and actuality?), although Aristotle does not specify how this can be achieved. Cleary (*Senses*, 51) also argues that all types of Δ 11's priority can be reduced to or expressed in terms of priority in nature or substance, sometimes with the help of the distinction 'in respect of potentiality'/'in respect of actuality'.

In my interpretation, the phrase κατὰ ταῦτα (ᵃ12), after the removal of the parentheses, does not refer back to κατὰ φύσιν καὶ οὐσίαν in [i] but to κατὰ δύναμιν and κατὰ ἐντελέχειαν in [iii]. To paraphrase: 'in a way, *all* ontologically prior or posterior things, which do or do not (respectively) satisfy [IC], are so *according to these last notions* (κατὰ ταῦτα, i.e. κατὰ δύναμιν and κατὰ ἐντελέχειαν just analysed in [iii]); for some *can be without* others in respect of generation, while the latter *can be without* the former in respect of destruction' (ᵃ12–14). The underlying connection between actual being and generation and between potential being and destruction has already been introduced implicitly through διαλυθέντος at ᵃ10.

So understood, the argument advanced in [iii]–[iv] implies that there is a systematic connection between ontological priority in respect of potential and actual being and priority in respect of destruction and generation respectively, a connection which I set out in Section 4.2 above. A schematic way in which to represent textually this systematic connection would run as follows: τὰ μὲν γὰρ [κατ' ἐντελέχειαν] κατὰ γένεσιν ἐνδέχεται . . ., τὰ δὲ [κατὰ δύναμιν] κατὰ φθοράν [ἐνδέχεται] (ᵃ12–14).

Just like πάντα τὰ πρότερον καὶ ὕστερον λεγόμενα at ᵃ11, so too the phrase ὁμοίως δὲ καὶ τἆλλα at ᵃ14 does not, in my interpretation, refer back to all types of Δ 11's priority. I think it is more plausible to take ὁμοίως δὲ καὶ τἆλλα as ranging only over the types of τὰ κατὰ φύσιν καὶ οὐσίαν [πρότερα] discussed at 1019ᵃ1 ff. If so, this phrase should, in the first instance, be conceived as generalizing over the rest of the examples at ᵃ8–10: 'what obtains in the whole–part example also holds good in the other examples [ὁμοίως δὲ καὶ τἆλλα], those of the line–segment and the substance–matter'.

246 *Michail M. Peramatzis*

At the same time, however, ὁμοίως δὲ καὶ τἆλλα should be seen as also generalizing over the type of ontological priority which belongs to subjects and substances (ᵃ5–6: what I called 'type (*a*)' ontological priority). For, in my view of the claim made at 1019ᵃ11–12, *all* ontologically prior and posterior items discussed at ᵃ1–11 (πάντα τὰ [κατὰ φύσιν καὶ οὐσίαν] πρότερον καὶ ὕστερον λεγόμενα), which do or do not (respectively) satisfy [IC], can be understood κατὰ ταῦτα, in terms of this last distinction between κατὰ δύναμιν and κατὰ ἐντελέχειαν. In particular, ontological priority of subjects (discussed at ᵃ5–6) can be set out on the basis of priority κατὰ ἐντελέχειαν. Further, since this last notion is parallel to priority κατὰ γένεσιν, it follows that priority of subjects-substances can also be understood in terms of priority κατὰ γένεσιν.

BIBLIOGRAPHY

Bostock, D. (trans. and comm.), *Aristotle:* Metaphysics *Books Z and H* [*Z & H*] (Oxford, 1994).

Burnyeat, M., *et al.*, *Notes on Eta and Theta* (Oxford, 1984).

—— *Notes on Z* [*Z*] (Oxford, 1979).

Charles, D., *Aristotle on Meaning and Essence* (Oxford, 2000).

—— 'Some Comments on Prof. Enrico Berti's "Being and Essence in Contemporary Interpretations of Aristotle"', in A. Bottani, M. Carrara, and P. Giaretta (eds.), *Individuals, Essence and Identity: Themes of Analytic Metaphysics* (Dordrecht and London, 2002), 109–26.

Charlton, W., *Aristotle's* Physics *I, II* (Oxford, 1970).

Cleary, J., *Aristotle on the Many Senses of Priority* [*Senses*] (Carbondale, Ill., 1988).

Dancy, R. M., 'Aristotle and the Priority of Actuality' ['Priority'], in S. Knuuttila (ed.), *Reforging the Great Chain of Being* (Dordrecht, 1980), 73–115.

Fine, G., 'Separation', *Oxford Studies in Ancient Philosophy*, 2 (1984), 31–87.

Fine, K., 'Essence and Modality', in *Logic and Language* (Philosophical Perspectives, 8, ed. J. Tomberlin; Atascadero, Calif., 1994), 1–16.

—— 'Ontological Dependence' ['Dependence'], *Proceedings of the Aristotelian Society*, 95 (1995), 269–90.

Gill, M. L., *Aristotle on Substance: The Paradox of Unity* [*Substance*] (Princeton, 1989).

Jaeger, W. (ed.), *Aristotelis Metaphysica* (Oxford, 1957).

Kirwan, C. (trans. and comm.), *Aristotle's* Metaphysics, *Books Γ, Δ, and E* [*Γ, Δ, & E*] (Oxford, 1971).

Makin, S. (trans. and comm.), *Aristotle:* Metaphysics*, Book Θ [Θ]* (Oxford, 2006).

—— 'What Does Aristotle Mean by Priority in Substance?' ['Priority'], *Oxford Studies in Ancient Philosophy*, 24 (2003), 209–38.

Maudlin, T., 'Substances and Space–Time: What Aristotle Would Have Said to Einstein', *Studies in the History and Philosophy of Science*, 21 (1990), 531–61.

Morrison, D., 'Separation in Aristotle's Metaphysics' ['Separation'], *Oxford Studies in Ancient Philosophy*, 3 (1985), 125–57.

Panayides, C. Y., 'Aristotle on the Priority of Actuality in Substance' ['Priority'], *Ancient Philosophy*, 19 (1999), 327–44.

Ross, W. D. (ed. and comm.), *Aristotle's* Metaphysics *[Metaphysics]* (2 vols.; Oxford, 1924).

Spellman, L., *Substance and Separation in Aristotle [Separation]* (Cambridge, 1995).

Wedin, M. V., *Aristotle's Theory of Substance: The* Categories *and* Metaphysics *Zeta* (Oxford, 2000).

Witt, C., 'The Priority of Actuality' ['Priority'], in T. Scaltsas, D. Charles, and M. L. Gill (eds.), *Unity, Identity, and Explanation in Aristotle's* Metaphysics (Oxford, 1994), 215–28.

—— *Ways of Being: Potentiality and Actuality in Aristotle's Metaphysics [Ways]* (Ithaca, NY, 2003).

EXCAVATING *DISSOI LOGOI* 4

D. T. J. BAILEY

I

I BEGIN with a necessary apology for the extreme obscurity of the text I shall discuss. The *Dissoi Logoi*, whose fourth chapter is the subject of this paper, is perhaps unique among texts in the history of philosophy for its murkiness. It is an anonymously authored philosophical work appearing to argue, among other things, for the sameness and then the difference of properties such as good and bad, just and unjust, true and false. Almost every aspect of it likely to interest scholars is monstrously undetermined. Thus:

(1) Its date is unknown. Many suppose it to be a Sophistic moot book or the like from around the late fifth/early fourth century BC.[1] Others take the location of its only manuscripts, always in the works of Sextus Empiricus, to indicate a dating anything up to six hundred years later. One scholar has suggested that it might have been written as late as the medieval end of the Byzantine era.[2]

(2) Its original dialect is unknown. It is largely composed in Doric, but with numerous Atticisms and dashes of Ionic. The relation between the first two is not sufficiently clear to indicate whether the work was written by a non-Doric speaker for a Doric audience, or whether the text we now have was composed entirely in Doric

© D. T. J. Bailey 2008

I am very grateful to Brad Inwood, David Sedley, and an anonymous referee for *Oxford Studies* for some extremely helpful criticism and advice. I should also like to express my gratitude to Robert Wardy, who encouraged this piece in its original form as an essay submitted for the Cambridge University M.Phil. in Classics in 2000.

[1] For a detailed discussion of one disagreement, even among those who view the text as belonging to the early Sophistic movement, see T. M. Robinson, *Contrasting Arguments: An Edition of the* Dissoi Logoi (Salem, NH, 1979), 34–41. I rely on this magnificent work of scholarship throughout.

[2] T. M. Conley, 'Dating the So-Called *Dissoi Logoi*: A Cautionary Note', *Ancient Philosophy*, 5 (1985), 59–65.

and then progressively Atticized by later scribes less and less familiar with the Doric dialect.

(3) Partly because of its content, and partly because of (1) and
(2), its purpose is unknown. Even for someone confident that the
work belongs roughly to the period during which the Sophists
flourished, there are several options. It could be a serious, and hence
disappointingly bad, treatise; a heavy-handed spoof of such works;
a spot-the-errors workbook for novice dialecticians; or a sample of
some Sophist's wares meant to persuade the unwary buyer that he
too will eventually be able to argue both sides of any argument.

Given (1), (2), and (3), it is almost impossible to say anything
about the *Dissoi Logoi* that goes beyond *mere* conjecture. But it
would be a pity to let caution silence all contributions to the understanding of this most mysterious text. In what follows, I discuss two
issues—the meaning of the word *logos*[3] in 4. 1–5, and the argument
of 4. 6—with a view to assessing just how Sophistic this chapter is,
and asking what there is about it that might have aroused interest
in later Sceptical traditions. I shall not count the exercise a failure
if all I can achieve is to make this text even more intriguing than
it has seemed beforehand.

II

Here is a complete translation, with some explanatory footnotes,
of chapter 4:[4]

(1) Twofold arguments are also asserted about what is false and what is
true. Some assert that the false *logos* is different from the true one, others
that they are the same. (2) And I affirm the latter view. Firstly, because
they are expressed in the same words; and then because whenever a *logos* is
expressed, if things have come to pass as the *logos* says, then it is true, but
if they have not come to pass then the same *logos* is false. (3) For example, a
logos accuses someone of temple robbery. If the deed occurred, the *logos* is
true, but if it did not, false. The same goes for the *logos* of the one defending
himself. Also, law courts judge the same *logos* to be both false and true.
(4) Next, if when sitting in a row we say 'I am an initiate', we all say the
same thing, but only I am right since I *am* an initiate. (5) It is clear that the

---

[3] I leave this word transliterated but not translated throughout so as not to pre-
judice the investigation.

[4] I am very grateful to David Sedley for help with the translation, and for making
me see that the text makes sense unemended (see the following footnote).

same *logos* is false when the false is present to it and true when the true is present to it, just as a man, too, is the same when he is a child and a youth and an adult and an old man. (6) But it is also affirmed that the false *logos* is different from the true one, the word differing.[5] For if someone were to ask those maintaining that the same *logos* is false and true which of the two[6] they mean, then if the answer were 'a false one', it is clear that there are two of them.[7] But if the person replied 'this same one is true and false',[8] and if he has ever said or sworn anything true, it follows that those same things are false too. And if he knows some truthful man, he knows that the same man is also a liar. (7) And on the basis of their *logos* they assert these: that if the event has happened then the *logos* is true, and if it has not happened the *logos* is false. In which case it makes no difference (8) later for the jurors what they judge, for they were not present at the events. (9) And even they agree that that with which the false is mixed is false, that with which the true is mixed, true. But this is an entirely different matter.

My thoughts about this chapter were partly inspired by a remark of Martha Kneale's. Writing about 4. 4, she claims that 'We may have here the origin of the Stoic distinction between *phōnē* and *lekton*.'[9] In the thought-experiment described in 4. 4, there is a sense in which everyone says the same thing in so far as everyone makes the same noise (the noise made by saying 'I am an initiate'), but also a sense in which the author says something different from everyone else in so far as he alone says something true. Kneale's thought was that if you can make this distinction, then you have not got far to go in making the distinction between a mere expression—a form of words—and a proposition—the meaning that a form of words can express. The Stoics made this distinction in terms of that between the part of an expression that is corporeal and hence perceptible— a *phōnē*—and that which is incorporeal and hence imperceptible,

[5] Here I follow the text and avoid the emendations favoured by Diels and Robinson. The point, already suggested by more explicit formulations earlier in the *Dissoi Logoi* at 1. 11 and 3. 13, is just that a difference of terminology indicates a difference in the world. Since 'true' is a different word from 'false', then supposedly a true *logos* will be a different thing from a false one.

[6] I take this question to be about the pair 'a true *logos*' and 'a false *logos*'.

[7] That is, it is clear that the true *logos* and the false one are *two* distinct things, and not one and the same *logos*, as the identity thesis maintains.

[8] I take the thought here to be that the proponent of the identity thesis cannot maintain that his thesis is false—for obvious reasons—but he cannot simply say that it is true either. For according to (this shifty interpretation of) the identity thesis, the true *logos* is the same as the *false* one. So if the identity thesis is true at all then it is true and false.

[9] W. and M. Kneale, *The Development of Logic* (Oxford, 1960), 16. I have transliterated the Greek expressions in the original text.

a *lekton*. A *lekton* is the Stoic bearer of truth and falsehood, an incorporeal meaning that gets expressed by a corporeal *phōnē* when the latter is both articulate and significant.

It is not my intention to say much about Stoic semantics in this paper, or to evaluate the arguments of those such as Fabricius who actually thought the *Dissoi Logoi* was written by a Stoic.[10] Instead, I want to exploit this distinction between the perceptible parts of language which are not meaningful taken by themselves (I shall call these *tokens*) and the meaningful imperceptible parts that they can express (I shall call these *propositions*) to investigate what our author means when he uses the term *logos*. Initially, my conclusion is negative. An analysis of *Dissoi Logoi* 4. 1–5, the 'identity thesis' attempting to establish that the true *logos* is the same as the false one, shows that he could be using *logos* to mean either a token or a proposition. But the transfer of these materials to the second half of the chapter, the 'difference thesis' attempting to establish that in some sense the true *logos* is different from the false, reveals some surprising consequences. They provide some evidence to support or encourage both those unconvinced that the writer is a pre-Platonic sophist, and for those curious about why the work might have been of interest to philosophical Sceptics in (supposedly) later antiquity.

III

At 4. 2 the author argues for the identity thesis with the claim that the true *logos* and the false one are said 'with the same words'. We might plausibly take *logos* here to mean a token, for something can be a word just by virtue of being composed of perceptible parts, sounds, or marks, without thereby having any semantic properties. For example, there are words, properly so called, such as *'blituri'*,[11] which we do not read as being meaningful, and surely any *logos* composed of such words will be itself a mere token, lacking semantic properties. Perhaps the sameness of this thing across true and

---

[10] Fabricius thought the author was Sextus of Chaeronea, Plutarch's nephew and a teacher of Marcus Aurelius. He held that it was the accident of having the same *praenomen* as later antiquity's most celebrated sceptic that explained why the *Dissoi Logoi* always appears in the latter's manuscripts. See Robinson, *Contrasting Arguments*, 2–3.

[11] The example is Stoic; it is taken from D.L. 7. 57. See A. A. Long and D. N. Sedley (eds.), *The Hellenistic Philosophers*, vol. i (Cambridge, 1987), 195–202.

false *logoi* reveals the sense in which the true *logos* is the same as the false. Alternatively, the author might think that something with semantic properties is the same in the true *logos* as the false one. With Robinson, I translated τοῖς αὐτοῖς ὀνόμασι as 'with the same words', but one might equally translate it as 'with the same names'. It is possible that the *Dissoi Logoi* antedates Plato's discovery in the *Sophist* that *logoi* are composed of logically heterogeneous parts, names and verbs. If that is so our author might well suppose that a *logos* can comprise just names. But names are not mere tokens like '*blituri*'. They are words used in a certain way, read as having the semantic property of referring (or at least in some sense trying or pretending to refer). In that case there would be more to the author's *logoi* in 4. 2 than the typographical or phonetic properties that constitute tokenhood. And whether he is familiar with Plato's discovery or not, we certainly need not suppose him to be talking about mere tokens in 4. 2 because in 4. 4, the passage which sparked Kneale's interest, any reference to words or names drops out altogether. All we get is the claim that in the thought-experiment 'we all say the same thing'. But this still leaves us in the dark about the author's *logoi*—we do not know precisely what the thing is *that gets said*. For all we know from 4. 2, the thing that is common to true and false assertions might be a mere token, or it might be what Kneale calls, in this context, 'the statement or proposition'.

The interpretation of *logos* in 4. 3 can be argued reasonably either way as well. Here the *logos* in question expresses an accusation against someone of temple robbery, where the same *logos* is true if the defendant robbed the temple and false if he did not. One could easily argue against taking *logoi* as tokens here. For it seems quite unlikely, at least when thinking of their oral performances, that the accuser and the defendant will introduce the same phonetic object. The defendant would not normally refer to himself in the third person, nor will his counsel be prohibited from referring to his client with pronouns. Rather, there will be something the prosecutor affirms when he utters the token 'Callias robbed the temple', and that very same thing will be denied by Callias when he utters the different token 'I did not rob the temple'. What is the same in each case, but affirmed in one, denied in the other, is not a mere token but a proposition. But there is still the possibility of a token reading. For it might be that there is some affidavit put before the jury, written on a scroll or wax tablet, in which case there would be a clear sense in which both prosecutor and defendant would be disputing about the truth-value of the same perceptible object. (Imagine them pointing, the former saying 'That's true', the latter 'That's false'.)

The investigation becomes more serious and interesting once we return to 4. 4. This contains the strongest evidence for understanding the author's *logoi* as tokens. For surely it is only the sounds, or how things would look when transcribed into a suitable language, that are the same when a group of people all say 'I am an initiate'. Once those sounds are understood as having semantic properties, then there is a sense in which they do *not* all say the same thing, for the author's 'I' refers to him and no one else, his neighbour's 'I' to his neighbour and no one else, and so on.

But this is not decisive. For there is a way of interpreting the thing that is the same in each utterance of 'I am an initiate' as having *some* semantic properties, while keeping the author's thought that everyone says exactly the same thing even without everyone being right. How?

Frege claimed in his famous paper 'The Thought', when discussing how 'I' refers, that 'everyone is presented to himself in a special and primitive way, in which he is presented to no one else'.[12] Colin McGinn has pointed out that there is a scope ambiguity in this claim.[13] Does Frege mean that, *for everyone*, there is some mode or other in which he presents himself to himself and in which he is presented to no one else? Or does he mean that *there is some mode or other* such that everyone presents himself to himself in that mode, and is presented to no one else in that mode? The former is compatible with there being as many different modes of presentation as there are people, while the latter is not. The latter says that if there is a mode in which I present myself to myself and no one else, then you present yourself to yourself in that mode and no one else, and Gottlob Frege presented himself to himself in that mode and no one else, etc.[14]

Which of these Frege meant does not concern us. The point is just that, if the second reading of his claim at least makes sense,

---

[12] In M. Beaney (ed.), *The Frege Reader* (Oxford, 1997), 323–45 at 333.

[13] C. McGinn, *The Subjective View* (Oxford, 1987), 58.

[14] In order to avoid contradiction here we should have to understand each individual's mode as being a token of the same type as everyone else's mode, or a trope of the same universal.

then there is a way in which even though the *reference* of 'I' varies from speaker to speaker, there is none the less something semantic common to every use of that expression. Even though my 'I' *refers* to me and yours to you, there is some meaning element common to both expressions because their senses involve the same mode for each of us.[15]

In this sense there will be *something* that all the people in a row say when each one says 'I am an initiate' that is not confined to the level of the mere tokens formed by their mouths. I see no reason to rule out in principle the thought that our author could have had a vague sense in which all those saying 'I am an initiate' *mean* the same thing even though one of those utterances is true and the rest false. So even in 4. 4 we cannot be precise about what our author's *logoi* are. Perhaps they are mere tokens, but perhaps in this context they are meaningful entities.

What about 4. 5? Here, the sameness of a *logos* across truth and falsehood is compared with the identity of a man across the different stages of his life—childhood, adulthood, and so forth. Here it might be important that a man is some material object, a perceptible public thing that we can see persisting over time. It is the same person who is now an adolescent, now an old man, because he has (albeit rather roughly) the same body. If corporeal facts determine the identity of a man across the changes wrought by age, perhaps the author's thought is that it is the corporeal properties of a *logos* that remain the same across changes wrought by the world, in which case he will be talking about tokens here.

There might be further grounds for taking 4. 5 this way. The same *relata* used for the argument in 4. 5 appear in Aristotle's *Categories* at $4^a10-{}^b25$. But here Aristotle is using the identity of a man over time as a *contrast* with the identity of his truth-value bearers, statements or beliefs, across truth-value changes. Aristotle is considering whether statements or beliefs qualify as substances just as men do according to his criteria. Initially it looks as if they do. For substances are things capable of receiving contraries while retaining their identity across the change. Dark and pale are contraries; one and the same man can go dark in the sun and pale again in

---

[15] Note that I write 'involve' rather than 'are'; for according to Frege sense determines reference. So if your way of presenting yourself to yourself when you use 'I' is a token of the same type as my way, whatever that token is had better not be *identical* with the sense of 'I'. Perhaps this is a reason for taking Frege to have meant the scope distinction to be clarified in the former way in the main text.

the shade; so men are substances. Likewise, the statement or belief that Callias is sitting is the same statement or belief when it is true as it is when it is false. True and false are contraries no less than dark and pale; so, the argument runs, the bearers of truth-values are substances.

Aristotle rightly rejects the conclusion of this argument by pointing out an important difference between the cases. When a man goes from being dark to being pale, it is the man who changes. Things are not like this when a statement changes its truth-value. When a statement about Callias changes its truth-value, what changes is *Callias*, and nothing else. The relevant change is not suitably describable as a change in the statement. So the bearers of truth-values are not substances.

The point of this discussion is that if, unlike Aristotle, you see the bearers of truth-values as being like men in terms of their capacity to sustain their identity over changes from one contrary to another, perhaps this will be because you see them as corporeal, perceptible objects no less than men. And if you think like this, you will probably think that *logoi* are tokens. Now I agree that this is implausible; not even the Giants of the *Sophist*, you might say, are the sort to think that what is now true but later false is *just* something you might hold in your hand on a piece of paper, or hear with your ears. But it is implausible simply because we are now powerfully aware of how many relational factors and values for variables—worlds, times, places, agents, etc.—affect the truth-value of a *logos*; and of how such relations and values cannot be reduced to the mere material properties of a written mark or spoken sound.[16] Such relations and variable-values do not figure in material bodies exchanging their contingent properties while remaining the same things over time. But if you can so much as recognize the relations and variable-values required for something logical to remain the same while something non-logical changes, like Theaetetus passing from sitting to not sitting, then you are well on the way to making the sort of distinction we have just seen Aristotle making. And if you are on that path, you will not think that *logoi* retain their identity in anything like the way in which men do over time.

---

[16] For instance, logical form must also be involved in the continuity of a *logos* when it changes truth-value; and logical form will not in general be reducible to any material properties of an expression.

But it will come as no surprise that we can take 4. 5's *logoi*
as having semantic properties as well. We could take the *relata*
of the analogy to be *logos* identity over truth-value changes and
personal identity over time. Here we can suppose without controversy that what sustains the latter over changes from one contrary
to another need not be anything perceptible like a material body.
For the Greeks could certainly imagine changes in personal identity that are not accompanied by any perceptible material changes:
the phenomenon of metempsychosis was, I dare say, a subject of
considerable intellectual interest whenever and wherever the *Dissoi
Logoi* was composed. Look, for example, at the peregrinations of
Pythagoras' soul described in detail at Diogenes Laertius 8. 4–5. It
is presumably an immaterial soul that successively determines the
personal identities of bodies named Aethalides, Pythagoras, Eu-
phorbus, and Hermotimus. And presumably there is no immediate
and perceptible difference in one of these bodies when this soul
leaves it. What determines personal identity lies beyond the perceptible. So it might be that the relevant analogue for a *logos* in 4. 5
has properties beyond the perceptible too, and counts as something
other than a mere token.

IV

So far the results have been negative. But they will become useful
later on in Section V of this paper. For the moment, I want to dwell
on what I take to be a surprising fact about the argument for the
difference thesis of 4. 6–9.

Semantics after Plato's *Sophist* was geared, quite rightly, to making a sharp distinction between the meaning of a truth-evaluable
expression, what I have so far been calling a proposition, and the
truth-value that it actually has.[17] This is part of the point Aristotle
is making in the passage mentioned above from the *Categories*.
At 4^b8–11 Aristotle says 'it is because the thing is or is not the
case that the *logos* is said to be true or false, not because the *logos*
itself can receive contraries. For quite simply no *logos* or belief is
changed by anything.' The point can be put as follows. When truth-

---

[17] You might say: Plato formulated arguments showing how there can be such a
thing as the truth-*conditions* of *p* even though there is nothing that actually *makes*
p *true*.

values change it is because matters in the world have changed. But meanwhile something essentially changeless persists throughout that change in things, what philosophers now call the content of a proposition or belief.[18] The content of the statement 'Theaetetus sits' is the same whether the referent of the name is sitting or not. The same considerations motivated the Stoics to theorize about non-material subsisting meanings, *lekta*.

It is precisely this thought—that there is some meaningful entity that is the same when it is true as when it is false, something that does not change when things in the world change—that we should expect to see under attack in *Dissoi Logoi* 4. 6–9. In 4. 6 the difference thesis is affirmed: the false *logos* is different from the true one because when the terminology differs, so does the thing to which it refers. An argument for this position might go as follows. The expressions 'true *logos*' and 'false *logos*' do not semantically have the '*logos*' bit in common any more than 'Socrates' and 'Cratylus' semantically have the 'rat' bit in common.[19] Such a difference thesis would treat them as unit names, identifying expressions like 'giraffe' and 'tarantula': and there is nothing that can be a giraffe and a tarantula, or now a giraffe, now a tarantula. As the names differ, so do their referents.

This version of the difference thesis would cohere well with the prevailing view that the second contrasting argument of *Dissoi Logoi* 4, like others throughout the work, represents a fallacious switch satirized in some of Plato's dialogues, that of trying to refute an argument that treated some predicate as expressing a contingent property of things by pretending that the property is part of the essence of things that have it. On this view, although it seems that 4. 1–5 treat truth and falsehood as contingent properties of *logoi* (4. 4 especially), 4. 6–9 should be expected to attack that thesis by supposing that the truth or falsehood of a *logos* determines what *logos* it is, from which it infers the truth of the difference thesis.

Now to maintain that truth-values are essential properties of the

---

[18] Modern philosophers ordinarily recognize at least two levels of linguistic content, in large part precisely because of the issues raised by indexicals such as 'I' in the discussion earlier in the main text. Such refinements are not directly relevant to the coarser Aristotelian distinction I am here mentioning.

[19] This may seem implausibly extreme. But we need something like this in order to make a difference of terminology sufficient for the falsity of the identity thesis. The expressions 'Water' and 'H_2O' are different items of terminology without that showing that nothing is both water and H_2O.

things that bear them is just to maintain an intolerably close relation
between *logoi* and how things stand in the world. It is how things
stand in the world, as Aristotle saw, that constrains truth-value.
But according to the imagined difference thesis I am describing,
the world also determines *what is said* about how those things stand
in the world. If the world determines truth-value, and truth-value
is an essential property of a *logos*, then the world determines what
is said about it. In effect the semantic relation between *logoi* and
what they are about has become as simple as that between a name
and its referent. But then we are plunged into familiar Sophistic
problems about how there can be any such thing as a false *logos* at
all.[20] For it will not now be clear how something's not being the
case can go towards determining the meaning of a *logos* that wrongly
says it is the case. *Which* thing that is not the case determines the
meaning of such a falsehood, if the truth-value of a *logos* determines
its meaning, and how? To use my analogy with terms: it is the
existence of giraffes and tarantulas that makes it the case that the
expressions 'giraffe' and 'tarantula' refer. But now what is it that
does *not* exist that makes it the case that the expression 'snark' does
not refer, and how does it do so? You had better not reply 'snarks',
since their non-existence prevents them from having any effects at
all, let alone the effect of making an expression non-referring.

But what is so striking about the second contrasting argument in
Dissoi Logoi 4 is that this is *not* what we get. Far from giving us an
argument that says that the true *logos* is different from the false one
in such a way as to suggest scepticism about falsehood, 4. 6 gives
us what appears to be a self-refutation argument. That is, it offers
an argument *depending* on the possibility of a false *logos*.

Our author can be convicted of the slide from (*a*) treating truth
and falsehood in the identity thesis as *contingent properties* of *logoi*
to (*b*) implying in the difference thesis that, were the identity thesis
correct, *all logoi would enjoy truth and falsehood together at the same
time*. This is the only explanation I can think of for the moves
made in 4. 6. The identity theorist is asked 'And which kind of
logos is *yours*, then?' There are four possible answers: 'true', 'false',
'true and false', or 'neither true nor false'. The identity theorist

---

[20] For an extensive discussion of this topic, see N. Denyer, *Language, Thought
and Falsehood in Ancient Greek Philosophy* [*Language*] (London, 1991). Chapter 3
shows that scepticism about falsehood was widespread among Plato's predecessors
and contemporaries; chapter 4 shows that even Plato himself was tempted by it.

wrecks his own position if he gives either of the second or fourth answers here. But he cannot give, as he might like, the first one, for according to this prejudicial reading of his slogan 'the same *logos* is true and false', no *logos*, including his own, is *just* true: if it is true at all it must be false as well, in which case, his sneaky opponent can infer, it is false.

The important point is that, for all the naughtiness of the moves in 4. 6, its conclusion depends on treating a *logos* as true or false depending on whether things are as it says they are. And here we just have a situation where, supposedly, things cannot at all be as a *logos* says they are, as in the traditional 'Liar' paradox. But to wonder whether things are how a *logos* says they are is pretty clearly to recognize a distinction between those things and what is said about them. In fact the perspective of the actual difference thesis involves treating *logoi* as true or false according to the theory of truth sketched in 4. 7, where a *logos* is true when the thing it is about has occurred, false if not. Such a formulation is not very distant from the fuller definition of truth given by Aristotle at *Metaphysics Γ*, 1011^b26–7: 'to say of what is, that it is not, or of what is not, that it is, is false; while to say of what is, that it is, or of what is not, that it is not, is true'. Aristotle's formulation is important in the history of semantics in part because of how cavalier he can afford to be when speaking of what is not, as if the problems of falsehood and non-being had not troubled him. The likely explanation for this, borne out by his claims about the heterogeneous parts of *logoi* in the *De interpretatione*,[21] is that Aristotle knew the *Sophist* and felt that it had solved once and for all the problems about non-being.[22] Hence he need not worry about them when it comes to giving a definition of truth. The author of the *Dissoi Logoi* looks no less carefree: and while this is certainly not hard evidence that he wrote after Plato, I think it does call into question the claims of those who take him for a Presocratic sophist labouring under the influence of Protagoras. For he does not follow a Protagorean way of establishing the difference thesis on the back of scepticism about falsehood.

To conclude this section, let me urge the thought that this is not the only feature of *Dissoi Logoi* 4 with a Platonic or post-Platonic flavour. The account of truth-values in 4. 5 sounds very much like

---

[21] For discussion see P. T. Geach, 'History of the Corruptions of Logic' in id., *Logic Matters* (Oxford, 1972), 44–61.

[22] This is the conclusion argued for by Denyer, *Language*, 183–5.

an instance of the general account of properties from the end of the *Phaedo*, where things are *F* when *F*-ness *is present* in them. More tellingly, my understanding of 4. 8 gives it a whiff of the jury passage from *Theaet.* 200 D–201 C. The latter tries to make the point that, since the jurors were not present at the events over which they deliberate, they can never *know* how things turned out. The best they can do is to acquire a true belief about those events. *Dissoi Logoi* 4. 6 is apparently making a related point: that jurors cannot come to know what happened just by inspecting a *logos*. For it is the events themselves, things by implication different from the *logos*, that make it true or false, and the jurors do not have access to those. These points, taken together with our author's comfort with the concept of falsehood, suggest to me that the *Dissoi Logoi*, or at least its fourth chapter, may well have been written after Plato.

V

Return to the fact that our author appears comfortable with the thought that *logoi* can be false. What is the connection between that and the investigation in Section III that showed we cannot pin him down in 4. 1–5 on whether his *logoi* are tokens or propositions? The last suggestion I want to make is that the neutrality of 4. 1–5 on that question might give us a clue about why at least the fourth chapter of *Dissoi Logoi* might have been of interest to Sceptical traditions in periods later than the generally agreed dating to the era of the Sophistic movement (on which Section IV above has tried to cast some doubt). Recall the identity thesis, 'The same *logos* is true and false'. Prescinding for the moment from the details of the text, is there anything substantial and genuinely informative to be gained from objecting to this claim? That is, is there something to be gained from denying that a *logos* is some third thing that can be expressed now by a contingently true token, now by a contingently false one? I think there is. Such a denial would amount to the claim that, whatever *logoi* are, they are not things capable of changing truth-value. Whatever truth-value they have, they have *once for all*. Nothing that is ever true can change from being true to being false, and vice versa. This claim is certainly consistent with the theory of truth sketched in 4. 7, which showed that our author is not susceptible to Sophistic problems about non-being, and quite different from the claim that both truth-values are always enjoyed at the same time together by every *logos*, the suppressed premiss that drives the self-refutation in 4. 6. Moreover, it is also a plausible claim. The thought that truths and falsehoods are once-for-all truths and falsehoods has been held in our own time by Quine. On this interpretation, the difference thesis would be a denial that the same *logos* is ever now true, now false, or true in one mouth but not in another. It is the thought that there is no further meaningful entity, such as a proposition, which is there to be expressed by different tokens. Quine holds something similar. He denies that there is some semantic entity which gets 'expressed' by true and false token sentences because he holds that such entities—propositions—would have identity conditions indeterminable by his method of radical translation. Such semantic items as propositions so understood are therefore well beyond the pale of his naturalism. Hence Quine's theorizing about so-called 'eternal sentences', sentences[23] whose truth-values are fixed for all time once they are read as being meaningful.[24]

Now if this idea can be retrieved from the murky details of the difference thesis, it might be that someone reading it in later antiquity saw 4. 6–9 as a claim that semantic properties enter *only* when we fix the truth-value of an utterance, and that the *logoi* whose nature we found underdetermined in 4. 1–5 are therefore *mere* tokens by the lights of 4. 6–9. According to this reading of the difference thesis, there is no independent thing whose meaning we express when we all say 'I am an initiate'. All that we have in common is an

---

[23] Quine's distinction between sentences and propositions is not the same as the one I have been using in this paper. For he holds that there are both token-sentences and type-sentences, both of which can be meaningful; and also that he can countenance both of these while rejecting the need to admit propositions into his ontology. But I have been contrasting propositions with tokens alone; I have treated the latter solely as individuals and not also as universals, and also as lacking semantic properties. I have done so in order to discuss this work in the light of the distinction between Stoic *phōnai* and *lekta*. But the difference between my framing of the issues and Quine's more elaborate theory is irrelevant to the main point here. Quine is responding to philosophers who have felt a need to suppose the existence of propositions as what tokens in different languages share, or as bearers of truth and the objects of propositional attitudes etc. Sometimes such philosophers, he claims, have argued in the following fashion: 'if we can speak of a sentence as meaningful, or as having meaning, then there must be a meaning that it has, and this meaning will be identical with or distinct from the meaning that another sentence has' (W. V. O. Quine, *Word and Object* (Cambridge, Mass., 1960), 206). Quine is rightly suspicious of this move; it is suspicion of a quite similar move in the inference to the existence of Stoic *lekta* that I claim might be fostered by my imagined reading of the difference thesis.   [24] Quine, *Word and Object*, 191–232.

object formed by our mouths. So, reading the whole chapter as a pair of contrasting arguments about the need to postulate semantic entities, one might read the identity thesis of 4. 1–5 as asserting that *logoi* can have semantic properties before reference is determined— the analysis in Section III shows that nothing rules out taking 4. 1–5 in this way, not even 4. 4—while the difference thesis of 4. 6–9 attempts to deny this, holding that *logoi* have permanent truth-values once they are read as having any semantic properties.

Of course, it would be much too far-fetched to attribute this position to the author of the *Dissoi Logoi* himself. He is nowhere near so subtle. The self-refutation argument of 4. 6 would need quite a few extra premisses spelt out in order even to look as if it was directed against the thought that there are meaningful entities which different tokens, true and false, are capable of expressing. But it might provide an explanation of why the *Dissoi Logoi* was associated with our major source for Pyrrhonism, Sextus Empiricus, in whose manuscripts the *Dissoi Logoi* is always found. It might also explain why, according to Diogenes Laertius 9. 106, the earlier Sceptic Zeuxis (a friend of Aenesidemus) wrote a treatise 'On *Dissoi Logoi*'. For regardless of when our work was written, if we can read *Dissoi Logoi* 4 as arguing for, then against, the existence of semantic items beyond perceptible tokens, then we can read it as something Pyrrhonian sceptics might have been seriously interested in, as urging (however incoherently) suspension of judgement about Stoic *lekta*.

As Burnyeat puts it, 'sober readers will suspend judgement on every question about [*Dissoi logoi*]'.[25] Quite so. I do not expect to have persuaded anyone that this chapter was written later than the scholarly consensus holds, or that and why it was of serious interest to later sceptical traditions. But I do hope to have uncovered a bit more evidence for these views.

University of Colorado at Boulder

BIBLIOGRAPHY

Burnyeat, M., '*Dissoi Logoi*', in E. Craig (ed.), *The Routledge Encyclopedia of Philosophy* (London, 1998), 106–7.

[25] M. Burnyeat, '*Dissoi Logoi*', in E. Craig (ed.), *The Routledge Encyclopedia of Philosophy* (London, 1998), 106–7.

Conley, T. M., 'Dating the So-Called *Dissoi Logoi*: A Cautionary Note', *Ancient Philosophy*, 5 (1985), 59–65.

Denyer, N., *Language, Thought and Falsehood in Ancient Greek Philosophy* [*Language*] (London, 1991).

Frege, G., 'The Thought', in M. Beaney (ed.), *The Frege Reader* (Oxford, 1997), 323–45.

Geach, P. T., 'History of the Corruptions of Logic', in id., *Logic Matters* (Oxford, 1972), 44–61.

Kneale, W., and Kneale, M., *The Development of Logic* (Oxford, 1960).

Long, A. A., and Sedley, D. N. (eds.), *The Hellenistic Philosophers*, vol. i (Cambridge, 1987).

McGinn, C., *The Subjective View* (Oxford, 1987).

Quine, W. V. O., *Word and Object* (Cambridge, Mass., 1960).

Robinson, T. M., *Contrasting Arguments: An Edition of the* Dissoi Logoi (Salem, NH, 1979).

PLOTINUS ON ASTROLOGY

1. Introduction

PLOTINUS was very interested in astrology. We know this because
Porphyry tells us so:

[Plotinus] devoted himself to the tables concerning the stars,[1] not much
with regard to the mathematical aspects, but with greater thoroughness
regarding the castings of horoscopes [τοῖς δὲ τῶν γενεθλιαλόγων ἀποτελε-
σματικοῖς ἀκριβέστερον]. And having discovered the unreliable basis of what
they profess he did not hesitate to refute many things in their writings. (*Life
of Plotinus*, 15. 21–6 Henry–Schwyzer)

Plotinus' own writings also testify to this interest. One of the first
works he wrote, *Enneads* 3. 1 [6], is a treatise on fate which criticizes
astrologers' claims alongside other deterministic systems. Some
time later, he devoted a lengthy section of a long treatise on the
soul, *Enneads* 4. 4 [28]. 30–9, to a discussion of astral causation.
And one of the last works he wrote, *Enneads* 2. 3 [52], is devoted
entirely to the question of whether the stars cause things to happen
in the sublunary world. These texts show a sustained engagement
on Plotinus' part, not just with the question of how the stars relate
to the sublunary world, but also with the more specific question
of whether it is possible for there to be a science that predicts
particular events by observing the heavens.[2] Or more accurately:

© Peter Adamson 2008

I am grateful to the Leverhulme Trust for its support while this paper was being
written. The paper has benefited from reading ancient philosophy with colleagues
at King's College London, especially M. M. McCabe, who has made me more alert
to methodological points such as those mentioned in the last two paragraphs of the
article. I am also grateful for comments received on the paper when I presented it in
London, Helsinki, and Leeds. Finally, I thank Bob Sharples, James Wilberding, and
Philip van der Eijk for their useful and detailed written comments and suggestions.

[1] For this translation see J. Wilberding, *Plotinus' Cosmology: A Study of* Ennead
II. 1 (40) [*Plotinus' Cosmology*] (Oxford, 2006), 4–5.

[2] For previous discussions of Plotinus' views on astrology, see J. M. Dillon, 'Plo-

Plotinus takes it for granted that astrologers do sometimes succeed in making such predictions, and asks how we are to explain this (supposed) fact.

This point bears further emphasis. In the various criticisms of astrology just listed, Plotinus does not focus on the idea that astrologers are often wrong in their predictions, or say that they get things right only by luck. Rather, he concedes that astrology is often successful. He is also happy to admit that other methods could genuinely tell us about future events, for instance prophecy based on the observation of birds. What interests him is rather the philosophical implications of astrology's success. And he is surely right to be interested in this. If it were in fact true that astrology could predict the future, this would raise major philosophical problems. One that leaps to mind is this: if an astrologer knows today that some event will happen in the future, does this imply that the event in question is already inevitable or necessary? This worry is of course similar to the sort of deterministic argument raised by Aristotle in his famous discussion of the sea battle at *On Interpretation* 9. But it does not seem to be a worry that Plotinus shares. At least, he never singles it out as a problematic consequence of astrology.

Plotinus is instead worried by the astrologers' causal accounts of why their predictions are accurate.[3] He seems to have been better informed about these accounts than other ancient critics of astrology. The discussion in 2. 3, especially, shows that he was acquainted with contemporary astrological theory to a high degree of detail—

tinus on Whether the Stars are Causes', *Res Orientales*, 12 (1999), 87–91, a brief but useful discussion focusing primarily on the early 3. 1; and A. A. Long, 'Astrology: Arguments Pro and Contra' ['Astrology'], in J. Barnes *et al.* (eds.), *Science and Speculation: Studies in Hellenistic Theory and Practice* (Cambridge, 1982), 165–92, which discusses Plotinus alongside numerous other ancient figures. For a development of the contrast between hard and soft astrology made by Long (on which see further below), see D. Rolando, 'L'anima e le Moire: Hard Astrology e Soft Astrology nel pensiero del Plotino', *Discorsi*, 10 (1990), 237–62. Despite the title, this article concentrates on situating astrology within Plotinus' broader metaphysics. For general context see T. Barton, *Ancient Astrology [Astrology]* (London, 1994).

[3] I would like to credit Porphyry with having understood this. I therefore take the phrase φωράσας τῆς ἐπαγγελίας τὸ ἀνεχέλλυον in the passage from the *Life of Plotinus* quoted above to refer not to the inaccuracy of astrologers' predictions (so Armstrong: 'when he had detected the unreliability of their alleged results'), but to the fact that the *grounds* they offer for the predictions are baseless. (Compare Wilberding's translation, quoted above: 'once he discovered that this pursuit is without foundation'.)

this in contrast to critics such as Cicero, whose notions about the astrologers' claims were comparatively vague.[4] But *any* theory that makes the stars causally responsible for sublunary events will have two dire consequences, from Plotinus' point of view. First, and most obviously, such a theory could impact negatively on human autonomy:[5] it would seem that if the stars cause me to perform a given action, then this action is no longer 'up to me'. Second, Plotinus holds that the stars are divine. So if we say that the stars cause evils, then we are making gods responsible for evil, which is absurd.

Plotinus could have avoided these two results by means of a distinction he himself draws, between what A. A. Long has called 'hard' and 'soft' astrology. Hard astrology is the view that the stars cause or make (*poiein*) things happen in our sublunary world. Soft astrology rejects this, but allows for the accuracy of astrology by admitting that the stars do symbolize or signify (*sēmainein*) sublunary things. Of course, soft astrology still requires an explanation for how it is that the stars signify other things within the physical cosmos. And Plotinus has such an explanation available to him. For he follows Plato and the Stoics in thinking that the entire physical cosmos is a united system, indeed a single living thing. It is bound together by *sumpatheia*.[6] Thus the astrologer may, by observing one part (the stars), be able to tell what is happening or will happen in another part (the sublunary world), just as an expert in dance can tell, by looking at one part of a dancer, what the rest of the dancer's body is doing or will be doing. (This image comes from *Enneads* 4. 4. 33.[7]) Here, then, we have a summary of what could easily have been, and in fact sometimes does seem to be, Plotinus' stance on astrology: 'hard' astrology, the idea that stars *cause* all sublunary things, is rejected; 'soft' astrology, the idea that stars *sig-*

---

[4] On this see Long, 'Astrology'. Sextus Empiricus, *M.* 5. 1–40, does survey astrology in a detailed way; many aspects of his presentation parallel that of Plotinus.

[5] I use the word 'autonomy' rather than, for instance, 'freedom', to avoid clouding the philosophical issue. The question is whether the human agent is in fact the *cause* of his or her own actions, or of the consequences of those actions. Hard astrology would deny this and make the stars the causes of the actions and their consequences (along with everything else in the sublunary realm).

[6] Cf. G. M. Gurtler, 'Sympathy in Plotinus' ['Sympathy'], *International Philosophical Quarterly*, 24 (1984), 395–406.

[7] Cf. 4. 4. 8. 45–9, 3. 2. 16. 23–7. For musical metaphors in Plotinus, see S. Gersh, 'Plotinus on *Harmonia*: Musical Metaphors and their Uses in the *Enneads*', in J. Dillon and M. Dixsaut (eds.), *Agonistes: Essays in Honour of Denis O'Brien* (Aldershot, 2005), 195–207.

nify all sublunary things, is accepted; and the latter is explained by appealing to *sumpatheia*.

Unfortunately, this summary of Plotinus' view purchases its simplicity at the price of its accuracy. In 3. 1 he seems more or less to defend soft against hard astrology, but without invoking *sumpatheia*. The same position is set out in the first eight chapters of 2. 3, this time with *sumpatheia*. But the remainder of 2. 3, together with the earlier 4. 4, shows that in fact he is willing to concede much more to astrology than just the claim that stars signify. Sometimes the concessions he makes look as though they may be merely dialectical. But in 2. 3 it is the authority of Plato himself that leads Plotinus to allow a significant degree of causal influence from the stars. Thus he develops a more nuanced position on astrology, which will admit causal influence but limit it in various ways, so as to safeguard human autonomy and astral benevolence. In what follows I shall explain Plotinus' evolving ideas about astrology by giving an overview of the discussions of 3. 1 and 4. 4, before providing a more detailed analysis of 2. 3. I privilege the treatment of 2. 3 not just because it is Plotinus' last word on the matter, but also because there he discusses astrology directly, not for the sake of pursuing broader aims, as happens in 3. 1 and 4. 4.

2. The early view: 3. 1 [6]. 5–6

Enneads 3. 1, to which Porphyry gives the title *On Fate*, is typically thought to be a scholastic, fairly derivative, discussion of physicalist causal theories.[8] One of the theories considered is hard astrology. Though Plotinus is anxious to reject physical determinism, he is happy to affirm that all things in the physical world do have a cause (3. 1. 1. 14–16, alluding to *Tim.* 28 A–C). (So if, as some hold,[9] it is correct to understand Aristotelian chance events as uncaused events, Plotinus here rejects the existence of Aristotelian chance events.[10]) Notice that this immediately rules out an obvious escape

---

[8] Thus Armstrong in the introduction to his translation of 3. 1 in the Loeb edition, following Bréhier. But for a judicious warning against seeing early Plotinian treatises as derivative scholasticism, see R. Chiaradonna, 'L'anima e la mistione stoica: *Enn.* IV 7 [2], 8²', in id. (ed.), *Studi sull'anima in Plotino* (Naples, 2005), 129–47.

[9] See R. Sorabji, *Necessity, Cause and Blame: Perspectives on Aristotle's Theory* (London, 1983), 3–25.

[10] Plotinus in fact alludes to Aristotle's discussion of chance in this very chapter,

from hard astrology, which would be to say that some things are
entirely uncaused and *a fortiori* not caused by the stars. But of
course in 3. 1 he does want to reject hard astrology; he refutes it
after attacking the atomist theory of the Epicureans and a World-
Soul theory that may be Stoic. What these three theories have in
common is not quite physical determinism, since the Epicurean
swerve (mentioned at 3. 1. 1. 16) is, famously, offered as a way
of avoiding this. Rather, his complaint would seem to be that they
make everything the result of a complex of causes that are *within* the
physical world—whether these be atomic motions, a variety of physical causes which can be traced back to an immanent World-Soul,
or heavenly motions. The word 'fate' (*heimarmenē*) is used, especially with reference to the Stoic theory, to describe the inevitable
workings of the network of causes within the cosmos. Plotinus, by
contrast, wants to make room for the efficacy of transcendent immaterial causes.[11]

In chapter 2 Plotinus makes his first reference to astrological
theory:

Others, holding that the circuit of the cosmos surrounds and causes all
things [πάντα ποιοῦσαν] by its motion and by the figures of the wandering
and fixed stars and their relative positions, and being persuaded by the
foretellings made on the basis of this, claim that all the individual things
[ἕκαστα] come about from that. (3. 1. 2. 26–30)

Here the crucial terms are ποιοῦσαν and ἕκαστα: according to the
astrologers the stars actually cause or make things, and they do this
to each and every thing in the sublunary world. (As this passage
makes clear, the 'stars' in question are both the fixed stars and
the 'wandering' stars or planets, which would include the sun and

but garbles the example so as to eliminate its point: 'if all things have a cause for
their happening it is easy to apprehend the causes which are immediately relevant
to each happening and trace it back to them: for instance, the cause of going to the
market-place is that one thinks one ought to see someone or to collect a debt' (3. 1.
1. 24–7, trans. Armstrong). Of course, the original version of the example in *Physics*
2. 5 has the person going to the market for some other reason, and just happening
to meet the debtor. Compare 2. 3. 14. 17–18, which similarly alludes to the famous
example of digging and finding treasure but says that this is to be explained because
'one of the things from the cosmos' has brought it about, in which case it is signified
by the heavens.

[11] Compare the contrast found, for example, in Pseudo-Plutarch's *On Fate*, between *heimarmenē* and *pronoia*: providence descends from superior principles and
includes within its working fate, which operates only at a lower level. See further
below on 2. 3.

moon.) As we shall see, Plotinus' response to astrology in later treatises focuses sequentially on these two ideas. His first line of attack is the one described above: deny that the stars *cause* things to happen, and say instead that they only signify. His second line of attack is to concede that they both cause and signify, but to deny that the stars are the exclusive cause for *all* things, even if they do signify all things. Already in 3. 1, both lines of attack are present, though the first is predominant.

As remarked above, there are two main reasons for Plotinus to object to hard astrology. First, because it is tantamount to denying human autonomy. Second, because the astrologers make the stars responsible for evils. These two complaints emerge in chapters 3. 1. 5 and 3. 1. 6, respectively. With regard to human autonomy, he has this to say:

ἐκείνοις ἀνατίθησι τὰ ἡμέτερα, βουλὰς καὶ πάθη, κακίας τε καὶ ὁρμάς, ἡμῖν δὲ οὐδὲν διδοὺς λίθοις φερομένοις καταλείπει εἶναι, ἀλλ᾽ οὐκ ἀνθρώποις ἔχουσι παρ᾽ αὐτῶν καὶ ἐκ τῆς αὐτῶν φύσεως ἔργον. (3. 1. 5. 16–20)

[Astrology] gives what is ours to them [the stars], deliberations and emotions, vices and impulses, giving us nothing and leaving us as stones that are moved, instead of men who have a function which is their own and comes from their own nature.

It is precisely those features of human life having to do with psychology that he wants to preserve from astral determination: volitions, emotions, desires. A few lines earlier he has reiterated that hard astrology would make 'each and every thing [ἕκαστα]' an effect of the stars, and added that this would be true 'not least [of] thoughts [καὶ διανοίας οὐχ ἥκιστα]' (3. 1. 5. 6–7). Here we see him alluding to a distinction that will be deployed more systematically in his later treatments of astrology. Such phenomena as human 'deliberations' and 'impulses' are not to be ascribed to the stars. This is because they are 'ours': 'one must distinguish between those things that we accomplish ourselves and those where we are affected by necessity' (3. 1. 5. 22–3).[12] The contrast between what is 'ours' and what is 'necessary' correlates with a contrast drawn later in 3. 1 (and frequently in other treatises) between what is 'internal' to us and what is 'external' to us. Causal influences from the stars, if there are any, fall into the latter category (3. 1. 9. 3–4).

Plotinus' reluctance to admit that the stars might give rise to evils

[12] Cf. S.E. *M.* 5. 41–2.

gives him a further reason to reject the idea of direct astral causation. As he says in chapter 6, 'how could viciousness of character be from [the stars] given that they are gods?' (3. 1. 6. 10–11).[13] But in fact the problem is somewhat broader than this. For as the subsequent lines make clear, he also finds it implausible that the stars devote their attention to the sublunary world, whether for good or ill, or that they react to their positions relative to each other by exercising causation on what is beneath them. The point here is not just that the stars cannot cause what is bad, but that they cannot *purposefully* cause anything at all in the sublunary world. If they did, their will would be directed towards what is worse than them—what is 'beneath' them in every sense of the word—instead of towards higher divinities.

Here Plotinus is in agreement with Alexander of Aphrodisias,[14] who likewise denied that the stars intentionally bring about sublunary things, on the basis that this would compromise the stars' nobility. This emerges with particular clarity from a work of Alexander's which is preserved only in Arabic, entitled *On Providence*.[15] It is worth giving a brief summary of Alexander's position here, because of the similarity of his position to that of Plotinus and the centrality of these issues for Plotinus' subsequent treatments of astrology. Alexander argues that the gods do not concern themselves with 'particular things [*al-juz'iyyāt*]'—compare Plotinus' ἕκαστα— and multiplies arguments against such divine concern.[16] One of these is that if the gods did exercise care for particulars, then they would thereby be worse than the particulars instead of better. For

---

[13] πονηρία δὲ ἤθους παρὰ θεῶν ὄντων πῶς ἂν δοθείη;

[14] Nothing in what follows presumes that Plotinus actually read the relevant works of Alexander, though it is not unlikely that he did. I mention Alexander primarily to clarify the philosophical issues, and secondarily to give a sense of the broader historical context of Plotinus' discussions of astrology.

[15] Edited and translated into German in H.-J. Ruland, *Die arabischen Fassungen von zwei Schriften des Alexander von Aphrodisias: Über die Vorsehung und Über das liberum arbitrium* [*Die arabischen Fassungen*] (diss. Saarbrücken, 1976). Edited and translated into Italian in S. Fazzo and M. Zonta, *Alessandro di Afrodisia: La provvidenza* (Milan, 1998). Edited and translated into French in P. Thillet, *Alexandre d'Aphrodise: Traité de la Providence* (Lagrasse, 2003). Thillet discusses the possible influence of *On Providence* on Plotinus at 46–54. The treatise exists in two Arabic translations, an early one from the Kindī circle and a later one by the Aristotelian philosopher and Christian Abū Bishr Mattā. The latter is certainly a more accurate source for Alexander's ideas and is the one referred to here, by citing page numbers from Ruland's edition, which are reproduced in the edition of Thillet.

[16] Ruland, *Die arabischen Fassungen*, 13 ff.

in that case the gods would exist for the sake of (*min ajli*) the particular things, and when one thing exists for the sake of another, the
latter is superior to the former (*Die arabischen Fassungen*, 21). In
these passages Alexander does not equate the heavenly bodies with
gods. But we find him later in the treatise using similar arguments
to deny that heavenly motions are for our sake (ibid. 51–9).

Now, all these considerations suggest that we should restrict the
scope of causal celestial influence. If we say that the stars have no
effect on human volitions, that they never cause evils, and that in
general they cause nothing in the sublunary realm on purpose, what
is left for the stars to do? Alexander's solution was to say that the
stars incidentally bring about a 'general' providence, by ensuring
the cyclical production of natural species.[17] But of course this would
not 'save the phenomena' of astrology's supposedly accurate predictions about particular things. So instead, we might take refuge
in soft astrology: give up entirely on the idea of astral causation,
but say that the stars do signify. This is what Plotinus seems to do
at the end of chapter 6:

ἀλλὰ μᾶλλον, ὡς φέρεται μὲν ταῦτα ἐπὶ σωτηρίᾳ τῶν ὅλων, παρέχεται δὲ καὶ
ἄλλην χρείαν τὴν τοῦ εἰς αὐτὰ ὥσπερ γράμματα βλέποντας τοὺς τὴν τοιαύτην
γραμματικὴν εἰδότας ἀναγινώσκειν τὰ μέλλοντα ἐκ τῶν σχημάτων κατὰ τὸ ἀνά-
λογον μεθοδεύοντας τὸ σημαινόμενον· ὥσπερ εἴ τις λέγοι, ἐπειδὴ ὑψηλὸς ὁ ὄρνις,
σημαίνει ὑψηλάς τινας πράξεις. (3. 1. 6. 18–24, trans. Armstrong, modified)

We must rather say that the movement of the stars is for the preservation of
the universe, but that they perform in addition another service; this is that
those who know how to read this sort of writing can, by looking at them as
if they were letters, read the future from their patterns, discovering what
is signified by the systematic use of analogy; for instance, if one said that
when the bird flies aloft it signifies some lofty deeds.[18]

This analogy between the stars and birds has already appeared
in chapter 5 (ll. 35–7), and will appear yet again in 2. 3 (2. 3. 3.
27–8; 2. 3. 7. 14–16). It seems to be a favourite rhetorical device
of Plotinus', and for good reason. Prediction by birds is a widely
accepted form of prognostication, but no one (Plotinus presumes)

---

[17] This position is also defended in his *On Fate*, for which see R. W. Sharples,
Alexander of Aphrodisias: On Fate (London, 1983).

[18] The example of the bird suggests that what we have here is a case of 'natural'
signification, rather than one in which the relationship between the sign and the
signified is arbitrary or by convention. The same, presumably, would be true for
astral signification, though Plotinus never seems to develop this idea.

would be so daft as to say that the birds actually *cause* the things that they signify.

Yet the neat story, which has Plotinus insisting on soft astrology in response to the various pressures we have identified, is already undermined in 3. 1 by the following passage:

ἀλλὰ γὰρ γίγνεται μὲν ἕκαστα κατὰ τὰς αὐτῶν φύσεις, ἵππος μέν, ὅτι ἐξ ἵππου, καὶ ἄνθρωπος, ὅτι ἐξ ἀνθρώπου, καὶ τοιόσδε, ὅτι ἐκ τοιοῦδε. ἔστω δὲ συνεργὸς καὶ ἡ τοῦ παντὸς φορὰ συγχωροῦσα τὸ πολὺ τοῖς γειναμένοις [accepting Armstrong's emendation], ἔστωσαν δὲ πρὸς τὰ τοῦ σώματος πολλὰ σωματικῶς διδόντες, θερμότητας καὶ ψύξεις καὶ σωμάτων κράσεις ἐπακολουθούσας. πῶς οὖν τὰ ἤθη καὶ ἐπιτηδεύματα καὶ μάλιστα οὐχ ὅσα δοκεῖ κράσει σωμάτων δουλεύειν . . .; (3. 1. 6. 1–9)

But the individuals come to be according to their natures, in one case a horse, because it comes from a horse, in another man, because it comes from a man, and a such-and-such because it comes from such-and-such. *Let it be granted that the circuit of the universe too is a co-operative cause*, handing most of it over to the parents, and that many bodily things are given [by the stars] in a bodily way, heatings and coolings, and the mixtures of bodies that follow on these. How, then, are the characters and pursuits [caused by the stars], especially those that are not obviously ruled by the mixture of the bodies?

Here the italicized phrase shows Plotinus making an important concession, albeit in the midst of a polemic against the claims of the astrologers. The concession is that the stars are a 'co-operative cause' (*sunergos*) of what is produced in nature. As we shall see, this idea of celestial causation as a *sunergos* will be an important component of his later treatments of astrology. Part of what he is already claiming here is that some things escape celestial influence entirely, as our analysis thus far has suggested (again, the example has to do with ethical character). But he is also saying that even when the stars do exert physical causation, they are not the *only*, not even the most important, physical causes in play: this is the sense of the *sun-* in *sunergos*.[19] His example, repeating a theme that he has already developed in chapter 5, is that one's general bodily condition is affected not only by the position of the stars when one is born, but also by the bodily conditions of one's parents. If I am of a phlegmatic predisposition, this is at least as likely to be caused

---

[19] See the useful discussion of συνεργόν at Wilberding, *Plotinus' Cosmology*, 133–5, which discusses 3. 1. 1. 32–5 alongside other passages, including 2. 3. 14.

by my being the child of a phlegmatic father as it is to be caused by the stars.

The upshot of 3. 1 would then seem to be as follows. Plotinus is critical of astrologers not so much for their predictive claims as for the causal theory that underlies those claims. He undermines the causal theory by saying that some things are not brought about by physical causes at all, but are rather 'ours'. He adds that even things that are brought about physically have a multiplicity of physical causes, so that any reference to the stars could provide only a partial explanation.[20] And he gives reasons for believing that the stars cannot in any case be responsible for many of the things that happen in our lower world, especially evils. Despite all this, he concedes that the stars may cause. On the other hand, perhaps he does so only because of the present context. The concession could be purely dialectical: some astral causation can be admitted so long as we stop short of the universal astral causation of hard astrology. This is all that would be needed for his present concerns.

3. Astral theodicy: 4. 4 [28]. 30–39

Our interpretation of 4. 4 will likewise need to bear in mind the context in which astrology is discussed. In this case, Plotinus is in the midst of an extensive discussion of various problems having to do with the soul. His immediate concern has been with the psychological capacities of the stars, for example whether they can see and hear. He affirms this but denies that they have memory (4. 4. 6–8, with reference back at 4. 4. 30. 1–2). This leads him to the question of whether the stars hear prayers, and thus bring about sublunary events intentionally. This question, whether the stars cause sublunary things (especially evils) by *prohairesis*, becomes

---

[20] This point is missed by Rolando, 'L'anima e le Moire', who thus speaks of hard and soft astrology 'fusing' (244), and writes: 'la soft astrology finisce così per includere l'hard astrology come un suo caso particolare', taking astral causation as just part of a broader system. But the claim that astral causation is (at least sometimes) an insufficient cause for things in the sublunary world does not amount to 'including' hard astrology within a broader, less deterministic framework. Rather it amounts to a straightforward rejection of hard astrology. Perhaps what Rolando has in mind is not really hard *astrology*, but rather a broad physical determinism that would invoke both astral and non-astral causes. Even then, however, there will be sublunary events (the results of human choices) which are not so determined by physical causes.

the dominant issue in 4. 4. 30 ff. Thus he frames the treatment of astrology as a dialectical problem, in the classical Aristotelian sense of a clash between opposing *endoxa*. On the one hand, it is generally believed (πεπίστευται) that the stars bring about many things, and are 'helpers [συλλήπτορας]' for both good and bad actions. On the other hand, many people are reluctant to concede this, because the stars would be 'co-operative causes' (*sunergoi*) for unjust things (4. 4. 30. 6–10). Given these terms of reference, Plotinus will be satisfied with any position that absolves the stars of blame for evils (ἀπολογήσασθαι, 4. 4. 30. 25). What he wants to do, in short, is to provide an astral theodicy. With Alexander in mind, we might expect him to do this by denying that the stars direct their *prohairesis* towards the sublunary realm at all.

Plotinus seems to begin by conceding a great deal to astrology:

ὅτι μὲν οὖν ἡ φορὰ ποιεῖ, αὐτὴν μὲν πρῶτον διαφόρως διατιθεῖσα καὶ τὰ ἐντὸς αὐτῆς, ἀναμφισβητήτως μὲν τὰ ἐπίγεια οὐ μόνον τοῖς σώμασιν, ἀλλὰ καὶ ταῖς τῆς ψυχῆς διαθέσεσι, καὶ τῶν μερῶν ἕκαστον εἰς τὰ ἐπίγεια καὶ ὅλως τὰ κάτω ποιεῖ, πολλαχῇ δῆλον. (4. 4. 31. 25–9)

That the circuit acts—first of all disposing variously itself and the things inside it—indisputably on the earthly things not only with respect to their bodies, but also with respect to the dispositions of the soul, and [that] each of the parts [of the heavens] acts on the earthly things and, in general, on what is below, is abundantly clear.

Part of what he means is that there are obvious effects from the heavens on the sublunary realm: it is 'obvious to everyone [εὔδηλοί που παντί]' that the sun produces heat and gives rise to the seasons, for instance (I take it that this is what is meant a little earlier, at 4. 4. 31. 12–13). He seems happy to admit that such things involve direct causation (*poiein*, used twice in the passage just cited). And that seems like common sense, more than anything else.[21] But it is a significantly larger concession to admit that 'dispositions of the soul [ταῖς τῆς ψυχῆς διαθέσεσι]' are brought about by the stars. Does this not contravene the stricture in 3. 1 against ascribing psychological phenomena to the stars? This is a difficulty we shall be able to solve below, when we examine 2. 3.

Plotinus' concessive mood does not last long. He immediately

---

[21] But a significant point nevertheless, since these 'obvious' effects were often invoked as the first stage of a slippery slope argument in favour of more subtle effects. See Long, 'Astrology', 172–3 for the point in Cicero, and 180–1 for the point in Ptolemy (for which also Barton, *Astrology*, 61).

goes on to say that it is hard to see how the manipulation of heat and cold could give rise to such things as fortune, wealth, and poverty, or—an allusion to Aristotle's discussion of chance—finding treasure (4. 4. 31. 43–6).[22] He repeats that it is also implausible that the stars deliberately (*prohaeresei*) cause vicious behaviour on the part of humans (4. 4. 31. 48–58). That seems to leave us more or less where we were at the end of the discussion in 3. 1: the stars may exercise some causality, but not as much as the astrologers claim, and certainly not enough to warrant our blaming the stars for evils. But he is no longer satisfied with this response. Nor should he be, since he has given no principled explanation for why the stars do indicate but do not cause, or at least, do not cause evils. Thus he starts afresh in chapter 32:

εἰ οὖν μήτε σωματικαῖς αἰτίαις ἀναθήσομεν μήτε προαιρέσεσιν, ὅσα ἔξωθεν εἰς ἡμᾶς τε καὶ τὰ ἄλλα ζῷα καὶ ὅλως ἐπὶ γῆς ἀφικνεῖται ἐξ οὐρανοῦ, τίς ἂν εἴη λοιπὴ καὶ εὔλογος αἰτία; (4. 4. 32. 1–4, trans. Armstrong, modified)

If, then, we are not to attribute all that comes from outside to us and the other living creatures, and in general to things upon the earth from the heavens, to bodily causes or the deliberate choices of the heavenly bodies, what reasonable explanation is left?

Plotinus answers the question by expounding a theory, namely that cosmic *sumpatheia* accounts for the success of astrological prediction. Inspired by the *Timaeus*'s description of the universe as 'one living thing with all livings things within it' (30 D 3–31 A 1), Plotinus says that just as in an animal or the human body, the universe can have parts that are not contiguous but are 'affected together' (*sumpathein*, 4. 4. 32. 22). The famous analogy to a dancer is given in chapter 33, as a way of explaining how the disparate motions of a living whole's parts may cohere into a unity. He concludes:

τοῦτον τοίνυν τὸν τρόπον καὶ τὰ ἐν οὐρανῷ φατέον ποιεῖν, ὅσα ποιεῖ, τὰ δὲ καὶ σημαίνειν. (4. 4. 33. 25–7)

One should say that this is the way that the things in heaven cause [*poiein*] the things they cause, but some things they also signify [*sēmainein*].

Notice that he does not here use the contrast between *poiein* and *sēmainein* to support soft astrology. Rather, he uses it to specify the sense in which the heavenly bodies do indeed cause: they cause

---

[22] See also above, n. 10.

in the way that one part of a living whole affects another part.[23] That is an idea with which a hard astrologer could agree—as is vividly shown by the fact that back in 3. 1 Plotinus mentioned *sumpatheia* as part of the astrologers' views, not his own (3. 1. 5. 8).[24] Indeed, the idea of *sumpatheia* should make us *more* ready to admit causation between heavenly bodies and sublunary bodies, not less. For as Plotinus says himself, in so far as they are parts of the same physical system the former may indeed cause the latter, just as one part of a dancer causes another part to move (the analogy reappears at 4. 4. 34. 28).[25]

But an astrologer would be less comfortable with the peroration that follows (introduced by μᾶλλον δέ at 4. 4. 33. 27). This passage gives us to understand that the interlocking parts of the cosmos are not the ultimate causes of other parts. Rather, the *whole cosmos* is 'arranged'[26] by acting upon itself, and at this level the agent and the acted upon are identical (μηδ' αὖ τὸν σχηματίζοντα ἄλλο ποιοῦντα ἄλλο ποιεῖν: 4. 4. 33. 35–6). This cosmic point of view will allow Plotinus, in chapters 34–5, to explain that the figures formed by the stars sometimes both cause and signify other things, and sometimes only signify (for an explicit statement see 4. 4. 34. 24–6). The idea that the heavenly bodies are just parts, albeit very important parts, of the system leaves room for other causes to affect what happens in the sublunary world (see especially chapters 37 and 38). Plotinus thinks we need to invoke a wide variety of causes to explain sublunary things. For instance, misbegotten creatures are

[23] This was already anticipated in the opening admission that the heavens do 'obviously' affect the earth, at 4. 4. 31. 12–13: what is obvious are the effects 'of parts on parts [μερῶν πρὸς μέρη]'.

[24] Cf. S.E. *M.* 5. 4, which likewise mentions *sumpatheia* as a core feature of the astrological theory.

[25] Thus I would disagree with Gurtler, 'Sympathy', 396–7, when he says apropos of 3. 1. 5 that the *sumpatheia* idea involves denying causality to the stars (cf. also 401: 'he admits the presence of sympathy in the physical universe, but denies it any causal efficacy'). Gurtler does not really explain what sort of causation (or lack thereof) would be present between two objects that are in sympathy. But the fact that Plotinus attempts to explain vision, for example, by means of sympathy suggests that some sort of causation is involved. Furthermore, Ptolemy and other ancient astrologers invoked sympathy as well as brute physical causation by the stars (e.g. by means of heating, cooling, and the like), which shows that they at least thought the two sorts of explanation were compatible.

[26] Here Plotinus repeatedly uses forms of the verb σχηματίζω, which brings out the intimate connection between the providential arrangement of the cosmos and the astrological 'figures' (σχήματα) formed by the stars, which are mentioned at l. 37 and in the next chapter.

to be blamed not on the stars, but on (for example) the inadequate 'underlying matter' used to form the animal. The general point is that we must not take away the efficacy of sublunary natures. The things with these natures do genuinely give rise to their apparent effects. Or at least, they cause in the same way the stars cause, namely by being a part of the single cosmos (4. 4. 37. 1–6). So the stars are partial causes in a twofold sense: they cause only because they are parts—so that they are not ultimate causes—and they are only part of the causal network within the cosmos—so that there is room for other, sublunary causes in Plotinus' cosmology.

But these same considerations guarantee that the stars will *always* at least signify what happens in the sublunary world, even if they do not always cause these things. This is admitted in the opening lines of chapter 39 (σημαίνεσθαι πάντα). Just as in 3. 1, then, Plotinus makes no attempt to deny that astrologers could (at least in principle) predict sublunary events. His critique consists rather in substituting a Platonist explanation for the astrologers' account of why these predictions work, and ensuring that the new explanation places limits on the causal influence of the stars. A welcome consequence of his explanation is that the stars signify in only an incidental way, the way a dancer's hand might tell you what his foot is doing. As he puts it, 'the signification is not in order that things may be signified in advance': it is just, as it were, a side effect of universal *sumpatheia* (4. 4. 39. 17–23). In principle it seems that sublunary things could also 'signify' the things in the heavens.[27]

Plotinus thus concludes, with satisfaction, that if this account is correct 'the problems [*aporiai*] would be solved' regarding whether the stars cause evil (4. 4. 39. 23–4). They do not, because they are not necessarily causes for evils at all. For as we just saw, Plotinus prefers to invoke other causes for these, such as inadequate material. Moreover, to the extent that they do cause, their *prohairesis* is not directed towards doing so.[28] But, one wants to ask here, what

---

[27] Rolando, 'L'anima e le Moire', 240, rightly notes that the 'signification' relation between material and immaterial is by contrast necessarily 'one-way': the material can signify the workings of the immaterial, but not vice versa. Could the sublunary world actually exert causality on the heavens? This question is raised, but deferred, at 4. 4. 31. 30. It is discussed again at 4. 4. 42, where Plotinus says that the heavens are subject to affections in so far as they have bodies. Compare the question of whether there is any material interchange between the heavens and the sublunary world, which Plotinus denies; on this see Wilberding, *Plotinus' Cosmology*, 59–61.

[28] One might wonder whether the cosmos itself exercises *prohairesis*. According to 4. 4. 35. 26–32, the cosmos directs *prohairesis* beyond itself, not towards its own

about our own human *prohairesis*? How does human autonomy fare within Plotinus' unified, self-acting cosmos—are we only parts of the larger system? He only gestures towards an answer in the present context. At the beginning of chapter 34 he mentions that we too are acted upon (πάσχειν) along with the body of the cosmos, because part of us belongs to this larger body. But, he says, this is only a part of us, and so we are affected only to a limited extent (μέτρια). His view would seem to be that although each one of us makes up a part of the cosmic whole, it is only a part of us that is a part. Autonomy, then, could belong to that part of us which is *not* a part. After making this proposal, he immediately drops the subject—again, his concern here is with absolving the stars of blame, not preserving human autonomy. But a more developed version of the idea expressed here will appear in 2. 3.

4. The final treatment: 2. 3

Prior to writing 2. 3 [52], Plotinus devotes a chapter (3. 3 [48]. 6) of his great work on providence to questions familiar from 3. 1 and 4. 4: how is it that people are able to prophesy future events, in particular the ones that are 'worse', by 'seeing the [heavenly] circuit of the cosmos'? His discussion here is more schematic than that in 4. 4, and is as close as he ever comes to a straightforward endorsement of soft astrology. He again invokes the unity of all things in the cosmos (here he does not use the term *sumpatheia*, though he does mention that the cosmos is a single living thing). But in this context he is willing only to grant that an astrologer could note an *analogia* between the heavenly things and the sublunary things. On this basis astrology will be able to determine the 'that' of what will occur, but not the 'because' (ὅτι but not διότι). This is because it is an art of reading the writing in the heavens, as suggested in 3. 1. This discussion, despite its relative brevity, might suggest that Plotinus' concessions to astrology in 4. 4 were simply for the sake of argument, or that he has changed his stance to a more complete rejection of astrology. But the evidence of 2. 3, written shortly

parts. Ultimately 'it seeks, or rather beholds, the good'. But the end of chapter 26 suggests that the cosmos may not act through *prohairesis* at all, being 'older' than *prohairesis*. These passages could be reconciled, I think: the cosmos does have a power of *prohairesis*, but it uses this only to look to higher principles, not to act upon itself.

after 3. 2–3, shows that during this late period he holds the same views on this subject as when he wrote 4. 4. The most plausible interpretation is that, for whatever reason, he has no intention of giving a nuanced discussion of astrology in the context of 3. 3.[29]

Actually, the first half of 2. 3 might also give the impression that Plotinus has now embraced soft astrology—or even that, despite the apparent concessions of 4. 4, he has embraced it all along since writing 3. 1. For the first eight chapters, 2. 3 represents itself as an all-out attack on contemporary astrological theory. The putative organizing principle of 2. 3, set out in the very first sentence, is the now familiar contrast between *poiein* and *sēmainein*:

ὅτι ἡ τῶν ἄστρων φορὰ σημαίνει περὶ ἕκαστον τὰ ἐσόμενα, ἀλλ' οὐκ αὐτὴ πάντα ποιεῖ, ὡς τοῖς πολλοῖς δοξάζεται, εἴρηται μὲν πρότερον ἐν ἄλλοις, καὶ πίστεις τινὰς παρείχετο ὁ λόγος, λεκτέον δὲ καὶ νῦν ἀκριβέστερον διὰ πλειόνων. (2. 3. 1. 1–5)

That the course of the stars signifies [*sēmainei*] in each case what is going to happen, but does not itself cause [*poiei*] everything to happen, as is believed by the many, has been said before elsewhere . . . but now we should discuss this more accurately and in greater detail.

Notice, though, that even here he is not necessarily endorsing soft astrology. His position is that the stars signify without causing *everything* (πάντα ποιεῖ), which leaves open the possibility that they do cause some things. But this is certainly not the impression given by chapters 1–8.

The argument of these chapters is detailed, well informed, and relentless, as Plotinus singles out various astrological claims for criticism and even mockery. Some sense of his umbrage at the theory is detectable already in his opening summary of the astrologers' view:

τοὺς δὴ πλανήτας φερομένους ποιεῖν λέγουσιν οὐ μόνον τὰ ἄλλα, πενίας καὶ πλούτους καὶ ὑγιείας καὶ νόσους, ἀλλὰ καὶ αἴσχη καὶ κάλλη αὖ, καὶ δὴ τὸ μέγιστον, καὶ κακίας καὶ ἀρετὰς καὶ δὴ καὶ τὰς ἀπὸ τούτων πράξεις καθ' ἕκαστα ἐπὶ καιρῶν ἑκάστων . . . (2. 3. 1. 6–10)

[29] Here is a hypothesis: Plotinus' reason for raising astrology in 3. 3 is entirely different from his reasons for raising it elsewhere. In 3. 3 astrological prediction appears not as a threat to Plotinus' view but rather as grist to his mill. The accuracy of astrology is treated as another piece of evidence for the key claim of 3. 2–3, namely that the entire universe is unified by a single order. (Hence he concludes 3. 3. 6 by saying 'So that the *logos* is one [οὕτω γὰρ καὶ λόγος εἷς]'.) This also helps to explain the *prima facie* surprising fact that in stark contrast to 4. 4, there is no discussion in this chapter of whether the stars would be responsible for evils.

They say that the planets as they move cause [*poiein*] not only the other things, namely poverty, wealth, health, and illness, but moreover ugliness and beauty and above all vice and virtue too, and indeed also the actions that proceed from these in each case and at each time . . .

This passage captures two of the points which he finds unacceptable. First, the astrologers claim that things of genuine value—so virtue, not just wealth—are caused by the stars. This is as close as Plotinus comes to expressing a worry about human autonomy in the early sections of this treatise. Second, the astrologers claim that astral causation is involved in each and every thing that happens in the sublunary world. We know from earlier treatises that Plotinus rejects this. A third sticking-point is mentioned further on in chapter 1: the astrologers say absurd things about the psychology of the stars. For example, they say that the stars are angered or pleased to find themselves in a certain configuration, and that they then express this anger or pleasure by giving rise to bad or good effects in our world.

It is this third point that drives the criticism of astrology up through chapter 6. Plotinus starts his attack (chapter 2) with a dilemma: if the stars were brute physical causes without souls, they could never give rise to the complex things we see in our world. But if the astrologers concede that the stars do have souls, then they will have to admit that the souls of the stars are divine, which, as in previous treatises, rules them out as a cause of evil. This begins a theme on which Plotinus presents numerous variations. For example, why would the stars be pleased to be setting or rising? Why would their 'mood' change at all? Rather, since they are divine,

οὐδὲ λυπεῖσθαι οὐδ' ἐπὶ καιροῦ χαίρειν αὐτοῖς δοτέον, ἀλλ' ἀεὶ τὸ ἵλεων ἔχειν χαίροντας ἐφ' οἷς ἀγαθοῖς ἔχουσι καὶ ἐφ' οἷς ὁρῶσι. βίος γὰρ ἑκάστῳ ἐφ' αὑτοῦ, ἑκάστῳ καὶ ἐν τῇ ἐνεργείᾳ τὸ εὖ· τὸ δὲ οὐ πρὸς ἡμᾶς. (2. 3. 3. 21–5)[30]

they do not feel grief and, when the occasion arises, rejoice, but maintain their graciousness at all times, rejoicing at the goods which they have and the things they see. For each of them has life from itself, and well-being for each consists also in its activity, but is not directed towards us.

This line is also taken by Alexander in *On Providence*, which avoids ascribing evils to the stars by saying that they intend nothing for us, whether good or ill. Plotinus underscores the point by saying:

[30] Cf. 4. 8. 2.

οὐδὲ ὅλως τὸ ἔργον πρὸς ἡμᾶς, εἰ ὥσπερ ὄρνισι κατὰ συμβεβηκὸς τὸ σημαίνειν. (2. 3. 3. 27–8)

What they do is not for us at all, if their signifying is accidental, like birds.[31]

As in 4. 4, the question is why the stars should be thought to signify even in this accidental way, given that astrologers' physical and psychological theories about the stars are incorrect. Again, the answer is to be found in cosmic *sumpatheia* (chapter 7). But here— reminding us more of 3. 3. 6 than of 4. 4—the *sumpatheia* theory is used only to support the signification required by soft astrology. The closest Plotinus comes to endorsing any astral causation in these chapters is this passage:

σημαίνει μὲν οὖν πάντα, ὅσα ἐν αἰσθητῷ, ποιεῖ δὲ ἄλλα, ὅσα φανερῶς ποιεῖ. (2. 3. 8. 8–9)

Thus [the stars] signify [*sēmainei*] everything which is in the sensible but they cause [*poiei*] other things, the ones they obviously cause.

But in the light of the word 'obviously' (φανερῶς), I believe he means only such things as the sun's effect on the seasons and the heat of daytime (cf. 4. 4. 31. 12–13, discussed above). If so, this passage gives no support for the less 'obvious' causal influences alleged by astrological theory.

At the beginning of chapter 9, however, the discussion takes a dramatic turn.[32] Plotinus has of course been drawing on Plato in the foregoing, especially the *Timaeus*'s idea of the cosmos as a single living thing. But he now explictly cites two Platonic passages that push us towards admitting a greater role for the heavenly bodies in determining what happens to us in our bodily existence. The first is the Myth of Er from *Republic* 10, the second *Timaeus* 69 C–D. With the introduction of this Platonic material the issue of human auto- nomy, barely present in chapters 1–8, is suddenly thrust on stage:

οὗτοι γὰρ οἱ λόγοι συνδέουσιν ἡμᾶς τοῖς ἄστροις παρ᾽ αὐτῶν ψυχὴν κομιζομένους καὶ ὑποτάττουσι τῇ ἀνάγκῃ ἐνταῦθα ἰόντας· καὶ ἤδη τοίνυν παρ᾽ αὐτῶν καὶ κατὰ τὰ ἤθη πράξεις καὶ πάθη ἀπὸ ἔξεως παθητικῆς οὔσης· ὥστε τί λοιπὸν ἡμεῖς; ἢ ὅπερ ἐσμὲν κατ᾽ ἀλήθειαν ἡμεῖς, οἷς καὶ κρατεῖν τῶν παθῶν ἔδωκεν ἡ φύσις. (2. 3. 9. 10–16, trans. Armstrong, modified)

These statements bind us to the stars, from which we get our souls, and

[31] For the comparison to birds, see above, n. 18.
[32] As also noted recently by C. Marzolo, *Plotino: Che cos'è l'essere vivente e che cos'è l'uomo? I 1 [53]* (Pisa, 2006), 55.

subject us to necessity when we come down here. From them we get our moral characters, our characteristic actions, and our emotions, coming from a disposition which is liable to emotion. So what is left which is 'we'? Surely, just that which we really are, we to whom nature also gave power to master our passions.

This passage is the fulcrum of 2. 3. It sets out a new challenge to Plotinus' scepticism regarding astrology. But, in the last sentence, it also offers a foretaste of how he will respond to this challenge. The rest of the present paper will be devoted to teasing out these two implications of the passage just cited.

First let us consider the two Platonic passages that Plotinus mentions, the Myth of Er and *Timaeus* 69. The myth is of course a fundamental text for Platonist ideas about fate and necessity. And it introduces fate in a heavily cosmological context, since, as Plotinus explicitly mentions, the spindle that sits on the lap of Necessity is the axis around which the heavenly spheres turn (*Rep.* 616 C; 617 B). The three daughters of Necessity are also present in the myth: they sing about the past, present, and future, and are involved in the dispensation of 'lots' which determine the sort of life each soul will lead when it returns to earthly existence. Having chosen, the souls are 'bound to the life by necessity [$\dot{\epsilon}\xi$ $\dot{a}\nu\dot{a}\gamma\kappa\eta s$]' (617 E). At 618 B we learn that the *taxis* of soul 'necessarily [$\dot{a}\nu\alpha\gamma\kappa\alpha\dot{\iota}\omega s$] becomes different because of the life it chooses'. On the other hand, the gods are free of blame ($\theta\epsilon\dot{o}s$ $\dot{a}\nu\alpha\dot{\iota}\tau\iota os$) for what occurs, since each soul is choosing its own fate, and 'virtue has no master [$\dot{a}\rho\epsilon\tau\dot{\eta}$ $\dot{a}\delta\dot{\epsilon}\sigma\pi\sigma\tau\sigma\nu$]' (617 E), a slogan which Plotinus quotes further on in 2. 3. 9. It is no surprise that he introduces this passage in the context of 2. 3. For the myth combines cosmology with allusions to the two themes that have been central in Plotinus' treatments of astrology: human autonomy and its relationship to necessity, and the question of divine responsibility for evil.

As for the passage from the *Timaeus*, it comes at the beginning of the section in which Timaeus describes the formation of the human body by the lesser gods. The context of this passage is less overtly cosmological than the Myth of Er. But the lesser gods have already been associated explicitly with the heavenly bodies at *Timaeus* 40 A–D, and here at 69 C Timaeus reiterates that the cosmos is 'a single living being'. What Plotinus actually quotes from *Timaeus* 69 is the statement that the Demiurge gives the 'principle of soul', but the lesser gods (which he calls $\phi\epsilon\rho\dot{o}\mu\epsilon\nu\sigma\iota$ $\theta\epsilon\sigma\dot{\iota}$, i.e. the gods borne along with the heavenly spheres) give the 'fearsome and necessary affections: angers, desires, pleasures and pains, and another kind of soul, from which these affections derive'.[33] What really strikes him about this passage, I would suggest, is the repetition of the term 'necessity' (ἀνάγκη), which appears in the passage quoted by Plotinus and twice more within 69 D. This creates a powerful link between necessity and the human body, which is the subject of the following pages in the *Timaeus*.[34]

Plotinus, then, can take from the *Timaeus* passage a message similar to the one he finds in the Myth of Er. Both passages subject human life to a necessity which is associated with bodily existence and which comes to us from the heavens. On the other hand, both passages take care to say that we are not entirely governed by this necessity: 'virtue has no master', and 'the principle of soul' comes from the Demiurge and not the lesser gods. This brings Plotinus finally to articulate a more considered view of physical necessity. His view is that the necessity is total for those who identify themselves with their bodily nature, but *need* not be total for anyone, because it need not affect a part of us, the part that, as he has just said, 'is that which we really are'.[35] He uses the term 'fate' (*heimarmenē*)[36] to refer to the necessity that afflicts our lower nature:

ἢ ἔρημος ταύτης τῆς ψυχῆς γενόμενος ζῇ ἐν εἱμαρμένῃ, καὶ ἐνταῦθα τὰ ἄστρα αὐτῷ οὐ μόνον σημαίνει, ἀλλὰ γίνεται αὐτὸς οἷον μέρος καὶ τῷ ὅλῳ συνέπεται, οὗ μέρος. διττὸς γὰρ ἕκαστος, ὁ μὲν τὸ συναμφότερόν τι, ὁ δὲ αὐτός. (2. 3. 9. 27–31)

The one who abandons this [higher] soul lives within fate. And then, not

---

[33] 2. 3. 9. 6–10: ἔν τε Τιμαίῳ θεὸς μὲν ὁ ποιήσας τὴν ἀρχὴν τῆς ψυχῆς δίδωσιν, οἱ δὲ φερόμενοι θεοὶ τὰ δεινὰ καὶ ἀναγκαῖα πάθη, θυμοὺς καὶ ἐπιθυμίας καὶ ἡδονὰς καὶ λύπας αὖ, καὶ ψυχῆς ἄλλο εἶδος, ἀφ' οὗ τὰ παθήματα ταυτί. Cf. *Tim.* 69 C–D. This is perhaps what Plotinus means when he says (2. 3. 9. 11) that we get our souls from the stars. In general, the *Timaeus*'s claim that each soul has a star associated with it lends strong support to astrology, but Plotinus does not emphasize the point in the present context. A related issue, which I shall not discuss further here, is the 'astral body' acknowledged by Plotinus at 4. 3. 15 and elsewhere. On this concept see E. R. Dodds, *Proclus: The Elements of Theology* (Oxford, 1963), 313–21, with Plotinus discussed at 318.

[34] Cf. the famous invocation of necessity (ἐξ ἀνάγκης) at 75 A–B, regarding the human head.

[35] See above, n. 33. Plotinus' doctrine of the 'undescended soul' in fact *guarantees* that some part of us remains unaffected. But here he seems to be referring to the descended but rational soul, since he adds that this soul has the role of 'ruling over the affections' (κρατεῖν τῶν παθῶν). The question of who 'we' are is the central issue in the slightly later *Enneads* 1. 1, as emphasized in a recent study: G. Aubry, *Plotin: Traité 53 (I, 1)* (Paris, 2004).

[36] See above, n. 11.

only do the stars signify for him, but he himself also becomes, as it were, a part, and is drawn along together with the whole of which he is a part. For each man is double, composite on the one hand, and himself on the other.

One advantage of this stance is that the solution to the problem of human autonomy is closely parallel to the solution to the problem of whether the stars cause evil. For the stars too are 'double' (2. 3. 9. 34), having divine souls whose *prohairesis* is directed towards the higher principles, not towards the sublunary world (2. 3. 9. 38–9).

We can say more to flesh out how it is that the stars impose a limited 'necessity' upon us. As becomes clear later in the treatise (2. 3. 15. 5–8), the 'lots' distributed to the souls in the Myth of Er symbolize the physical conditions at the moment of our birth. These conditions are summarized as 'externals' (τὰ ἔξω).[37] As in 3. 1, the stars are not the only causes in play here. It also matters whom one has as parents, for instance. And in general, the underlying nature of what is affected by the stars tends to be more powerful than the stars' influence. Thus horse makes horse, man makes man, and in both cases the sun is only, as we have seen before, a *sunergos* (2. 3. 12. 5).[38] When the stars do cause, what sorts of things do they cause? Perhaps the most interesting example is what one might call our ethical predispositions, e.g. our inborn tendency towards lust, anger, or villainous cleverness (πανουργία). Plotinus names these as worse versions of the characteristics of the stars (2. 3. 11). He uses the word *diathesis* for such predispositions.[39] This, I believe, clears up the troubling passage at 4. 4. 31. 25–9 (quoted above), where he also refers to the 'dispositions of soul' as coming from the stars. There, as here, what he means is not that the stars determine whether or not we are virtuous, but that the ethically significant

---

[37] Cf. already at 2. 3. 8. 13, as well as e.g. 1. 4. 14. 14. Plotinus plays with the idea of being 'outside', which can also be applied to the higher soul in so far as it is 'outside' the body (2. 3. 9. 25).

[38] There is a possible textual problem with 2. 3. 12. Starting at l. 12, there is a passage providing greater detail about astrological theories, with apparent approval. Armstrong finds plausible Ficino's placement of this material following chapter 5, and admits that it may even be an insertion by another author. While I have no firm view on the matter, there are some reasons to think that the passage belongs where it is. First, as my interpretation suggests, Plotinus is now at a stage in the argument which allows greater scope for astral influence. Second, it may allude back to ideas from chapters 9–11, such as the 'mixture' of influences from the stars and the production of θυμός. The emphasis on the stars as part of a cosmic whole in this passage is also consistent with Plotinus' own view.

[39] Compare the use of διάθεμα by Sextus Empiricus, *M.* 5. 89–90.

tendencies with which we are born are, to some extent, caused astrally. Still, it is possible for us to overcome such tendencies (2. 3. 15. 14–17), which is unsurprising since these tendencies arise from the features of the body which the soul enters.

We should also bear in mind that the soul's choice of lot in the Myth of Er is made precisely at the moment when the soul is not embodied, and is thus unaffected by bodily states. So the soul itself chooses the astral influence that will be exerted upon the body it enters, by virtue of choosing its life. This fact already guarantees us a degree of autonomy.[40] It remains important, though, that Plotinus makes provision for overcoming the physical tendencies that are chosen.[41] For one thing, it ensures that the soul is not inevitably in thrall to the body it chooses—which for Plotinus would be a metaphysical impossibility. For another, from the point of view of preserving autonomy in our present *embodied* condition, saying that our souls have made a choice for this life which is now irrevocable yields the same result as saying that our lives are determined by physical causes. Either way, the soul would have no influence on its fate once it was embodied.

Notice also how closely Plotinus associates astral influence with the condition of the body and physical environment *at our birth*. This is partly because he is responding to the Myth of Er, but also because in his discussions of astrology he seems to have in mind mostly the casting of horoscopes. When he entertains the possibility that the stars cause or signify 'everything' (e.g. at 4. 4. 39.

---

[40] On the other hand, Plotinus believes that each soul receives a body suited to it. This point emerges several times in 4. 3. See 4. 3. 6. 11–15 ('there is a difference between souls . . . [and] the individual souls, since body exists already, received their allotted parts when their sister soul [sc. the World-Soul], as we may say, was already ruling, as if it had already prepared their dwellings for them', trans. Armstrong); 4. 3. 8, where Plotinus emphasizes that in the myth the souls choose according to their previous lives; and especially 4. 3. 13. 10: the soul 'enters into the appropriate body [εἰς τὸ πρόσφορον σῶμα]'. In that chapter Plotinus goes on to say that the 'choice' of body is in fact not so much deliberately selected as the result of a natural process or unreasoning motion; fate is also mentioned (4. 3. 13. 18–21). Even this unusually fatalistic passage may not rule out some degree of autonomy on the part of the soul choosing its lot. But at a minimum it shows that the choice is not immune to the effects of previous embodiment.

[41] James Wilberding has pointed out to me that Porphyry's *Life of Plotinus* §11 is relevant here: Plotinus diagnoses Porphyry's suicidal thoughts as deriving 'from some melancholic malady [ἐκ μελαγχολικῆς τινος νόσου]' rather than from reason. This shows the relatively complex tendencies that could be produced by bodily temperament, but also our ability to thwart such tendencies by recognizing and overcoming them.

2: σημαίνεσθαι πάντα), this would seem usually to mean that everything that will happen in a person's life is already shown by their
horoscope. Whether this means literally everything, down to the
most trivial detail, is unclear. Perhaps he means only to consider
whether astrologers can predict the things they actually claim to
predict by casting horoscopes, whether these be our ethical predispositions or the events we shall experience. In the latter case these
will presumably be significant events, such as someone's becoming
a general or king (mentioned at 2. 3. 2. 15–16). Again, this suggests
that the dialectical context is important: on this reading, what he
means by 'everything' is determined by the claims of his astrological opponents.[42]

Nevertheless, hard astrology suffers a double blow in these chapters. First, as in previous treatises, the stars are not the only physical
causes. They signify everything, but they do not cause everything.
Second, even the totality of physical causes does not determine
everything for us, since our higher soul is unaffected by such
causes.[43] The following passage seems to sum up his considered
view, as far as the contrast between *poiein* and *sēmainein* goes:

εἰ δ' οὕτω, τὰς σημασίας καὶ νῦν δοτέον· τὰς δὲ ποιήσεις οὐ πάντως οὐδὲ τοῖς
ὅλοις αὐτῶν, ἀλλὰ ὅσα τοῦ παντὸς πάθη, καὶ ὅσον τὸ λοιπὸν αὐτῶν. καὶ ψυχῇ μὲν
καὶ πρὶν ἐλθεῖν εἰς γένεσιν δοτέον ἥκειν τι φερούσῃ παρ' αὐτῆς· οὐ γὰρ ἂν ἔλθοι
εἰς σῶμα μὴ μέγα τι παθητικὸν ἔχουσα. δοτέον δὲ καὶ τύχας εἰσιούσῃ [τὸ κατ'
αὐτὴν τὴν φορὰν εἰσιέναι]. δοτέον δὲ καὶ αὐτὴν τὴν φορὰν ποιεῖσθαι συνεργοῦσαν
καὶ ἀποπληροῦσαν παρ' αὐτῆς ἃ δεῖ τελεῖν τὸ πᾶν, ἑκάστου τῶν ἐν αὐτῇ τάξιν
μερῶν λαβόντος. (2. 3. 10. 1–10)[44]

[42] In fact it is difficult to separate Plotinus' considered view from the sophisticated
astrological theory of an author such as Ptolemy. Ptolemy emphasizes that astrology
is an inexact science and that the stars are *not* the only physical causes (*Tetr.* 1. 2;
see further Long, 'Astrology', 182–3). Ptolemy is of course a proponent of astrology,
and Plotinus a critic, but both make concessions that bring their positions close to
one another. None the less, they would disagree on the validity of specific claims in
the astrologers' causal theory, for instance the power of the planets to manipulate
the lower world by heating and cooling, and the relevance of the relative position
of the planets.

[43] A nice example of the flexibility of Plotinus' considered view comes at the
beginning of 2. 3. 14: if someone is rich because his father was rich, the stars merely
signify this. If he is rich because of his outstanding character (ἀνδραγαθία), and the
body was a co-operative cause (*sunergos*) for this character, then the stars may be
part of the explanation. But if he has 'virtue without body [ἄνευ σώματος ἡ ἀρετή]',
then there is no explanation in terms of physical causes: virtue itself is the cause.

[44] The bracketed phrase is excluded by Armstrong and Henry–Schwyzer. The
passage καὶ ψυχῇ μὲν καὶ πρὶν ἐλθεῖν εἰς γένεσιν δοτέον ἥκειν τι φερούσῃ παρ' αὐτῆς is

If this is so, then signifyings are still to be admitted. But causings are not [to be admitted] without qualification or with respect to them as a whole but with respect to those things which are affections of the universe, and with respect to what is left over [i.e. which are not caused by higher principles?]. And it is to be admitted that even before the soul comes into generation, something comes to it as it is travelling away from itself. For it would not come into body without having some important thing that is subject to affections. But it is also to be admitted that it enters into chance. And it is to be admitted that the astral motion itself acts as a co-operative cause and completing factor by itself, for the things that the universe must bring to completion, with each of the parts in it taking a role.

This passage is a good place to end our examination of Plotinus on astrology, embodying as it does the arc of his argument as a whole. The concessive strategy of this argument is brought out in the passage by the repetition of δοτέον ('to be admitted'). First *sēmainein* is allowed, which accommodates widely held views about the success of astrological prediction. *Poiein* is also allowed, contrary to initial impressions. But it is then severely restricted in scope. The different layers of Plotinus' argument are most plausibly seen as addressing different concerns. If he were worried only about the problem of human autonomy, he could have admitted that the stars are the only efficacious physical causes, saying, for instance, that whom one has as parents is in fact itself caused by the stars. After all, he preserves autonomy by pointing out that the higher soul is unaffected by *any* physical causes, so it would make no difference if all physical causation were ultimately astrological. But this would have made it more difficult for him to explain why stars are not causes of evil, especially since he would still less wish to blame the higher soul for evils. The stress on the merely partial character of astral causation allows him to absolve both the stars and our higher selves of evil: evils are brought about by our lower souls and by physical causes other than the stars. And, of course, even these evils are for the best when seen from the cosmic, providential point of view.[45]

---

difficult to understand; it seems to mean that the soul acquires its passive part as it descends. My thanks to James Wilberding for discussion of the passage.

[45] As emphasized at 2. 3. 18. Note that I have said nothing about the concluding sections of 2. 3, which principally attempt to reconcile evils with cosmic providence. It is obvious why this problem arises. Plotinus has absolved the stars of evil by saying that they cause only incidentally, the real ultimate cause of everything being the soul. But then evils will be the fault of this soul instead of the stars. Plotinus' strategies

5. Conclusion

In conclusion I would like to dwell briefly on the methodology of the treatises we have examined. As I have been stressing throughout, Plotinus' methods are highly dialectical. Let me say more clearly than I have so far what I mean by this. First, I mean that he is satisfied if his arguments deal effectively with the problem at hand. Thus in 3. 1, 4. 4, and 3. 3 the treatments of astrology differ in emphasis and in the extent to which he makes concessions to astrology. This is because in each case astrology is discussed only to support his various wider aims in those treatises. His approach is also dialectical in a second way, familiar from Aristotle: Plotinus sets up problems in terms of simple contrasts, leading us to expect that he will opt for one view or the other. But in fact a more nuanced middle position emerges in the subsequent discussion.[46] This is most clear in 2. 3, where he begins by asking, effectively, '*poiein* or *sēmainein?*' The answer turns out to be 'the latter, but also the former, albeit in a circumscribed way which is not problematic'.[47]

Furthermore, there is the role played by Plato in this dialectical procedure. Obviously there are themes from Plato that underlie all these discussions of astrology, especially the *Timaeus*'s idea of the unified, living cosmos. But in 2. 3 something more surprising happens. The quotation of Platonic material overturns an initial solution, which was to embrace one of the two simple options set out at the beginning. Plotinus uses Plato to replace the false dichotomy of the original *aporia* with a deeper *aporia*, namely: given that the stars *are* involved in necessitation, in what way do we none the less escape this necessity?[48] And this paves the way for a more adequate

for dealing with this in 2. 3 are largely familiar from other discussions of providence in the *Enneads*.

[46] Cf. the observation of Rolando, 'L'anima e le Moire', 255, regarding the method employed in 2. 3: Plotinus seems at first to give 'l'impressione di una contrapposizione di tesi, quando, in effetti, il suo intento è quello di giungere alla conclusione finale attraverso un progressivo ampliamento della tesi iniziale mediante successive elaborazioni di tesi complementari'.

[47] The concessions made to astrology make it easier to understand why astrological causal theories are so plausible. As in Aristotle, the dialectical procedure explains why *endoxa* are widely accepted (or accepted by experts), but without ultimately giving the *endoxa* full endorsement. My thanks to Miira Tuominen for this point.

[48] For an interesting recent discussion of *aporia* in the Platonist tradition, see I. Männlein-Robert, 'Die Aporien des Kritikers Longin: Zur Inszenierung der

and nuanced solution, which is itself suggested by the same Platonic passages. *Enneads* 2. 3 is thus a good example of how complex and sensitive Plotinus' use of philosophical authority can be. He does not, for example, quote selectively in order to shore up standard Plotinian doctrine. Rather, he quotes precisely what seems at first to be problematic or puzzling about Plato, in order to show that the puzzles are productive.

King's College London

BIBLIOGRAPHY

Armstrong, A. H. (ed. and trans.), *Plotinus:* Enneads ['Armstrong'] (7 vols.; Cambridge, Mass., 1966–88).

Aubry, G., *Plotin: Traité 53 (I, 1)* (Paris, 2004).

Barton, T., *Ancient Astrology [Astrology]* (London, 1994).

Chiaradonna, R., 'L'anima e la mistione stoica: *Enn.* IV 7 [2], 8²', in id. (ed.), *Studi sull'anima in Plotino* (Naples, 2005), 129–47.

Dillon, J. M., 'Plotinus on Whether the Stars are Causes', *Res Orientales*, 12 (1999), 87–91.

Dodds, E. R., *Proclus:* The Elements of Theology (Oxford, 1963).

Fazzo, S., and Zonta, M., *Alessandro di Afrodisia: La provvidenza* (Milan, 1998).

Gersh, S., 'Plotinus on *Harmonia*: Musical Metaphors and their Uses in the *Enneads*', in J. Dillon and M. Dixsaut (eds.), *Agonistes: Essays in Honour of Denis O'Brien* (Aldershot, 2005), 195–207.

Gurtler, G. M., 'Sympathy in Plotinus' ['Sympathy'], *International Philosophical Quarterly*, 24 (1984), 395–406.

Henry, P., and Schwyzer, H.-R. (eds.), *Plotini opera* ['Henry–Schwyzer'] (3 vols.; Oxford, 1964–82).

Long, A. A., 'Astrology: Arguments Pro and Contra' ['Astrology'], in J. Barnes *et al.* (eds.), *Science and Speculation: Studies in Hellenistic Theory and Practice* (Cambridge, 1982), 165–92.

Männlein-Robert, I., 'Die Aporien des Kritikers Longin: Zur Inszenierung der Platonexegese bei Proklos', in M. Perkams and R. M. Piccione (eds.), *Proklos: Methode, Seelenlehre, Metaphysik* (Leiden, 2006), 71–97.

Marzolo, C., *Plotino: Che cos'è l'essere vivente e che cos'è l'uomo? I 1 [53]* (Pisa, 2006).

Platonexegese bei Proklos', in M. Perkams and R. M. Piccione (eds.), *Proklos: Methode, Seelenlehre, Metaphysik* (Leiden, 2006), 71–97.

Rolando, D., 'L'anima e le Moire: Hard Astrology e Soft Astrology nel pensiero del Plotino', *Discorsi*, 10 (1990), 237–62.

Ruland, H.-J., *Die arabischen Fassungen von zwei Schriften des Alexander von Aphrodisias: Über die Vorsehung und Über das liberum arbitrium* [*Die arabischen Fassungen*] (diss. Saarbrücken, 1976).

Sharples, R. W., *Alexander of Aphrodisias:* On Fate (London, 1983).

Sorabji, R., *Necessity, Cause and Blame: Perspectives on Aristotle's Theory* (London, 1983).

Thillet, P., *Alexandre d'Aphrodise: Traité de la Providence* (Lagrasse, 2003).

Wilberding, J., *Plotinus' Cosmology: A Study of* Ennead *II. 1 (40)* [*Plotinus' Cosmology*] (Oxford, 2006).

POWER, ACTIVITY, AND BEING

A Discussion of *Aristotle:* Metaphysics Θ,
trans. and comm. Stephen Makin[1]

CHARLOTTE WITT

STEPHEN MAKIN's contribution to the Clarendon Aristotle fits
well with the series' intention to provide accurate translations of
important texts to students and scholars supplemented by an introduction and a commentary that focus on philosophical issues
and problems. This book has many virtues, including a smooth,
intelligible translation, a sensible and largely helpful orientation
in the introduction, and a detailed, philosophically sophisticated
commentary. Because of these virtues this volume will make an
important contribution to the recent flowering of scholarly and
philosophical interest in book Θ, where Aristotle introduces the ontological distinction between potentiality and actuality. Since this
distinction appears in many different contexts in the Aristotelian
corpus, its elaboration and defence are of considerable consequence
for our understanding of Aristotle's thought.

Despite book Θ's intrinsic importance to Aristotle's metaphysics,
and to many other subjects, it is sometimes not read with the attention it deserves. One reason for this benign neglect is the difficulty
in understanding the unity of the book, which seems to be discussing one topic in its first five chapters (the powers or capacities
of substances) and another topic in subsequent chapters (the ontological distinction between potentiality and actuality). Given this
uncertain thematic unity, scholars have doubted the intrinsic philosophical importance of book Θ as well, and, in particular, its relevance to our understanding of Aristotle's metaphysics of substance.

[1] *Aristotle* Metaphysics Θ, trans. and comm. Stephen Makin (Clarendon Aristotle
Series; Oxford, 2006), pp. xlii+289.

Makin's introduction tackles both problems. In 'An Overview of
Metaphysics Θ' and in his commentary on the first chapter, Makin
follows a suggestion originally made by Michael Frede to solve the
problem of thematic unity.[2] Frede had suggested that the powers or
capacities of substances (discussed in chapters 1–5) are themselves
exemplars of the distinction that Aristotle draws between potentiality and actuality (in chapters 6–8) and so chapters 1–8 turn out
to have a single basic theme. The earlier chapters introduce and
clarify one central example that Aristotle uses in chapter 6 to introduce the ontological distinction between potentiality and actuality,
namely that of an inactive power of a substance and the correlative
active power or activity (the power of sight and seeing). Moreover,
Aristotle's argument for the priority of actuality in relation to potentiality, in chapter 8, makes use of many of the distinctions among
kinds of power drawn in the first five chapters. Read in this way,
book Θ exhibits strong thematic unity, which is a powerful argument in favour of Frede's interpretation.

With the thematic unity of book Θ secured, it might seem that
we should look to the argument of the book in order to determine
its central topics and claims. Two obvious candidates emerge in
Aristotle's argument. The first topic is the existence of the powers
or capacities of substances (my ability to cook or to sew) when they
are inactive (when I am not cooking or sewing). Aristotle tells us
that some philosophers ('the Megarians') had denied the existence
of inactive powers. Since Aristotle's notion of a power or capacity of
a substance is of something that exists both when it is inactive and
when it is active, the Megarian position poses a serious challenge to
Aristotle's philosophy. Aristotle acknowledges the significance of
the Megarian challenge by presenting several complex arguments
against their position in Θ 3. Makin's commentary on these arguments is detailed, imaginative, and philosophically sophisticated.

The second claim Aristotle develops in book Θ is the priority of
actuality in relation to potentiality. The second claim is general in
two ways. First, actuality is prior to potentiality in every sense of the
term 'prior': it is prior in time, in definition, and in being. Second,
Aristotle argues that the three kinds of priority hold of all the different examples of potentiality and actuality he has introduced in

---

[2] M. Frede, 'Aristotle's Notion of Potentiality in *Metaphysics Θ*', in T. Scaltsas,
D. Charles, and M. Gill (eds.), *Unity, Identity, and Explanation in Aristotle's Metaphysics* (Oxford, 1994), 173–93.

the preceding chapters. Hence, as I mentioned above, Aristotle's argument for the priority of actuality in Θ 8 both establishes a central metaphysical thesis and provides a unifying terminus for the preceding chapters. One important crux of interpretation is how to understand the claim that actuality is prior to potentiality in being. Is this a claim about the asymmetrical, existential dependence of what exists potentially on what exists actually? Or is there some other, preferable interpretation of priority in substance?

Makin describes these two central claims of book Θ in his introduction, and he explores their philosophical nooks and crannies with great energy in the commentary. His clever exploration of the Megarian position, concerning which virtually nothing is known, is particularly noteworthy for its intrinsic philosophical interest. There can be little doubt that the existence of capacities or powers is of central importance both to Aristotle's metaphysics and to his natural philosophy broadly construed. Aristotle's theory of causation in nature rests upon the notion of causal powers or capacities; they are central to his thought in biology, to his understanding of change, and to his understanding of soul. Hence, the Megarian position threatens to rend the fabric of Aristotelian philosophy, and Aristotle's response to it sheds important light on a foundational concept in his thought. Moreover Makin's commentary on this text opens it up to contemporary philosophers, which is particularly timely given current interest in the notion of causal powers and how to understand them.

The significance of the priority of actuality for Aristotle's metaphysics is also undeniable, as it is a crucial thesis for Aristotle's theology. As Makin notes, it is in book Θ that Aristotle introduces the puzzling concept of an activity or actuality that is not correlated with a power or potentiality, and this is a notion that he uses elsewhere to characterize the being of his deity. But the priority of actuality in relation to potentiality is also an important thesis for other areas of Aristotle's thought as it inflects the relationship between capacity and exercise, between matter and form, and between incomplete substance and complete substance. Indeed, the teleological character of Aristotle's metaphysics is expressed by the relationship between potentiality and actuality, and it is integral to the priority relations that Aristotle establishes in book Θ.

Because Makin's introduction and commentary do such a good job of exploring the philosophical significance of book Θ, it is somewhat surprising that Makin thinks he needs to do even more to mo-tivate the reader's interest in book Θ. To that end he develops two connections between the philosophical issues explored in book Θ and those discussed elsewhere in the *Metaphysics*. He remarks:

Such problems motivate us to work through the difficult internal structure of Θ. They give a sense of purpose to Θ. And, if the problems are of inde-pendent philosophical appeal, they will engage those who are not already drawn to Aristotelian exegesis. (xxxvi)

Very wisely, Makin does not try to answer the question of how book Θ relates to the rest of Aristotle's investigation of substance in the *Metaphysics* since that is a topic that would require elaborate argument and interpretation. Makin does make the more modest claim that book Θ contributes in two ways to Aristotle's investi-gation of substance. First, it provides a solution to the problem of the unity of form and matter in perishable substances. This is what we might expect given Aristotle's explanation of the unity of the immediate or concurrent matter and the form of a perishable substance in H 6. In that text, their unity is explained by iden-tifying the concurrent matter with potentiality and the form with actuality. Second, as I noted above, Aristotle deploys the idea of an actuality that is independent of any correlative potentiality in Θ 8, and this idea is important for his discussion of non-sensible substance in book Λ.

But, as I have argued elsewhere,[3] readers who look to book Θ for an explicit and definitive answer to the question of how form and concurrent matter are united in the composite substance are bound to be disappointed. Θ 6–8 does not contain a discussion of the unity of form and concurrent matter in perishable substances. First, the topic of their unity is never explicitly broached in these chapters, or at all in book Θ. The examples in Θ 6 which Aristotle uses to introduce the distinction between being x potentially and being x actually (1048^a30–$^b6$) do not include examples of the relationship between concurrent matter and form. Rather, Aristotle's examples of potentiality and actuality contrast an inactive capacity with its exercise (sight and seeing) and either an incomplete substance with a complete substance or the pre-existing matter from which a sub-stance originates and the complete substance. Missing from these

[3] C. Witt, *Ways of Being: Potentiality and Actuality in Aristotle's Metaphysics* (Ithaca, NY, and London, 2003).

examples of the relationship between being x potentially and being x actually is the example of concurrent matter in relation to form.

Interestingly enough, Makin notes this difficulty in his commentary (168). There he makes a case for extending Aristotle's discussion of when the pre-existing matter of F is potentially F to cover the case of the concurrent matter of F. He makes several points in favour of the extension, but the fact that he needs to do so undercuts the claim in the introduction that book Θ is centrally concerned with explaining the unity of concurrent matter and form in the composite substance. Given Aristotle's examples in Θ 6 and 7, it seems rather that he is centrally interested in explaining when the pre-existing matter from which a substance comes to be is potentially that substance, and in expressing the relationship between an incomplete substance and a complete substance.

Let me summarize the issue. If book Θ's major contribution to the investigation of perishable substance were to elaborate how the distinction between being x potentially and being x actually resolves the problem of the unity of concurrent matter and form in perishable substances, then we would expect to find a discussion of this issue in book Θ. But, we do not. What, then, do we say about H 6 and its apparent resolution of the question of unity using the notions of potentiality and actuality? How should we interpret this text? My suggestion is that rather than focus either on Aristotle's examples in Θ 6 or on the discussion of when x is potentially F in Θ 7, we should focus on Aristotle's argument for the priority in substance of actuality. And, indeed, Makin seems to agree that we need to devise a solution to the problem of unity indirectly, in relation to the claim that 'the organism which is actually human is prior in substance to its immediate matter, which is potentially human' (207). Hence, Aristotle's solution to the problem of the unity of concurrent matter and form in perishable substances depends on how one interprets the priority in substance of actuality; the problem of unity is not directly addressed in book Θ.

Moreover, the question of what is meant by priority in substance in Θ 8 has received various interpretations, and remains the topic of vigorous scholarly debate. Makin argues that priority in substance means an asymmetrical relationship of existential dependence, and he provides a detailed and original explanation of Aristotle's justification of the claim that actuality is prior in substance to potentiality. Without settling the issue, Makin's discussion makes an important contribution to the ongoing debate on the topic of the priority in substance of actuality.[4]

I would like to close this review by considering two issues that Makin's book raised in my mind. The first concerns translation, and it is inspired in part by Makin's useful overview of several translation issues in his introduction. There are significant questions about how to translate both Aristotle's terminology of power, potentiality, and possibility, and his terminology of activity and actuality. In his translation, Makin follows a traditional approach in translating *energeia* as 'actuality' (as I have in this review and elsewhere) rather than as 'activity', which is the literal translation. One reason for this decision is that Aristotle's examples of *energeia* in chapter 6 are not all activities, which might be suggested by that translation. Still, there is a puzzle as to why Aristotle would use a word that means 'activity' to refer to a way of being that includes both activities and complete beings. Aristotle's choice of terminology is especially puzzling given that he coined another term, *entelecheia*, that he might have used to refer to all of his examples. Hence, Aristotle's preferred term for actuality throughout book Θ, i.e. *energeia* (or activity), raises serious questions for an interpretation which takes actuality to be the genus and activity to be one of the kinds of actuality. Makin asks:

Since the original meaning of *energeia* is 'activity', why should it come to seem sensible to Aristotle to express the idea that something exists actually (*entelecheia*) by saying that it exists 'in activity' (*energeia*)? These questions are to be answered by working through Aristotle's text, rather than deciding points of translation. (xxx)

But someone might fairly object that in making the translation decision he has, Makin makes it difficult for the reader to work through the text keeping this question in mind.

The second issue I would like to discuss is how to understand chapter 9, which discusses the normative dimensions of potentiality and actuality. Makin suggests that chapter 9 is 'a folder' comprising text that 'gathers material which is relevant to, but not integrated with, the structured argument of the surrounding text' (221). Fold-

---

[4] On this see R. M. Dancy, 'Aristotle and the Priority of Actuality', in S. Knuuttila (ed.), *Reforging the Great Chain of Being* (Dordrecht, 1981), 73–115; S. Makin, 'What Does Aristotle Mean by Priority in Substance?', *Oxford Studies in Ancient Philosophy*, 24 (2003), 209–38; C. Y. Panayides, 'Aristotle on the Priority of Actuality in Substance', *Ancient Philosophy*, 19 (1999), 327–44; Witt, *Ways of Being*, 75–96.

ers are like appendices in modern texts. Contrary to Makin's suggestion, however, I find chapter 9 to have several points of integration with chapter 8, viz. in relation to the priority in substance of actuality, and in its mirroring of chapter 8's treatment of both perishable and imperishable substances. Finally, I think it is not at all clear that the normative dimension of potentiality and actuality is not part of Aristotle's 'structured argument' in book Θ. If we think about the book as focused upon introducing the notions of potentiality and actuality, and establishing certain relationships between the two, including priority relations, it seems just as plausible to read the material on normativity as rounding out the discussion as it does to file it away in a folder. For it may well be that a consideration of the normative implications of the argument in chapter 8 is part of the goal or purpose of book Θ, and that something important would be omitted from our understanding of Aristotle's teleological metaphysics without its inclusion.

The publication of Makin's translation and commentary makes an important and timely contribution to the ongoing reconsideration of the significance of book Θ for our understanding of Aristotle's metaphysics. With its useful introduction, clear translation, and sophisticated philosophical commentary, the volume will also be of value for graduate students and philosophers with an interest in Aristotle's thought.

University of New Hampshire

BIBLIOGRAPHY

Dancy, R. M., 'Aristotle and the Priority of Actuality', in S. Knuuttila (ed.), *Reforging the Great Chain of Being* (Dordrecht, 1981), 73–115.
Frede, M., 'Aristotle's Notion of Potentiality in *Metaphysics* Θ', in T. Scaltsas, D. Charles, and M. Gill (eds.), *Unity, Identity, and Explanation in Aristotle's Metaphysics* (Oxford, 1994), 173–93.
Makin, S., 'What Does Aristotle Mean by Priority in Substance?', *Oxford Studies in Ancient Philosophy*, 24 (2003), 209–38.
Panayides, C. Y., 'Aristotle on the Priority of Actuality in Substance', *Ancient Philosophy*, 19 (1999), 327–44.
Witt, C., *Ways of Being: Potentiality and Actuality in Aristotle's Metaphysics* (Ithaca, NY, and London, 2003).

INDEX LOCORUM

Notes for Contributors to Oxford Studies in Ancient Philosophy

1. Articles should be submitted with double or 1½ line-spacing through-out. At the stage of initial (but not final) submission footnotes may be given in small type at the foot of the page. Page dimensions should be A4 or standard American quarto (8½ × 11″), and ample margins should be left.

2. Submissions should be made as a file in PDF format attached to an e-mail sent to the Editor. Authors are asked to supply an accurate word-count (*a*) for the main text, and (*b*) for the notes. The e-mail which serves as a covering letter should come from the address to be used for correspondence on the submission. A postal address should also be provided. If necessary, arrangements for alternative means of submission may be made with the Editor. Authors should note that the version first submitted will be the one adjudicated; unsolicited revised versions cannot be accepted during the adjudication process.

The remaining instructions apply to the final version sent for publication, and need not be rigidly adhered to in a first submission.

3. In the finalized version, the text should be double-spaced and in the same typesize throughout, **including displayed quotations and notes**. Notes should be numbered consecutively, and may be supplied as either footnotes or endnotes. Any acknowledgements should be placed in an unnumbered first note. Wherever possible, references to primary sources should be built into the text.

4. **Use of Greek and Latin.** Relatively familiar Greek terms such as *psychē* and *polis* (but not whole phrases and sentences) may be used in transliteration. Wherever possible, Greek and Latin should not be used in the main text of an article in ways which would impede comprehension by those without knowledge of the languages; for example, where appropriate, the original texts should be accompanied by a translation. This constraint does not apply to footnotes. Greek must be supplied in an accurate form, with all diacritics in place. A note of the system employed for achieving Greek (e.g. GreekKeys, Linguist's Software) should be supplied to facilitate file conversion.

5. For citations of Greek and Latin authors, house style should be fol-lowed. This can be checked in any recent issue of *OSAP* with the help of the Index Locorum.

6. In references to books, the first time the book is referred to give the ini-tial(s) and surname of the author (first names are not usually required), and the place and date of publication; where you are abbreviating the

title in subsequent citations, give the abbreviation in square brackets, thus:

> T. Brickhouse and N. Smith, *Socrates on Trial* [*Trial*] (Princeton, 1981), 91–4.

Give the volume-number and date of periodicals, and include the full page-extent of articles (including chapters of books):

> D. W. Graham, 'Symmetry in the Empedoclean Cycle' ['Symmetry'], *Classical Quarterly*, NS 38 (1988), 297–312 at 301–4.

> G. Vlastos, 'The Unity of the Virtues in the *Protagoras*' ['Unity'], in id., *Platonic Studies*, 2nd edn. (Princeton, 1981), 221–65 at 228.

Where the same book or article is referred to on subsequent occasions, usually the most convenient style will be an abbreviated reference, thus:

> Brickhouse and Smith, *Trial*, 28–9.

Do *not* use the author-and-date style of reference:

> Brickhouse and Smith 1981: 28–9.

7. Authors are asked to supply *in addition*, at the end of the article, a full list of the bibliographical entries cited, alphabetically ordered by (first) author's surname. Except that the author's surname should come first, these entries should be identical in form to the first occurrence of each in the article, including where appropriate the indication of abbreviated title:

> Graham, D. W., 'Symmetry in the Empedoclean Cycle' ['Symmetry'], *Classical Quarterly*, NS 38 (1988), 297–312.

8. If there are any unusual conventions contributors are encouraged to include a covering note for the copy-editor and/or printer. Please say whether you are using single and double quotation marks for different purposes (otherwise the Press will employ its standard single quotation marks throughout, using double only for quotations within quotations).

9. Authors should send a copy of the final version of their paper in electronic form by attachment to an e-mail. The final version should be in a standard word-processing format, accompanied by a note of the word-processing program used and of the system (**not just the font**) used for producing Greek characters (see point 4 above). This file must be accompanied by a second file, a copy in PDF format of the submitted word-processor file; the PDF file must correspond **exactly** to the word-processor file. If necessary, arrangements for alternative means of submission may be made with the Editor.